Dan Duryea

Dan Duryea

a career appreciation

by Joseph Fusco

BearManor Media
2017

Dan Duryea: A Career Appreciation

© 2017 Joseph Fusco

All Rights Reserved.
Reproduction in whole or in part without the author's permission is strictly forbidden.

BearManor Media
P. O. Box 71426
Albany, GA 31708

bearmanormedia.com

Typesetting and layout by John Teehan

Published in the USA by BearManor Media

ISBN—978-1-62933-195-9

Dedicated to Sarah and Beth

Table of Contents

Introduction 1

The Early Years: Hollywood's Finest
Man Behind the Lion's Roar... 33
The Freelance Market 46
Prestige Pictures and Shadow Plays 64

Universal Studios
Crime and Punishment 87
Period Pieces, Westerns and Costume Dramas 105
Crime Bosses 120

New Directions
Old Heels and New Blowhards 135
Indies, Radio and TV 150
China Smith 166

TV Anthologies, On the Big Screen and In the Old West
50's Television 185
Sidekicks, Ciphers, Heroes and Bums 203
Western Gold, Steel Rails and Brass Bells 217

The Old Standby System
More of the Same 229
1957: The Underbelly of the Golden Years 238
New Marquee Economics 262

The Golden Age of Television Westerns
Wagon Train 275
Laramie, Rawhide and Bonanza 287
Prairie Shadows 305

TV: 1958-1963
All American Role Models 327
The Dysfunctional Relative 336
Glimmers of Hope and Renewal 347

Western Twilight
Retro Cowboys 357
Sundown 366
Western TV Reprise 378

The Cold War
Crime: Post Script 391
Espionage: Adventures and Thrills 404
All Roads Lead to Eddie Jacks 418

Conclusion
The Bamboo Saucer 433

List of Credits 439

Endnotes 483

Index 485

A sleek portrait of Dan Duryea, an actor who created characters that embodied suave gentility with cunning depravity. 1954, Universal Pictures Company, Inc.

Introduction

CRIME DRAMAS AND WESTERNS have produced many villains but few have been as effective and memorable as Dan Duryea. Standing at a fit 6'1" with blond hair, brown eyes and a mid-range voice, he would have been at home playing the nice guy next door, the hero's best friend or the guy a woman could trust implicitly. Instead, he excelled at playing odious sociopaths who made life miserable, not only for the hero, but for a score of women, too.

The bulk of his villains were mean-spirited sadists who made life rough for anyone who got in their way. They could be cold-blooded crime bosses or psychotic Western gunslingers. It didn't matter whether the terrain was urban or country, the dead-panned expressions, clipped threats and hyena laughs often resulted in death for someone. Many big time stars of his era had to contend with Dan Duryea's cynical arrogance before they got the upper hand in the film's showdown. It was rare that his villain walked away from a confrontation and that was because he was the quicker draw.

The menacing heel screen persona became so pervasive that Dan Duryea changed character-type to broaden his range. His first attempt was a comedy, *White Tie and Tails*, made in 1946. Fan mail favored his tough guy roles and he stayed with this type for a while. Television helped him to expand his characterizations and enabled him to translate this adjustment to the big screen. Despite his excellent acting ability, audiences still wanted him to be the man they loved to hate. Suffice to say, even his good characters had a touch of larceny to them; if they didn't, they wouldn't have the Duryea touch.

Dan Duryea was a rare actor who had the knack of creating an impressive array of characters from a limited range of emotions. He used this array in different combinations and frequencies to create heroes and villains from the same patterns. It was a matter of degree pertaining righteous behavior versus malicious cowardice. Sometimes, the touches were subtle; other times they were stark contrasts. That meant there were times when tags like hero and villain meant nothing.

Similar expressions and reactions could mean one thing or its opposite according to Duryea's acting technique. It was more complicated than the villain doing the sniveling boot licking routine or the hero with the in-your-face sarcasm. A snarl could be a whine for a spineless deadbeat or a warning from a hardnosed crime boss. A stare could mean abject surrender or an ultimatum that meant certain death. Temper tantrums could be the futile flare-up of a helpless loser or a triumphant outburst of someone

In Fritz Lang's Scarlet Street, Dan Duryea created his first impressionable villain, Johnny Prince, an amoral cad who abuses and exploits his lover, Kitty March (Joan Bennett). 1945, Universal Pictures Company, Inc.

mighty. Timid two-faced cowardice and gorilla mandated chest beating could be the cry of the concrete jungle or the whimpering surrender of a spoiled nobody.

Dan Duryea was a durable actor who was able to carry a solid supporting role or hold down the lead in a boisterous Western or pulp melodrama. He's held his own with many leading actors and actresses besides working for many notable directors. Whether or not he was working in a classic film or a low budget pot boiler, he always gave an engaging performance. That is especially true of his expansive television credits.

He was also an actor who benefited from the character lines and rueful expressions that came from decades of experience. This gave the characters of his later years the emotional depths and shady demeanors of the underdogs who rose above the fray for awhile before their luck ran out.

Producer Aaron Rosenberg summed up his talent when he said, "As far as being an actor's actor, this means that Dan doesn't demand that he dominate every scene. He may be a scene stealer because of his ability, but never because he thinks only of his own performance. He's smart enough to know that the people around him are what make a scene good or bad."[1]

Duryea's unique style was highlighted in classic dramas, crime *noirs*, pulp Westerns, soap opera romances and low budget independents from the 40's to the late 60's. He also had a television resume that covered all of the dramatic, comedy and Western genres of the 50's and 60's, including his own adventure show in the 50's and a recurring role in a 60's prime time soap opera.

Dan Duryea is identified chiefly with portraying screen villains who menaced their victims before being brought down by ironic twists of fate. Conniving, vain, sniveling, and overconfident to a fault, these characters epitomized the sleazy con-artists whose oily smoothness and soprano intonations dominated a group of stooges until they were ruined by a bitter conclusion to one of their own failed schemes.

These villains suffered the pangs of karmic payback so many times they had to develop night vision to suit the shadows of their crime drama hells. That was true of Johnny Prince in *Scarlet Street* in 1945 and twenty years later for Carl Lutcher, the hired killer, in *Walk a Tightrope* in 1965. It was the same thing for anyone with similar intentions who came along in between.

In most film profiles, Dan Duryea has a bad reputation as an abusive lout, which came in part from the two films he made for Fritz Lang, *Woman in the Window* and *Scarlet Street*. In both films, he menaced Joan

Dan Duryea plays Ralph Cobb, a Southern gentleman who loses his manners in *That Other Woman*, a comedy of errors. 1941, 20th Century Fox.

Bennett and dominated her with a creepy relish. Although it was a type he would occasionally play again in his career and was a small addition to a larger scope of his characters, its impact on Duryea's image cemented his reputation as a larcenous opportunist.

Dan Duryea may have been typecast by the 40's label of being a mean-spirited heel but his overall behavior towards women is more chivalrous than the handful of movies that cemented his back-handed reputation. On some occasions, he has been the dupe or on the short end of things.

The Little Foxes and *Mrs. Parkington* had strong matriarchs to bend his weak sniveling characters. Bette Davis and Greer Garson were wheelers and dealers in a male dominated business world. His characters—a nephew and a grandson—were weak and vain-glorious in comparison.

On a more intimate level, *That Other Woman* and *Man from Frisco* show suitors that become the X factor by the final reel. Dan Duryea plays Ralph Cobb, a cuckolded suitor, in *That Other Woman*. In a coming-of-age comedy about a secretary in love with a womanizing playboy architect, Ralph is her proper Southern gentleman beau. He is a Yankee-hating man who gets caught up in a convoluted scheme started by his fiancé to net her boss. He becomes an ex and an odd man down and out for the count. The real insult to his Southern etiquette is being ridiculed by a sweet child of the South.

The Man from Frisco depicts a shipbuilder with new ideas and a means of production to increase the manufacture of battleships needed for the war effort. Duryea is part of the old scheme, someone who supports the former boss who now seems antiquated because of the revolutionary production methods created by the man from Frisco. Jealousy spurs him into sabotaging a shipbuilding project to humiliate the hot shot architect who stole his girl. His disregarded love blows up into a disaster where his ex-fiancé's brother is killed.

He plays the alcoholic husband in a spouse-sidekick act that accompanies a sharpshooter played by Erich Von Stroheim in *The Great Flamarion*. A fatal misstep during the act is attributed to alcohol but is really the clever scheming of a fed-up wife and ambitious sidekick to the steel-willed Prussian marksman.

Things changed when Dan Duryea appeared in his second film for Fritz Lang, *Woman in the Window*. The role of Heidt only took up twelve minutes of screen time, but it was enough for viewers to take notice of a different type of screen peril. That set the momentum that would lead to a greater notoriety with *Scarlet Street*.

It didn't hurt that his tragic femme-fatale was played by a dark haired beauty with a kittenish sensuality. Joan Bennett gave gravity to Dan Duryea's character and it was especially true in their next pairing. As a scheming and insensitive beast in *Scarlet Street,* Duryea once more harasses the lovely Joan Bennett and hustles the timid Edward G. Robinson into compromising his honor for the sexy vamp. The milquetoast is a timid cuckold who becomes a mother hen because of Bennett's domineering allure. Death and blackmail are Duryea's forte until he becomes a victim of his own scheme.

Not only was the Johnny Prince character morally repugnant but the film was banned in New York. After appeals and editorial changes, the movie still received criticism from the Legion of Decency. Coupled with movie magazine articles explaining the psychological allure of forceful brutes, Dan Duryea was tagged with nicknames like "The Merchant of Menace" and "Heel with Sex Appeal."

Adverse real life reactions impelled the actor to broaden his range and show the sympathetic side of his characters but none of these figures gained approval from the movie audience. In the 40's, it was difficult but it is something that Dan Duryea finally achieved by the end of his career. Until then, it was a case of trial and error.

There were attempts by Universal to broaden Duryea's type with *The Black Angel* and *White Tie and Tails*. Martin Blair is a piano player

"The Merchant of Menace" was the title for a typical Dan Duryea magazine profile.

whose hit song was playing the night his ex-wife, a nightclub singer, was murdered in *The Black Angel*. June Vincent is the angel who leads him to a bleak redemption at his own expense during the investigation of the crime. The same thing can be said about his perilous association with a nightclub in *White Tie and Tails*. Ella Raines is the steady influence this time around. She gets him into a jam and uses it to make him see the light about day jobs and the night life.

Then there were the power molls whose magnetism wielded a power that dominated even the most hardened crime bosses. Most of the time, they survived their successful emasculation rituals but on one occasion each actress paid the price of pushing too fast and too hard.

The various degrees of mean trio were temporarily tamed by Yvonne De Carlo in *Black Bart*, *River Lady* and *Criss-Cross*. In similar circumstances, Shelley Winters captivated them in *Larceny*, *Johnny Stool Pigeon* and *Winchester '73*. However, there was no viable exit for either actress in *Criss-Cross* and *Larceny*. That might seem like an improvement according to his standard as a scoundrel but it didn't matter when Dan Duryea repeated the odious physical tormentor in two new films, *Manhandled* and *Too Late For Tears*, both made in 1949.

Dorothy Lamour has a rooftop dance with Duryea in the former and Lizabeth Scott squares off with him in the latter. Karl Benson, the seedy private investigator and Danny Fuller, the blackmailer vying to get his mislaid money back, synthesize all of the traits Duryea imbued his trademark sleaze ball characters with.

The villains from the Fritz Lang melodramas come to mind and these two films are perfect matches for the earlier movies. An unpleasant connection to the Lang films is the anti-woman behavior of the villains. The private investigator has no qualms in framing an innocent woman for murder and the blackmailer plays rough with Lizabeth Scott to get his money back from her. But things were changing. Danny Fuller rues his rough house tactics when his victory toast backfires and he misses a fun-filled trip to Mexico.

With the 50's, Dan Duryea began to shade some of his characters with contradictory traits, eventually leading to a hybrid type that blended heroics with dubious motives. Even when Duryea played heroes, their virtues were suspect and their manners somewhat seedy. If they championed a worthy cause it was because they were likely to reap a formidable profit with civic duty a coincidental afterthought. Duryea's heroes also chiseled, connived, and did all that they could to pull off a scheme.

An upbeat photo of Dan Duryea and four starlets (left to right, Louise Jones, Alva Lacy, Shirley Mathison and Dee Van Enger) at Ocean Park, Coney Island of the West. The publicity photo was the studio's attempt to soften Dan Duryea's screen image, something many fans resisted. 1947, Universal Pictures Company, Inc.

Duryea's good guys are hard-boiled anti-heroes with soft insides. Their weaknesses make them repugnant, but all of them are redeemed by shouldering the responsibilities of victory and being given little from the spoils of its success. There were even hints of chivalry in some of Duryea's characters. It is the defining deed that is the reward for these rapscallions with hearts of plated gold.

The term 'hero' was often ambiguous when applied to any of Dan Duryea's protagonists. That is because these characters were virtuous by default, having to deal with characters with motives and sins more disreputable than their own. The only exception was a group of television roles he played in the 50's and 60's. Usually, the heroics were at the behest of a beautiful woman or an intriguing set of circumstances. In the end, all that mattered was self-glory and a reward. It was all done with respect to breeding and circumstance, something that his devilish alter-egos on the range never understood.

Mike Reese was an unscrupulous newspaper editor who uses his big city tabloid instincts to energize a small town newspaper in *The Underworld Story*. 1950, United Artists Corp.

Think about Mike Reese, the duplicitous newspaperman in *The Underworld Story* or *World for Ransom*, with an adventurer loosely based on Duryea's television character in *The Affairs of China Smith*. They are shady opportunists whose crowning achievement is accomplishing a heroic deed at the behest of a woman who really doesn't like him at all. That is why Mike Reese and Mike Callahan come up winners despite having been good guys in sordid crime melodramas.

They operate from more perspectives than most people could handle and that makes them mercurial personalities. They infuriate everyone they come in contact with, but always get the job done because their lives depend on it. They save the very systems that were trying to destroy them by taking out the enemy. Mike Reese bags a murderer and his gangster buddy, while Callahan takes down nuclear spies that threatened the free world.

Image modification became possible with Dan Duryea's entrance into television and no evaluation is complete without considering his television performances. Unavailability and the pompous prejudice that it is only television precludes the chance of enjoying many performances that are not only variations of his big screen characters but also experiencing a battery of characters that are the polar opposites of his merchant of menace roles.

China Smith may be an annoying gadfly that many considered a bottom feeder but he was a princely fellow when it came to any woman who needed his services. Even if his clients' motives were a tad shady he still found the need to please. Oddly, many of Dan Duryea's television roles from this period reflected the connubial and domestic bliss motif that came to typify 50's American home life.

He was the valiant chief surgeon at a Yakima Hospital who creates order out of chaos in *Four Hours in White*. In *Comeback*, he plays an ex-ball player down on his luck and who is resurrected by a little league team's faith in him. *Tiger on a Bicycle* has Dan Duryea as a cop trying to solve an armored car robbery. He knows what it's like to be a justice of the peace who finds his life in jeopardy when an escaped lunatic vows to return to kill him in *The Vengeance*. In each story, Duryea plays a man who acts without strings attached to his intentions.

This residual good charm was now tolerated and even enjoyed to some extent on the big screen. The good-natured sidekick is a fair assessment of his parts in *Thunder Bay*, *Foxfire* and *Battle Hymn*. Of course, being Duryea's big screen characters meant there had to be some degree of ambiguity; in this case it was rash judgments, hard drinking and wartime wheeling and dealing.

In Climax: Four Hours in White, Dan Duryea plays Dr. Sullivan, the chief of surgeons who faces a night of challenges that define his integrity. 1958, NBC.

Johnny Gambi likes the idea of trampling all over the Old World customs of a small Louisiana fishing village. He is drilling for oil with his partner, Steve Martin. Doc is just as hard drinking as Gambi, but he is not nearly as ambitious, bold, or successful. He runs a clinic in a mining town. He is a sidekick to Jonathan Dartland, the enigmatic and super-strong lead, but he is far from being an asset.

Gambi and Doc are sidekicks to two leads who are mustering the forces of nature to create a legacy for themselves. *Thunder Bay* and *Foxfire* deal with the water and the earth, but they share the common theme of the outsider who plans to tap into nature's reserves and make it his personal stake. Gambi will reap part of the rewards because he has a vested interest, but Doc will become bone-dry because of his small dreams.

In *Battle Hymn*, he plays Sgt. Herman, the resourceful supply sergeant. He chomps on a cigar and gets what is needed while leaving the worrying to the film's lead, played by Rock Hudson. Duryea's character is sympathetic, laid-back and in good spirits as he wheels and deals his way through the war to keep the unit strong.

It would not be a stretch to declare that Dan Duryea has the most impressive Western resume of any Hollywood actor. It is necessary to add his television roles to his feature length film portrayals to prove this. His choice of roles includes every imaginable characterization in the Western genre except Native American portrayals. Prairie heroes, vicious gunslingers, sly town bosses, grizzly mountain men and honest settlers are some of Dan Duryea's contribution to Western movies and television programs. His characters have embodied the admirable personality traits that made honor a code in the building of a nation and also portrayed the adversaries that impeded law, order and justice.

Duryea's sagebrush villains were the Western forebears of their urban crime brethren. Few of them rose to be the crime boss of the range, but even the big men who did failed to escape ironic twists of fate when they lost the opportunities to save their hides.

The hired gun was a man without a past who had a mean reputation for gunning down people and taking things over when he had a mind to. It took more than a sheer arrogance and a fierce bloodlust to make a good gunslinger. He had to have a quick wit, a sardonic philosophy, and a keen way of getting things done. If that meant bribery, murder, and mayhem, then so it was because all his hoods had a bloodthirsty gang at their beck and call.

Duryea's first Western bad man was in *Along Came Jones* (1946), starring Gary Cooper. His last gunslinger was in *Incident at Phantom Hill* (1966). That's twenty years of terror and marauding, a repetitious loop of dying in the dust. No one can beat the good guy and that includes the legion of Black Bart roles Duryea played throughout his career. The only one who got away was Mr. Denton in *The Twilight Zone*'s episode of *Mr. Denton at Doomsday*. He is aided by a magic potion that the others do not possess. That is why they wound up on Boot Hill and Mr. Denton didn't. He got to live in *The Twilight Zone* and that was television.

Monte Jarrad was Duryea's first Western gunslinger and he had to square off against Gary Cooper in *Along Came Jones*, a Western satire spoofing Cooper's tall-in-the-saddle image. It took four years before Dan Duryea got back into gear as a Western villain: the memorable character of Waco Johnny Dean in *Winchester '73*. The 1950 Western classic relates a captivating story about the rifle's history as it passes hands, usually after violent confrontations.

Waco Johnny Dean morphed into Whitey Kincaide, perhaps Duryea's finest bad man because of his twisted sense of ethics. Three years later Whitey Harbin becomes the new kindred spirit when he gets his chance to have a showdown with James Stewart. He also has the added thrill of a gunfight with Audie Murphy. Harbin wins one and loses the other.

Dan Duryea's high standing as one of the movies' premier Western bad men cast him against many popular screen heroes. He was the foil to James Stewart in 1950's *Winchester '73* and *Night Passage* in 1957. John Payne faced off with him in *Rails into Laramie* and *Silver Lode* in 1954. Audie Murphy was aided and abetted by him in *Ride Clear of Diablo* in 1954, *Night Passage* in 1957 and *Six Black Horses* in 1962. He acted with Tom Tryon in Disney's 1959 *Texas John Slaughter* tele-movie and a Universal TV remake of *Winchester '73* in 1966. He also stuck around in between to needle Tony Young in *He Rides Tall* and *Taggart*, two retro-oaters made by Universal in 1964.

Dan Duryea had the Western bad man patented before long. That does not mean that he was strictly repetitive, because he also added a twist or a turn to each character to make him new and unlike any of his forebears. That is true from when he started to play a series of prairie mad men to many of the heroes-in-residence on Hollywood's best Western back lots.

A distance of eight years presents two different hired guns who become Audie Murphy's strange benefactors. In *Ride Clear of Diablo*, Whit-

Monte Jarrad was Dan Duryea's first Western villain and he set the template for a vast collection of Western portraits. 1945, International Pictures Company, Inc.

ey Kincaide still has the hair-trigger temper and maniacal laugh, but has now developed a sardonic sense of humor. Eight years later in *Six Black Horses*, Frank Jesse is a philosophical gunman. In both cases, he assists Audie Murphy in his mission and pays dearly two times around.

In the movies, it was a requisite for the Black Bart villains to return to the dust. It all ended in the dust that created the gunslinger in the first place, and that includes the variations on the gunslinger, such as the maverick marauders or town bosses, the gunmen made good and gone respectable. They owned the towns that they once terrorized but still managed to die the gunslinger's death.

The next step in the evolution of the gunslinger is the shooter with a grand plan. Besides being a quick draw, this takes intelligence. Few prairie gunmen can think beyond the showdown or make it to the catbird seat.

Beauvais was a smooth sharpie who tried and failed to rise above his nature and become a player in *River Lady*. Years later, Ned McCarty is a gunslinger with a grand plan in *Silver Lode*. Shanessy also has a plan—and the catbird seat!—in *Rails into Laramie*. McCarty and Shanessy may be

After *Black Bart*, Yvonne de Carlo and Dan Duryea became Universal-International's top box office draw. 1947, Universal Pictures Company, Inc.

the same person on different rungs of the ladder, but they still wind up falling off the same way as Beauvais.

In *Silver Lode*, McCarty tries to pull the wool over a town's eyes through deception and this backfires because he does not have a real backup plan. His only backup is two gunmen, and their extra firepower proves to be useless. Shanessy is a gunman who finally makes it to the catbird seat in *Rails into Laramie*. He also wants a cut of the new railroad system besides pieces of the town he lives in. Shanessy has the same razzle-dazzle that McCarty has, but he has boosted it up a couple of notches. He, too, has two gunmen at his beck and call, plus the wife of his former best buddy.

Dan Trask and Bart McAdam are two town bosses on opposite sides of the law. Trask is the boss of an outlaw town south of the border and McAdam is a big shot in Dodge City. They both have to deal with Tom Tryon in two different ways. One does it at Disney in 1959 and the other plays it for Universal TV in a 1966 remake of one of Duryea's best Westerns.

Dan Duryea created some poignant Western villains late in his career when he appeared in several retro-oaters and shoestring prairie tales. *The Bounty Killer*, *The Hills Run Red*, and *Incident at Phantom Hill* are the sunsets of Duryea's Western villainy. The movies are low-budget films filled with Western legends who had seen better days, but Duryea's performances are powerful enough to broaden his Western villain portfolio.

In *The Bounty Killer*, Willie Duggan is a city slicker who goes West and becomes corrupted by the bounty tradition in a tale full of irony and hopeful desperation. Getz is not who he appears to be, but that does not change his heroic code, the one that forces him to lend his protective aid to a cowpoke with a motive for revenge in *The Hills Run Red*. He appears throughout the movie as a laconic outlaw whose support of the film's hero is an obstacle to the chief villain, played with emotional gusto by Henry Silva.

The villain in *The Incident on Phantom Hill* is Joe Barlow, the last of Duryea's gunslingers and a man to be reckoned with. He is freed from a prison sentence for masterminding a payroll robbery of cavalry officers that ended in the death of several troops. Barlow is needed as a guide to the loot he stole, but he has ulterior plans other than re-claiming his freedom.

Willie Duggan, Willy Getz, and Joe Barlow are worthy additions to Dan Duryea's Western bad man credentials, adding seasoning and subtle touches of humor and regret to the shady, shifty high-plains gunmen of previous decades. Duggan, Getz, and Barlow have that wily country charm and psychopathic need to deceive and deter their adversaries while riding the range with a clear conscience because that's what the system decrees.

Dan Duryea even changed his Western villains for a couple of heroic rascals. *Black Bart* and *Al Jennings of Oklahoma* are two righteous gentlemen whose honor forces their hands at playing dishonor as their vocations. They have points to make and lose their grips because of the "true love and let's settle down" factor. This is what softens them up and brings them down. One goes down in flames, and the other rises from the ashes.

One way to appreciate the variety and textures of roles that make up Dan Duryea's Western credits is to contrast two of his characters that are separated by a considerable length of time. A decade's span shows an evolution of maturity and diminution of power in men who once survived the frontier boom because of the instincts that finally made them go bust.

The General and O.E. Hotchkiss are men who wear the law on their holsters. They are driven by a mania separated by various degrees and time spans. A timid bookkeeper becomes the power-hungry General in *The Marauders* (1955). O.E. Hotchkiss is a near-sighted, elderly deputy to a hired lawman in a frontier railroad town in *Stranger On The Run* (1967), an allegory of the changing turn-of-century West.

Another facet of Dan Duryea's career that has not been given enough consideration is his work with the independent production companies during the 50's. Duryea continued to work for Universal-International and appeared in many entertaining films for the studio during the 50's. He also appeared in many bizarre independent films that are brutal, cutting, and weird in their normalcy.

Dan Duryea appeared in many independent films that were made off the beaten track of Hollywood. *Storm Fear* and *The Burglar* are two offbeat crime dramas that have heists as major plot elements. In the first movie, it is a bank robbery turned sour. The second film boasts a successful theft that creates its share of problems for the thieves.

Duryea's roles in the two movies are on opposite sides of the law. In *Storm Fear*, Fred is the hermit writer whose soul has provided respectability for his shotgun bride and bewildered son. He confronts a dark and angry part of his past when gangsters on the lam hide out at his desolate, snowy ranch after a robbery gone bad.

Nat Harbin is a down-on-his-luck burglar who hatches and pulls off a peculiar jewelry robbery with his gang in *The Burglar*. It is a successful theft even though it spells tragedy for the jewel thieves.

Storm Fear and *The Burglar* share a common claustrophobia aggravated by two sets of sociopaths that bet against house odds and lose. Both films are originals because they take familiar conventions and reinvent them through the unique lens of their directors, Cornel Wilde and Paul Wendkos, respectively.

Bill Cannon is a disintegrating man who has lost his wife and daughter and faces a life threatening crisis in *Chicago Calling*. Major Bill Rogers must clear himself of his estranged wife's murder while on leave in *Terror Street*. Failure to meet their deadlines will be the cause of their demise.

Dan Duryea and Tony Young take a break with Claudia Barrett during the filming of *Taggart*, one of Duryea's latter day Westerns. 1964, Universal Pictures Corp.

Bill Cannon and Major Rogers are as disparate as two people can get but they share a common goal and that is to beat the clock to solve a crisis that will make or break their lives. Confinement, the need to make life altering decisions, and a race against time are the things that unite them, along with being downtrodden men who still cling to a vague code of ethics. That is the sentence that puts each man in the box, and how he ends his gambit depends on whether or not he lands on a period, a question mark, or an exclamation point.

Sky Commando is a low-budget quickie about war and honor, snap judgments, and the military chain of command. It has the flat look of a dull documentary and uses stock combat footage to supply the thrills. The movie starts with a flying mission during the Korean War that becomes a flashback story set in WWII. The common point is Colonel Wyatt, a hated officer who has the courage to make on-the-spot decisions concerning life and death.

Dan Duryea plays an ex-dancer confined to a wheelchair in *This is My Love*, a strange and depressing soap opera with Faith Domergue as his wife. 1954, RKO Pictures.

This Is My Love is an obscure oddity and fills the category for the whiners and the wimps, the drunken wastrels who think they deserve more than what they have. There is no charity of strangers for Murray Myer, a former dancer confined to a wheelchair. There is also no love in a family driven to the verge of a breakdown by his whining and bickering. A soap opera that poisons the souls of everyone in it thanks to Murray's knockout medicine.

Dan Duryea continued to work for Universal-International during his independent projects and he made three movies for the studio between 1957 and 1960. One was *Kathy O*, a coy comedy about a lovable husband who shills for a living and gets caught up in the world of Hollywood publicity run amok. It is a color film with Patty McCormick, a reigning child star of the time. The movie features Duryea in a secondary role as a flustered second banana to a rebellious child star that has bolted the system and found sanctuary in his family's home. Another 1957 film was *Night Passage*, an excellent James Stewart Western, and the last was *Slaughter on Tenth Avenue*, a hard-core labor union drama produced by Albert J. Zugsmith.

Albert J. Zugsmith was a producer who wavered between the righteous and the profane during the 1950's. *Slaughter on Tenth Avenue* was made during his pinnacle, a period that also included *The Incredible Shrinking Man* and *Touch of Evil*. By 1960, he was ending his run as a producer for Universal-International and one of his last films for a major studio was *Platinum High School*, made for MGM. It still had his old stamp because it was a twisted and tormented overture in teen angst and military discipline.

Corruption, intimidation, and murder are some of the ingredients of the crooked hierarchy of these movies. A labor union and a military school are two settings where shady policies have claimed innocent lives and it takes the honest outsider to straighten things out.

In *Slaughter on Tenth Avenue*, Dan Duryea plays the counsel for the crooked labor union. He heads a murderous goon academy in *Platinum High School*. Richard Egan and Mickey Rooney are the troubleshooters. Egan is a green assistant district attorney investigating the shooting death of a dock foreman. Mickey Rooney is a concerned father looking into his son's death at the academy. He is an ex-Marine so it's not wise to try to strong arm him when he comes looking for answers and explanations.

Although Dan Duryea continued to make movies in the 1960's, the bulk of his appearances were on television. He supplanted his screen appearances with a trove of television performances that added shades and

Platinum High School is one of producer Albert Z. Zugsmith's teen exploitation flicks. 1961, Cinema Associates, Inc.

dimensions to his big screen roles. Still, it is of no small measure that his last movie roles were charming sociopaths.

John Hopta is a Yank living in England during the swinging sixties in *Do You Know This Voice?* Life for him is anything but swinging as a hospital orderly and he uses his spare time to botch an ill-executed kidnap attempt that ends with the death of the victim. In *Walk a Tightrope*, he is still the dissolute Yank living below the radar in a bleak England. This time around he is named Carl Lutcher and he sells his soul to a woman who pays him to kill her husband. The trouble is Lutcher uses his silencer on the wrong husband.

Dan Duryea's last louse may not have killed anybody but he belongs to the long list of heart breakers and deadbeat dads. Eddie Jacks disappeared from *Peyton Place* for what should have been the fruition of his marriage and the formative years of his daughter's life. He returns eighteen years later to extract promises from the people who forgot about him a long time ago. Eddie Jacks is the last illegitimate link to Johnny Prince.

The irony of Dan Duryea's career is that the man who created a roster of scoundrels, connivers, murderers, and thieves was actually a mild mannered man who enjoyed a fulfilling home life and a marriage that lasted 36 years and produced two sons, Peter and Richard.

Dan Duryea was born on January 23, 1907 in White Plains, New York. He attended White Plains High School, where he had to contend with the reputation of Hewlett L., his older brother, an honor student whose standard created a high bar for the youngster. His attendance was so uneventful that the only incident of merit was being disparaged by an English teacher when his answer to what book and play he would select if he was stranded on a desert isle was The Bible and Robert Browning's *Pippa Passes*. She thought that her disinterested student's answer was disingenuous and humiliated him in front of the class.[2]

His high school years may not have been eventful but Dan Duryea kept himself busy with extracurricular activities. He was the manager of the basketball team and belonged to the following clubs or committees: the Boys' Mandolin Club, Amphictyons, Orange Board, G.O., Cheerleader, Secret Three, Class Prophecy, W.P.H.S. Club and Delta Alpha.

Duryea had a mild interest in dramatics in high school and belonged to the Stage Club. He noted that in all of the plays that he appeared in, his roles were "always the honest, upright, law-abiding hero." It was not until he graduated and attended Cornell University that he developed a keen interest in theater. English was his major at Cornell and he still insisted that he was a disinterested student. He joked about passing one history course because of his resemblance to his professor's deceased brother.[3]

Dan Duryea earned his way through Cornell by waiting on tables at a fraternity house. He also performed in two plays a semester. In his senior year, he succeeded Franchot Tone as the president of Cornell's Dramatic Society.

Dan Duryea graduated in 1928 and began work at The N.W. Ayer advertising agency in New York. In 1931, he married Helen Bryan. Their families had known each other but the couple never met. Dan was busy earning his degree at Cornell when Helen was attending a finishing school with a high school curriculum. She didn't even know that he had returned with a degree and had obtained a job with a New York advertising firm after his parents opposed their son's plans to become an actor.

It was happenstance that Helen's father was making the same morning commute to the city as Dan. One day he recognized the young man and offered to drive him home when they returned to White Plains. Helen met her father at the train station and accompanied them on the drive

A detail of the Cornell High School's Mandolin Club with Daniel Duryea sitting front and center. 1924, The Oracle (Perfection to the Finish), White Plains High School Yearbook.

where they dropped Dan off at his house. When she got home she received a phone call from Dan asking her for a date that very night.

She put him off for a couple of weeks because the dating etiquette of the time dictated that a girl should not be too eager to date a man. Propriety was the rule of the game and it was part of the courting ritual to take it slow and easy. As Helen explained, "Mother thought that it would be good for me to accept a house party invitation—the flock-of-girls-type—from a friend who moved to Birmingham, Alabama. Each morning I received a special delivery (from Dan); sometimes, two."

That was enough to suggest to prospective beaus that Helen was spoken for and it set the stage for a long courtship that lasted for two years. This may seem unthinkable to modern men but Dan Duryea did not mind. His advice to young women was, "If you intend to be courted only once in your life, why not draw out those beau-days a little? I found them fun."[4]

After Dan Duryea and Helen Bryan were married the newlyweds moved to Philadelphia where he was to open an office for the advertising agency. Instead of finding success, he suffered a mild heart attack that ultimately forced him to seek a career change. Doctor's orders inspired him to seek out an enjoyable career so Dan Duryea headed for the summer stock straw circuit to seek work that led him to the New York stage. He appeared in *Stepping Sisters*, a play that turned out to be short-lived. Around this time, Duryea made his film debut in an Argentine film, *El tango en Broadway*. He has an uncredited bit part as the boyfriend of the female lead. The film was made during the summer in New York.

In 1935, the playwright Sidney Kingsley—a former classmate at Cornell—gave Dan Duryea a bit part as a G-Man in *Dead End*, a hit Broadway play about New York slum life that created the legend of The Dead End Kids. The inexperienced Duryea eagerly signed a one-year lease on a New York apartment, not realizing that the play could fold like *Stepping Sisters*. He needn't have worried because *Dead End* became a phenomenal hit, not only in the scope of the theater but from a sociological perspective because of its commentary on slum life and cause for legislative action.

The play ran for eighty five weeks, and when it closed he was playing one of the leads, Gimpty, the idealistic architect. Sam Goldwyn bought the rights to the play and brought it to the Hollywood sound stages. The principal cast members—The Dead End Kids—traveled West but the rest of the cast was replaced by Hollywood actors and actresses. William Wyler was slated to direct the movie.

Dan Duryea (right, pictured with Maurice Hunt, Peter Van Buren, and Wendell Phillips) played a divinity student in the short-lived play, Many Mansions. 1937, Ben Pinochot.

His next part was a divinity student in *Many Mansions*, which ran for twenty one weeks. After the play folded, Dan Duryea returned to summer stock at Westfort, Conn. He was paid $25.00 a week because he was a junior member of Equity, despite having worked steady on Broadway. The meager salary was all the Duryeas had to live on and he wondered how they would make it through the summer when he remembered a small rundown estate he had seen not far from Westport. The owners were former missionaries and they resided in California. They were delighted when Dan Duryea contacted them to ask them if he could renovate the summer house. The couple agreed to let him clear off the grounds and allowed him and his wife to live there rent free. That summer he did the gardening chores during the day and acted in the barn playhouse at night.[5]

Shortly thereafter, Duryea played his first Western bad man in the Guthrie McClintic produced *Missouri Legend*, at The Empire Theatre. The play was written by E.B. Ginty and was a comedy about Jesse James' later years as a domesticated family man and a devout Baptist. The names have been changed, I suppose, to protect the guilty.

Dan Duryea appeared as Bob Johnson (Bob Ford), the coward who shot Jesse James. Brooks Atkinson, the theater critic for The New York Times, described Duryea as "a treacherous tin-horn sport with horrible validity." The play starred Dean Jagger as Thomas Howard (Jesse James). According to Atkinson, Jagger "…in the pivot role of an episodic play, … now shows that he has the strength and magnetism to hold a play together and the boyish charm to give it the relish of romantic acting."

Dorothy Gish, as his wife, "has the right sort of pout and spirit for the part of Jesse's middle-class wife." Mildred Natwick played the Widow Weeks, who is "admirably comic, endowing the part with drollery and personality", even though she is about to be dispossessed. Russell Collins, as Jim Cummins, "acts well the boorish doubts of a member of the James gang." Jose Ferrer, "as Jesse's most loyal satellite, is extraordinarily good, full of rude devotion and raffish sentiment." Karl Malden, in one of his earliest theater roles, plays Johnson's brother, Charlie.

The play had a short run but it was enough to impress Herman Shumlin, the theater impresario and the playwright Lillian Hellman. Shumlin cast Duryea as Leo Hubbard, the young weakling son and nephew, in Hellman's *The Little Foxes*, starring Tallulah Bankhead. He played the part for 763 performances in New York and eighty nine on the road tour. The drama's title comes from the Old Testament's Song of Solomon (11:15): "Take us the foxes, the little foxes that spoil the vines; for our vines have tender grapes."

"As a theatrical story teller Lillian Hellman is biting and expert", wrote Brooks Atkinson in his review of February 16, 1939. "In *The Little Foxes*, which was acted at the National last evening, she thrusts a bitter story straight to the bottom of a bitter play. As compared with *The Chil-

dren's Hour, which was her first notable play, *The Little Foxes* will have to take second rank. For it is a deliberate exercise in malice-melodramatic rather than tragic, none too fastidious in its manipulation of the stage and presided over by a Pinero frown of fustian morality. But out of greed in a malignant Southern family of 1900 she has put together a vibrant play that works and that bestows viable parts on all the members of the cast."

A photo from the stage version of *The Little Foxes*, later made into a film that featured Dan Duryea in his stage role. With him is Tallulah Bankhead (seated) and Charles Dingle and Carl Benton Reid.

Atkinson wrote four more glowing paragraphs, including "There are also vivid characterizations in the other parts by Charles Dingle, Abbie Mitchell, Carl Benton Reid, Dan Duryea, Lee Baker, and John Marriott."

Dan Duryea repeated his role of Leo Hubbard in William Wyler's 1941 film version of the play, starring Bette Davis as Regina Giddens.

"That picture started me off on the road to hell as a bad man", Duryea stated. "And ever since, I've been portraying the most hateful screen characters you can think of."

The Little Foxes started a film career in 1941 that continued until 1968 with *The Bamboo Saucer*, a Cold War science-fiction adventure. Dan Duryea's last television role was Eddie Jacks on the successful night-time soap opera, *Peyton Place*. He appeared during the show's 1967-1968 season, playing a sly home wrecker who returns to his wife eighteen years after he went out for a pack of smokes and didn't return home.

Eddie Jacks was a far cry from the man who portrayed him. Dan Duryea was a soft-spoken individual who prided himself on his successful marriage and dedication as a concerned father. When asked how he was able to have a long-lasting marriage while being in a business that was not conducive to conjugal bliss, he replied, "Simple. Marry a girl like Helen."

The Duryea family lived a quiet and unassuming life, far from the maddening din of Hollywood. They occupied a Mediterranean-style home in the Hollywood Hills that overlooked Hollywood and the San Fernando Valley. They also had a home on Lake Arrowhead, where Duryea and his sons built boats and raced them on the lake.

Dan and Helen Duryea were active in civic affairs and were members of the local PTA. Dan Duryea even served as an executive committee member for his sons' Cub Scout troops. He was also an avid gardener and once boasted about his roses and prize winning peas to his publicist, who was dismayed because it clashed with his image as a screen villain.

Dan Duryea did his best to distance himself from his original screen persona, which was a mean-spirited misogynist who liked to slap around women. In a fan magazine interview given later in his career, he stated, "Inside, I'm really a nice guy. I really don't know what it is that makes me look nasty. The first part of my career consisted of playing all the rats in the world. It got so that ladies, upon encountering me on the street, felt almost compelled to hit me across the face with their purses."

However, he did mention an upside to playing dead beats and scoundrels. "Playing villains is not only a living. It's therapy! I can get all my nastiness out of my system in front of the camera, and be an absolute angel at home."

The downside was the inevitable encounter with the bully who wanted to square off with him: "Being a happy and contented professional heel has its occupational hazards, too. In public places, some wise guy always tries to show off by wanting to find out how tough I am. When I can't smile my way out of a fight, I usually run like hell in the other direction. But now and then I've had to flatten out a wise guy to protect my reputation as a heel."

It was also the reason why he forbade his children from watching his movies. He did not want them to get the impression of their father as "the man who took pot shots at Gary Cooper." As he explained it, "I took one of my sons, when he was just a little kid, to see one of my pictures. I was playing the 'heavy.' In the middle of the show, during a big fight scene, my boy shouted, 'You better not dare shoot my daddy.' It was funny, but it was serious, too, because it sometimes takes a child a long time to realize that it isn't real."[6]

It also took adults some time to realize that Dan Duryea was merely playing a part. Comments in movie theaters or stares in restaurants or hotels were unnerving and gave the actor and his wife the impression that people thought that he was a bad man in real life. Soon, he had to convince the neighborhood kids and their parents that he was not a real life villain. That is one reason why he decided to become involved in community affairs.

He and Helen established Friday night film festivals at his house. They bought a 16mm projector and showed the neighborhood kids current comedies, Westerns or historical features. One night, up to 42 little kids were lying on the floor watching the movies. Duryea would explain to the children about the art of portraying a role and that playing a villain was an actor's job, just like portraying the hero.[7]

It was a philosophy that he reinforced by not letting his children become infatuated with

Hollywood. Peter and Richard visited Hollywood sets only three times during their childhood. Dan Duryea stated that it was usually to see special things like a stagecoach or a Western scene being filmed. He was not an advocate of child actors, believing that children who grew up around the studio and spent their childhood with actors and adults became emotionally stunted because they matured too fast. He did not believe that it was normal for a child to grow up before they were ready.

A candid portrait of Dan Duryea and his loving wife, Helen.
1950's, Fan Collection.

His oldest son, Peter, became an actor but that was after he graduated college. He was never pushed in that direction and it was a decision he made on his own. His younger brother, Richard, became a tour manager for The Beach Boys, among other entertainment acts. Neither of the sons was pushed into their careers and they were independently made choices because the Duryeas believed in letting their children mature naturally.

"I think basically I grew up in the same way that I tried to bring up my kids", he said. "My father was very good with his hands, making things and I'm pretty good at it too. I built a beautiful work shop with all the power tools and the boys and I have spent some wonderful hours there, making things together."[8]

The many photographs that show the Duryea family enjoying home life are not staged accompaniments for movie magazine puff pieces. They were honest slices of their family life. In one of his last interviews, Dan Duryea insisted that it was possible to raise normal kids in Hollywood.

"Sure, there were long hours involved and the travel and the location work. But we were always close, the boys, their mother and I. I somehow managed to find time to be with them because it was important."

A casual photo of Dan Duryea tending to the gardening chores. 1940's, Fan Collection.

Still in control behind the wheel.

It was a sound philosophy that endured a busy career in the movies and on television. Dan Duryea always credited his wife with being the soul of the family. Their blessed marriage ended when Helen Duryea suffered a fatal heart attack on January 21, 1967. The support of his loved ones helped Dan Duryea make the adjustment in his life and he helped to fill the void by accepting the role of Eddie Jacks on the first prime time soap opera, *Peyton Place*. He initially rejected the part several times until it was rewritten to his satisfaction. It was somehow fitting that his penultimate role would embody all of the dubious qualities of Duryea's best villains. Eddie Jacks was a shifty ne'er-do-well whose only virtue in life was that people dealt with his loathsome personality.[9]

Dan Duryea died on June 7, 1968, at the age of 61. Three months earlier, he had undergone surgery for a malignant tumor. Dan Duryea was interred beside his wife at Forest Lawn Memorial Park. Helen Duryea's commemoration is, "We loved everyone." Dan Duryea's memorial declares, "A man everyone loved."

The Early Years: Hollywood's Finest

MAN BEHIND THE LION'S ROAR

During the first half of the 20th century, the studio system created dream factories that comforted the public during the Great Depression and the WW II years. Hollywood had several major studios, others known as the major minors followed by the low budget companies called poverty row studios.

It was rare that an independent producer operated on the A level of film making but Sam Goldwyn was one of the exceptions. He is associated with MGM in name only, having become part of the new studio when Marcus Loew acquired Metro Pictures, Goldwyn Pictures and Louis B. Mayer Pictures. Sam Goldwyn occupied a strange position at MGM, having been ousted after the merger.

Leo the Lion was his creation and it found itself on firmer fitting with the studio than Goldwyn did. He became an independent producer whose films were distributed by several studios, including MGM. It was Goldwyn who brought Dan Duryea to Hollywood and the actor's contract was with the producer.

Goldwyn liked to snap up Broadway plays and adapt classic novels for film productions. Dan Duryea appeared in one such play, *Dead End*, but was not among the cast members who made the trip to Hollywood. He fared better with *The Little Foxes*, a screen adaptation of Lillian Hellman's 1939 play. Sam Goldwyn was impressed with the play but felt that its tone was too harsh and he asked Lillian Hellman to revise it as he had requested her to do with her treatment for Sidney Kingsley's *Dead End*. One of the revisions was adding David Hewitt, the young newspaperman, as a love interest for Regina's daughter. He was considered a less controversial social critic than the play's African-American maid. When

Regina Giddens (Bette Davis) is the rapacious matriarch of a southern family trying to adapt to the 20th Century in *The Little Foxes*. 1941, Loew's Inc.

Goldwyn asked for more revisions Lillian Hellman suggested that he use the writers Arthur Kober, Alan Campbell and Dorothy Parker. The final product is still sullen and downbeat but the acid was diluted with salt water.[1]

Bette Davis was loaned from Warner Brothers (in return for Gary Cooper, who was used for *Sergeant York*) to play the role that Tallulah Bankhead had acted on stage. Teresa Wright, in her first movie role, was hired to play Alexandra Giddens and Charles Dingle, Carl Benton Reid, Dan Duryea, Patricia Collinge and John Marriott were imported from the original Broadway cast.

Sam Goldwyn often used director William Wyler and was rewarded with Oscar-nominated pictures like *Dodsworth* ('36), *Dead End* ('37) and *Wuthering Heights* ('39). He also teamed the skilled cinematographer Gregg Toland with Wyler and they made many fine films together. *The Little Foxes* is one of them.

William Wyler's mature direction is masterful in the way he brings out the nuances of the characters' inner anguish, including the dark sides of the socially redeeming characters. Gregg Toland's deep-focus camera work gives the film a rich-textured, brooding atmosphere. His scene compositions resembled turn-of-the-century photographs come to life. Wyler and Toland plus an expert cast created a three-dimensional world on a flat screen.

The Little Foxes focuses on the members of a dissipated Southern family trying to make a successful transition to the twentieth-century machine age. They are a second generation of carpetbaggers and all they have left are dreams of past glory. Desperation and crass measures are some of the things they stoop to in order to make a lucrative investment in a cotton mill.

Regina (Bette Davis) is a strong-willed opportunist who has the business acumen and power of veto that allows her to outmaneuver her brothers, Oscar and Ben (Charles Dingle and Carl Benton Reid). They are desperate and kept in line by her resolute manipulation. She becomes the creative force behind the plan to adapt to the industrial age because only she has the vision to see the benefits of a partnership with Mr. Marshall (Russell Hicks), an industrialist and opera patron.

All the deal needs is the financial support of Regina's ailing estranged husband, Horace Giddens (Herbert Marshall). To Regina and her brothers, Horace is the period at the end of the sentence, as his approval is needed to make the deal final. His daughter, Alexandra (Teresa Wright), loves him dearly and is used to lure him back to the estate so he can be persuaded to kick in his share.

Regina controls her invalid husband even though he is the only person who understands her. His ailment makes him vulnerable to her will

Regina (Bette Davis) is catered to by her weak nephew Leo (Dan Duryea) and her scheming brothers (Carl Benton Reid and Charles Dingle [l – r]). 1941, Loew's Inc.

and that is the reason that she dominates him. She uses his aversion to the merger as a bargaining tool with her brothers. The weaklings can't deal with the suspense and will resort to larceny to make the partnership work. This includes temporarily appropriating some of the bonds that Giddens keeps in a safety deposit bank at the bank where nephew Leo Hubbard (Dan Duryea) works.

Regina's nephew is a rude, lazy, good-for-nothing until he tells his father about the valuable bonds in a safety deposit box. That is when he becomes a player by being a pawn. Leo is supercilious, a lazy man with grand ambitions who stands in his father's shadow and picks the old man's pockets when he can get away with it. Leo is weak, a pile of leaves swept around by the wind blown by his father and uncle. Easily manipulated by his father's ambition to be the main player in the family, Leo Hubbard is a vacillating parasite, but then so are most of the players in this drama.

Bette Davis is remarkable as the cunning yet vulnerable matriarch of the Giddens clan. She may be conniving and manipulative, but she is running on empty and is in desperate need of a refill. Failure to gain a controlling share in the prospective cotton mill will mean becoming a cipher in the new century. She is full of as much fear as she is hopeful, because her youth (and the dreams that went along with it) has slipped away.

Her pancake makeup and haggard reflection show her that she is trapped in a Limbo that will turn her into something worse than her dissipated sister-in-law or spineless brothers. Limbo will become Hell if she does not secure the finances she needs from her estranged husband.

Herbert Marshall excels at portraying a vulnerable man with a steel will. He has a conscience and realizes that the enterprise would ruin the town due to the investors' aim to pay substandard wages and secure land rights that do not belong to them.

His goodness and strong moral character are preserved in his daughter, Alexandra, played by Teresa Wright. Wright earned her place in 40's films by playing young, optimistic adolescents on the verge of womanhood. Her post-Gibson Girl-type characters were flowers blooming at the onset of spring, possessing an uplifting charm that was often a balm to the sickness that pervaded the lives of her supporting players.

William Wyler directs Teresa Wright (l) and Bette Davis (r) in a scene from *The Little Foxes*. 1941, Loew's Inc.

Patricia Collinge gives the most remarkable performance of the film as Birdie, Leo's mother and Alexandra's aunt. She is preserved by alcohol and fond memories of a proud past. Watching her performance is like seeing an ornate vase dropped to the floor and shattering in slow motion. Birdie's family were once true southern aristocrats, their honor well-preserved through adherence to a strict social code.

The Civil War changed their fortunes and they fell prey to the rapacious merchant code of the Hubbard family. Charles Dingle plays the crude and uncouth Oscar Hubbard, the man who married Birdie in order to snap up what was left of the family dynasty. Alexandra is warned by her aunt that she will suffer the same fate if she does not break away from the family. Her escape route is provided by an aspiring newspaperman played by Richard Carlson. Alexandra runs off with him at the end of the movie, leaving Regina to wallow in her ill-gained success.

Dan Duryea recreates his stage role of Leo Hubbard, a dunce who is lazy and greedy, willing to reap the benefits of unrealized dreams or live on someone else's fortune. Supercilious and rapacious, he is a spoiled brat turned loquacious bore. A schemer made of dough, Leo is the grifter who sells out himself every time he makes a score.

Leo wants to be rich and successful but does not have the drive to work for it. He has his father's dark heart, which makes him reckless because he does not think before he acts. His impulsiveness inspires small dreams and that's what his life is—a small dream. He needs to be rich in order to survive. Without money, he would be a casualty of life. That is also true of his father, aunt, and his Uncle Ben, who is portrayed as a frivolous bore by Carl Benton Reid.

There is a little touch of Leo Hubbard in the majority of Duryea's big screen roles. This applies to many of the heroes, too. It was Duryea's shadings and accents that produced the moral fiber of his characters and the degree of anguish they caused others in order to achieve an end that was either sanctified or damned. That is the only way his characters can be identified.

The Little Foxes received favorable reviews from the critics and was a success with the film public. The movie garnered 11 Oscar nominations, including Best Picture, Best Director, Best Actress, Best Supporting Actress (Patricia Wright and Patricia Collinge) and Best Adapted Screenplay. It was Sam Goldwyn's first movie since he departed from United Artists.

Of the stage originals imported by Goldwyn only Dan Duryea was awarded a term contract. Sam Goldwyn also had Gary Cooper under contract and the mogul was frustrated because his star's hits had been with loan-outs for other studios. One such instance was loaning Gary Cooper to Warner Brothers in return for Bette Davis. Cooper made *Sergeant York* and it was a sensation. Goldwyn had a mind to borrow Billy Wilder from Paramount studios so he could write a bright comedy for Gary Cooper. Paramount pointed out that they loaned out actors and, occasionally, directors, but not writers. Goldwyn solved this dilemma by offering Gary Cooper to Paramount for its production of Ernest Hemingway's *For Whom the Bell Tolls*.

In return, Paramount loaned him the writing team of Billy Wilder and Leigh Brackett, Oscar winners for their script for *Ninochka*. The team wrote a screenplay based on a short story Wilder and Thomas Monroe had co-written called *From A to Z*. The original story was written in German before Wilder left Germany. Monroe helped him to adapt it to American sensibilities.

From A to Z was the original title of the script before it was changed to *Blonde Blitzkrieg* and *The Professor and the Burlesque Queen*. The final title was *Ball of Fire* and Barbara Stanwyck starred opposite Gary Cooper. Dan Duryea had a small part as Duke Pastrami, a low-level thug who appears on the fringe of things.[2]

Romantic comedy is one of the film genres where a tight script is necessary for a successful result. The same goes for expert direction and tight editing, coupled with disciplined but zany acting and whimsical musical phrases that accent, not detract from, a scene. This perfect combination produces a snappy picture; anything less than this produces a strained result.

The degree of a romantic satire's success depends on whether or not the audience thinks that it fulfills the strict requirements of such a comedy style. It is one of the few genres where every facet has to work if the final result is to appear natural and not strained. A strong script is a necessity, but cannot be used to coast by on. It is hard to go wrong with the script supplied by Wilder and Bracket.

Ball of Fire is a rare combination of drawing-room farce, screwball comedy, gangster movie, and class satire. Dan Duryea has a small part as Duke Pastrami, a low level hood who speaks the jargon of the streets. He gets some screen time during the expository scene where he and another goon hold professors and a sanitation man hostage while an underground marriage is being performed across the river.

Ball of Fire is a treatise on the courting etiquette of the times. Barbara Stanwyck plays Sugarpuss, an earthy burlesque dancer kept under wraps by a gangster who has her living among the private world of a group of elderly professors. Duryea's part is small; he plays a sort of justice of the peace to insure Sugarpuss' wedded bliss with his boss.

In *Ball of Fire*, a nightclub chanteuse wanted for questioning by the police finds sanctuary in a brownstone where eight professors are writing an encyclopedia. She serves as an authority on slang for Professor Potts (Gary Cooper), an awkward English professor who falls in love with her. He does not realize that she is the moll of a gangster who wants to marry her so she can't testify against him in a murder trial. The professor complicates things by wanting to marry her after she teaches him how to kiss.

The staid routine of the professors' lives is interrupted by the ball of fire. They begin to think of love in the antiquated styles of their youth, from wearing spats to singing golden oldies. The only person not impressed by the burlesque queen is the maid, who believes that women like her cause the crumbling of civilization. She aims to do something about it when she reads the headlines reporting that the entertainer is wanted for questioning.

Gangsters enter the picture when they want to use her wedding with the professor as a pretext for a wedding between her and a crime boss, the gist being that a wife can't testify against her husband. It is when academia meets the underworld that a clash of attitudes produces a series of comi-

Title lobby card for Howard Hawks's *Ball of Fire*, starring Gary Cooper and Barbara Stanwyck. 1942, Loew's Inc.

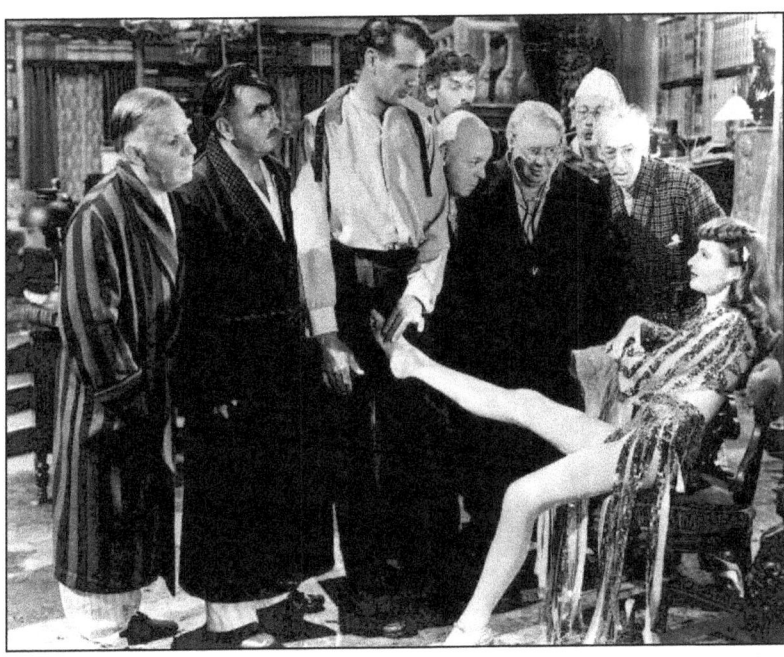

Sugarpuss (Barbara Stanwyck) casts a spell on the bookish professors (Henry Travers, Oscar Homolka, Gary Cooper, Aubrey Mather, Leonid Kinskey, S.Z. Sakall, Richard Haydin and Tully Marshall[l – r]). 1942, Loew's Inc.

cal mishaps. True love triumphs when the professor and the singer marry, proving that the illogical forms the backbone of screwball comedies.

Mix your verbs and strangle your malapropisms and you have a *Ball of Fire*, a war of the words, a comedy drama that demonstrates that words have power and that a nation's stability rests on respect and proper usage of its language. The question of who has the clout to codify proper usage and what does communication matter is the final cause of *Ball of Fire*, a pleasant gangster comedy with the flair of a Damon Runyon yarn.

Fortunately, *Ball of Fire* is top-notch. The first rate script by Billy Wilder and Charles Bracket is perfectly balanced between mirth and pathos. Language has always been an expression of status and class. Street talk and proper English are only tolerated in their own milieu. Billy Wilder and Leigh Bracket spent time in drug stores, pool rooms, burlesque houses and racetrack to research street idioms.

Barbara Stanwyck plays Sugarpuss with a brash and feisty sensuality. She is perky and frisky, relishing the way she disrupts the staid lives of the cloistered professors. She handles them with the ease and skill of a club hostess hustling a customer into buying an endless round of drinks for the house. It's all based on her sexual allure, something most of the professors know nothing about.

Gary Cooper displays his ability to play a shy, awkward man whose honest heart and decent moral code set him apart from the ruffians Sugarpuss is used to associating with. He falls in love with her, not realizing that she is a flirtatious tease who is leading him on.

Plot mechanics bring them together by the end of the film and it is not the first time that a cynical woman is won over by an innocent Cooper character. His righteousness impresses Sugarpuss, but he wins her over the old fashioned way by beating up his rival and bringing down his crime syndicate.

Picaresque characters have always been an asset to screwball comedies. It is one of the film genres where they fit in as normal characters. The professors and the working class players are a colorful bunch, but the groups are linguistic oddities. The professors are experts in the usage of modern English, and the working class characters communicate with neighborhood colloquialisms. It's a polite confrontation between two class systems but the gentility turns bombastic in the film's final reel.

Dana Andrews is the crime boss and Dan Duryea has a small role as Duke Pastrami, one of the wise-cracking, small-time hoods working for the big guy. The professors are played by the top character actors of the era. Among them are Henry Travers, Oscar Homolka, S.Z. Sakall, Tully

Duke Pastrami (Dan Duryea) is one of the two gangsters who keep the professors and guests hostage so his boss can marry Sugarpuss without their interference. 1942, Loew's Inc.

Marshall, Richard Haydyn, Leonid Kinskey, and Aubrey Mather. Allen Jenkins plays a sanitation man who tutors Professor Potts in jive-talk, doing so with a snappy verve.

Speaking of snappy verve, Ms. Stanwyck sings *Drum Boogie* with Gene Krupa and his orchestra. She has a skillful interlude with him where she sings *sotto voce* and he solos with Blue Diamond Tip matchsticks.

Howard Hawks is in top form in a role akin to that of a traffic cop in Times Square during rush hour. He repeated this formula with a remake, *A Song Is Born*, with Danny Kaye and Virginia Mayo, which tells the story of a stripper on the lam and a college professor who has to invent a new lexicon when they meet.

Goldwyn finally got his hit with Gary Cooper. The movie was among the 20 top grossing films of 1942. *Ball of Fire* earned four Academy Award nominations, including one for Best Actress (Barbara Stanwyck) and Best Adaptation. Lux Radio Theatre put on a version that starred Barbara Stanwyck and Fred MacMurray.

Sam Goldwyn put Gary Cooper's folksy charm to good use in his next picture, *Pride of the Yankees*. Working titles for the movie included *The Lou Gehrig Story*, *The Great American Hero*, *The Life of Lou Gehrig* and *Lou Gehrig*. The picture was a tribute to a popular folk hero, Lou Gehrig, the first baseman for the New York Yankees. He was known as The Iron Horse because of the string of consecutive games that he played for the team—2,130.

He was struck down by amyptrophic lateral sclerosis in the prime of his life and the height of his career. The disease eventually became known as Lou Gehrig's disease and it was the way he handled its devastating effects that defined his character. Lou Gehrig died one year before the release of the movie and his legend still loomed large in the public's mind.

Actors considered for the part were Spencer Tracy, Eddie Albert, Brian Donlevy, Cary Grant, Billy Soose (former middle-weight boxing champion) and Waite Hoyt, a former pitcher for The New York Yankees. MGM announced that Dan Duryea and Walter Brennan would be added to the cast as sports writers. Brennan was originally to have played Miller Huggins, the manager of the Yankees. In his new role, Brennan was playing Gehrig's ghost writer and confidante. Duryea's role would be a little more cynical as he was to serve as Babe Ruth's ghost writer.[3]

Pride of the Yankees is the sentimental and emotional story of Lou Gehrig (Gary Cooper), the Yankee legend known as The Iron Horse for his long consecutive streak of games played. Gehrig is the shy and unas-

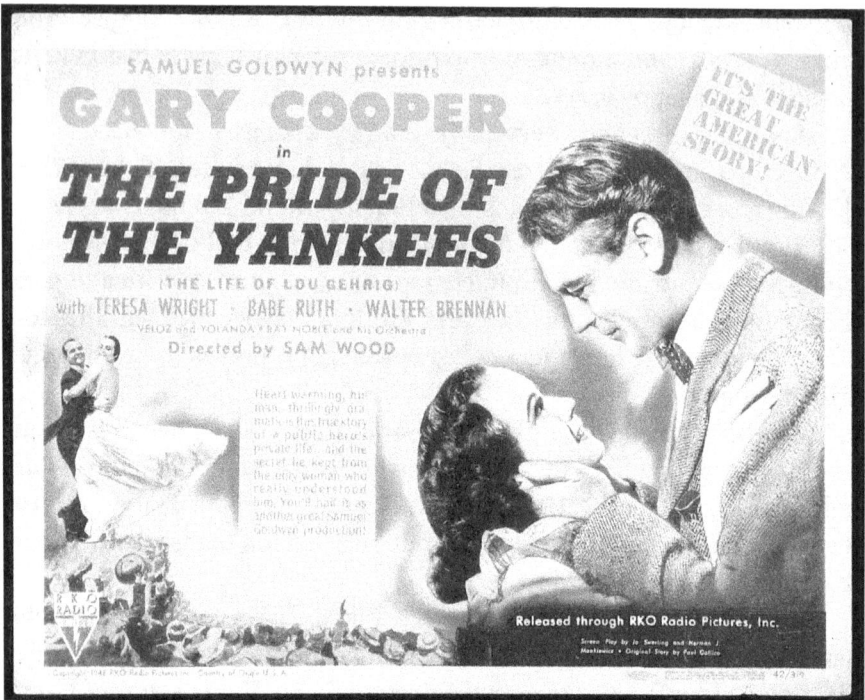

Title lobby card for *Pride of the Yankees*, starring Gary Cooper and Teresa Wright. 1942, Loew's Inc.

suming child of German immigrants. His mother's dream is for Lou to become an architect, so he works his way through Columbia University. He excels at baseball, attracting the eyes of a scout for The New York Yankees. *Pride of the Yankees* could very well be seen as a profile of courage in the immigrant chronicles.

Gehrig makes it to the big leagues but he is afraid that his mother will be disappointed when she finds out that he is a ballplayer instead of an architect. He is right; despite his fame and success, she is upset that he hasn't fulfilled her dreams for him. It is not until he becomes an American legend that she can accept the life that he has carved out for himself.

Gehrig's success in the game turns him into a superstar of the time. He gets to battle Babe Ruth for the supremacy of the sports pages. They are two larger-than-life figures that represent the two extremes of human nature. Ruth is convivial and Bacchus-like in his rapacious appetites, while Gehrig is the picture of quiet reserve, possessing a refined grace under pressure. Their rivalry creates a basis for a fairy tale that has its sadness within the charm.

Pride of the Yankees has all of the clichés, inanities, and apocryphal messianic episodes that make Hollywood biographic films fun to watch. What makes this film remarkable is the success of the actors in affecting the pathos, empathy, and soft heartedness of the audience by cutting through the sappy dialogue.

Gary Cooper, Teresa Wright, and Walter Brennan deliver the corniest lines to the dippiest musical accompaniment, but they still elicit the same type of catharsis you would get from a classical Greek tragedy. Gary Cooper delivers corn-pone dialog and Teresa Wright is too pure to be true, but they go beyond the cornball conventions to give powerful performances. Their courtship, marriage, fame, and tragic travail are all portrayed convincingly.

Pride of the Yankees is a storybook, feel-good film that celebrates legends such as Lou Gehrig and the New York Yankees. Babe Ruth is on hand to lend authenticity to this weepy sudser. Despite the way the film tugs at the heart strings it shows the greatness of the man, especially in the finale when Gehrig gives his famous farewell speech at Yankee Stadium.

Dan Duryea is a disparaging press box reporter who rebuffs Brennan's positive copy about Gehrig. Duryea's reactions and feelings about Gehrig change as the film progresses as he is seen mostly from the press booth, mixing it up with Brennan.

Lou Gehrig (Gary Cooper) and Babe Ruth (Himself) humiliate a couple of press box critics, including one played by Dan Duryea (r). 1942, Loew's Inc.

Sam Goldwyn was once again rewarded when *Pride of the Yankees* received 11 Academy Award nominations and won three, including Best Actor and Actress awards. Film editor Daniel Mandell won the Oscar for Best Editing. It was the Goldwyn touch and was an example of a maverick producer working within the studio system at its apex.

THE FREELANCE MARKET

Dan Duryea's contract with Goldwyn allowed to him to work on the freelance circuit. His first outside picture was a screwball comedy called *That Other Woman*. The director was Ray McCarey, the younger brother of Leo McCarey, the famous director. Ray McCarey had worked his way up from prop boy to assistant director until he received his big break with Hal Roach Studios in the 1930's. He directed several two-reelers with Our Gang (The Little Rascals) and Laurel and Hardy. He moved to Columbia Studios, where his best known work was with the 3 Stooges. His workload was basically B-movie programmers and *That Other Woman* was typical of his output.

The screenplay was written by Jack Jungmeyer, a prolific director, writer and producer. It was called *Leap Year*, the title of an original story by Lamar Trotti. Like *Ball of Fire*, *That Kind of Woman* is a romantic farce with a Damon Runyon-like flavor. Both movies have clever scripts but they do not share adept players, appropriate musical accents, seasoned direction, and rhythmic editing. *Ball of Fire* and *That Other Woman* are at the opposite ends of the scale and serve as two studies of the comedy-drama where daffiness and logic have to blend to create laughs and pathos.

That Other Woman has a tight script, but it is reduced to college level hi-jinks because of the two dull leads and uninspired direction. Everything is present for a formidable comedy but it does not happen. James Ellison, Virginia Gilmore and Dan Duryea are a romantic triangle. Mistaken identity, romantic double-crosses, and clever writing shuffles them around town in a fox hunt that ends with a toe-to-toe blowout between Ellison and Duryea.

Henry Summers (James Ellison) is a narcissistic architect who is irresistible to women and too weak to stave off the temptation that goes along with his magnetism. It has given him a mercurial attitude towards his work, where reaching a deadline means cramming three weeks' worth of work into a maddening night.

Poster for *That Other Woman*, a romantic comedy starring James Ellison and Virginia Gilmore. 1943, 20th Century Fox.

Emily Borden (Virginia Gilmore) is his perfect secretary because she is a Gal Friday who excels at arranging schedules, juggling clients, and evading paramours. She is an attractive woman who has fallen in love with Summers, but feels helpless because she believes that she lacks sex appeal.

Grandma (Alma Kruger) is a southern matriarch who is proud of her Victory Garden because it is her patriotic duty. She is a conspirator who looks out for the interests of her granddaughter, whom she believes is wasting her time with her suitor, Ralph Cobb (Dan Duryea), even though he is a southern gentleman with a sense of hospitality and an inbred mistrust of Yankees.

The dowager regales her granddaughter with tales of how she snagged Grandpa, telling of ruses that included letters of flattery and seduction, something she suggests her granddaughter should attempt if she wants to land Mr. Summers as her husband. The family tradition boasts the anonymous love letter gambit as a surefire way of fortifying the blood line.

It is fitting that a deceptive mash letter should get things moving with Mr. Summers because he is vulnerable to perfume-scented love notes with ornate penmanship. Grandma's advice becomes Miss Borden's burden and she mails it more out of compunction than compulsion.

This leads to a chain of events that fosters love while encouraging discouragement. This is done in screwball style, with clever lines and synchronized slapstick bits to enliven a subplot about a lover's misunderstanding and the fun of life-and-death chases based on mistaken identities.

Henry Summers, the narcissist, is knocked down a couple of pegs when he realizes there is more to a woman than a line on the expense account. Emily Borden discovers the inherent power of a plain Jane who becomes a lady on a court balcony.

Chivalry wears out easier than it used to when Ralph Cobb is cuckolded and cut out of the deal completely. Grandma maintains matriarchal status and has successfully passed down the tradition of the poisoned pen letter as being more prudent than an invitation to a shotgun wedding.

James Ellison plays his part like a wind up doll going through the motions. He never runs out of energy, playing his part well enough to get his character's intentions through to the audience. Virginia Gilmore is another wind-up toy playing her part the way it was written, so she compliments her lead as they run circles round each other in a game of charades mixed with masquerades. Lynn Bari played the role for eight days before she got the lead part in *China Girl*.

Ralph Cobb (Dan Duryea) and Henry Summers (James Ellison) are about to fight over Emily Borden (Virginia Gilmore). 1943, 20th Century Fox.

Dan Duryea is Ralph Cobb, a Southern gentleman who courts Borden in the way of a Southern gentleman, only to be knocked on his pride by his rival. He plays it honest and noble throughout the movie and winds up confounded by a game of errors. Duryea plays it well as the suspicious suitor who follows his fiancé upstate while her boss thinks that he is being shadowed by a gangster. Duryea plays it both ways, as a jealous shadow and a Southern cuckold.

Janis Carter is the other woman vying for the architect's attention and Alma Kruger is the know-it-all snoop who starts the chain of events that ends with the architect and his secretary falling in love. Minerva Urecal plays a suspicious landlady who eyeballs Ellison and Borden as they try to book a room in her hotel in a small upstate town.

On January 25, 1943, Columbia Pictures announced that Dan Duryea was signed to appear in *Sahara* with Humphrey Bogart. The announcement noted that Duryea was a Broadway actor who was brought West by Samuel Goldwyn to recreate his stage role in *The Little Foxes* for the film version. In August, when the trades noted that J. Carroll Naish and Richard Lane were added to the cast, it was revealed that the title was temporarily changed to *Gung Ho!* The movie was inspired by an incident in the Soviet film, *Trinadstat (The Thirteen)*, a 1937 Amkino Soviet production directed by Mikhail Romm. This is acknowledged in the movie's opening credits.

The casting and preparation for a movie often reads like a who's-who? of Hollywood players. Glenn Ford and Melvyn Douglas were introduced as the original stars of *Sahara*. It was also revealed Bernard Nedell was tested for an important part. Then, the movie was supposed to have been a vehicle for Brian Donlevy but the actor balked because he was tired of making war movies.

The role was then offered to Gary Cooper but he turned it down. Humphrey Bogart played the part because he had just signed a new contract with Warner Brothers that allowed him to make one picture a year for other studios. The other studio was Columbia Pictures because Bogart admired and liked Harry Cohn. Bogart made other movies for Cohn and he provided the star power that the studio sorely lacked.

It was the fourth movie that Humphrey Bogart made with a war theme. The other movies were *Action in the North Atlantic*, *Casablanca*, and *Across the Pacific*. *Sahara* is an intriguing movie, a minor gem set in the desert during the Allied campaign against Rommel. Sgt. Joe Gunn (Humphrey Bogart), Waco Hoyt (Bruce Bennett), and Jimmy Doyle (Dan Duryea) pilot the tired tank Lulubelle, whose saga is about to become part of war history. Before it does, it will give a boost to the morale of a group of marooned Brits, an Italian P.O.W., and a downed German flyer.

Lulubelle and her pilots are the central characters in the drama, the only reason for the others to hope that they'll survive being stranded in the desert. The ragtag outfit consists of Bogey and his two men, a group of Brit soldiers they pick up at a derelict oasis, an Indian officer, a contrite Italian soldier, and a defiant, grounded German flyer. They brave the desert elements and their common enemy is thirst. Their water is running low and rationing is driving them mad.

Sgt. Gunn is the boss and he makes the life and death decisions that eat at his insides and irritate the others. The trouble is that beneath his tough guy exterior is someone who prizes life. That is why the German and Italian soldiers are allowed to accompany the stranded British troops and the Indian officer. He would have left them if not for the beckoning of his subordinates, international troops included.

It is this motley arrangement that adds more strain to the mission of survival. One Axis prisoner is overt in his loyalty, but the Italian seems to be appreciative, although he is not fully trusted by the others.

A Belgian movie poster for *Sahara*, an exciting WWII drama set in the African desert. 1943, Columbia Pictures.

The survival equation is changed when they pick up the remnants of a British squadron. It becomes weakened when two more survivors turn out to be fascist soldiers. That is why questions of conscience pop up, including natural survival instincts and nationalism. Everyone gets to vent their spleens and they represent their sides of the story well.

Their salvation is an abandoned oasis where the well still drips a little water from the rocks. The Indian officer spends hours filling canteens and cups and sending them to the surface. That is how they survive. There are the sub-stories, such as that of the Italian P.O.W., who begs for his life in the name of his family. His is despised by the arrogant German soldier, who is defiant and cunning to the end. The Brits are righteous guys who agree to let Bogey call the shots.

They brave the desert looking for a water hole that will revive them. What they find is a devastated outpost that will serve as their fortress against an advancing and parched German division. Bogey and his boys will fight a fierce battle, but not without paying a price. The survivors leave behind the silent heroes, whose helmets hang on the butts of rifles dug into their memorial graves.

Director Zoltan Korda, cinematographer Rudolph Mate and set designer William Kiernan have created an impressive desert vision for the eyes and added a compelling atmosphere to the movie. 2,000 tons of sand was used to create a desert with wind machines and paint used to produced the rippling swirls that highlight the desolate landscape.

Sgt. Gunn (Humphrey Bogart) is a regular guy from Brooklyn who finds himself in an extraordinary desert survival drama. 1943, Columbia Pictures.

The Sarge is one of those characters that become flesh and blood because of Bogey's acting. He plays a man with no past or origin. It's more than blood and guts that makes Sgt. Gunn a leader. He calls the shots because he has what it takes to coax Lulubelle to fight the desert's elements.

Bennett is the strong and silent type, someone who drives the tank and makes bets with Duryea about short term standoffs. He is doing it as it comes along; dealing with time as if it were something as endless as the sand.

Duryea is a happy-go-lucky optimist, someone who keeps things going with his farm boy energy. He is the machine gunner and can handle the rough stuff, but is able to smile and joke with Bogey and Bennett. Easygoing to a fault, he and Waco make bets with each other on the outcome of Sarge's decisions. He is one of the war memorials left behind.

J. Carrol Naish and Kurt Krueger give passionate performances as the captured P.O.W.s. Louis Mercier is poetic and philosophical as Frenchie. Rex Ingram keeps a stiff upper lip as a British officer. Richard Nugent imbues his character, an Indian officer, with the solemn pride and determination that inspires the rest of the cast.

Jimmy Doyle is the mid-Western machine gunner for Lulubelle, a nuts and bolts tank on its last mission. 1943, Columbia Pictures.

After making two movies for Columbia Pictures, Dan Duryea's next stop was Republic Pictures, the legendary studio whose impressive output belied its low budget assembly line production methods. The tagline for *Man from Frisco* read, "Nothing's impossible... for this red-headed tornado! He launched ships by the thousands... and had a love affair to go with each!"

Man from Frisco is the story of an innovative builder (based on Henry J. Kaiser) who turns his mercurial genius toward building government ships for use in the European war effort. His revolutionary methods of production can increase output, earning him a trial period at the shipyards of the nation's most prominent shipbuilder. The clash between old and new, tried and true, versus bold and innovative creates a lot of friction in a movie that is Frank Capra-esque Americana mixed with industrial film footage of the shipyards.

Matt Braddock (Michael O'Shea) is an arrogant genius with a mission. Nothing will stand in his way, not even knowing that his new methods will forever change the small town by erasing the residents' lives and replacing them with a mad, mechanical world of his making.

Dan Duryea, Gene Lockhart, Anne Shirley and Michael O'Shea (l – r) star in *Man from Frisco*. 1943, Republic Pictures Corp.

An old-world icon, an old-world political system, an old-world way of life is usurped by the government when they give the mad genius total control of the shipyards so he can produce his revolutionary, pre-fabricated ships for the European war effort.

The old-school network, whose figurehead is the iconic Joel Kennedy (Gene Lockhart), is ordered to accommodate Braddock, but they offer subtle resistance. The only support comes in the form of the old guardian's young son, Russ (Tommy Bond). He is optimistic and supportive of Braddock and his pre-fabricated ship-building plan. Russ offers a strange midpoint in labor relations when he works for Braddock and lives at home.

The odd cog in the network is Jim Benson (Dan Duryea), the would-be son-in-law of the icon, who is in love with Diana Kennedy (Anne Shirley). The balance of romance changes when the arrogant and aggressive Mr. Braddock throws his weight around. He brings in over a thousand workers and risks arrest by the town elders until a broadcast of the bombing at Pearl Harbor makes the old guard realize that they are obsolete.

The megalomaniacal Braddock builds his shipyards and pre-fabricated ships, but not without treachery and tomfoolery by Jim Benson, who is the cuckolded, would-be son-in-law suddenly squeezed out of the picture. He supervises the shipbuilding, but becomes purposely negligent due to his jealousy. This has tragic results, and Braddock is blamed for Tommy's death until Benson owns up to it in the end.

The home wartime effort ends with Braddock and Diana united in a tacked-on ending. The industrial drama that showcased the destruction of an old-time American town ends with a few cornball jokes about raising kids.

Man From Frisco is a hometown war drama. This story of shipbuilding is full of history and rich tradition. The clash of production methods is a contest of wills. It is almost stupefying to see the way Kennedy's world is washed away by Braddock's rude stampede. He is trampled under Braddock's brash new enterprise, the construction of a world that is built on his own terms.

No one has asked him to move, but he makes himself fair game when he challenges Braddock in the opening moves. Benson was Kennedy's loyal assistant before he became Braddock's hesitant foreman. His integrity is blinded by jealousy; it costs the life of youthful vision. Benson is still manipulative, although this time it is because he saw his girl kissing the arrogant interloper.

Once the balance of power tips in Matt Braddock's (Michael O'Shea) favor he becomes a mover and a shaker in the munitions industry. 1943, Republic Pictures Corp.

This results in sabotage that temporarily darkens Braddock's name. A heroic comeback thanks to strong scripting has him building the ship that will be christened in the name of the youthful visionary who lost his life to petty jealousies.

Michael O'Shea is irritating, but he accomplishes the mission. Along the way he wipes out a sleepy little town, destroys the old political regime, and dethrones the preeminent shipbuilder who once ruled the town and was an icon. O'Shea plays it arrogantly and effectively as if he expects success and obeisance as part of his reward for being a genius.

Gene Lockhart plays a shallow icon, one whose stature is more like a statue in the park. He is obsolete but still deserves the reverence of past accomplishments. He also plays the role of the past being thrust aside by the necessity of innovation.

Ann Shirley is caught between her father and Braddock, not to mention her relationship with Duryea. Shirley is the all-American, true-hearted, heartland girl. Whomever she chooses becomes the steer that leads the stampedes that trample anything that gets in their way.

In the end, Michael O'Shea stampedes Lockhart and Duryea while claiming Tommy Bond as his inspiring angel. He is played with the sincere earnestness that was supposed to epitomize the future captains of industry bred in American suburbia.

The next studio stop for Dan Duryea was RKO Pictures, where he appeared in *None but the Lonely Heart*, starring Cary Grant and Ethel Barrymore. Crisis and old-world resolve are the themes of *None but the Lonely Heart* and this profile in courage is played out in the shadows of a small obscure town in England, a place haunted by the Reaper when it's time for him to pay a visit.

Ernie Mott (Cary Grant) is a loner and a vagabond who is fond of describing himself as someone with a heart that is "blacker than the Ace of Spades." His boon companion is a scraggly dog and they roam the countryside without a care in the world. He occasionally touches base in his hometown, where his mother runs a secondhand shop. It is where he recharges his batteries before he hits the road again.

It does not take long for the viewer to realize that Mott is a selfish Cockney blackheart instead of the free spirit that he pretends to be. A crisis of conscience upsets his world when he finds out that his mother is dying of cancer. Mott's struggle lies in curbing his wanderlust and fitting into the routine of running the shop while caring for his ill mother, Ma Mott (Ethel Barrymore). The challenge is staying in one place long enough to confront the biggest enigma of his life: himself.

He assumes the responsibility of running his mother's thrift shop. He is a Handy-Andy and the jack-of-all trades. The colors of his life turn into shades of gray when he copes with the burden of his mother's crisis. The only sure thing in his life is his perfect pitch.

Economic pressures force the mother and son to operate outside the law. Ma Mott becomes a fence and Ernie Mott a petty thief as he gives in to pressure from Jim Mordinoy (George Coulouris), the local gangster. Mott is dating Ada (June Duprez), the gangster's ex-wife and this makes for a strange triangle.

The shady areas and ambiguous spots are balanced by the three women in Ernie Mott's life. Ethel Barrymore is a towering figure, Jane Wyatt is pure optimism, and June Duprez is callous remorse. They inhabit the world that Ernie Mott has settled in, and they expect a lot from him. They are selfish in the way they use him to nurture their feeble lives. He becomes middle-class yet accepts their sorrow. His foray into crime ends disastrously for him, but what makes things tragic is his mother's arrest

Ernie Mott (Cary Grant) is a selfish vagabond with perfect pitch and a black heart. 1944, RKO Pictures.

for fencing stolen goods. This shock sends tremors through Mott's cocksure attitude and he begins to feel unsure as he faces the terror of making split decisions about long-term affairs.

Cary Grant is to the point as the attitudinal wayfarer. He receives a lesson in humility that brings out a dark side to Grant's acting ability. He rekindles his relationships with towering arrogance, only to give into the supporting players.

As Mott's mother, Ethel Barrymore has a quiet strength and mettle reserve that is stronger than anything Grant can come up with, which is why they work so well together. Barrymore is a quiet, but deep reservoir of joy and sorrow.

Jane Duprez is sharp and defiant while being vulnerable and frightened. She hates the gangster life and promises to cut off Grant if he hooks up with her ex-husband. Duprez is desperate but not reckless.

George Coulouris is chilling as the gangster who gets what he wants and acts however he likes. He is brazen, brutal, and defiant. He sets himself up by being so tough, but it only takes one misstep to bring himself down. Coulouris is a successful small time crook who crosses wires and short circuits.

Jane Wyatt is Aggie Hunter, the cellist with the heart of gold. She is the lit hearth and spring fever aiming to please. Her true-heart, homespun charm is what attracts Mott after all is said and done. It's the wholesome middle-class life that attracts the jack-of-all-trades who has tired of his wanderlust.

Barry Fitzgerald pulls out his leprechaun disguise in his role of Henry Twite, the family friend who is a font of old-world wisdom that sets Ernie Mott straight.

Ernie Mott (Cary Grant) provides the music for a neighborhood dance. Dan Duryea is part of the dancing couple, second from the left. 1944, RKO Pictures.

Dan Duryea plays Lew Tate, a snide fry cook at a fish and chips shop. He is a pampered mama's boy and shows it when he backs up his mother's criticism of the refrigerator that she received as a gift from Ernie. Duryea has two short scenes, one at the shop and the other in the apartment of Ernie's mother.

This was Cary Grant's chance to play a serious role and it was something that the public did not want to see. Author Richard Llewellyn originally wrote Ernie Mott as a young man barely out of adolescence and he strenuously objected to the casting of Cary Grant. Famed playwright Clifford Odets adapted his screenplay to suit Grant and directed the film with an emphasis on the lower class ambience of the London working class.

The movie lost money although it received critical acclaim and four Academy Award nominations, including Best Actor for Cary Grant. The only winner was Ethel Barrymore, who won a Best Supporting Actress Oscar. It apparently changed her mind about working in Hollywood. The theater legend had long felt that movies were inferior to the stage but moved West after her Oscar win.

Man from Frisco was released when Dan Duryea completed filming *None but the Lonely Heart*. Dan Duryea considered returning to the stage with a role in *Tucker's People*, a play written by Elmer Rice. It was slated for a November opening in New York but nothing was finalized so he continued making movies.

It was 1944 and Dan Duryea had been making pictures for three years. He had seven credits to his name and was about to take his career to the next level with a step into the crime genre. Before he did that, Dan Duryea signed with MGM to make *Mrs. Parkington* starring Greer Garson and Walter Pidgeon. When his MGM picture was completed, there would be two films directed by Fritz Lang, *Ministry of Fear* and *Woman in the Window*. They would take Dan Duryea into a shady terrain and give his screen identity a dark side that would enthrall movie goers.

Greer Garson was the reigning queen of MGM during the war years and was an Oscar winner for *Mrs. Miniver*. She was one of the movie's top box office winners from 1942 to 1946 and was nominated for the Academy Award seven times, including five years in a row. Greer Garson combined a breathtaking aristocratic beauty with a strong-willed, working-class bravado. She plays the lightning rod for two scions of the Gilded Age in *Mrs. Parkington* and *Valley of Decision*. The movies are MGM spectacles that brilliantly chronicle the rise to power of families whose fortunes were made during the Gilded Age, an era of sumptuous wealth for the newly-formed American aristocracy.

Tay Garnett's films deal with a time when the robber barons were born, men who controlled the elements that created the new Industrial Revolution. The Gilded Age started with the post-Civil War years and reached its peak around the turn of the century. The Great War changed the world economy and the Gilded Age began to tarnish, eventually collapsing with the Great Depression of 1929.

The first of the films, *Mrs. Parkington*, is the history of Susie Graham's marriage to the Major, a wealthy industrialist whose fortune was built on the mines. Major Augustus "Gus" Parkington's story is that of a time when the American frontier was being shaped into an empire by a handful of ambitious, if avaricious, men. It was an era when opportunists became industrialists and created an age of ostentatious wealth, and with it, a class system to rival Europe's.

The Major's investments in shipping, railroads, and the new automobile have made him rich beyond most men's dreams. He uses this wealth as a way to commemorate his wife's beauty. Susie "Sparrow" is his muse

Susie Sparrow (Greer Garson) and The Major (Walter Pidgeon) are dismayed at another telegram expressing regret at not being able to attend his prestigious ball. 1944, Loew's Inc.

and motivation, the only person who is his equal in cunning and compassion.

Mrs. Parkington is a woman with a clear sense of morality. She was a helper in her mother's rooming house when she met the gregarious Major. Marriage followed shortly after her mother was caught in a cave-in and killed while delivering lunch to miners. Their marriage is the beginning of a journey that will span several decades, well into the early 20th century.

Greer Garson projected a strange charm: wise, sensual, and cunning. She had a strong sex appeal made more alluring by her strength and wisdom. Mrs. Parkington is a noble woman of humble means who inherits the kingdom when she marries a dashing entrepreneur who creates an empire based on natural resources, the railroad, and the emerging automobile. In the film she starts as an octogenarian who takes a trip down memory lane when a family crisis makes her think about the man who started it all.

Walter Pidgeon is sublime as The Major. He is tall and debonair, gregarious and boorish, charming and obnoxious, spiteful and tenacious. The Major's upbeat ego offends many of the old world moneybags and they show their disapproval by shunning him. This proves to be their fault because he takes their snobbery and uses it to destroy them, one by one, on Wall Street. His wife is the only person who can stand up to him and make him come back for more.

Agnes Moorehead is delightful as Baroness Aspasia Conti, a French coquette who is more like the Major's mistress. She begrudgingly accepts his marriage to the servant girl and acquiesces to his wish that she educate Sparrow in the ways of the world.

Moorehead is worldly and charming, a bundle of elegant energy and French sensuality.

Cecil Kelliway plays the Prince of Wales with a lighthearted humor. He is also observant and respectful of customs when he steps in to favor Sparrow in a delicate situation regarding the Major and the Duchess after a fox hunt on the English estate.

Edward Arnold plays the son who has a financial scandal on his hands. It threatens the inheritances of his brothers and sisters. He is a flatterer who is on the verge of being exposed as an embezzler.

Gladys George plays a dissolute relative, one whose nerves are shattered by booze and neurosis. She is acerbic, quite a contrast to her role as the mother in *Valley of Decision*.

An elderly Mrs. Parkington (Greer Garson) welcomes her daughter's cattleman beau (Rod Cameron) while the rest of the family condescends to acknowledge his presence. 1944, Loew's Inc.

Duryea again plays a spoiled heir whose dependence on the family fortune has rendered him useless in the ways of independence and ambition. Roger Stillwell is the complete opposite of his grandfather, the Major, who started out as a gambler with a silver mine and wound up a Wall Street scion before his death in an automobile race.

Roger Stillwell is lazy, lanky, and lachrymose. Unlike his grandfather, there is no need for him to leave his mark on the world because he will inherit part of his grandmother's fortune. This safety net is why Roger is a rude and selfish do-nothing. His impertinence fits in well with the second and third generation Parkingtons because most of them are decadent, hollow people.

Roger lacks the manners, bearing, and temperament of a wealthy man, electing instead to act like an ignorant boor. He refuses to shake the hand of his new brother-in-law (Rod Cameron), a cattle rancher. Instead, he whistles *Home on the Range* as he saunters across the room, marking his distance from the new family member.

He also callously rejects his father when the elder tells the family that he is about to be exposed as an embezzler. The rest of the family, with the exception of Mrs. Parkington and his daughter, could not care less about his predicament. They are worried about the family name being fed to the press.

Later, when Mrs. Parkington announces that she will use her fortune—their inheritances—to bail him out, the family protests, threatening legal action. Roger, showing no respect, accuses her of experiencing a second childhood. The thought of losing his safety net appalls him and it seems as if he will do anything to prevent his grandmother from carrying out her promise.

Mrs. Parkington was another success for Sam Goldwyn and received two Academy Award nominations, one for Best Actress (Greer Garson) and Best Supporting Actress (Agnes Moorehead).

Prestige Pictures and Shadow Plays

After Dan Duryea completed *Mrs. Parkington*, it was announced that he would report to the set of MGM's *Women's Army (Keep Your Powder Dry)* starring Lana Turner and Lorraine Day. That didn't pan out so it was back to independent negotiations. The result was linking up with the legendary director, Fritz Lang.

Fritz Lang was an Austrian-German filmmaker whose work with German Expressionism created a new cinema language during the Weimar Republic years. He made the *Dr. Mabuse* Trilogy, *Die Nibelungen* ('24), *Metropolis* ('27), *Woman in the Moon* ('29) and *M* ('31), his first talkie. Lang fled Germany in 1933 when Adolf Hitler and the Third Reich came to power and he found temporary asylum in France, where he made a film with Charles Boyer.

He immigrated to the United States, where he signed with MGM in 1936 and made *Fury* starring Spencer Tracy. Lang made 23 movies in America, mostly crime dramas, but he did not enjoy the artistic freedom that he once had in his homeland. It was stifling for him to work within the studio system and make movies by committee. Many critics have dismissed his Hollywood films as being formulaic programmes, but he had a supporter in Francois Truffaut, who lambasted film critics and historians for not recognizing Lang's genius in "the spy movies, war movies or simple thrillers" he made in Hollywood.

Graham Greene was one of Fritz Lang's favorite writers and the filmmaker wanted to make a film out of *Ministry of Fear* but could not outbid Paramount Pictures for the rights. That is why he was pleasantly surprised when his agent called him to say that Paramount wanted him to direct the movie. Usually, Lang had the power to tinker with a script but this requirement was unwittingly left out of his contract and he was unable to convince a resentful writer to change a script that the director claimed had no relation to Graham Greene's novel.[4]

A fake spiritualist (Hillary Brooke) uses natural charm to bedevil Stephen Neale (Ray Milland). 1945, Paramount Pictures.

Ministry of Fear is a pocket-book espionage thriller where the action flows in and out of conflicts and resolutions with little or no trouble. There is a beginning, a middle, and an end with a bewildered hero, good and evil blonde seductresses, treasonous villains, and colorful supporting characters. It is well-made in a paint-by-the-numbers fashion by Fritz Lang.

Ray Milland is Stephen Neale, a troubled man who has served time in a mental hospital for the mercy killing of his wife. He becomes embroiled in a Nazi plot involving smuggled microfilm when he inadvertently intercepts the microfilm in a cake. It happens at a county fair where a fortune teller sets things up such that Neale wins the cake by guessing its weight. He is the wrong rigged winner and it sets off an intense manhunt in which Nazis and British authorities pursue Neale, who is aided by Marjorie Reynolds playing Carla Hilfe, a reluctant Fraulein.

It is the cat-and-mouse chase scenes that add suspense to the plot. Outwitting two pursuers does not give Neale much room to operate. Fair-handed law officer Inspector Prentice (Percy Waram), and pat scriptwriting enable Neale to scour a bombed-out field for the microfilm in the cake. Of course, he finds it in a bird's nest! This clears him in the eyes of the law, but does not get him out of the sight of the Nazis' scopes.

Ministry of Fear is a wartime film that has split sides with heroes and patriots intermingling with each other and arousing antipathy and sympathy with every ploy or maneuver. There are those who have a split vision of Neale, who is considered a crazy American by some and a dangerous, patriotic spy by others. He is still needed because he can be used against the Axis powers.

Ray Milland's earnest performance gives the character credulity. Marjorie Reynolds is the Austrian freedom fighter who aids him in his escape. Rex Ingram is her wimpy brother, a man who reluctantly aids Milland before turning him over to the authorities. Percy Waram plays a vacillating top cop who is suspicious but obliging in Neale's attempts to clear himself.

The distinguished Alan Napier plays Dr. Forrester, who works for National Security but secretly heads a Nazi spy ring that uses a charitable organization as its front. Hillary Brooke is a phony psychic who adds to the confusion that creates another front for the traitors.

Erskine Sanford adds color as George Rennit, an eccentric investigator who does not stick around to collect his fee. Dan Duryea plays Cost, a small-potatoes tailor who fails to get the cake and winds up a fall guy and

The tailor and his scissors. 1945, Paramount Pictures.

a frame-up at a séance. The séance was not meant for him, and it lays him out with a phantom punch. He makes a comeback as a tailor whose scissors make a point that costs him his life. This time it's for real.

Ministry of Fear is an entertaining movie even though it is performed on stilts. Fritz Lang has given some of the scenes a mysterious ambience, but otherwise it's full of phony theatrics, such as the suitcase bomb in the hotel room, the phony subway bomb-shelter setting, and the bombing of the fields. The microfilm in the cake is a cheap enough gimmick, but finding the microfilm after the Nazi bombing stretches credulity a bit. The fortune-telling angle adds a touch of parlor-game amusement, but the presence of Hillary Brooke makes it hypnotic and worthwhile.

Fritz Lang may not have been totally satisfied with *Ministry of Fear*, but he was approving of the séance scene with Hillary Brooke and pleased with Dan Duryea's scissors-stabbing scene. He was also impressed by the performances turned in by Marjorie Reynolds, Percy Waram and Dan Duryea. It was Duryea's performance as the traitorous tailor that landed him a role in Fritz Lang's next movie.[5]

Fritz Lang was pleased with the script for *Woman in the Window*. Nunnally Johnson had based it on a short story by J.H. Wallis called, "Once Off Guard." There was only one element that bothered Lang and that was the lack of youth among the three male leads. Lang remembered Dan Duryea's performance in *Ministry of Fear* and liked the way he handled the scissors in his role as the tailor. He believed that Duryea would bring a youthful zest to the role and he convinced the studio brass to hire the actor for the role of Heidt, the blackmailing former bodyguard of the murdered lover. He also changed the ending to a dream ending because he did not believe that the audience would accept the plausibility of the series of killings. He believed that making the movie a dream would justify the over-the-top action.[6]

Alice Reed (Joan Bennett) is *The Woman in the Window*, a portrait of a seductive woman that inspires three middle-aged professional men to question their own virility. Professor Wanley (Edward G. Robinson) is a mild-mannered psychology professor who faces his mid-life changes with a sex-fantasy that turns into a bone-chilling nightmare. It starts with a captivating portrait on display in a gallery next to the men's club that he frequents.

The lobby card for *The Woman in the Window*. 1944, RKO Pictures.

One night, the painting inspires a conversation among the three friends at the social club. The DA (Raymond Massey) believes that a middle-aged man is like an unconditioned athlete who cannot rise to the task at hand. Many cases that cross his desk attest to the foibles of over-the-hill stallions that still pass themselves as colts. The doctor (Edmund Breon) reluctantly agrees, but Professor Wanley does not concede the point so easily.

The DA and the doctor leave their colleague to ponder his conceit, a perspective that leads to a chance encounter with the model. This leads to a round of cordials and a late night review of her portfolio. Murder, blackmail, and suicide follow, all because of an innocent flirtation with a painting.

The Woman in the Window is a gimmick-laden blackmail melodrama whose chief interest is the mesmerizing Joan Bennett. To look at her allows you to tolerate a pat plot development based on cardboard figures given life by the principal players. Edward G. Robinson and Dan Duryea breathe life into the stock characters of a milquetoast and sleek villain. They add a seedy vitality to Bennett's veneer of sophistication. A twist ending befits a morality tale where murder and suicide are suitors for the hand of a bored socialite-for-hire.

The Woman in the Window is a compact and compelling movie, expertly acted and directed with Lang's concise flair. The viewer is swept along with the fluid plot development that flows like dream logic. The repressed sexual fantasy unfolds naturally even though the plot seems illogical when examined. The forbidden impulse lies in falling in love with the sexy portrait. Self-censorship comes in the form of not wanting to take the cordials beyond a casual encounter. Fantasy and temptation are shown by giving in to her invitation of viewing her portfolio in the privacy of her apartment. Denial and chaos occur when he tries to deny his feelings and confronts her jealous keeper. Condemnation and punishment is manifested with a blackmail scheme and a sordid way to find absolution.

The first half of the movie plays like a police procedural, with the DA assuming the pompous, professorial tone of Sherlock Holmes. He reveals clues, deduces motives, and lays out assumptions that make Professor Wanley feel uneasy. The movie's tone changes once Dan Duryea shows up as the blackmailer, an ex-cop turned private eye who has been shadowing the murder victim. The moment Duryea enters the movie, the DA disappears and it becomes Duryea's show. He becomes the character who calls all of the shots and decides which way the plot will develop.

Prof. Wanley (Edward G. Robinson) disposes of the weight of his guilt. 1944, RKO Pictures.

The Woman in the Window has a special allure because such by-the-numbers movies are designed to make clichés enjoyable. Forget loose ends and a novelty ending, 'no questions asked' is the way to digest the movie's logic. So Alice Reed has nothing better to do than to look at the reactions on strangers' faces when they match her visage to the portrait in the window?

Of all the strangers she encounters, she invites the bulldog man up to her apartment. The seedy man in the straw hat can bluff his way into a blackmail scheme without resistance from Reed. The professor will dig a grave for himself when he buys poison for Alice Reed to use on the blackmailer. It all does not matter because a shaggy dog story is just a shaggy dog story, especially if it is a dream.

Prof. Wanley is likeable although it is unlikely that Bennett would take an interest in him, especially when she is the kept woman of a millionaire. The jealous outburst of the sugar daddy is extreme, but lays the groundwork for the scissors-in-the-back bit and the body-in-the-rug disposal. There is always a creepy peeper around to witness the disposal of the corpse. In this movie, it's Heidt (Dan Duryea). He insinuates himself into Reed and Prof. Wanley's life, complete with blackmail demands and a Plan B that serves as his magic carpet ride to a noisy fade-out.

The ease with which he accomplishes his threats, demands, and set-ups is convenient but unrealistic. Reed agrees to come with part of the money, and also uses poison in a cocktail toast. It does not work because Heidt is too smart for that.

However, he is not smart enough to avoid the shootout with cops that results in his death and accusations of being the original murderer. It is a smooth if implausible turn of events that clears Alice Reed. Too bad that the professor did not have nerves of steel and opted instead for a poisonous bromide. It's all a joke when the sandman collects the leftover laughs from a doorman, a porter, a lady in a painting and a professor who realizes that he is middle-aged and there's nothing he can do about it.

Joan Bennett is the main reason to disregard the absurdities of the plot. She is one of the last of the original dark-haired *femmes fatale* before they became dominated by peroxide blondes. Her hypnotic eyes and neurotic manner legitimize the illogical dreamlike simplicity of the action.

Edward G. Robinson's inner satyr makes him a slave to Bennett. It's not just the painting; it's the polite come-on in the genteel form of a sidewalk pickup. It is abstract rudeness to him and it drives him crazy. He becomes a cuckold gone cuckoo in need of a Mickey Finn prescription.

Dan Duryea comes off like the shadow of Bennett and Robinson's skewed moral compasses. He is the built-in nemesis created by the loopholes of their plan. They killed Zeus, the great sugar daddy, and Duryea was the rude jester who appeared on the scene to exact payment for their folly.

Heidt (Dan Duryea) is the shadow player who upsets the balance of power with a blackmail scheme. 1944, RKO Pictures.

Duryea witnesses the activities of the crime and deduces that the guilty parties are a model and her slave. He cashes in on it with sly inference and dream logic. Being justified in his attempt to collect a tariff on Bennett and Robinson's secret gives Duryea the liberty to break the law with impunity. The principal players reunited for a radio broadcast of *The Woman in the Window* for The Lux Radio Theater on June 25, 1945.

If *Main Street After Dark* looks like a padded educational film, it might be because the director, Edward L. Cahn, once made shorts for the studio. His previous movie was a short called *Main Street Today*. Cahn was a prolific maker of low budget films of every genre. He started out as a cutter for Universal and became a director in 1931 and directed a total of 127 movies. He is recognized mainly for the type of movies he made during the 1950's because they were popular exploitation movies with teenage juvenile delinquents, small time mobsters and sci-fi monsters.

The original title for *Main Street After Dark* was *Tell-Tale Hands* and it was described as a film about a shakedown racket "pulled by unscrupulous B-girls on servicemen." The script was tinkered with a bit to tone

The Dibson family is a clan of hustlers consisting of Lefty (Tom Trout), Jessy Bell (Audrey Totter), Poesy (Dan Duryea), Ma (Selena Royale), and Rosalie (Dorothy Ruth Morris). (l–r). 1944, Loew's, Inc.

down the sensationalism. In *Main Street After Dark*, the quickie master directs Dan Duryea in a movie about a crime family of paddy rollers. Ma (Selena Royale) heads the gang that rousts gullible servicemen in the military town the family operates in. Duryea is smooth and slips easily into the darkness after hustling innocent soldiers. He gets in over his head and nabs a bellyful of "crime does not pay" by the final credits.

One could look at *Main Street After Dark* as an educational film padded with crime drama vignettes. The subject is the police crackdown on con artists in a military town. The focus is on a family and Lt. Lorgan (Edward Arnold), the detective who hounds them to keep them in line. Thanks to the detective, the drama veers off into educational segments on surviving the scams the servicemen will face in town.

Selena Royale plays Ma Dibson, the matriarch of a family of crooks that thrives on the easy marks in their military service town. Their dupes are mainly servicemen, and the family plies a variety of methods to snare their prizes. It all comes apart for the crime family when the eldest son is released from the pen after serving his stretch.

He cannot wait to get back in the game and eyeballs a payroll drop as his one big score. It is bungled and turns into a murder rap when he murders his boss. Lt. Lorgan dogs the family in a way that makes it seem like harassment until the film's climax. It becomes apparent that he knew what he was doing and that the villainous kin will be split up to face separate raps.

Edward Arnold is aggravating as the detective hot on the beat. He comes off like a patronizing big brother, but he is always there to make a bust. He is always smiling, whether he is giving a pep talk, conducting an unofficial interrogation, or cracking down on someone with the iron cuffs.

Selena Royale is the matriarch that rules the gang with an iron fist. She knits sweaters while listening to a police band and calls the shots that net wallets, knick-knacks, and other odds and ends. She is strictly a small-town crime queen, but one that uses her street savvy to stay one step ahead of the law.

Posey (Dan Duryea) pulls an ingenious but heartless scam on two unsuspecting servicemen. 1944, Loew's, Inc.

Lefty (Tom Trout) is a two-dimensional cartoon tough guy right out of the funny pages. The main difference is that he does not have a five o'clock shadow until his final shot when it turns into a twenty-year stretch. The cartoon tough guy has a wife, and she is played by Audrey Totter.

Totter has a bitter deadpan expression and a sexy pout that brings life to the stereotypical character of Jessy Bell Gibson, a hard-bitten, dime-a-dance girl. She resists his attempts to get her back into a life of crime, but she gives in to the pressure.

Dan Duryea is Posey, the pampered younger son who is the apple of his mother's eye. He is a pickpocket who is fawned over by his mother, turning him into a lazy good-for-nothing. He is soft, and that is what works against him in the big holdup.

Hume Cronyn plays an unsettling and morbid antiques shop owner. He is a front and he is there to finance the undercurrent of the hustler squad's world. Lloyd Corrigan is his usual friendly boisterous self. This time his charm is not enough to impress everyone as his payroll robbery is a countdown to his death.

Even though *Main Street After Dark* was produced with the MGM logo it was hardly a prestige picture. The studio produced its share of B-movies but they still had that sumptuous look indicative of their quality movies. So it was not such a stretch for Dan Duryea to work in a melodrama at Republic Studios.

Considered part of the Poverty Row studio system, Republic Pictures still had an admirable reputation of getting the most out of the least and that included an eclectic output that ranged from serials to musicals with the occasional high-brow production, such as Orson Welles' stark version of *Macbeth*, on its itinerary. It was also a studio where a temperamental genius like Erich Von Stroheim could eke out a living starring in low budget melodramas.

Von Stroheim was a cinematic innovator whose genius created a legend around itself. Director, actor and producer, he was an auteur long before the theory was espoused in any cinema journal. His vision, style and temperamental was too big for the silent era and his creations were severely edited to conform to the standard running times of movie houses.

He entered the talkie era as an actor, starting out with a classic like *Le Grande Illusion*, and he made a series of movies in France before he came to America. Once he arrived in Hollywood, he played stereotypical Austro-Hungarian aristocratic martinets. Some of his 40's American movies

Al Wallace (Dan Duryea) makes another empty promise to his wife Connie (Mary Beth Hughes) about giving up alcohol. 1945, Republic Pictures.

were *I Was an Adventuress* ('40), *Five Graves to Cairo* ('43[as Rommel]) and *The Lady and the Monster* ('44).

Anthony Mann had the dubious task of directing Erich Von Stroheim in *The Great Flamarion*. He conceded that Von Stroheim was a genius and he was not, having added that his lead was difficult to work with. Von Stroheim's assertion was that no moviegoer would be interested in a movie where the lead character was killed in the introduction. He also detested non-linear scripts and abhorred the use of the flashback as a story telling technique.

The Great Flamarion is a Prussian marksman who showcases his shooting prowess by shooting at the husband-and-wife team who play an adulterous couple to his enraged cuckold. Offstage, the wife eventually ingratiates herself to manipulate the great showman into shooting her husband in a drunken misstep while going through this act.

If the dated histrionics of yesteryear's romanticism aren't enough to keep you in stitches, the ham acting of a once-upon-a-time great film director doing the Mad Prussian routine will have you in hysterics.

The Great Flamarion seems old for its time and is reminiscent of early films of the sound era because it is overly melodramatic and has a tinny soundtrack. It has its odd attraction because of the talent associated with it. The director is Anthony Mann and the star is Erich Von Stroheim. The *Sturm und Drang* of betrayed love in the theatre world makes it an interesting companion piece to the *Blue Angel*, although it is a minor connection.

Flashbacks were the rage of many films in the 1940's, chiefly because of Orson Welles' masterful use of the technique in *Citizen Kane*. It eventually became a cheap gimmick among its many imitators after it became a standard storytelling method. The use of the flashback in *The Great Flamarion* is basic.

The movie begins with a murder in a Mexican theater. A woman had been killed and her husband is the chief suspect. The real murderer is a wounded mystery man who falls from the rafters after everyone except the clown has left the wings. The dying man tells the clown his story, the legend of *The Great Flamarion*.

The legend is an expert marksman who showcases his shooting prowess in an absurd stage show. He plays the cuckolded lover who returns home to find his wife with another man. He shoots at them with his pistol, popping buttons, straps, and bottles. His aim is hair-raising and the audience is enthusiastic. *The Great Flamarion* enters and exits to thunderous applause every time he performs his act.

His assistants are played by Mary Beth Hughes and Dan Duryea. Al Wallace, the husband, is a drunkard and Connie, his wife, strives for a better life. She contrives a plot where the Great Flamarion would accidentally shoot her husband when he stumbles drunkenly onto the stage. The murder would be deemed an accident because of Wallace's drinking problem.

At first, Flamarion is a tough nut to crack. He is the stereotypical, highly-disciplined Prussian aristocrat. The act is the only thing that matters to him and his only concern is Wallace's drinking. His life consists of practicing to strengthen his eyes.

Flirtation and exhibitionism fail to excite Flamarion. He is immune to female wiles because of a failed relationship many years ago that turned him into the man of stone. His work is now his life and it occupies all of his time. It takes time to wear him down, but when Connie does, he is silly putty in her hands.

It does not take long to convince him to shoot her husband and make it look like an accident. The coroner rules the death accidental because of the high amount of alcohol in Wallace's blood. The successful plot is

The Great Flamarion (Erich Von Stroheim) and sidekick Connie (Mary Beth Hughes) plan to murder her husband during a performance. 1945, Republic Pictures.

a pact to temporarily separate and meet at a later date where they can resume their love.

It is when Connie fails to show up at the designated spot, a hotel in Arizona, that Flamarion realizes that he was deceived. He becomes obsessed with revenge and becomes destitute during his nationwide search for Connie, who has run off with the cyclist from their last act together.

The tip-off is that Connie is in Mexico and it is all settled at the theater when he strangles her backstage and she shoots him twice. He uses the wings to make his escape before he comes down to earth to tell the clown his story. The movie ends when Flamarion finishes his story and the flashback turns into the sympathetic clown nodding as the cops arrive to solve the crime.

The Great Flamarion is a shrill affair with overblown performances. Backstage rivalries make for great mystery and intrigue when handled with lurid melodramatics and ham acting. Histrionics and cliché dialogue comprise a noteworthy genre when a good cast and experienced crew squeeze the thrills and chills out of bits that have been reliable standbys since the silent era.

The movie benefits from the sinister character of Von Stroheim, a one-time cinematic giant whose career flourished in pre-Nazi Germany and Hollywood during the silent era. He later attained success in B-movies typecast as Mad Prussian types in post-war American melodramas. Erich Von Stroheim is hilarious as Flamarion, especially when he acts like a schoolboy in love.

Dan Duryea plays a dupe to the great Von Stroheim and attempts to keep himself from being the losing side of a lover's triangle. Duryea plays the spineless jelly-man, one who keeps his promises in a bottle. The goofball is Leo Hubbard under dire circumstances. Dissipated and cheapened by his spoiled sense of superiority, he now acts like a stooge in a marksman's side show.

He is a spineless drunkard in every scene and his promises ring hollow because they are fueled by liquor. He is a liability to the act, which infuriates the Great Flamarion and he no longer serves a purpose to Connie. In the end, Duryea's main nemesis is the bottle. It is no wonder that the ruined genius should push him out of the picture and lay claim to his wife. Mary Beth Hughes is a formidable vamp, although it is Flamarion's pent up desperation, not her seductive power, that makes her effective.

Dan Duryea returned to the MGM lot to make his last film for the studio. *Valley of Decision* was a book by Marcia Davenport chronicling four generations of the Scott family, scions of the Pittsburgh steel mill industry. It covers the years 1873 to 1945, a pivotal epoch in American history that included The Industrial Revolution, The Gilded Age, WWI, the Great Depression and WWII. The title of the book comes from a verse in the Old Testament's Book of Joel (3:14). It is about the Day of Reckoning when God will pass judgment in the valley of decision.

The movie could be considered a companion piece to *Mrs. Parkington*, not only because it also stars Greer Garson or has Tay Garnett as the director; like *Mrs. Parkington*, *Valley of Decision* is about the new robber barons of the Gilded Age. *Valley of Decision* depicts the time when steel mills took over America and a Scottish immigrant who created a steel empire deals with the changes it has brought in production methods as well as Irish workers' grievances. Greer Garson again stars as a noble woman of humble means who inherits the kingdom, but not without heartache and misery.

She plays Mary Rafferty, the daughter of an embittered steel worker who was injured in an accident at the steel mill. She exacerbates her father's anger when she accepts a job as a maid in the house of the mill owner. It does not help matters that she falls in love with Paul (Gregory Peck), the eldest son. The tension provides for a Romeo-and-Juliet type of romance. In this version, happenstance reunites the lovers and they do it right the second time around after having been separated by family politics and feelings of guilt.

The movie is an incisive portrait of the formation of the steel mills. Rugged individualism pervades a movie filled with sons of thunder and lightning, spinners with steel backbones and fiery spleens. One wonders if a genetic code is responsible for the working and ruling classes. The thing they have in common is the smokestacks that belch billowing, voluminous smoke. The difference is that the son of Scottish immigrants lives in the house on the hill and the progeny of the Irish immigrants live in the shanties of the valley.

William Scott, Sr. (Donald Crisp) is a fair-minded man who did not become corrupted by his enormous success. He is a sober-minded individual who is aware of his social status and the responsibilities that come with it. Scott is the immigrant son who made a fortune, but is still considered new money by the industrialists he competes with. Independent and proud, he is unwilling to lose his bearings by becoming part of a steel syndicate headed by Andrew Carnegie.

His noble character is reflected in the way he treats his workers, especially the irascible Pat Rafferty (Lionel Barrymore), who was crippled in an accident at the factory. Mr. Scott has compensated Rafferty with a weekly stipend, but the victim's pride has made him bitter and vengeful.

Lionel Barrymore is to be given a lot of credit for creating a full-bodied figure with the tempestuous nature of a raging tornado. He leads the strikers in a confrontation on the bridge and shoots the elder Scott to death, only to be shot dead by one of the strike breakers.

The two men represent the two factions that forged steel out of their own blood. Both adversaries are children of the immigrants who dug into the mountains to create the mines. Now, one prides himself on hard work and visionary ideas while the other relies on cunning and ambition to compensate for his inability to earn a decent wage to support his family.

The essence of dissolution, the bitter old man in the wheelchair is the impediment to the future. Pat Rafferty leads his working-class ruffians against the effete founder of the steel mills. It appears to be class war-

Patrick Rafferty (Lionel Barrymore) strongly disapproves of the relationship between his daughter Mary (Greer Garson) and Paul (Gregory Peck), the son of his arch rival. 1945, Loew's Inc.

fare, but what it is comes closer to being mob rule. Through an unforeseen miscalculation, the sides collide with deadly consequences during a strike. The patriarchs are killed, but their offspring eventually marry. It is a new dawn in the age of industrialism.

The underlying industrial theme is a sub-plot to the personal stories and relationships that are interwoven into the social studies lesson. The setup is similar to the family rivalries in Romeo and Juliet.

Greer Garson is mesmerizing as the lady in ascension. She does it through humility, beauty, and a quick and sharp tongue. She appeals to the benignly arrogant Sir Paul, who admires the servant girl, but things go wrong between them because of caste restrictions.

Gregory Peck plays Paul, the son of the steel magnate. He is steadfast and strong, inheriting his father's vision for the future of the steel mills. It does not hurt that he is aided by a rustic genius, played by Preston Foster. Foster is the odd man out, an engineering genius who develops a blueprint for a new type of mill.

Marshall Thompson is the popinjay son with the drinking problem. He causes the cataclysm that kills the heads of the families in the confrontation at the bridge. He was entrusted with the task of informing his brother, Willie, to call off the strike breakers because an agreement had been reached between the workers and the elder Scott. While waiting for his brother to arrive, he passes the time with a few drinks that eventually make him too drunk to carry out the task.

His sister, Constance, is played by Marsha Hunt. She, too, is a spoiled brat but is taught about responsibility by Mary Rafferty, especially after she marries into royalty and goes to live abroad. Mary accompanies her out of fealty to the Scott family, who hope that Paul will marry his well-to-do fiancée, played with icy frippery by Jessica Tandy.

Dan Duryea is Willie, the middle son, the one who tires of the workers' demands. Duryea plays a decisive and brash younger brother of a fledgling Scottish steel magnate played by Gregory Peck. His break with the family in the way of useful politics ends with a mini-revolution that kills its captains. Willie butts heads with Paul and winds up losing it all when his kid brother has one too many send-me-offs at the bar.

William Scott, Sr. (Donald Crisp) breaks up a row between his sons, Willie (Dan Duryea) and Paul (Gregory Peck). 1945, Loew's Inc.

Willie does not believe in progress and would readily sell the mines if it means that he would net two million dollars. He also does not believe in family honor, and he shows little gratitude to his immigrant grandfather or the toll that had to be paid to make the mines the meat of the family's matter.

Willie Scott is the exception to the rule of the decadent aristocratic offspring. He is the son of a steel magnate, but does not rest on his father's laurels. He is more active and outspoken than the other roles played in the industrial jungles. That does not mean that he will not sell the family mines and factories if the price is right.

Dan Duryea's contract ran out and he did not renew it. He told a Hollywood reporter that, "Acting is a business with me, and I want to handle my own affairs. If I was under one contract I might be going into one picture after another and then what would happen? This way I can limit myself to about three pictures a year and I don't have to do a part if I don't like it."7

One of Dan Duryea's new projects was to have been an Eddie Cantor-Joan Davis musical Western called *Come on Along*. He signed with RKO in Oct., 1945 and his part was the romantic lead of The Calico Kid, a Robin Hood type of bandit. Eddie Cantor and Joan Davis were the stars of a traveling theatrical troupe in the 1900's. Eddie Cantor returned to New York and the shooting was postponed. Dan Duryea asked for and received his release from the film, which was never made.

Duryea was signed by International Pictures to star in Gary Cooper's next film, a Western that also featured Walter Sande and Frank Sully from Columbia. Loretta Young and William Demerest were added to the cast and Stuart Heisler was slated to direct from a screenplay by Nunnaly Johnson. The movie's title was *Along Came Jones*, and it was Gary Cooper's first film as a producer. His company, Cinema Artists Corp. and International Pictures financed the movie and RKO agreed to distribute it.

In *Along Came Jones*, Melody Jones is mistaken for Monte Jarrad, a gunslinger, and he encounters all sorts of trouble and awkward situations when he and George Fury (William Demarest), his sidekick, arrive in a town called Payneville. Jones matches the description in the wanted poster and also has the same initials as the killer bandit. It is a mystery to Jones why townsfolk defer to him but his false pride turns to fear when gunmen and a posse hunt him down.

The real bad man is holed up in the house of his showgirl sweetheart, Cherry de Longre (Loretta Young). She sees a formidable dupe in Jones

Lobby card for *Along Came Jones* starring Gary Cooper and Loretta Young. 1945, International Pictures.

Monte Jarred (Dan Duryea) keeps a tight rein on Cherry (Loretta Young). 1945, International Pictures Company, Inc.

and plans to use him as a diversion to the boyfriend in hiding. Trouble starts when she falls in love with Jones, starting a feud between him and the real bad man. The rivalry ends in a classic Western shootout.

Along Came Jones is a good-natured spoof of Westerns, where the strong, silent lawman romances a petticoat beauty while contending with a ruthless Black Bart. It does not hurt that the star of the movie is known for playing lone hero types. Gary Cooper is the laid-back Melody Jones, and he spoofs his image well. He gets plenty of support from a humorous William Demarest, a seductive Loretta Young, and a villainous Dan Duryea, who creates his first Western bad man in the role of Monte Jarrad.

The movie may be a Western spoof but it is still Duryea's prototype gunslinger. It's a stagecoach that he robs at the beginning of the movie, passengers that he shoots, and that is Gary Cooper and a posse that he shoots it out with in the finale. Gary Cooper may have been spoofing himself, but Dan Duryea was carving a new niche in his cast of characters.

Cooper and Duryea are a study in opposites, even though they are both tall and lanky. Cooper is tentative and self-effacing and Duryea is blunt and ruthless. This creates a riveting rivalry between the characters. Loretta Young is leather and lace as the frontier woman whose hardness is softened by Cooper's lanky heroics. Her character once loved the outlaw because he was wild in his youth. The wildness was supplanted by meanness, and this change is what causes the rift between them.

Loretta Young possessed a strange sex appeal that was a blend of gawkiness and eroticism. It was an unusual blend, along with presenting the illusion of helplessness mixed with total control.

William Demarest is humorous as the hero's sidekick. He is tough and funny, mainly because he is bewildered by his saddle sidekick. Demarest provides comic relief, but he is also there for the final showdown, lending moral support even though he was wounded by the bandit.

Along Came Jones was adapted by Nunnally Johnson from Alan LeMay's novel, *Useless Cowboy*. Stuart Heisler directs the film with a light-handed manner in a dark and foreboding atmosphere. It takes a special talent to blend humor and drama, and Heisler achieves the balance by providing a humorous satire that is also an earnest Western.

Universal Studios

Crime and Punishment

Universal Studios was considered one of the major minors. That was the term for big studios that did not own movie theater chains to spool their movies. In 1945, it did not matter because Hollywood's anti-trust debacle was not far off and even the major studios would no longer have the benefit of a movie theater chain to play their products.

Universal was always riding the crest of one genre wave or another. In the sound years, they revived the horror picture cycle in the 30's and the war years keep them going with other film series, mainly Abbott and Costello, Sherlock Holmes and later Francis the Talking Mule and Ma and Pa Kettle. They also profited from the Deanna Durbin years, a series of films with the singing child star. Deanna Durbin's reign ended when she grew up. Like other child stars, she was given a chance to act and perform as an adolescent. Surprisingly, she chose to retire after *Lady on a Train* despite having given an excellent performance and seemingly being capable of playing adult roles.

Lady on a Train is a whimsical murder-mystery, an attempt by Universal to alter Deanna Durbin's screen image without straying too far from her persona as a singing ingénue. She plays Nikki Collins, a lover of mystery novels who witnesses a Christmas Eve murder while riding a train into Grand Central.

The police don't believe her claims so she undertakes the task of investigating the murder, eventually persuading mystery writer Wayne Morgan (David Bruce) to reluctantly help her. She finds out through a newsreel that the victim was Mr. Waring, a wealthy shipping magnate who is reported to have died from an accident at his Long Island estate. This inspires Nikki to visit the estate for the inquest, where she unwittingly assumes the role of Margo Martin, a nightclub singer who is the disputed heir to the victim's estate.

Poster for *Lady on a Train*, a comedy-drama starring Deanna Durbin. 1945, Universal Pictures Company, Inc.

This leads to a cat-and-mouse tale of mistaken identities as the schemers try to dissuade Nikki from continuing her investigation. This includes numerous murder attempts on her life, although her persecutors are not responsible for the original murder. The whole investigation becomes a trail of false leads and a string of red herrings.

Lady on a Train is typical of the films Universal turned out during the 1940's. It is a professionally-made movie, created by expert craftsmen who knew how to do their jobs well. It is entertaining because it follows a formula and evenly dispenses the thrills and humor.

Deanna Durbin is attractive and personable, showing a flair for sex appeal and comedy. She sings "Silent Night" over the phone to her father and performs "Night and Day" in a nightclub.

David Bruce was a bland star of the 40's and he plays the mystery writer who is drawn into a real mystery. His pencil mustache has more character than he does and he ambles his way through the film with an affable manner.

Dan Duryea again dons a trench coat and a fedora for *Lady on a Train* as a suspect who is sinister and suggestive of menace, although he is a diversion to the real murderer. His performance netted him six offers

Nikki Collins (Deanna Durbin) mesmerizes two brothers (Dan Duryea [r] and Ralph Bellamy [l]) at an inquest. 1945, Universal Pictures Company, Inc.

from different Broadway producers and his fan mail also skyrocketed to 1,000 fan letters a week.

Ralph Bellamy plays his older brother and they are drawn into the scheme when they become infatuated with the nightclub singer who was the bait for their uncle, the murder victim. The brothers are the two swings of the pendulum, only one of them cuts for real.

George Coulouris is a nightclub owner who is responsible for the original extortion scheme that led to the murder of his lure, Margo Martin. She is a nightclub singer played by Maria Palmer and is used as bait to snare the aging millionaire. It becomes a case of mistaken identity when Nikki Collins temporarily assumes the singer's identity, implicating her in the shady goings-on, only one of them gets roses and the other winds up colder than chilled champagne.

Allen Jenkins is menacing as the nightclub owner's chauffeur and strong-arm thug. Edward Everett Horton is charming as a befuddled attorney for Collins' father. William Frawley has a comic bit as the cop who refuses to believe Collins' claims at the beginning of the movie. Lash LaRue, the future Western legend, has a small part as a waiter at the club where Margo Martin sings.

After the filming of *Lady on a Train* was completed Dan Duryea contributed to the war effort. The war was winding down in 1945 and performers were still making tours with the USO shows. Dan Duryea went on a hospital tour with Frank Faylen and Gale Sondergaard among others. They wrapped up the tour at the end of May and Duryea took a well-deserved vacation.

Dan Duryea's next role for Universal would be the one to stamp him with despicable louse and manhandler. Johnny Prince would create enough notoriety for Dan Duryea to steer his career in the direction of his choice even if it meant having a less than honorable standing with the movie-going public. The movie would also reunite him with the nucleus of *Women in the Window* and that resulted in creating a curious bookend with similar themes.

Fritz Lang had a desire to film the French novel and play, *La Chienne* ("The Bitch") by Georges de la Fouchanliere. Jean Renoir had filmed it in 1931 and it would be the first film made by the newly formed independent production company, Diana Productions. The principal stock holders were producer Walter Wanger and his wife, Joan Bennett, plus Fritz Lang. The company was a private corporation with Fritz Lang as the largest stockholder and in charge of the artistic side of things. Walter Wanger was the associate producer and was in charge of all the financial aspects of production.

There were many clauses and provisions to protect the studio from any over running costs caused by Lang's substantial artistic ego. This included studio interference if the project went over budget, taking control of the final cut after sixty days and the right to re-edit the movie if there

Christopher Cross (Edward G. Robinson) is a star-crossed milquetoast in *Scarlet Street*. 1945, Universal Pictures Company, Inc.

was any problem with the censors. The deal would have Diana put up half the cost of *Scarlet Street* via the Bank of America and Universal would provide the rest. This was a new type of movie making where independent companies would make films that were distributed by established studios.[lcv]

Scarlet Street reunites Fritz Lang's three principal players from *Woman in the Window* in a similar, ill-fated triangle. Dan Duryea and Joan Bennett play a sleazy couple that hustles Robinson for his paintings. Robinson is so love struck and timid that he considers it an honor that his paintings can bring wealth to his lover.

Three on a match leads to a streak of bad luck for Chris Cross (Edward G. Robinson). He is an honest and well-respected cashier for a prestigious banking firm. His life begins to fall apart on the night of his testimonial dinner after an act of heroism turns into a downward spiral. He rescues a woman from her abusive boyfriend only to become a hapless victim of their heartless manipulation.

A friendly drink and a conversation peppered with two-sided exaggerations leads to a strange affair between the timid painter and Kitty (Joan Bennett), the outgoing "actress." It turns into a tragic and violent scam because of the nefarious Johnny Prince (Dan Duryea), the sleazy boyfriend of the low-class femme fatale.

Prince is forever concocting get-rich-quick schemes, usually at the expense of his girlfriend, who is madly in love with the abusive heel. His dream is to buy into a garage and force out the partners. The dream is given substance by Cross, the quiet cashier who also is a devoted Sunday painter.

His paintings become the focal point of the drama because they bring out the hidden personalities of the characters. They are something out of Rod Serling's *Night Gallery* because they have a quality that makes people feel differently about them.

Cross loves his paintings, but he is self-effacing when it comes to his talent. His wife thinks that they are garbage and they only make her more of a shrew. Prince thinks that they are the work of a hop-head, but becomes giddy with ambition when they command the attentions of an art critic and a gallery owner. Kitty is put off by them but finds self-worth when she takes credit for them. They will bring her fame in the art world, as will her grisly murder.

A series of clever plot twists worthy of a good pulp novel leads to a downbeat conclusion for all of the principals. Kitty is murdered by Cross. Prince is accused, convicted, and executed for the crime. Cross is driven

Johnny Prince (Dan Duryea) is the rotten apple of Kitty March's (Joan Bennett) jaundiced eye. 1945, Universal Pictures Company, Inc.

insane by guilt and becomes an unhappy wanderer. The final irony comes in the final scene when his portrait of Kitty commands $10,000 as the deluded bum passes the gallery where it has just been sold.

The plot to *Scarlet Street* is convoluted but the movie is captivating, mainly because of the three principal characters. Joan Bennett sizzles as usual. She is crude and vulgar this time around, possessing a rude sex appeal that overshadows her rough edges. She is crazy about Duryea, an abusive heel who sometimes hustles her to make money. In his straw hat and striped jacket, Dan Duryea looks more like a song-and-dance man from vaudeville than a pimp. He has a dancing partner, but she is no Irene Castle. Her love for Duryea is matched by her well-disguised contempt for Robinson.

Robinson again plays the kind-hearted milquetoast. He has celebrated twenty five years working as a cashier with a prestigious banking firm, has a nagging wife at home, and his friends are considerate of him. It all changes when he becomes involved with the woman he saved from a brutal attacker.

The rescue becomes a polite drink and a strange relationship is formed, a perverse marionette play with Duryea pulling the strings. It is not enough that Cross offers his paintings to Bennett; he has resorted to embezzling money from the firm that recently held a testimonial dinner in his honor. This is a convoluted way to dissolve his marriage.

Robinson is too dense to notice that Duryea is Bennett's paramour. The unsavory lover controls Bennett in every way and uses her to con the old man. It all unravels when Bennett can no longer conceal her contempt for the old man. She ridicules him and basically lets the whore inside chew the old man up and spit him out. It is the one time that Robinson cracks up and he does so with a creepy gusto.

Duryea created his first really vicious sleaze ball character with the role of Johnny Prince. He was the template of the conniving heel, akin to Leo Hubbard's prototype of the vacillating weasel. Prince is a low-brow cad with a well-honed personality and a pimp's mentality.

Scarlet Street has a strange charm to it and works well as a cheap and tawdry thriller. It is part music-hall crudity, part German Expressionism, part minimalism and part exploitation flick. Lang's direction gives the movie a quaint touch, like a German silent movie with sound added to it. There are the usual Fritz Lang parlor tricks, visually and plot-wise. The first husband of Robinson's wife shows up after having been presumed drowned in the river. The circumstances of his survival stretch one's credulity although his demands for getaway money and how he gets it are comical. His temporary intrusion interrupts Bennett and Duryea's vicious hustle.

It is also implausible that Duryea can pass off Bennett as the painter of the popular masterpieces that Robinson willingly gives her. An eccentric painter and a pompous art critic attest to her genius although one

Kitty March (Joan Bennett) and Johnny Prince (Dan Duryea) confront an ironic twist of fate. 1945, Universal Pictures Company, Inc.

never sees a painter's studio in her home. The paintings are in the ludicrous style of a Sunday painter but they cause a rage in the art world.

Adding to the absurdity is Robinson's first wife believing that he copied his style from the female impostor after she sees a painting in an art gallery window. One of the movie's charms and highlights is the rustic Greenwich Village neighborhood where Bennett has her love nest. Margaret Lindsay adds a sanitized sex appeal as Kitty's roommate. She has contempt for Prince, which Kitty mistakes as jealousy.

Scarlet Street may have been considered a standard thriller by many of the critics of its time but it caused a minor commotion when it failed to obtain an exhibition license from the New York Censor Board. *Scarlet Street* was ruled "indecent and tending to incite to crime and tending to corrupt morals."

The film makers and the studio appealed to Dr. Irwin A. Conroe, the acting director of the Motion Picture Division of the State Education Department. A personal review by Dr. Conroe could result in an upholding of the ban or suggestions of certain editing changes. The Loew's Criterion

Theatre was supposed to show the movie but held over "*What Next Corporal Hargrove?*" for another week.

Dr. Conroe admitted that public opinion had some sway on his decision to release the film and it opened at the theaters to mixed reviews. The only taint of the temporary ban was The National Legion of Decency's B rating to protest the dubious moral tone of the movie.

Censorship problems and tepid reviews did not hurt the box office of *Scarlet Street*. It turned out to be one of Universal's biggest hits of 1945 and affirmed the studio's commitment to distributing outside productions to compliment its own output.

Cliff Work, the head of production at Universal, declared that *Scarlet Street* "was the best picture that has ever been made at Universal, and will measure up to the standard of any picture made in the industry in past years."[2]

The Johnny Prince character was odious but Dan Duryea's fan mail grew and reflected a strange fascination with the amoral lout. Many letters came from women and this fact was played up in movie magazines and newspaper articles. There was actually a story with the headline, "Women Like to Get Slapped" and a couple of pseudo-psychological profiles emphasizing a presupposed propensity to masochism in women. One fan article described a psychiatrist visiting the set of a Dan Duryea movie and coming to this conclusion. It seemed like a good publicity gimmick apropos of the times but it proved a little unsettling when fans actually believed that Dan Duryea was the man he portrayed on the screen.

Universal Studios was on the verge of one of its periodic changes. It was on the verge of merging with International Pictures and this would result in revamping its production methods and general output. In 1946, Universal-International signed Dan Duryea to a seven-year exclusive contract. His previous contract called for two pictures a year with the option of having the right to work for other studios. His first picture under his new contract was to be the screen version of Dorothy B. Hughes' latest novel, *Ride a Pink Horse*. Ben Hecht and Charles Lederer were tapped to write the screen play about a New York murderer who seeks anonymity south of the border in a Mexican town during a fiesta.

Production was to start in early 1947 but the role and directing chores eventually went to Robert Montgomery as part of his profit-sharing agreement with the studio. Originally, he was supposed to have starred in and directed *Lights Out*, produced by Joan Harrison. Instead, she would produce *Ride a Pink Horse* and they would follow it with *Lights Out*.

Dan Duryea renegotiated his contract and signed a two year contract for Universal, agreeing to do a picture a year for the studio. The first movie under his new contract was *The Black Angel*, based on a novel by Cornell Woolrich. *The Black Angel* is a nightmare that plays like a weird cabaret act with all of the thrills of an old pulp crime novel. Some of the hooks and clichés served up in this mystery are blackmail, the innocent

Martin Blair (Dan Duryea) is a successful song writer and cabaret pianist who harbors a dark secret that eventually destroys him. 1946, Universal Pictures Company, Inc.

man on death row, the persistent wife who tries to find the truth, amnesia as a part-time alibi for murder, and the helping hand of the victim's rum-pot, piano virtuoso husband.

Martin Blair (Dan Duryea) is the hard-drinking ex-husband of Mavis Marlowe (Constance Dowling), the victim in a murder that Catherine Bennett's (June Vincent) husband has been tried and convicted of. He is sent to death row to await execution while Mrs. Bennett enlists Martin Blair's help to clear her husband of the crime.

Marko (Peter Lorre), the sweaty, cigarette-smoking owner of The Black Angel club, becomes their chief suspect because Blair identifies him as the man who entered his wife's apartment building shortly before her murder. Blair and Catherine get jobs at The Black Angel as a piano man and his chanteuse, respectively. It is their way of keeping tabs on Marko, who, it turns out, is keeping tabs on them.

The movie asks if a murderer can be a hero if he turns himself in. It seems so only if he can turn back time. If not, then alcohol and amnesia are useful alibis until they cave in. That is when Martin Blair becomes a hero and a louse whose act of chivalry violates the Fifth Commandment. His alcohol-induced amnesia is cured by the dry heaves, and a guilty conscience outweighs his upset stomach.

Alcohol frees Blair from his inner pain but imprisons him because of the dreams they inspire. Benders allow him to live in the past, but waking up returns him to his lonely present. Booze blends the past and the present to create a hellish future that creates the fog that enables him to commit the perfect crime. An alcoholic haze also allows him to recall a repressed memory that saves an innocent man from execution and forces them to trade places.

The solution lies in "Heartache," a song that can heal wounds or open them up. Who was playing the song the night of the murder, the victim or the killer? For one of them, it was a piece of passionate nostalgia. Its symbol is a brooch that becomes the real trace to the killer. Missing from the murder scene, it winds up being found by the confused mystery killer who becomes the guilty party when death row gives a rare reprieve to a lucky innocent man.

Dan Duryea's Martin Blair is a complex character, a civilian detective whose investigation leads him to the face in the mirror. He has been destroyed by alcohol, but retains his brilliant talent for playing the piano. Blair has a fraction of morality left within him, because he is the one who saves Catherine Bennett's husband at a dear cost.

Blair is a classic tragic figure, a component of a mystery whose solution leads to his own demise. He is a man who is ruined by unrequited love, a sucker who surrenders his soul to a siren. His hit song, "Heartache," was written for his ex-wife who despises it, even though she recorded it with him. It is a tune Blair plays every night until he passes out at the honky-tonk bar where he works.

Martin Blair's courtliness is a disguise for love on the rebound in *The Black Angel*. Blair earns dubious honors in the hero category because he sacrifices himself for someone wrongly accused of his crime. Martin Blair sees that justice is served even though it means that he will be the main course. It is his offering of good tidings to Catherine Bennett.

The dizzy gent of *Black Angel* is a step in two directions when it comes to character labeling. He has the weak traits that make him vulnerable to a frame-up while being good-natured with a will to survive the nightmare. Blair also has a nagging guilt so strong that it blocks out the details of the murder that he is trying to solve.

His angel inspires a loyalty in him that turns out to be a legal death sentence, something that never occurred to him when he was first awakened from a drunken slumber by the wide-eyed innocent blonde seeking help to clear her husband.

Constance Dowling exudes the bitchy sexuality of a woman who would ultimately be strangled with her monogrammed scarf. She has the face of a young Marlene Dietrich without the strong toughness to it. She plays it cool and mean, the way a blackmailer would if she thought her scheme would last forever. It's too bad she hedged her bets and lost her life because of unabashed arrogance. It was the night the doorman happened to look the other way.

June Vincent looks like a Veronica Lake clone. She has the same silky beauty that makes her at home in a drama with a cabaret setting. She is like a caged bird in her lackluster marriage but regains her freedom when she resumes her singing career with Blair. She is sultry without being tawdry, alluring without being cheap, and inviting without seeming promiscuous. It is her perseverance that gets the unofficial investigation underway.

Peter Lorre had a distinct personality that made him a marvel to watch no matter what type of role he was playing. He was diminutive, with a reptile's tortured face and eyes that popped when he spoke. He has a leering voice that was the hallmark of many voice impersonators' careers. In the movie, he is an obscene piece of putty in a tuxedo.

Martin Blair (Dan Duryea) is the black angel who aids Catherine Bennett (June Vincent) in clearing her husband of a murder he did not commit. 1946, Universal Pictures Company, Inc.

Broderick Crawford's police captain belongs to an age when cops could break constitutional amendments with impunity. He walks into a house without being invited and rifles a lock box without a search warrant while the owner points out the illegality of his actions. He also has the gumption to call the governor's mansion to rouse him from his sleep so that he can halt the execution of an innocent man.

Kirk Bennett (John Phillips), the man who is the cause of this noble campaign, is little more than a bewildered face who deserves to be wrongly convicted. He is married to a beautiful ex-singer and why he should want to cheat on her is a mystery that is never explained.

Wallace Ford is still playing the faithful sidekick at Universal, ready to put his life on hold if it means helping out a buddy in distress. In *The Black Angel*, he spends his life like a museum figure in the shadows, ready to come to life when his buddy needs him.

Martin Blair showed a sympathetic side to Duryea's good-for-nothing but he was still a murderer. His fan mail grew and he was one of ten actors chosen by the Motion Picture herald's "Stars of Tomorrow" contest. The owners of the nation's movie houses chose the following ten players and they are listed according to the amount of votes they received: Joan Leslie, Butch Jenkins, Zachary Scott, Don De Fore, Mark Stevens, Eve Arden, Lizabeth Scott, Dan Duryea, Yvonne DeCarlo and Robert Mitchum.

Women still wrote in to Duryea asking him to find the time to slap them around between movies. Then there were the women who thought deep in their heart that they could uncover the noble Dan that was buried deep within him. There was also the British woman who periodically mailed him intimate photos slashed into puzzle pieces.[3]

Dan Duryea tried to explain the fatal attraction in terms outlined by a psychologist who observed him for a magazine profile. It had something to do with a dichotomy that ran through Dan's life. Dan added, "One of his notions was that there was something about the way I walk— 'lackadaisical and carefree'—he called it, that gives a dame a whollop. And he figured that even the way I'd worn the flat straw hat in *Scarlet Street* handed them an emotional belt. He called it 'disturbingly jaunty.' He said that my voice has nasal overtones that do things to women, in spite of the fact that I've been trying to get rid of those nasal sounds for years. And he allowed as how my eyes have a hypnotic quality."[4]

Not all women were bowled over by Duryea's screen Neanderthal Lothario. An incisive letter to the New York Times by an irate female moviegoer states her case: "Recently while sitting placidly through some previews I saw one of the pictures, *The Black Angel*. In it Dan Duryea is again the vicious hero that he played in *Scarlet Street*.

The preview inquired how does this man fascinate women? Men will never know for women will never tell them.

I just want to state for the record that one will never know either. Outside of a script writer's fertile imagination, the no doubt very estimable Mr. Duryea, could scarcely be called fascinating.

After seeing a preview of *Scarlet Street* I decided that Miss Bennett must be very short of male friends and after seeing the beautiful Miss Vincent bewitched by the same Mr. Duryea I gave thanks that I, as a much plainer woman, had never been driven to such desperate straits in my search for male companionship."

N.Y. Times; letters to the Editor; Dec. 15, 1946

Even Dan Duryea numbered himself among the critics of his typecasting. It included an attempt to make serious changes in the public perception of his screen image. A change was due and what better way than to use publicity? In the September 23 issue of Variety one could read, "Regeneration of Dan Duryea is complete. Once a particularly nasty villain on the screen, Dan is now an honorary deputy sheriff in Nevada. They went that-a-way, sheriff." Another article in a fan magazine recounted how Dan Duryea was made an honorary member of the Oglala Indian tribe of the Sioux Nation in Deadwood, South Dakota. He was named Na-Ta-Opi, which means "wounded head."

This led to his insistence that the studio cast him in a light-hearted comedy. It would be something to break the spate of Alpha lunatics that he was noted for. They gave him the lead role of the erudite butler in *White Tie and Tails*.

In *White Tie and Tails*, Dan Duryea is a gentleman's gentleman masquerading as the gentleman himself. He gets involved in an oddball adventure with a dark haired femme and a loony-tunes mobster. White tie and tails is the disguise used by Charles Dumont, a major-domo, to en-

Charles Dumont (Dan Duryea) is the perfect gentleman's gentleman, much to the delight of the well-heeled Louise Bradford (Ella Raines). 1947, Universal Pictures Company, Inc.

joy the high life from the other side of the tracks. Dumont is the perfect butler, one who can coordinate clothes, mix drinks, talk knowledgeably about art, and bring order to the chaotic world of teenagers.

The butler is a brilliant man who enjoys the finer things in life and believes that the only way he'll ever enjoy them is by being butler to a wealthy family. This leads to a walk on the wild side. He gets the chance to play the boss when the Latimer family he works for takes a holiday in Florida. Dumont dismisses the staff for a holiday of their own, only retaining the services of the chauffeur, George (Frank Jenks).

Dumont's first night on the town is the first of many missteps that will end with his ignominious dismissal, but happy days await him as befits the ending of a sophisticated comedy bordering on lunacy. His misadventure is actually a belated coming-of-age drama intended to work up the creativity and individualism that lie within him; all it took to bring it out was love.

On his first night out on the town, Dumont meets Louise Bradford (Ella Raines) at a nightclub and he is instantly smitten by her. There is an air of mystery to her that only makes his attraction stronger. George cautions him about taking the masquerade to the next level, but Dumont does not heed the advice.

Love and a heavy sense of chivalry implicate the butler in a crime of passion. He vouches for a gambling debt incurred by Louise's sister and winds up surrendering two paintings to Larry Lundie (William Bendix), the nightclub owner, as collateral. This theft becomes the basis of a series of wrong conclusions for the butler posing as the master. It all seems okay until the real master returns and notices something amiss about his prized paintings. The gangster mucks up things with his intrusion, the butler is fired and becomes reborn again. All's well that ends well when Dumont is dismissed for abusing the master's trust, but he gets to start a new life with Louise Bradford.

Dan Duryea is spry and sleek as Charles Dumont, the imposter *bon vivante*. Dumont is sophisticated and knowledgeable about the finer things in life. He has the charm to pull off his scheme but crumbles under the pressure when Lundie swipes two paintings as security for the check he has written.

William Bendix is funny as Larry Lundie. He is a flummoxed apeman who wants to expand his vocabulary and become a fashion plate. He is dim but still can see straight to the point. He gets things done the old fashioned way, with muscle based on I.O.U.s. He offers to hire Dumont as a tutor about the finer things in life.

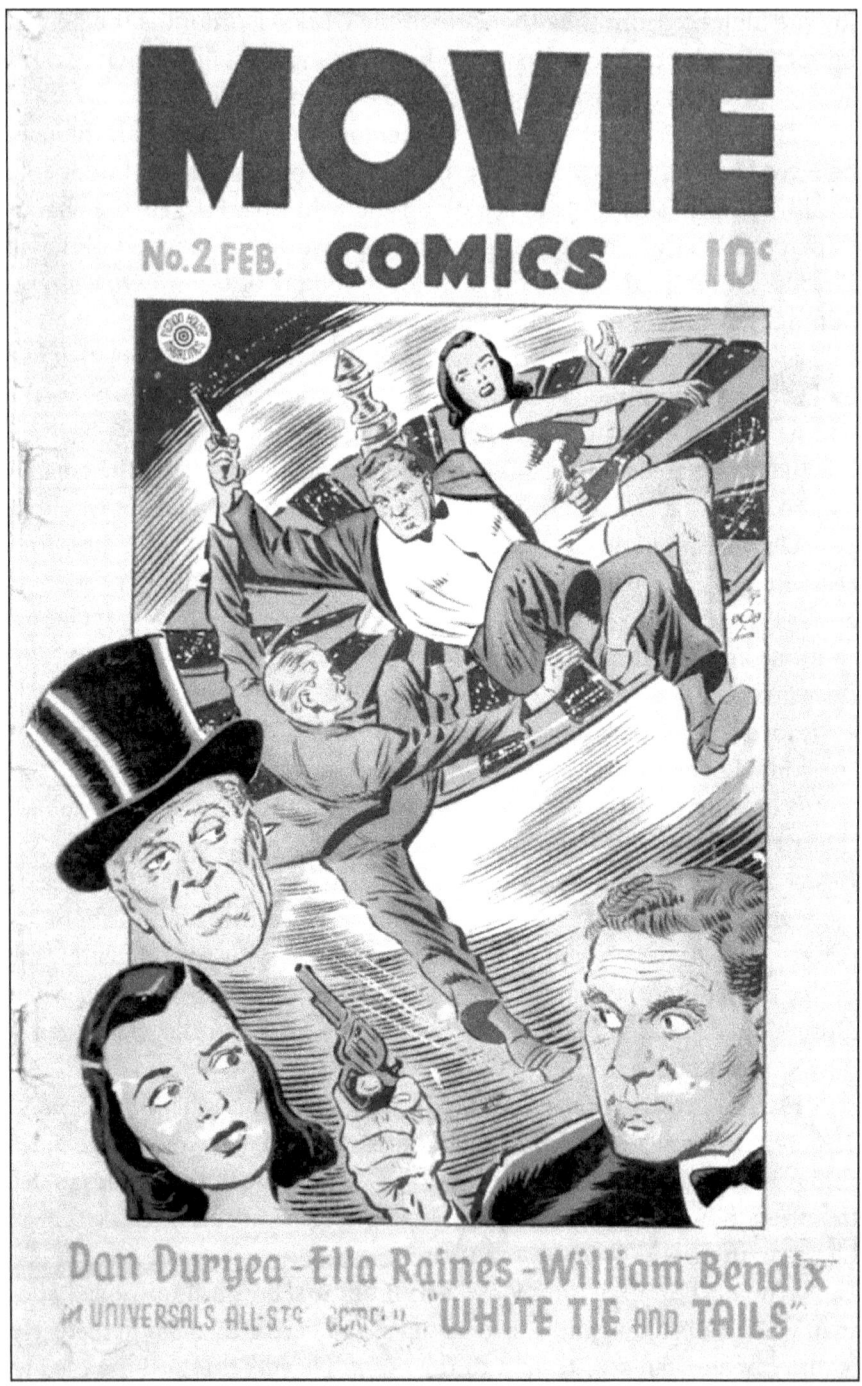

Cover for a comic book rendition of *White Tie and Tails*. 1945, Universal Pictures Company, Inc. 1947, Universal Pictures Company, Inc.

Ella Raines has a vampish quality to her. She is delightful but droll and seems to be off in a dream state. She encourages Dumont to seek his artistic muse and start painting again. Her younger sister, played by Patricia Alphin, owes a gambling debt to Lundie and this is the reason that Dumont has overextended himself.

Donald Curtis plays Bendix's henchman and exudes menace as he intimidates the younger Bradford daughter. Frank Jenks excels at playing wise guy, working-class types from the old neighborhood, although here, he is a rational font of wisdom to whom Charles Dumont won't pay any mind. Charles Kolb plays the gruff and stuffy society scion that earmarked his career. Scotty Beckett and Nita Talbot are the children of the man of the house.

Black Tie and Tails was considered a disappointment by the studio. Ticket sales were down from previous Duryea movies and it became apparent that his fans preferred his malicious villains. Fan mail urged him to revert to his evil self and there were fan features that implored him to stay his same old mean self. A synthesis was the order of the day.

"I almost got away from the label they've hung on me in a movie called *White Tie and Tails*", he later said wistfully, "but the fans wouldn't go for me as Dapper Dan. They kept writing me to ask what happened to Dangerous Dan. Maybe someday they will let me play romantic heavies, like Bogart. Maybe even romantic leads, like Gable."[5]

Before that would happen, Dan Duryea returned to radio for two performances on *Suspense*. At the beginning of the year he starred with Cathy Downs in *Will to Power*. At the end of the year, he returned to Suspense for *The Man Who Couldn't Lose*.

Period Pieces, Westerns and Costume Dramas

Universal Studios owned the rights to a story called *The Highwayman* and it was a costume drama set in the 19th Century West. They had planned to turn it into a movie but shelved it when the studio merged with International Pictures. New studio policy included making crowd-pleasing, storybook-costume dramas that were a compendium of old Hollywood's used storylines redone in Cinemascope. One crowd pleaser was the romantic adventure triangle made up of a mysterious Robin Hood figure and a desirable, exotic, and quixotic dark beauty hampered by a wily and conniving ex-partner out to benefit from a perceived double cross in the past. *The Highwayman* was taken off the shelf and became *Black Bart*.

Dan Duryea, Yvonne de Carlo and Edmond O'Brien were announced as the stars of *Black Bart*. Luci Ward and Jack Natteford were assigned to write the script and Leonard Goldstein was the producer. Charles Barton directed. By the time of filming, O'Brien had schedule conflicts and was replaced by Jeffrey Lynn, who had just ended a long term contract with Warner Brothers.

Yvonne de Carlo was riding the crest of her career and gave Duryea a chance to express his gallant and cavalier side while still maintaining a dose of banditry. It was the first of three pictures he would make with the beautiful actress. They would ultimately become Universal-International top box office attraction.

Black Bart has Dan Duryea as a new kind of banker, one who steals from the rich and invests it in the birth of a new banking system. All it takes is nerve, a fast horse, and a lucrative target: Wells Fargo and its payload routes. The new kind of banking believes in establishing credit with someone else's money. It is especially satisfying because Charles E. Boles,

Title lobby card for *Black Bart*. 1947, Universal Pictures Company, Inc.

aka Black Bart, and his friendly lawyer, Clark (John McIntire), have declared themselves fair competition for Wells Fargo's payload.

The story unfolds as three thieves decide to go their separate ways to prevent the law from capturing them. Charlie, Lance Hardeen (Jeffrey Lynn), and Jersey (Percy Kilbride) go their separate ways after agreeing to meet at a secret location so they can split the money. Charlie trusts his buddies to do the right thing by holding on to the money and bringing it with them for the split. They do not possess the honor their ex-partner has and decide that a two way split is preferable to a three-way bargain.

In time, Charlie becomes the respectable businessman, Charles E. Boles. He reverts to a life of crime when Clark, his cunning lawyer, comes up with a scheme to rob Wells Fargo of their gold shipments. He does all of the planning and Boles does the night riding as Black Bart, a masked desperado with a flowing cape.

A change in fortune occurs when Lola Montez (Yvonne DeCarlo) arrives in town for a series of performances. They develop a two-sided relationship; the first is when Black Bart robs her stagecoach and the second is when Boles falls in love. She is dismayed to learn that Boles is the notorious bandit that stole her jewels, but love softens her anger. However, she gives him an ultimatum if he wants to wed her: either give up his life of crime or lose her.

He does not mind settling down because he would be foolish to risk their future because of his criminal behavior. His decision is complicated by the arrival of his former partners, who blackmail him into committing a series of robberies so they can collect a commission.

The careers of Charles E. Boles and Black Bart collide and cancel each other out. A shootout at a bonfire is fate's way of saying things are even between him and his ex-partner and that love conquers all.

Is it Lola Montez the dancehall queen, or Lance Hardeen, his former partner in crime, who brings down Black Bart? It is too easy to say a little of both or blame it on one of them. The final draw is Black Bart's responsibility because he tried to satisfy both his past and his future simultaneously.

He does not owe Hardeen a thing and could have increased all that he had by sharing it all with Lola Montez and freezing out his phantom past. Black Bart and Lola Montez are a power couple in the making, the king and queen of a burgeoning gambling town.

Bart's fidelity to the past and his generosity to the former partners who betrayed him are his own undoing. They are small time by their own making, which is why they belong to the past. With Lola by his side, Black

Black Bart (Dan Duryea) robs dance hall star Lola Montez (Yvonne De Carlo) of her jewels. 1947, Universal Pictures Company, Inc.

Bart could have driven Hardeen and Jersey Brady (Percy Kilbride), the third gang member, out of town.

They would have had no choice, especially since they were already under suspicion by the sheriff. His ex-partners felt wronged because they had lost out the first time around. They tried for a second piece of the action. That was when it all fell apart, the former partners bonding again in a blood ritual called the shootout.

For them, hoof-and-mouth disease is a desert treasure and a lucrative side job that buys respectable dreams for low down criminals. Black Bart and Hardeen square their differences in a fiery showdown with the law and only Lola Montez lives to benefit from it, this being just another colorful tale to add to her legend.

Black Bart presents Duryea in a unique light as a romantic Robin Hood of the open West as he robs Wells Fargo and pays homage to a wealthy entertainer played by Yvonne DeCarlo. Dan Duryea has the smooth moves and prairie lightning that it takes to play a genteel bandit. He is the sharp and sophisticated businessman and the prairie outlaw who plunders Wells Fargo. When the tallies from Black Bart came in, Yvonne de Carlo and Dan Duryea were considered Universal-International's top box office couple.

Yvonne DeCarlo is the seductive Lola Montez. She is a dance hall queen with the power to make things happen on her own terms. Black Bart courts her love with his gallant, devilish commissions, but winds up going up in flames himself.

Jeffrey Lynn is the interloper who messes up things when his small ambition threatens the strange empire of his former partner in crime. It didn't matter to Lynn that he was the one who first double crossed Duryea.

Percy Kilbride is the third wheel who rode into the sunset, living in a cell to tell the tale of Black Bart. Kilbride would later hit pay dirt as Pa Kettle in the famous Universal-International "Ma and Pa Kettle" series.

Dan Duryea took a break from movie making to return to radio for a couple of *Suspense* episodes. He also starred in a straw hat version of *The Front Page* at a Medford, Conn. regional theater. Dan Duryea may have

Lou Costello takes a break from filming *The Wistful Widow of Wagon Gap* to pay a visit to the set. Producer Leonard Goldstein seems jaded while star Dan Duryea takes an interest in Lou's scratch sheet. 1947, Universal Pictures Company, Inc.

not returned to Broadway but he did revisit Lillian Hellman when he was contracted to appear in *Another Part of the Forest*, the prequel to *The Little Foxes*. He was supposed to play Ben Hubbard but Edmond O'Brien took over the role when he was signed for the picture and Duryea was switched to Oscar, the father of Leo Hubbard.

Another Part of the Forest provides a history of the Hubbard family twenty years before their attempt at resurrection in *The Little Foxes*. It is Universal-International's attempt at making a serious picture, but runs into trouble because very little about it can compare favorably with the film it is setting itself up to. The script, for the most part, is good. The performances range from excellent to perfunctory. What dooms it in comparison is the lack of style provided by the original's direction and cinematography.

In The Little Foxes, the remnants of a family of ruined Southern aristocrats try to recapture lightning in the bottle again, a power surge they enjoyed during the years shown in Another Part of the Forest. In the prequel, Ann Blyth is supposed to turn into Bette Davis and Dan Duryea gets to play his character's father. Originally, he was hired to play Ben Hubbard but was switched to Oscar when Edmond O'Brien joined the cast and took over the role.

The Hubbards are from the merchant class and they are resented by some of the townsfolk. There is whispering and backbiting about the success of their business. The elder Hubbard's moral character is an ink blot to some, and how this perception affects his family sets the tone for this post-Civil War drama.

The family's history is clarified and it is an ignominious one, at that. Klan tales, war profiteering, and atrocities are the ingredients of the merchant family that escaped its class through dark secrets of treachery. The family skeleton is responsible for the shift in the balance of power within the Hubbard family. To risk exposure, Pop relinquishes his fiefdom to Ben, his avaricious elder son.

Frederic March is excellent as the elder Hubbard and he does what he can with a few startling character faults and an unraveling and fall from power that happens too fast. It is hard to imagine that he would not try to wheel and deal with his eldest son to keep him from informing the town elders about who was responsible for the atrocities committed in the town during the war.

Edmond O'Brien is the strong son who steps out from his father's shadow when he hears his mother misspeak about the old man's skeleton in the closet. His threats, demands, and rise to the seat of family power are too swift and could have provided grist for a family power play worth expanding on.

This sudden change of events shifts the balance of power from the father to the eldest son. The most startling thing about the new power scheme is the way Regina is reborn as a selfish manipulator in order to cozy up to the new head of the household.

Ann Blyth is beautiful and somewhat defiant as Regina Hubbard, but cannot give credibility to a character that will develop into Bette Davis. One can imagine Bette Davis eating Ann Blyth as if she were an after-dinner mint. The only thing that links the two performances is the cold and deliberate look Blyth displays when she realizes that the family power has passed from her father to her elder brother.

The only way to accept Ann Blyth is to believe that Regina was once as innocent as Alexandra, her daughter. Her fortune's loss and her brother's gain taught her a new meaning to survival. From that point onward, it is possible to accept Blyth's sweet character eventually turning into Bette Davis' bitter crone.

The Hubbard clan: Marcus (Frederic March), Regina (Anne Blyth), Lavinia (Florence Eldridge), Oscar (Dan Duryea) and Ben (Edmond O'Brien) (l-r). 1948, Universal Pictures Company, Inc.

Regina's first step toward one day becoming the family's matriarch occurs in the last scene of the movie, which is stolen by Florence Eldridge. She plays the matriarch of the Hubbard clan and she is part Rock of Gibraltar and part pillar of salt. She scores the film's focal point with her declaration, one that ends the movie and puts a cap on the family that was to evolve into *The Little Foxes*.

Duryea gives a fleshed out performance of the lanky, bilious coward that he played in *The Little Foxes*. Father and son are hardly distinguishable, so weak and mealy-mouthed. Duryea plays the father much the same as he played the son. His part in the prequel is larger so we can get a fuller portrait of the devilish, ne'er-do-well wastrel of a hated Southern family. The elder Hubbard, too, is a dim-wit, a flippant popinjay in love with a Can-Can girl and one who dresses in Klan regalia when driving Yankees out of town under the cover of night.

Having Duryea play the father of his character from *The Little Foxes* is interesting casting, but one of the things that work against the film. Duryea expands on Leo Hubbard, but it is unlikely that his father, so cold and manipulative in *The Little Foxes*, could have been anything like his son.

Laurette Sincee (Dona Drake) is a spirited Can-Can dancer who puts some pep in Oscar Hubbard's (Dan Duryea) step. 1948, Universal Pictures Company, Inc.

Universal Studios • 113

A magazine ad for *River Lady*. 1948, Universal Pictures Company, Inc.

This also applies to Edmond O'Brien's performance as the young Ben. He is a chip off the old man's block in this film, but is portrayed as a sad and weak bachelor in *The Little Foxes*. It's as if the brothers exchanged personalities when they matured.

The genesis of Aunt Birdie depicts a twit with a loon's perspective of life. She is nothing like that in the Wyler film. As played by Betsy Blair, she is a genteel Southern doyenne weakened through attrition, her husband's family takeover of her family legacy due to a deal she asked for when things were rough.

This is played out in *Another Side of the Forest* and it becomes clear that she will lose everything her family has. The impact in this movie is nothing compared to the sane effect achieved by an unsettling performance of her older self by Patricia Collinge in *The Little Foxes*.

Dona Drake has a small part as Laurette Sincee, a Can-Can girl being romanced by Oscar Hubbard. She gives a vivacious performance as a simpleton bimbo who does a mean Can-Can. Oscar wants to marry her but his father will not hear of it. She irritates him to the point of his being stupefied by her.

Before Yvonne de Carlo struck box office gold with Dan Duryea, she made several successful films with Rod Cameron. It seemed only natural for Universal-International to use the three stars for a movie. They appear together in *River Lady*, an eye-catching colorful adventure story.

The next step in the evolution of the prairie gun man is the town boss. That takes economic power backed up by showdown dexterity. Beauvais is the first character to take the next step in Duryea's Western bad man's climb to power. Beauvais wears the fancy suits and smokes the finest cigars while wheeling and dealing, but he still knows how to kill a man and has not lost his killing instincts.

Beauvais is not yet the town mayor but he is a player nonetheless, and he goes for the catbird seat in *River Lady*. Duryea plays a morally corrupt wannabe town boss who does not come up to Yvonne De Carlo's river lady snuff. She is being wooed by a hero played by Rod Cameron, a do-right kind of guy who is Duryea's main headache.

River Lady is a rousing, Technicolor, romantic tale of the logging industry, business ambition, and hostile takeovers. It is a moral story of integrity versus chicanery and the perils of using each trait as a means to an end. Machiavelli would have been proud of the four main players as they do what they have to in order to get what they want: power and respectability. Are they victims of Darwinian circumstance, or agents of Christian free will? It does not matter because as in all contests there are two clear-cut winners and losers when the movie rolls its final credits.

Sequin owns the *River Lady*, a floating saloon and gambling den. She is a heavenly angel for the loggers who will gladly spend all of their hard-earned wages in her den of iniquity once their season is over. Her popularity is an empty mark of distinction for her.

She dreams of being a lady of leisure because she is angry about being avoided by proper women. Sequin does not like to be considered cheap and desires social prestige and economic stability. The only way for her to live on the largest house on the hill is to settle down and marry Dan Corrigan, a logger who thinks like an executive.

Corrigan loves Sequin, but he would rather stick to the outdoors because he does not mind being a river rat. He knows that Sequin wants to domesticate him and he is cynical because he has seen too many men worked to death because of ambitious women. They don't see eye-to-eye because he wants to be one thing and she wants him to be another. He is honest with himself and believes that Sequin is delusional about her dreams of becoming a society lady. She is offended when he tells her that all the money in the world won't make her a refined lady. She says that he learned everything he knows about women in kindergarten. Opportunity knocks the day H. L. Morrison, the owner of a small mill, arrives to seek financial support from Sequin. His business is being squeezed by the dastardly Beauvais, a front man for an emerging logging syndicate. Beauvais informs Morrison that the days of the small mills are over and that he had better sell his business while the price is right. This disturbs Morrison and he offers Sequin a percentage of his mill if she will offer some clout against the syndicate.

Sequin agrees to purchase 49% of Morrison's mill if he will offer Corrigan an executive post without telling him that Sequin is responsible for his new opportunity. This is Sequin's attempt to civilize Corrigan and lay the plans to a successful life as a power couple.

Corrigan is reluctant to accept Morrison's offer because he still likes the outdoors. He relents because he does not want to look a gift horse in the mouth. His new career will enable him to marry Sequin to fulfill her dreams, not knowing that they have turned into a scheme. Things fall apart when he meets a woman who is as manipulative as Sequin.

Stephanie Morrison is the boss's daughter. She has just returned from school and is dismayed to find that her arrival coincides with the end of the logging season. She considers the loggers an uncouth lot, but is won over by Dan Corrigan when he saves her from the clutches of a Swede. She had been accosted by him on the docks when the loggers arrive to vent their pent-up passion.

Chivalry is an aphrodisiac for the society woman, and she develops a rapacious appetite for Corrigan, making her intentions clear at a picnic in the countryside. Stephanie shows that a society dame can wrestle in the mud when she learns of Corrigan's impending marriage to Sequin. She spoils the plans by informing Corrigan of Sequin's deal with her father.

Corrigan is infuriated that his good fortune was financed by Sequin's wealth. He confronts Sequin and calls off the wedding, prompting her to threaten him with financial ruin. This is Stephanie's chance to move in for the kill. Stephanie takes advantage of the rift between Corrigan and Sequin by offering a shoulder to cry on when she visits a hard-drinking Corrigan in the local saloon. He wakes up the next morning with a hangover and a wife.

Stephanie proves that she is as tough as she is conniving when she lives the frontier life with her new husband. He has promised her the house on the hill but only after he has earned it on his own. His brainstorm is to create a new syndicate with the independent miners who are about to be taken over by Beauvais and his clique.

Jim Beauvais (Dan Duryea) has big dreams for Sequin (Yvonne De Carlo) and himself. 1948, Universal Pictures Company, Inc.

Corrigan and Sequin are now bitter enemies and she gives her support to Beauvais, who is thrilled because he desires her. He constantly reminds her that they are two of a kind and that she will never be the school type that Corrigan likes. Sequin gives him insider information on a logging deal Corrigan has engineered that will mean a resounding financial success if the timber can be delivered on schedule. It is a pretty big "if," because Beauvais plans to sabotage the deal by creating a logjam.

The logjam creates the violent climax of the movie when the two opposing forces collide. Beauvais is aided by the bitter Swede who is aided by his buddies and confidants. It looks as though Beauvais will succeed until the confrontation boils down to a fight between him and Corrigan. If Beauvais does not stop Corrigan from dynamiting the logjam, he will be ruined. It turns out worse for him because he loses his life in the explosion that frees the timber.

The final scene has Sequin making a last ditch attempt to win back Corrigan with a passionate apology. He does not forgive and forget, reminding Sequin that he is married, even though his wife will step aside if that's what her husband wants. By the movie's end, the new syndicate is born, Corrigan and Stephanie will have the life that Sequin sought, and the *River Lady* sails away to her next destination.

In 1948, Dan Duryea renegotiated his 1946 seven-year contract. Revisions included being committed to the studio for one picture a year for the next four years. Another alteration was the right for Dan Duryea to work on outside projects. It was his intention to make two independent films for every one for Universal-International. Marshall Grant tried to interest Dan Duryea for his production of *The Quantrills are Coming* but nothing became official.

Monte Jarrad was Duryea's first Western gunslinger and he had to square off against Gary Cooper in *Along Came Jones*, a Western satire spoofing Cooper's tall-in-the saddle image. It took four years before Dan Duryea got back into gear as a Western villain the memorable character of Waco Johnny Dean in *Winchester '73*. The 1950 Western classic relates a captivating story about the rifle's history as it passes hands, usually after violent confrontations. It stars James Stewart, along with Shelley Winters, Rock Hudson, Charles Drake, and John McIntire.

Winchester '73 is an episodic movie that tells the stories of the people who temporarily own the rifle that built the West. The violent vignettes range from the heroic to the tragic as the rifle passes hands from one owner to the next. Some of the people whose lives are changed by the rifle include two brothers on opposite sides of the law, a rebellious Indian chief inspired by the Battle of Little Big Horn, a gun merchant (John McIntire) whose admiration of the rifle costs him his life, a petty criminal who is not man enough to own it, and a wily gunslinger whose sarcastic humor makes him the last laugh.

The story starts in Dodge City, where Wyatt Earp is hosting a shooting contest for the rifle, a top of the line Winchester '73, one of a thousand perfect in every respect. Other men who own a perfect Winchester '73 are President Grant and Buffalo Bill Cody.

The two top contenders are Lin McAdam (James Stewart) and Dutch Henry Brown (Stephen McNally), two men who hate each other and have a score to settle. It's not until the story gets underway that we find out that the men are brothers and Dutch is guilty of patricide.

The brothers compete in overtime until Lin wins, but Dutch steals the rifle. He does not hold it for long because he trades it for a cache of guns that a merchant has promised an Indian chief (Rock Hudson). The gun merchant, in turn, loses it to the Indian chief, who wants it because of the efficiency of the repeating guns used against General Custer at the Battle of Little Big Horn.

Poster for *Winchester '73*, featuring James Stewart and Shelley Winters. 1950, Universal Pictures Company, Inc.

The Indian chief is killed in a raid on a Cavalry camp and the rifle is given to a civilian (Charles Drake) who fought bravely in the battle. He, in turn, is killed by Waco Johnny Dean, who reluctantly turns it over to a partner-in-crime, Dutch Henry Brown. The rifle ultimately winds up in the hands of the rightful owner, who settles his vengeance in a desert shootout.

Gimmicks such as the rifle passing hands have often been used to tell an episodic story. It takes a credible script and expert direction to make the story a success or else it descends into paperback-novel commonalities. *Winchester '73* works because it has several things going for it. Lin McAdam is a likeable lead because he is a decent man with a moral mission. He is brave without being foolhardy and kind without being weak. He earns respect and has no problem showing it. His sidekick is a likeable fellow, too. He is an experienced frontier man and reflects all of the admirable qualities of the leading man.

The story is multi-textured because the only thing in common with the characters is the rifle. They all have different lives that depend on survival on the prairie. The Indian chief wants to live free on the home of his people. He believes that the white man is a devil who is stealing what does not belong to him. He is inspired by Chief Crazy Horse and will do what he can to acquire the repeating rifles.

The gun merchant is a low-down cuss because he will sell his guns to anyone who has the money. He does not care that the Indians are fired up at Chief Crazy Horse's success at Little Big Horn. He does what he has to do to survive.

Waco Johnny Dean (Dan Duryea) is a psycho with a hair-trigger temper. 1950, Universal Pictures Company, Inc.

The young couple acquires the gun through default, but it costs the young man his life when he tangles with Waco Johnny Dean. He is a crazed outlaw who lives to kill and takes what he wants without asking. He is part of a plan to rob a bank and had acquired the rifle through force.

The man he hooks up with is Dutch, who immediately reclaims his gun. It does not matter for either man because they will be killed in the course of the robbery. The man who shoots both of them is Lin McAdam. He gets to show his shooting prowess, not only in town with Waco Johnny Dean, but on a mountaintop when he has a unique gun battle with his brother. Fate is the underlying theme of the movie and it proves that everyone engineers their own death. It is how a man dies that determines his worth. James Stewart is excellent as the trail beaten cowpoke stalking his evil brother. Stephen McNally plays his part well as the oily, snake-like villain. Charles Drake is jelly as a coward who dies while wearing an apron. Shelly Winters is sexy and touching as the saloon girl whose life changes for the better because of her hair-raising ordeals. Jay C. Flippen is a wizened Cavalry sergeant who can add one more gunfight with the Indians to his legacy and Tony Curtis is one of his young charges.

Dan Duryea sinks his teeth into Waco Johnny Dean. He is boldfaced, boisterous, and bad to the bone. He loves shootouts because they make him feel alive. There is no hesitation in killing a man, because that's what he does best. As is the case with prairie gunman, there is always one more cowpoke that is faster on the draw. He is the righteous lead who cuts the bad man down to size in public. The last laugh is on Waco Johnny Dean because he ran out of laughs of his own.

Crime Bosses

Universal-International created an impressive body of crime dramas that have never properly received their critical due. The critics of the time were pompous and considered crime dramas and film noirs shocking melodramas. Tawdry, tepid, lurid and venal were not traits that these bloodless scribes found redeeming. There was also the stigma of them being B-movies that were meant to occupy the lower half of a double bill. Viewed through a modern lens, they embody the American sensibility that the highbrow critics always accorded legitimate movies. The crime dramas of 1946 through 1961 chronicled three American eras: The Post-War Years, The Nuclear Age and the Jet Set Era.

Dan Duryea was able to put a slant on his nefarious reputation with a series of mob bosses that rivaled their ancestors on the range. The major difference was that, for the most part, Duryea's crime bosses had a vulnerable side. They may have rough, but with one exception, they didn't slap around their women.

Duryea's bosses were soft on their molls in ways that made them vulnerable to challenges when the ladies decided to take a powder on them. Slim Dundee was the only one who had something going on in the shadows, but the other boss men took it on the chin when it came to their ladies. Such was the case with the trio of crime bosses when they mixed their women with confidence games, armored car heists, and clever employees.

Silky Randall is just what you'd expect him to be, a smooth con artist. His one hang up is the insane love he has for Shelley Winters. It makes him soft, and her hard-headed enough to derail a heartless scam in small town USA.

Silky Randall (Dan Duryea) lays the groundwork for a war memorial scam as Duke (Dan O'Herlihy) and Rick Mason (John Payne) wait to hear the details in Larceny. 1949, Universal Pictures Company, Inc.

Larceny is Silky Randall's game as he masterminds stings that use Rick Mason (John Payne) as a front man. His latest scam is building a phony war memorial in a small California town. It all goes smoothly until his moll (Shelly Winters) upsets the balance because of her unbridled passion.

Larceny may have been a popular programmer but it had a serious undertone that made the movie jolting at times. Con men and smooth talkers were nothing new to drama but the two smoothies who cooked up the war memorial scam register with more conviction for their callousness. Rick Mason (John Payne) and Silky Randall (Dan Duryea) have just bailed out of a blown yacht-club hustle in Miami and have now set their sights on a small town that still reels from the combat death of a local hero.

Mason is a masterful and heartless masquerade artist who impersonates a fictional buddy of the local hero. He ingratiates himself with the kids at the youth center with a speech about honesty and giving the task at hand one's best. He is an instant hero with the kids, a welcome relief for Deborah (Joan Caulfield), the hero's widow and an object of deification for Charlie (Percy Helton), the froglike man who runs the youth center and directs all of its activities.

Mason's instant welcome allows him to become a popular man about town, especially when he sows the seeds of the memorial in the widow's sentimental reminiscences. The movie belongs to Mason, who presses the irony of being an upstanding, righteous, top-notch kind of guy. Everyone looks up to him and appreciates the way he has added a shock to the dull everyday type of sameness of their lives. Mason has them eating out of his hand and doesn't go soft until after he has the scam money in the form of a check.

His con is moving as scheduled until it is derailed by Tory, Randall's moll. She is an empty-headed, hot-blooded sex machine whose passion for Mason clouds her judgment and makes her the loose cannon of the gang. Silky sends her to Havana, but she makes a detour to the California coastal town to be near Mason. Tory is impulsive and reckless, possessing a tunnel vision that prevents her from seeing the bigger picture, an intricate high stakes scam that revolves around raising the investment money for building a war memorial.

She is the spoiler and it is not just because of her impetuous behavior, it's also the effect she has on Silky. His jealousy may turn out to be well-founded but he lets it cloud his business judgment and that begins to foul things up. Another monkey wrench in the works is good old-fashioned

Tory (Shelley Winters) is a bold inamorata who upsets the equilibrium of Silky (Dan Duryea). 1949, Universal Pictures Company, Inc.

love. It happens to the weary war widow who has become a living statue for the townsfolk to pity.

It is also Cupid's arrow for the con man when the little innocent melts his heart and ruins his chance for a clean getaway. Everything runs its course because of Tory's hysterical behavior. Her payoff is very funny because she creates the possibility of a new scam at her expense when she becomes a prop in the grifters' final gambit. The little innocent wins out and it's the paddy wagon for the con artists, the noble Mason included.

John Payne is convincing as the phony chum of the fallen soldier and eases into the confidences of the people who knew and loved his Army buddy. Joan Caulfield is the innocent small town war widow who conquers the con man with her wholesome sensuality.

Dan Duryea has a smooth smile and a hard tone of voice in a role that sets him up as the mastermind and sometime-player of the hustle team. Shelley Winters is the cloudburst that dampens the spirits of the two con men. Her electricity short-circuits the team and has every man scrambling for himself.

Tory's (Shelley Winters) unbridled desire distracts Rick Mason (John Payne) and eventually derails the war memorial scam. 1949, Universal Pictures Company, Inc.

Dan O'Herlihy lends a dash of charm as one of the cultured hustlers. He is in for the long haul but backs off at Payne's request. This costs him a bundle but he does not complain or demand recompense. Dorothy Hart is wolfish as a receptionist on the make. She takes baby steps that she thinks are giant strides. Percy Helton displays his eccentric quirks as a big-hearted director of a YMCA-like organization.

Slim Dundee is a cruel gang boss and a keeper in *Criss-Cross*, a warped love story where Duryea's crime boss and Burt Lancaster's inside man cancel each other because of Yvonne DeCarlo's ill-fated spell. Dundee is an extreme example of Duryea's abusers. He not only uses force, he keeps tabs on his wife and her ex-man in an armored car caper that has him blowing it all in the end with a double-homicide crime of passion.

In *Criss-Cross*, the ex-husband and current spouse of a confused femme fatale plan to double-cross each other and the woman they love prepares to betray both of them. It is a criss-cross, a double cross taken to the next level where more than two people plan to cut each other out of the lucrative haul of a successful heist.

The heist is an intricate armored truck robbery, something that has never been successful in the past. The twist is utilizing an inside man, someone with a thorough layout of routes and procedures. His name is Steve Thompson, played by Burt Lancaster.

Thompson is a man without roots and someone who lacks ambition. He has a past but no prospects for a successful future. He is a man ruined by the love for a woman who was his wife for seven months. He left California after the divorce and worked for a trucking outfit in Chicago, did construction work down South, and toiled in the Oklahoma oil fields.

He returns under the illusion of helping his aging mother with her responsibilities and overseeing the marriage of his younger brother. No one believes him, not even his mother or childhood friend Lt. Pete Ramirez (Stephen McNally). They know that he has returned to see Anna (Yvonne DeCarlo), his ex-paramour.

Thompson visits the Rondo, a nightclub that was the old hangout. It is the first in a series of missteps that end tragically for the three principal

Lt. Ramirez (Stephen McNally) prevents a drunken Steve Thompson (Burt Lancaster) from flattening Frank the bartender (Percy Helton) for refusing to serve him another drink in *Criss Cross*. 1949, Universal Pictures Company, Inc.

characters. The club is owned by Slim Dundee (Dan Duryea), a small-time gangster who runs a gang of two-bit crooks.

Slim has a placid face with a pensive stare. He speaks in a slow, deliberate monotone when he is angry, which is most of the time. He is rail-thin, but given an imposing presence by a jacket with padded shoulders. You know he means business because he likes to wear black shirts and white ties.

He has eyes for Anna and is insanely jealous and possessive. One thing leads to another after Steve and Anna meet again. That is where the double-crosses begin. It is the lovers' triangle trying to become a twosome with the payoff being the take of the armored car robbery. Dundee and Thompson plan to cross each other with Anna as the stable element in each other's plans. They base their success on who she will stick with and each man thinks that he is the taker. Both men are mistaken.

Criss-Cross is a tight crime drama where flashbacks, first person narration, and clever dissolves are used to make the action seamlessly flow from one scene to the next. The film was the second collaboration between Burt Lancaster and Robert Siodmak. The first one was Lancast-

Slim Dundee (Dan Duryea) lays down the law to his girl Anna (Yvonne De Carlo) about ex-husbands and infidelity. 1949, Universal Pictures Company, Inc.

er's debut film in 1946, *The Killers*, based on the short story by Ernest Hemingway.

The film was originally about a racetrack robbery as envisioned by the first producer, Mark Hellinger. He died before filming started and the project was in Limbo before Siodmak and Daniel Fuchs, the screenwriter, changed it to an armored car heist that takes second stage to the intense and ill-fated lovers' triangle.

Steve Thompson's plan for the armored car robbery can be seen from two angles; first as a way to get enough money for him and Anna to start a new life on the run, or it could be seen as Steve's way of talking his way out of being caught alone with Dundee's wife. It is more likely that his plan was hatched on the spot when Dundee and his men invade the privacy of the Thompson family's home.

Anna gains the audience's sympathy throughout the movie by pretending to be a victim of unfortunate circumstances. She has been hound-

Lt. Ramirez (Stephen McNally) breaks up a fight between Slim Dundee (Dan Duryea) and Steve Thompson (Burt Lancaster) while Vincent (Tom Pedi) diverts the cop's suspicion from a planned payroll heist. 1949, Universal Pictures Company, Inc.

ed by an amorous gangster since her divorce from Steve and she is threatened with a frame-up by Lt. Ramirez if she does not stay away from her ex-husband.

She shows her true, rapacious nature in the film's last scene when she tells Steve that she had planned to cross both him and Slim. Anna was going to leave town with the money because she believed that Steve would have to spend weeks recuperating from his wounds in the hospital and Slim would have to stay underground until things cooled off. Neither she nor Steve escapes the heat of Slim Dundee's passion-fueled revenge at the cottage by the moonlit sea. A walking stick and a smoking gun are the gangster's grim-faced nod to the electric chair. Steve and Anna become a Method Pieta.

Dan Duryea and Howard Duff had the chance to act together in *Johnny Stool Pigeon*, whose working title was *Contraband*. Johnny Evans is a temperate hoodlum who finds redemption in a woman. Evans plays narc in order to earn a chance to go straight with Shelley Winters, the girl of his dreams. His redemption is anything but bleak, but his past is what makes him someone who lives on the dark side of the street.

Johnny Stool Pigeon is an effective cops-and-robbers thriller with Howard Duff as George Morton, a cold hearted cop; Dan Duryea as Johnny Evans, a likeable Alcatraz inmate sprung for a special job; and Shelley Winters as Terry Stewart, a tarnished yet innocent *femme* in Limbo. It's the story of two hard-boiled eggs and a tomato in a sting operation aimed at destroying an international dope ring with points of operation in Mexico, Tucson, and Winnipeg.

George Morton is a special agent whose mission is to bust a drug ring. His only chance of success lies in springing a con he once put away. Guilt and some latitude persuade the bitter inmate to aid the brusque cop. Morton needs some underworld muscle so he secures a parole for a convict named Johnny Evans. They are a contentious pair posing as dope smugglers. Terry Stewart is an inamorata on the outs of the action and cuts herself in on the action when she plucks the strings of Evans' harp, thereby complicating the dope sting.

Evans is the stool pigeon of the title, but he is anything but a stoolie. He may be an Alcatraz hood but he is the hero of the movie. He languishes in prison until the cop who put him away needs him to bust a dope smuggling ring. Evans is sprung into action to avenge the drug-related death of his wife. Freedom means nothing to him until he meets and falls in love with Terry Stewart, who brings out his inner gentleman.

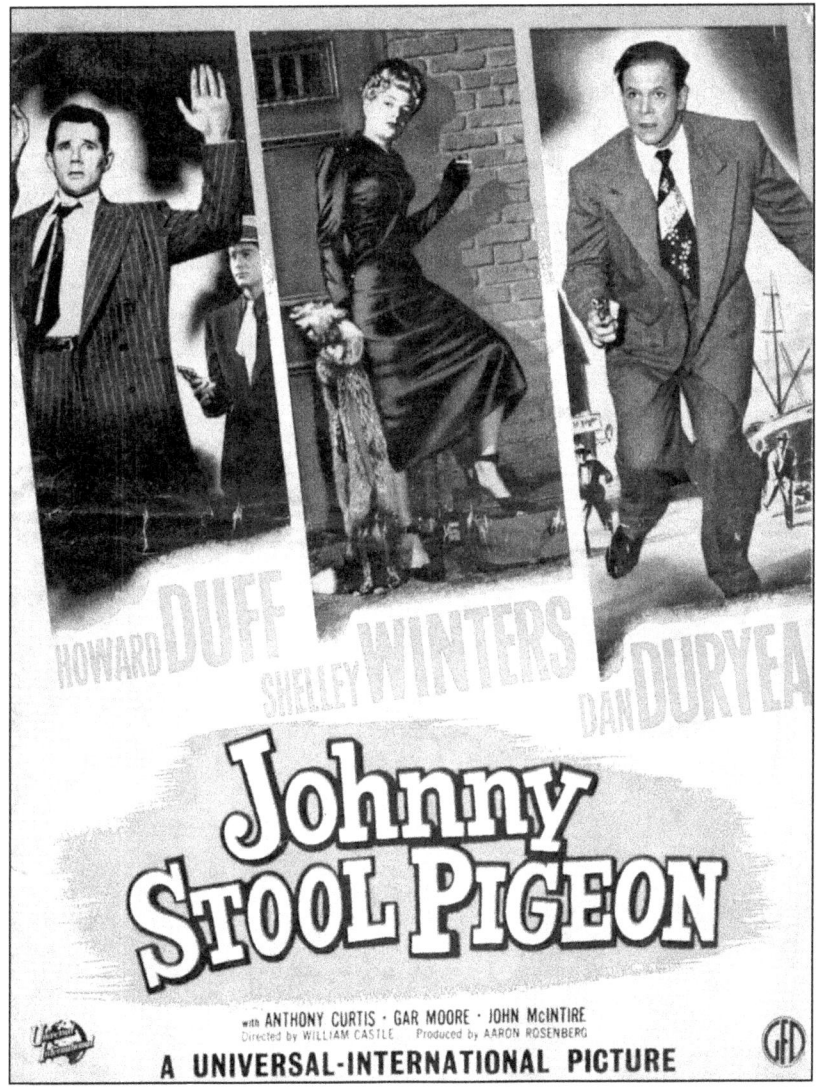

Movie poster for *Johnny Stool Pigeon*, starring Howard Duff, Dan Duryea and Shelley Winters. 1949, Universal Pictures Company, Inc.

Stewart is arm candy for one of the drug suppliers in Canada and she follows the men after they meet with the Canadian point of the drug connection. Morton is contemptuous of her but Evans takes a liking to her and makes it clear to the cop that if she goes, he will follow.

In *Johnny Stool Pigeon*, Johnny Evans is the only one who appreciates the power of a woman because absence makes the heart grow fonder. His stint in Alcatraz makes him feel that way. It's something that makes him a hero. Evans is a caustic man when it comes to dealing with Morton but his heart is a-flutter when it comes to Terry Stewart. He plays the game with Morton in order to get his freedom.

Evans is really the guy who gets things done. His quick thinking and firm rough housing gets things done in Mexico, Canada, and the mid-

Johnny Evans (Dan Duryea) falls in love with fly girl Terri Stewart (Shelley Winters). 1949, Universal Pictures Company, Inc.

A wounded Johnny Evans (Dan Duryea) is determined to warn Morton (Howard Duff) about a sudden change in plans by the drug smuggling kingpin. 1949, Universal Pictures Company, Inc.

Western states. He is the one going undercover for the deal, too. He uses his name and reputation to set up deals but crosses the wires at the right time. His sense of righteousness is too much for Morton to take.

George Morton depends on Evans' underworld contacts to accomplish the bust. He puts his life in the hands of a man he sent to Alcatraz. There are several opportunities for payback and it seems that one of them ruins the scheme towards the end. Johnny Evans isn't so primal and has a wide streak of principle that seems to elude Morton. Quick thinking, good luck, and perfect timing get the job done.

Morton is self-righteous and smug, but he learns humility from Evans and Stewart. He looked down his nose at them at the beginning of the film but he could not have accomplished the mission without them. Johnny Evans and Terry Stewart are the ones who take the victory walk in the film's last frame. George Morton remains as bewildered as ever.

John McIntire and Tony Curtis have supporting roles as criminals on opposite rungs of the ladder.

Dan Duryea played his last Universal crime boss in *One Way Street*. John Wheeler (Dan Duryea) is also soft on his lady, a Mediterranean beauty who abandons him for the greedily successful family doctor. Wheeler's tough guy authority is challenged by a minion who sees a soft heart as an invitation to take it all.

One Way Street is another U.I. crime parable set in Mexico. The gist is showing the senselessness of greed in the concrete jungle when nature's challenges are blessings to be appreciated. It is a road movie until the end, which is when it becomes a one-way street, and a slick, rainy one at that!

Poison and an antidote are an original variation on the bargaining power of an ambitious underling. In this case, it's the cultured Dr. James Malton (James Mason) who wants to take the boss's grand bundle, including his girlfriend Laura (Marta Toren), when she offers to go along for the ride. John Wheeler, the boss, is powerless to get his button men to take out the doc because the physician leads him to believe that he has given him poison instead of medicine for a headache. A phone call will be the subscription for the antidote along with providing enough time for a safe getaway.

Laura and the doctor make strange bedfellows and road companions as they elude Wheeler, the double-crossed mob boss. The time they spend in the small Mexican village is a purge for their big city mania. They become people of the soil and this is what upsets the balance that they seek.

Wheeler's persistent quest to track them down leads to a stand-off in Mexico City. Dr. Matson and Wheeler suffer from sardonic twists of fate. They survive each other, but succumb to themselves. Only Laura gets to wash her soul off in the rain.

James Mason had a restrained and cultured character that was more suited to a pedantic college professor with heartburn than to any character faced with a dilemma that could cost him his life. Mason played many such characters, and he did it with flair. Maybe it was his pained elocution or his stern and troubled expressions.

In *One Way Street*, he totally trumps Duryea by devising a powerful hook for a brazen swindle. It is sentimentality that brings him down, not a wronged crime boss or a determined woman. The epiphany of generosity eclipses the value of the dirty money. To be rid of it, Mason has to return it to its original abductor.

His second plan is more risky than the first and just as successful. Both encounters had to do with Duryea, who loses on both accounts. It was Mason's third plan—the intention of returning to a pastoral past with Toren—that did not pass the muster with fate.

For crime boss John Wheeler (Dan Duryea), there is only one way of dealing with insubordination in *One Way Street*. 1950, Universal Pictures Company, Inc.

Duryea's dependence on Toren is what brings him down. She was the daughter of one of his underlings and was brought to maturity under his watchful eye. She was molded and shaped into the type of woman he desired. His Pygmalion fantasy was a complement to wishful thinking, but losing the money and having his woman run out on him were the insults that became defiant blows to his empire. It's something that resonates with one of his men (William Conrad), whose double cross nets him more than the money.

Dr. Frank Matson (James Mason) and Laura Thorson (Marta Toren) try to blend in with local populace in Mexico. 1950, Universal Pictures Company, Inc.

Marta Toren picks up in *One Way* where Yvonne DeCarlo left off. She, too, inspires betrayal in a doctor played by James Mason. He has an ingenious ruse to keep Duryea's crime boss at bay, and only fate and circumstance bring down the doctor. The same cannot be said about Duryea's character. He is the only crime boss whose vulnerability sets him up for a payback for all the others' indiscretions.

Marta Toren has a Mediterranean charm that sizzles when she gets to Mexico. She understands the mendacious guidance of the itinerant priest, played by Rodolfo Acosta. The priest is solid oak, a bulwark traveling through the jungle, spreading his faith and helping others. William Conrad is a wise guy with dreams that are more than he can handle. King Donavan and Jack Elam play quirky gangsters who make early exits because of greedy thinking and small minds.

New Directions

Old Heels and New Blowhards

There were many interesting opportunities for Dan Duryea in 1949. Producer Bryan Foy of Eagle-Lion Productions offered him a deal to star and direct *Port of New York*. The actor would have received his usual $25,000 minimum salary for a six week shooting schedule. He also would have received the same amount for directing plus 10% of the gross. Dan Duryea turned down the offer. He believed that actors should not direct themselves unless they were geniuses, as he would claim in an interview he gave later in his career.[1]

The same year Universal-International purchased a screen treatment written by Nat Dallinger and Don Martin called *The Red Carpet*. It was about the rise and fall of a newspaper photographer who uses blackmail to pit two gangsters against each other. The studio had Dan Duryea in mind for the lead but nothing came of it. Martin Goldsmith and Alfred Lewis Levitt turned the story into the screenplay for *Shakedown*, with Howard Duff as the scheming shutterbug and Brian Donlevy and Lawrence Tierney as rival mobsters.

Lassor H. Grosberg and Richard Krakeur finalized a deal with the E. Henry Lewis West Coast Agency to present Leonard Lee's *Sweet Poison* for the stage. They were hoping for a Fall opening on Broadway. Dan Duryea was set to play the lead and Richard Whorf was tapped for the directorial chores. Rehearsals were scheduled to start on Labor Day and the show was to go through West Coast previews before opening in the East.

20th Century Fox had acquired the rights to the play and announced that they were delay filming for at least a year. The plot revolves around a woman's plan of action when she discovers the identity of her husband's

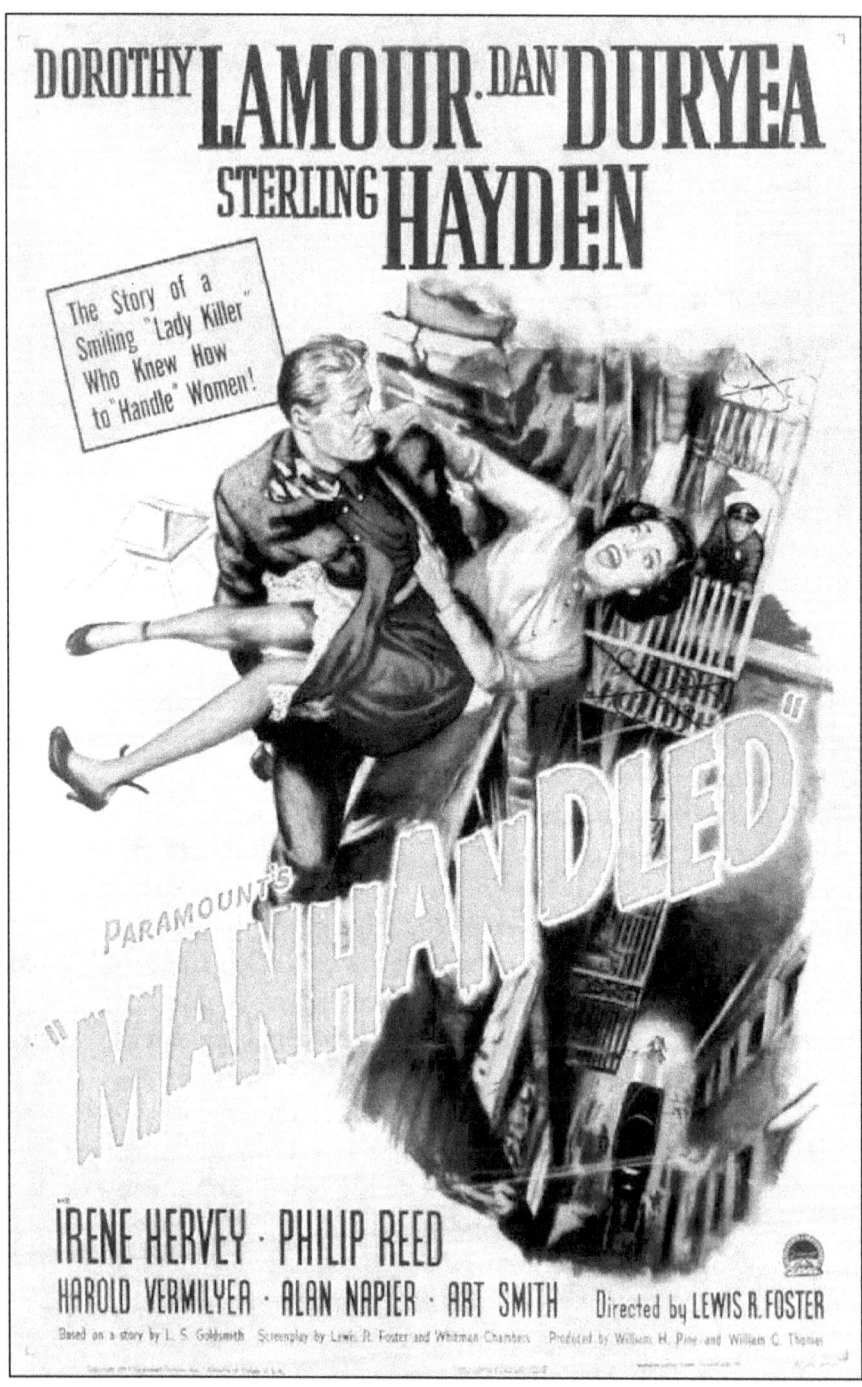

Movie poster for *Manhandled*. 1949, Paramount Pictures Inc.

murderer. At the time, the producers were searching for a well-known actress for the female lead. Nothing came of the project because Dan Duryea opted for a role in *Manhandled*. 20th Century Fox eventually made a film based on the play called *Along Came a Spider* starring Suzanne Pleschette. It was made for television in 1970.[2]

In the late 40's, Dan Duryea had the opportunity to fine tune his crime drama resume thanks to Universal-International. He also visited familiar territory when he took on two roles that referenced Tim Heidt and Johnny Prince. Karl Benson is a sleazy and manipulative private investigator in *Manhandled*. Danny Fuller is a sardonic wise guy that bites off more than he can chew when he's up against Lizabeth Scott in *Too Late for Tears*.

Pine and Thomas Productions at Paramount was a prolific production team that made profitable low budget movies. Bill Pine and Bill Thomas were known as The Dollar Bills because none of their productions ever lost money. After making *Dynamite* and *El Paso*, the duo announced that Sterling Hayden would be joining Dorothy Lamour and Dan Duryea in *Betrayal*, a melodrama scripted by Lewis R. Foster. *Betrayal* was changed to another working title, *A Man Who Stole a Dream*, before becoming *Manhandled*.

In *Manhandled*, Alton Bennett (Alan Napier) is a pompous author whose unfaithful wife (Irene Hervey) is bludgeoned to death with a cologne bottle. During the crime investigation, it is discerned that her jewels are missing from the murder scene. This brings Joe Cooper (Sterling Hayden), a wise-guy insurance investigator, into the crime investigation, much to the chagrin of Lt. Dawson (Art Smith) and Sgt. Foyle (Irving Bacon), two dumb detectives. Add Karl Benson (Dan Duryea), a tricky private eye, and Dr. Redmond (Harold Vermilyea), a wily phony psychiatrist, to the convoluted mess, and they add up to a clever murder frame-up for Merl Kramer (Dorothy Lamour), the pseudo-shrink's secretary.

The cops are not impressed with the forged credentials and blurry past of Miss Kramer, who has relocated from California to New York and used the credentials to gain employment with the fastidious fake psychiatrist. Her situation isn't helped by Karl Benson, the former cop turned deceitful private eye who is manipulating evidence against her, mainly because he has most of the stolen jewels hidden in his water cooler.

Benson is low-brow and obnoxious, a lazy detective who idles on his cot and sticks his used chewing gum wherever he wants to. He is also a sneak thief and he has made a haul that is ruined by the woman's murder.

Joe Cooper (Sterling Hayden), Merl Kramer (Dorothy Lamour) and Karl Benson (Dan Duryea) are the three principal players of *Manhandled*. 1949, Paramount Pictures Inc.

Her death makes fencing certain items forbidden because of the heat they generate.

The wise-cracking investigator is relentless in keeping the bumbling cops off his trail. Benson settles for small cash for some spangles and baubles and covers his tracks by planting false clues that point to Miss Kramer. She has access to the shrink's files, including records of sessions with the husband and his murdered wife. This is enough to cast suspicion on Kramer's motives.

The odd angle of the transcripts is the husband's recounting of a recurring nightmare where he bludgeons his wife to death. The police deduce that this knowledge plus a desire for the jewelry provided motive and opportunity for the stranger with the forged past.

Joe Cooper is a brazen insurance investigator who won't take no for an answer and has a natural disdain for cops. He believes that Merl Kramer is innocent and he is suspicious of Benson, whose wise-cracking, gum-chewing arrogance trips him up because someone in Cooper's business is alerted to a fast-talking wise guy.

Kramer's boss is the real king of frame-ups, and nothing he can do can get him out of the one he made for himself. His attempt to regain the stolen jewels from the private eye (who hijacked them from him in a surprise assault) ends with his own murder.

Manhandled could have been a palpable crime *noir* if not for the feeble attempts at humor that belabor the action. Most of the script is solid, except for a couple of scenes. A running gag about failed brakes is unnecessary as is an attempt to squeeze laughs out of Cooper's theory on the sleeping tablets that serve as an alibi for the husband/author.

The acting is good and would have been more effective without the strained attempts at humor. Sterling Hayden is his usual forceful and commanding self, propelling the action and plot development with his imposing personality. Dorothy Lamour acts like a comatose shrinking violet, which befits a tired character trying to lay down roots in a new environment so she could send for her daughter.

Dan Duryea is exceptionally obnoxious, even by his own standards. The scheming private detective is as sleazy as his habit of sticking his chewing gum wherever he wants.

Karl Benson (Dan Duryea) bears false witness against his neighbor (Dorothy Lamour), strengthening Lt. Dawson's (Art Smith) case against her. 1949, Paramount Pictures Inc.

He is a low rent private investigator without any discernible clients. A possible case is a client who wants him to frame his wife so that he can divorce her. He detects Kramer's disapproval and tells her that it is legitimate business. He idly languishes in his office, lounging on a sofa while watching his hamster work the treadmill. Benson is an ex-cop so he knows all of the tricks, including how to frame someone.

He cozies up to Kramer because she is a fragile woman. An invitation to a meal of Chow-Mein turns into a come-on because he does not want to wait for dessert. He only takes an interest in her because she inadvertently tells him about a client who may be obsessed with his wife's jewels. They are valued at $50,000 and that is all Benson needs to hear before he concocts a plan to rob the jewels and frame Kramer. He makes a copy of her key, robs the jewels and plants a signet ring in an overstuffed chair.

Benson actually sets himself up because he is too eager to please and is always offering an opinion, whether on how to change Kramer's life or adding bits and pieces to solve the police's dilemma. He is in over head because a murder was committed at The Grayson Arms. This will make fencing the expensive pieces impossible. His fence tells him this and Benson replies, "You're not talking to a cluck, Charlie. You're talking to a guy who knows all the angles. I got everything all planned out. Very, very carefully."

That includes trying to wheedle into the insurance investigator's territory when he offers to find the jewels if there is a reward. There is, but for Benson it will be the electric chair when his scheme falls apart. Along the way, he has framed Kramer and sold her out by denying not backing up her alibis. He even murders the psychiatrist in a pulse-pounding scene where he chases him with a car and grinds him into a wall. The shot of Benson's foot slamming on the accelerator rates well with Duryea's list of rub outs. It is of no avail to Benson, who is busted by Lt. Dawson, who sums up his suspicions with, "I've never known a congenital wise guy yet that didn't outsmart himself. They always bear down too hard."

Such is the way of a sleazebag. Equally sleazy is Harold Vermilyea as the psychiatrist, once his veneer is stripped away. His scenes with Duryea are the highlights of the movie as they try to outwit each other. The best scene in the movie is a death scene where the roles are reversed and the shrink is killed with his own car.

Art Smith is mostly effective as the intrepid detective who is an imp with a Brooklyn attitude. His character is undermined by some of the comic bits that he has to perform but he is not nearly as inane as Irving

Poster for *Too Late for Tears*. 1949, United Artists Corp.

Bacon, the sergeant who is his sidekick. The sergeant's character is what nearly sinks the movie and is responsible for the lame attempt at humor that ends the film. The ending dampens any grim satisfaction from a closing where justice is served with a healthy dose of old-fashioned irony.

After completing *Johnny Stool Pigeon*, Dan Duryea was borrowed from Universal-International by Hunt Stromberg for *Too Late for Tears*, with Lizabeth Scott and Don DeFore. The filming started at Republic Studios for a release by United Artists.

Old-fashioned irony is served with style in *Too Late for Tears*, a low budget crime drama that is satisfying because of the sincerity of the leads, chiefly an amazing Lizabeth Scott. Scott had a hypnotic effect on her marks because of her intense eyes, deep-set voice and the kind of smoky moves that had a way of making things go in her favor, at least until this movie's finale demands a swift, clean penance that proves crimes of passion do not pay.

It was always crimes of passion with Lizabeth Scott, a dame with moxie during an age when being called that was a sign of respect or a thing to be dreaded by everyone except the mark that prevented itself from being erased. If the protagonist resisted her evil charm, he was considered the hero of the drama; if not, he painfully died in service of the woman who inspired misguided trust in her stooges.

Danny Fuller and Jane Palmer are ill-fated reluctant partners in crime. 1949, United Artists Corp.

That's the setup for Alan Palmer (Arthur Kennedy) and Danny Fuller (Dan Duryea) in *Too Late for Tears*, an ambiguous and intricate thriller that delivers more twisted character development and fateful exits than is usually expected from a crime melodrama. Illicit fortunes always provided a great head start for movies about greed, where the accidental factor is an unhappy couple who unexpectedly receive a blackmail payoff for an underworld deal. This happens to Alan and Jane Palmer (Lizabeth Scott) while they are taking a drive along a road. A satchel of cash is tossed into their car from a vehicle that almost sideswipes them on an oceanside road.

The mishap opens a new world for the Palmers not only because of the sudden riches, but their opposite reactions to the occurrence and how they want to deal with the money. Alan wants to turn it over to the police, but she has other uses for the money. For Jane, it is a way out of her boring and hopeless marriage, something that Alan was not aware of before the rift.

Jane's fantasies are derailed when she is rudely reminded that the money already belongs to someone else, blackmailer Danny Fuller. He tracks her down and lays down the law about his money in an afternoon visit that includes a slap in the face for her and a rude awakening for him.

After their first drink, they become partners because of her quick thinking and the lack of resistance she shows to the idea of getting rid of a husband who has become superfluous due to his determination to turn the money over to the police.

Jane thinks of a plan to eliminate her husband during a boat ride on a dark lake where the boat attendant would be the only witness to the married couple boarding and alighting from the craft. Fuller would double for her husband on the ride back. The attendant does not realize that it is a case of bait and switch and, of the three participants, only two—Jane and Fuller—live to talk about it.

Shadows from the past haunt the lake as Kathy (Kristine Miller), Alan's sister, wants to search for her missing brother. She refuses to believe Jane's explanation that he deserted her to be with another woman. Kathy is aided by the sudden appearance of Don Blake (Don DeFoe), who claims to be a war buddy of Alan's from their European tour of duty. The couple hound Jane until she is about to crack and even put Danny Fuller under surveillance.

The blackmailer had become Jane's dupe during the commission of the murder and becomes the victim of his own farewell when he gets choked up during a toast to Jane. She uses the sole proceeds of her good

Don Blake (Don DeFore) and Kathy Palmer (Kristine Miller) question a boat attendant (Billy Halop) when they search for her missing brother. 1949, United Artists Corp.

fortune to enjoy the decadent life of a rich American debaucher in Mexico, where she buys the company of young men and the servitude of maids and butlers. It is the conflicting philosophy of low hems and high heels that determines her faith as a slap in the face becomes nothing compared to a long tumble through space.

Too Late for Tears is a dark, brooding thriller with seedy characters that add a dark dimension to the drama. Kennedy is a downbeat, honest dullard who gets iced in a crime drama triangle. Scott is deadly because of her insecurities. She kills because it is an easy way to deal with a problem. Duryea is protective of the secret that remains uncovered by the hush money intercepted by Scott and Kennedy.

Kristine Miller is sensual without being showy, a trait that could be a ruse or the real thing. Ruse is what comes to mind when DeFore shows inconsistencies with his story. He becomes a hero in the end and takes off with Miller. The boat attendant is an unaccredited Billy Halop, former leader of the Dead End Kids, before he took a temporary hiatus from the film industry.

Danny Fuller is another blowhard who gets tangled up in a web he helped spin. He becomes an unwitting pawn in his scheme and winds up bargaining for the money that belongs to him. His percentage decreases as the movie progresses and he winds up in arrears because he is no match for the lady he slapped to make a point.

Dan Duryea accepts the Heel of the Year Award from villainess Andrea King (1949).

Fuller may be in charge when he steps into the picture to reclaim his money but it does not take long for him to lose his grip and become a manipulated fall guy. Jane Palmer is too tough for him. Her transformation from docile housewife to greedy murderer is extreme and so is the effect it has on Fuller. He slowly tempers his arrogance with a drink or two before he begins to depend on the booze to calm his nerves. That is what leaves him open for Jane's final knockdown punch. A friendly toast turns into a silent memorial as Fuller's lifeless body relinquishes its ownership of the money, something that puts Jane's ill-fated dream within arm's length.

Mitchell Hamilburg, Dan Duryea's agent, started discussions in late 1949 with Hal E. Chester about *"The Big Story"*, a picture the independent producer was preparing for United Artists. On August 9, Hal E. Chester announced that he was going to produce *The Whip*, formerly *The Big Story*. Dan Duryea and Gale Storm headed a cast that included Harry Shannon, Gar Moore and Mary Anderson. Chester completed his casting when he signed Herbert Marshall, who had been inactive since 1947. Cyril Endfield was named as the director and the screen play, based on a murder mystery written by Craig Rice, was written by Henry Blankford. The movie was scheduled to be made at Monogram Studios with the poverty row studio supplying part of the financing. United Artists would handle the distribution.[3]

The Whip became *The Underworld* Story and it was a B-movie mulligan stew whose ingredients are the staples of various subjects and genres. We have a newspaper setting with two sides of the business, the cynical and the idealistic. A gangster connection and the genteel privileges of old money are the other two worlds that come together courtesy of the press. The three worlds are the playing board for characters caught up in the murder of a publishing magnate's daughter-in-law.

There is the disgraced reporter fighting the system, the newspaper baron covering up a scandal in the family, an idealistic small newspaper woman publisher, a light skinned African-American female scapegoat, a spoiled dissolute rich kid, a boorish gangster trying to make the next notch a social occasion, and a DA whose wounded pride has it in for the disgraced reporter.

Mike Reese (Dan Duryea) has fallen from the big time when a story he wrote leads to the shooting death of a gangland witness. Reese is blackballed and finds a way out of his shame when he invests in a suburban newspaper. The owner has a change of heart when she finds out who he

A poster for *The Underworld Story*. 1950, United Artists Corp.

is and the scandal that engulfs him. That changes when a newspaper publisher's daughter-in-law is murdered.

Reese's instincts kick in and pretty soon he moves into high gear and takes center stage in the running of the country paper. Catherine Harris (Gale Storm) and "Parky" (Harry Shannon), her typesetter, are swept up by his enthusiasm and authority, but it does not take long until his dark side emerges again when he starts wheeling and dealing at the expense of others.

He uses his contacts at the big city presses and news wires to attract attention to the small town scandal. Reese devises schemes that make him the center of attention, all the while pretending to help out the accused killer, Molly Rankin (Mary Anderson), a light-skinned African-American maid. Rankin has been arrested for the murder of her mistress and Reese begins to exploit her by forming a citizens' committee on her behalf.

Things begin to gain momentum when everything collapses because of Reese's hustling. Mike Reese connives with the defense lawyer on splitting fees, even it means sending Molly up the river. The DA exposes Re-

Mike Reese (Dan Duryea) is an amoral reporter who finds redemption in running a small town newspaper that cracks a local murder. 1950, United Artists Corp.

ese's motivation of getting the reward money. This sours many people on Reese and he becomes a pariah in the small town, an outcaste just as if he were in the city.

He makes amends for selling Molly out when he finds a witness who can corroborate Molly's contention about leaving flowers on a bus. Suspects become apparent to Reese and he has a run-in with the gangster. He arranges a meeting with E. J. Stanton (Herbert Marshall), the father of the real murderer (Gar Moore). There is a showdown with the publisher, his son, and Carl Durham (Howard Da Silva), the gangster. Reese is roughed up but wins in the end. He is called a hero and even complimented by DA Munsey (Michael O'Shea) as he is loaded into the ambulance.

The onerous urban newsman Mike Reese in *The Underworld Story* saves an innocent woman from the electric chair by earning a stripe for his incredulous partner, a suburban newspaperwoman. Reese is a disgraced reporter whose weasel-like personality overcomes a struggling small town newspaper and forces it to become an influential scandal sheet when a grisly murder occurs in the community. He wheels and deals with the outside press organization and wrangles deals that count the suspect out so many times that she goes from a beloved victim to the public to a convicted murderer who deserves to burn.

Reese proves her innocence, exposes the real killer, and pulls off the ultimate scoop in slam dunking a press magnate into the crime section.

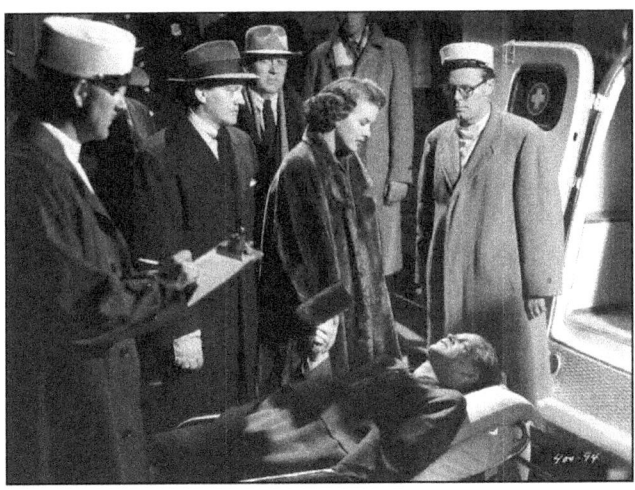

A. Munsey (Michael O'Shea) gives Catherine Harris (Gale Storm) a chance to ride in an ambulance at the conclusion of *The Underworld Story*. 1950, United Artists Corp.

He is wounded in bringing down a loathsome gangster who dealt himself into the power games of the rich and infamous. Reese is a hero, and even the DA who hates him has to give him the stamp of approval as his junior partner becomes a junior miss in her first ambulance ride.

Hal E. Chester was impressed with the push and exploitation United Artists gave his picture. He proposed a deal where he could deliver four "realistically budgeted" movies a year. One of the projects was a movie called *Models, Inc.* and was to have starred Dan Duryea but it was filmed with Dennis O'Keefe instead.

Indies, Radio and TV

Dan Duryea almost had the chance to work with William Wyler again when Paramount sought him for the part of Drouet in the production of *Sister Carrie*. He was close to inking the deal but the role went to Eddie Albert. Dan Duryea's next movie project was based on the memoirs of Al Jennings, a colorful Western outlaw who gained notoriety around the turn of the 20th century as a lawyer turned robber of trains and banks. He was imprisoned several times for various crimes and went straight after President Teddy Roosevelt pardoned him. He then embarked on several careers that included evangelist, politician, writer, actor and film producer. Only his life as a Western bandit is chronicled in the film. At the end of the movie, the narrator informs the audience that Al Jennings returned to Oklahoma and resumed his career as a lawyer. He became one of the leading proponents of statehood for Oklahoma.

Al Jennings of Oklahoma is a proud child of the old South, someone whose adversities inspired him to reach for the stars. Twisted fate and bad luck intervened, inspiring him to become a desperado instead of a brilliant lawyer. His fortune changed in 1863, a turning point for the South in the Civil War. The Union Army forces the Jennings family to flee their plantation while their father, a Confederate Major, fights the war.

Dan Duryea exudes charm and sophistication as Al Jennings. He is an American patriot fighting for the rights guaranteed by the Constitution. Duryea plays it hot and cold. He possesses a mean temper that cannot be quelled when his ire is raised. This is displayed throughout the movie when he cannot have his way. He is always bickering with an authority figure because it is either his way or the highway.

Al Jennings (Dan Duryea) is a lawyer who turns to banditry when the Fates conspire against him. He meets and falls in love with Margo St. Clare (Gale Storm). 1951, National Screen Service Corp.

The turning point in his life comes when he will not accept that his brother's murderer is free on bail. Murder is not an offense that allows bail and the only reason Mardsen is released is because he is a town bigwig. This does not sit well with Jennings, who shoots him in self-defense when the lawyer tries to shoot him after he refuses to write and sign a confession to the murder.

Al Jennings (Dan Duryea) rides to the home of Tom Marsden (John Dehner) to get a written confession from his brother's murderer. 1951, National Screen Service Corp.

Gale Storm plays Margo St. Clare, a society dame of her time. She desires Al Jennings, but feels that he is socially inferior because of his underworld activities. Ironically, it is the same criminal behavior that creates the allure. Margo plays hard to get while leaving openings for advances and praise from Jennings. She is not thrilled by his attention but does not discourage him from making overtures. It is she who first makes the suggestion that he set up shop in New Orleans, something Jennings considers unappealing at the beginning of the movie but reconsiders when he is on the lam. Margo may be frills, buttons, bows, and corsets, but she stands by Jennings, not only by aiding him to escape from the detective, but by attending his trial.

Dick Foran has always been a tower of strength. In this movie, he is Al's older brother. He sticks by his brother's side when he becomes a desperado and does not abandon him when the net tightens and he is caught.

Frank Jennings tempers brother Al's irrational emotionalism. Frank may be quiet, but he stills rides with his brother and shares in the danger. He is a quiet thinker, one whose rationality adds logical perspectives to Al's grand plans.

Frank is given five years and Al is sentenced to life in prison. However, improprieties in the arrest and trial of Al Jennings impel President Theodore Roosevelt to pardon him.

Raymond Greenleaf plays Judge Jennings, the family patriarch. He is a respected jurist who fought valiantly in the Civil War. Ed Millican and Louis Jean Heydt are the other Jennings brothers, Ed and John, respectively. Harry Shannon is the shady cattleman, John Dehner is the unscrupulous lawyer, and William "Bill" Phillips is his ornery henchman. John Hamilton and Myron Healey have small unbilled parts.

While *Al Jennings of Oklahoma* was playing in movie theaters fans could listen to Dan Duryea play a police detective on *Man from Homicide*, a radio crime drama that was a summer replacement for *Inner Sanctum*. Radio programs had diminished in popularity and were nowhere near their zenith years of the 30's and 40's. Television had just exploded thanks to the phenomenal popularity of Milton Berle and many radio formats and shows were developed into television versions.

Some of the old and cherished radio formats still continued into the 50's but they wouldn't last long. Their television counterparts would eventually lure away listeners and then the sponsors would follow suit. *Man from Homicide* rode the last of the line for crime dramas with other shows like *Defense Attorney, Richard Diamond, Private Detective* and *The Casebook of Gregory Hood*.

This was not Dan Duryea's first participation in radio. He had starred in a radio version of *Woman in the Window* in 1945. He also appeared in episodes of *Suspense* and *Family Theater*. *The Will to Power* and *Man who Couldn't Lose* were the *Suspense* programs. *Toledo Smith* and the *Postmistress of Laurel Run, Lodging for the Night* were *The Family Theater* shows. He was also interviewed by columnist Hedda Hopper for her show in 1950. Then came *Man from Homicide*.

Louis Vittes created the show. He was a radio writer who was on the staff for *The Thin Man, Barry Craig, Confidential Investigator* and *The Shadow*. He also created and wrote *Peter Salem* from 1949 to 1953. Louis Vittes knew the crime genre well and his writing crackles with the gaudy patter of pulp fiction.

Lou Dana was a detective although he was not a private shamus from either coast. He was a police lieutenant who played by the book and his refrain, "I don't like killers" is something that he believed in. It didn't matter who it was or whether or not he even suspected the guilty party; whoever committed the crime was brought to justice by Lt. Dana.

There were thirteen episodes of *Man from Homicide*, but only nine are extant, including the audition episode with Charles McGraw. It's the best of the lot because the gravelly voiced actor fits the battle weary cop to a tee. It's Dan Duryea's role and you accept his interpretation but that's only after you set the unofficial first show out of your mind. Duryea's Lt. Dana may not be made of crags and gravel but he was still tough and tenacious.

Duryea's Lt. Dana may not have had the asset of Charles McGraw's magnificent voice, but he didn't need it when it came to breaking down a guilty suspect. He was dogged, determined and persistent. The cop kept

Dan Duryea portrayed police detective Lou Dana, star of the radio series *Homicide Squad*. 1951.

Dan Duryea and Lawrence Dobkin played Lt. Lou Dana and Sgt. Dave, aka Pappy, for the summer replacement detective drama. 1951.

hammering—either with his questions or his fists—until the suspect cracked open and became liable to self-incrimination.

Lt. Dana was aided by his corpulent sidekick, Sgt. Dave (Larry [Lawrence] Dobkin) aka Pappy. He was a garrulous partner who always got things wrong. That's one reason why Lt. Dana seemed so smart. Another one was that he was always right. It didn't matter what the mystery was about because the common thread was that it was committed by someone and that person had an identity. It was his job to figure it out and there was no stopping him once he was on a trail.

Duryea premiered as Lt. Dana on June 25, 1951. The episode's title was *The Muriel Smith Case* and it was about solving the murder of a classy night club singer found lying on a bed in a cheap hotel. Was she shot to death by Blakey (Bill Bouchey), her boss? Maybe it was Michael Carter (Howard Culver), her lover? Or was it his wife, Susan (Jean Bates)? She was the one found standing over the body.

The investigation becomes a round robin of false leads until the least likely suspect becomes the name on the crime blotter. It was the wife, after all, which does not mean anything to the nightclub owner who killed the husband because he thought he was responsible for the murder of his beloved canary.

The Franklin Kelso Case shows the reverse snob in Lt. Dana when he is told that Mr. Kelso, a multi-millionaire, has been receiving death threats. He protests that the department would not have sent him to check out death threats made against a fruit peddler. The detective is told by his boss, Capt. Sherman (Bill [Willis] Bouchey), that a multi-millionaire rates that attention because of social etiquette. It's still not right but that's the way things are, especially when the multi-millionaire later turns up very dead.

What would a cheesy detective drama be without the notorious gang of gang robbers that wreaks havoc and creates mayhem for each other? *The Eddie Kent Case* has that and more. The police are on the lookout for Eddie Kent, a career criminal that pulled off a bank robbery that netted him $80,000 and a murder rap for the person killed during the holdup. The *Eddie Kent Case* is routine except for Dan Duryea finally getting a voice for his character. His projection no longer seems clipped and his intonation and stresses are more natural. From here on in, it's Duryea's role and he proves that he can be just as forceful and natural as Charles McGraw.

There is something about Lt. Lou Dana that makes him question normalcy. It has no place in homicide so when he runs across a scenario that appears pat he knows that he will have to do some serious snooping to reconstruct the real picture. That is the way it is in *The Drowned Girl Case*.

Sgt. Dave always trusts his eyes and believes that they have an open and shut case of suicide. Things are not so simple for Lt. Dana. Experience has taught him that suicides are tired, worn and, sometimes, bitter. The young victim recently had her hair done and had a face untouched by experience. That, plus the fact that she screamed before she jumped into the bay makes the detective reject the suicide explanation. All it takes is an ornate hat found at the crime scene to put Lt. Dana on the trail of the killers, a gang of thieves led by a milliner turned fence and murderess.

The Willie Baines Case is when the show found its voice. Dan Duryea developed the perfect intonation, the sound effects were more professional, and the music, always a strong point of the show, was amped up a couple of notches.

Willie Baines is a low-level thug who is found murdered. He was supposed to testify against a crime boss. When Scuyler, the man who subpoenaed Baines, is also shot to death Lt. Dana puts the pieces of the puzzle together and they add up to a beautiful nightclub pianist named Clare Mason. She is the innocent link between the killer and the victims.

She was the lover of Scuyler and he told her of Baines' upcoming deposition against Welch, the owner of the Orange Turban nightclub, where Clare works. She, in turn, told Welch, who then hired a hit man from Detroit to eliminate his liabilities, including Clare. Lt. Dana gets Clare to sign a dying declaration that will send Welch to the death house.

The Steve Morton Case is an odd sort of mistaken identity case. The corpse was found with two shotgun blasts to the face. The victim is tentatively identified as Steve Morton. A little background check uncovers that he is being investigated by the IRS for income tax evasion. Initially, Lt. Dana thinks his wife colluded with their lawyer to kill Morton.

Further investigation proves that the body was someone else who was lured to a rendezvous with the missus for a clandestine affair. It ended with a double-barrel shotgun surprise. The gist of the scheme was to have the missus inherit the insurance money so the couple can live a new life.

An apparent suicide turns out to be murder in *The Lucille Forbes Case*. That is nothing new for Lt. Dana. If Sgt. Dave comes to a hasty conclusion it can only mean something else. In this case, the lovely young woman who was found with her wrists slit in a theater lounge could only have been murdered.

Several trails lead to suicide but the road traveled by Lt. Dana leads to murder. The young victim was once married to a Hollywood star. She refused to give him a divorce and this unsettled his lover, the assistant who drugged the woman and slit her wrists. All it takes is a little pressure from Lt. Dana to make the woman crack.

Although the series was meant to be a summer replacement Dan Duryea was interested in continuing the show but the usual red tape and hierarchy changes prevented anything from materializing.

Shirley Temple hosted *The Family Theater* where Dan Duryea appeared in Toledo Smith with Skip Homeier. 1951, Family Theater Productions.

Dan Duryea would make a couple more radio appearances during the 1950's. In 1952, he would return to *Suspense* for two more episodes, *Remember Me* and *The Driven Snow*. His last radio appearance would be in a 1954 episode of *Family Theater* called *Sideman*.

Dan Duryea's next project was at the other end of his scale and it was not only a change of pace but a new direction. Arrowhead Productions was a fledgling independent company and their first project was *Chicago Calling*. The producers, Peter Berneis and John Reinhardt, arranged a deal for United Artists to distribute the movie. It was the only movie made by the company. A second movie, *The Girl from Astoli*, was planned, intended to be a European made film with American and Viennese funds. Still, the uncertainty of business reality did produce an interesting movie. *Chicago Calling* is an oddity, an almost pre-reality show exhibitionism that results in the defeat of the protagonist.

Alcohol is the demon that figures big in *Chicago Calling*. Bill Cannon (Dan Duryea) is an alcoholic photographer whose life has turned into a downward spiral. His wife, Mary (Mary Anderson), has tired of his failed attempts to reform and has decided to move to Baltimore with their daughter, Nancy (Melinda Plowman), in order to live with Mary's mother.

The situation becomes a crisis when the daughter is seriously hurt in a car accident outside Chicago. Cannon receives a telegram from his wife promising to call him at a certain hour to inform him of the outcome of an operation to save their daughter's life. There is no return address. His bad luck worsens when he receives a turn-off notice for his telephone. The

Bill Cannon (Dan Duryea) comforts his daughter Nancy (Melinda Plowman) before she leaves home with her mother. 1951, United Artists Corp.

drama hinges on his efforts to keep the service active so he can receive the news of the operation's outcome.

His drinking buddy, a charitable organization, and a finance company can't help him in his time of need. His only hope is Bobby (Gordon Gebert), a little orphan boy whom he persuades to filch the money from

Bill Cannon (Dan Duryea) and his lifeline, the telephone, in *Chicago Calling*. 1951, United Artists Corp.

his big sister. A change of heart has him convincing the boy to return the money.

His salvation is a kind-hearted phone service man (Ross Elliot) who lets him have one more call. It is in vain because the news is bad and that makes him suicidal, but his little buddy saves him from killing himself.

Chicago Calling could very well be a reality show chronicling the last days of a man on the verge of extinction. It has a *cinéma vérité* quality to it, mainly due to its blue-collar cadence and the low-key performances of the players. It is a peculiar movie whose merit lies in elements extraneous to the plot.

The premise is slight yet it turns the movie into a weird adventure and Duryea's performance only heightens the bizarre proceedings. He delivers a performance that is so ordinary that it makes it seem as if you are spying on his life as he runs into obstacles in his attempts to keep his telephone service running.

The odd characters, the gritty cityscape, and the main plot device—the telephone—are archaic by today's standards. They make the movie fascinating because it is like looking into another world. The best thing about the movie is its on-location filming. The Los Angeles slums are really as squalid as some of the street characters.

A drinking buddy, a pretty hash-slinger, a small boy and a dog, plus a kind-hearted telephone man, figure big in a small adventure at the end of nowhere. These are characters that nobody pays attention to, the work force that keeps the machinery going at the grassroots level during the post-war years. In this world, even the bureaucrats are odd, including the stoic banker, the hyena-like loan-man, and the kind-hearted zombie woman of the welfare office. They all provide a brick wall for Connor to bang his head against.

Dan Duryea worked without a salary, electing to take a profit sharing agreement. That the movie did not make any money did not faze the actor. The critics called it a slight movie with a soap opera plot that was worthy of the second half of a double feature bill. Dan Duryea called it his favorite movie and he was satisfied with it because his wife cried when she saw the film. He said that he trusted her judgment without reservation.

In October, Dan Duryea joined several American and British performers for the Command Film Performance at the Odeon, Leicester Square. The live show preceded the spooling of Ealing Studio's *Where No Vultures Fly*. It was produced by Ben Lyon and raised around $85,000 for the Cinematograph Trade Benevolent Fund. The production received lukewarm reviews and it was generally felt that it failed to live up to the quality of the previous year's show.

The show opened with a filmed segment featuring TV commentator Leslie Mitchell interviewing Zachary Scott, Jane Russell, Dan Duryea, Fred MacMurray, Peter Lawford and Van Johnson as they descended the gangplank at South Hampton. That was followed by the live show with the first sketch with Michael Wilding and Peter Lawford spoofing customs agents. Burt Lancaster was on hand for a sketch in a wax museum. Other British talent involved included Richard Attenborough, Anne Crawford, Herbert Lom and Sir Ralph Richardson.

The general consensus was that the show suffered from mediocre writing. Despite a bevy of American-British talent, the biggest ovation went to Nat Karson's Empire Girls for their flawless Charleston number. Kudos was reserved for Dan Duryea and Jane Russell's comic skit about a mobster and his moll. Orson Welles resurrected his USO magic show, aided by Lizabeth Scott and Van Johnson and he thrilled the audience with his sleight-of-hand tricks and dazzling illusions. Peter Ustinov and John Mills inspired laughs in a bit about two ham actors from the 1920's.[4]

In 1952, Dan Duryea paid homage to his dramatic roots when he added his name to "Cornellians on Broadway", a collective letter of congratulations to Prof. Alexander M. Drummond, organizer and director of the Cornell Dramatic Club. Among the other signers were Sidney Kingsley, Franchot Tone, Dorothy Sarnoff and William Prince. They expressed their gratitude to their former teacher and mentor and wished him well in retirement. The letter was read at a testimonial dinner attended by more than 125 alumni.

Dan Duryea's career entered a new phase with the new decade. He had amassed an eclectic collection of roles even though he was typecast as a hard-edged charmer with a menacing appeal. The opportunity to broaden his talent was due to his entrance into television. He continued to play boisterous psychos but added other characters that he had not played on the big screen.

He appeared on many of the premier anthology shows, such as *Climax*, *Studio 57*, *Schlitz Playhouse of Stars*, *The Ford Television Theater*, and *General Electric Theater*.

Dan Duryea was a flexible actor who was comfortable in either medium. He was able to fill in the nuances of a solid supporting role or hold down the boisterous lead in an independent Western or pulp drama. Duryea also benefited from the character lines and rueful expressions that came from decades of experience. This gave the characters of his later years emotional depths and shadings that made him a durable supporting player.

Dan Duryea made his television debut on *The Kate Smith Evening Hour*. Kate Smith was a popular songstress during the 40's and her rendition of *God Bless America* was once the standard. Dan Duryea starred in a short scene called *Land's End*. Vengeance and retribution are meted out

Dan Duryea made his television debut on *The Kate Smith Evening Hour* with a live dramatic presentation about the torment of a lonely man driven insane by revenge. 1952, National Broadcasting Company (NBC).

in a solitary diner at the end of the trolley line. It is where a dupe gets to take it out on his former boss, a mayoral candidate on the eve of election victory. The embittered ex-con's just dessert will get him the hot seat but it does not matter to him so long as personal justice is served with a strong dose of cynical irony.

It is a rainy night when a sickly man pours out his heart to the proprietress of an all-night diner. The man relates to nature's turbulence and tells her that he will quell the squall within his soul by committing an act that will stay with him for the rest of his life. That may be short lived because of his premeditation but it will be worth the long wait that turns into an answered prayer.

The Candidate's limo breaks down outside of the diner and the chauffeur is off on a rain-soaked hike to the nearest filling station. This makes for a convenient confrontation between the party boss and the stooge whose political patronage job time served.

A small exchange of accusations, pardons and promises leads to the shooting death of the candidate as news of his victory is broadcast on the radio.

The diner owner gives him three miles before the cops will catch up with him and makes an emergency call about a fatal shooting at the diner at the end of the trolley line. A post-midnight victory turns into a post-mortem beat down as the stranger with the bad lungs breathes in the wind and rain. The neon 'eats' sign blinks behind him.

Dan Duryea's next television appearance was on *The Schlitz Playhouse of Stars*, an anthology series sponsored by the brewing company. "If you like beer, you'll love Schlitz" was the slogan of the sponsor of Playhouse of Stars. The self-promos appeared half way through the dramas and reminded the audience of who was backing the show in case they forgot the musical opening that already made the point.

Dan Duryea starred in two dramas for the playhouse, *P.G.* and *Souvenir from Singapore*. *P.G.* was a prisoner-of-war drama set in a German P.O.W. camp. Dan Duryea shared the acting chores with John Forsythe and Teresa Celli. It deals with subjects and themes later dealt with in *Stalag 17*. Duty, honor and country are balanced against survival and self-preservation becomes the rule book for survival. Dan Duryea's next appearance on Schlitz Playhouse was more memorable.

The China Smith character was introduced in *Schlitz Playhouse: Souvenir from Singapore*. He is an Irishman on the run from the law in his native country because he is accused of treason and has taken up residence in Singapore. China Smith is a shady beachcomber and back alley dealer, someone who stays one step ahead of the law and a couple of steps behind the criminal gentry. The setting is Singapore in 1952, the midst of the Communist invasion and the waning days of British colonialism. Both factors figure in a peripheral way.

China Smith is a scrappy survivor who finds himself in a comic strip adventure involving stereotypes from Far East mystery thrillers. The hero's mission is to defend the Crown and break up a ring of rubber hijackers known as the Blue Tigers. He has to negotiate the Singapore underworld with its treacherous back alleys and ominous opium dens. Smith even has his own Dragon Lady to tempt with a jade necklace.

Critics may have derisively dismissed the second offering from *The Schlitz Playhouse of Stars* but the premise was enough to interest Bernard Tabakin in producing a series based on Robert C. Dennis' character. Dan Duryea started shooting his new series on July 9 for Edward Lewis Productions at Motion Picture Center. Douglas Dumbrille repeated his role as the British police inspector and blonde femme fatale Myrna Dell was added to the cast as the Empress Shari. 52 episodes were planned. The

Robert C. Dennis created the character of China Smith for his anthology drama, *Souvenir from Singapore*. 1952, Meridian Productions.

show was set in twelve markets and had sponsors like Cribben & Sexton, Inc., for Universal Gas Ranges and Falstaff Brewing Company.

China Smith

William 'China' Smith was an Irish émigré living in Singapore. He was a con man who operated on the borderline of honesty and petty larceny. His adventures were right out of a comic strip and the characters he encountered all came from central casting. The show is a period piece, a post-war colonial satire in spite of itself. The series' plots, dialogue, and characterizations give it a humor that was peculiar to the quirky personality of the star.

He was lanky and sardonic and wore a white fedora and matching suit. China Smith liked to smoke cigarettes and drink hard liquor. When he hunched his shoulders and smirked with glee, it was usually to deliver a sardonic conclusion to an ironic turn of events for his chief adversary. It was all done in the lyrical tones of an Irish brogue. China Smith was lazy but enterprising, shifty yet truthful, and braved any odds if it meant pleasing a beautiful woman with dubious intentions or dealing with ancient mysteries that challenged him to come and fight it out in the jungle.

Dan Duryea played China Smith in two versions of the show, one in 1952 and the other two years later. Both seasons had twenty six episodes. The difference with the old and new adventures was a change in the show's opening theme music, different empresses and a shift in locales. There was also the matter of the dogged British police inspector who wanted to have Smith deported in the first season. He was absent from the show's revival. The first show filmed episodes in Mexico and the second used San Francisco's Chinatown for a backdrop.

Some of China Smith's adventures included being hired by English run companies that needed a solution to blackmail or sabotage. Smuggling was a theme that ran throughout the series and he found himself doing business with cutthroats and double-crossers. Blackmail and death-threat cases put his life at risk on more than one occasion and there were others where an eastern custom made him the guardian of an orphan, monk or helpless widow. Being the sentimental Irishman that he was, China Smith always found time for tracking down old lovers and had an eccentric knack for reuniting parted suitors or exposing con artists passing as imaginary relatives.

China Smith may have been a friend to underdogs but he was painted as a petty criminal by Inspector Hobson (Douglas Dumbrille), the chief of British Police. Only Smith's nemesis was aware that the shady vagabond was really William Fitzgerald, a fugitive wanted for treason in Ireland.

China Smith was a self-styled private eye who worked the shady side of Singapore to aid the powerful and the powerless. He was a con artist with a righteous soul and a shady sense of justice. 1952, National Telefilm Associates (NTA).

The inspector's vehement threat to have Smith/Fitzgerald deported back to Belfast always fell on deaf ears and Smith succeeded in outsmarting the inspector for a whole season.

That's not to say that China Smith was not without sympathizers. In the first season, Smith's ally was Madame Shari (Myrna Dell), referred to as the Empress. She ran The Trade Winds Hotel, a hostel that was a front for every shady scheme and illicit deal in Singapore. She maintained her integrity as an honest business woman but she and Smith had an understanding between them. The Empress and China Smith formed a mutual alliance and provided assistance to each other in exchange for money and special favors. They used each other for their own purposes and agreed on the price of betrayal.

In the new adventures, Madame Shari was nowhere to be seen and The Countess Steffi (Regina Gleason) was the new lady power broker. She was the daughter of Count Von Idyll, a wealthy racketeer and crime merchant and she inherited the power and the glory when her father died. The Countess shared a cordial relationship with China Smith. It was less barbed than the pact he had with Madame Shari. China Smith and The Countess enjoyed a rare rendezvous as China Smith was a wily rascal who plied his charm whenever he could.

Dan Duryea takes a break from filming with Marian Carr, who appeared on the show several times as an exotic beauty with a dark past. 1952, National Telefilm Associates (NTA).

The second season also expanded the show's locale from Singapore to include surrounding cities like Hong Kong, Macao and Shanghai. An occasional adventure in the jungle also gave China Smith a chance to risk his neck in places other than the seedy waterfronts, colonial business enterprises or black market circuits. The change was academic because China Smith still contended with the same adversaries and dilemmas and walked the same crowded sidewalks, bandied with the same hustlers in the bustle, and was bamboozled by the same mysterious women in distress, zealous revolutionaries trying to make a point and broken-hearted lovers separated by fate.

The general tone of the storylines may have rendered China Smith a real-life cartoon but that was half the fun of the show. The other half was the strange characters that he had to deal with. That could include a gaggle of popular character actors who periodically showed up or anonymous people playing colorful parts.

Semi-regulars like Nestor Paiva, Victor Sen Young, Keye Luke and Clarence Lung popped up in an assortment of bit parts. Among the women who lent their charm were Marian Carr, Maxine Cooper, Rita Moreno, and Claudia Barrett.

The budget was very low and the short shooting schedule gives the episodes a certain amateurish feel to them. In a 1962 interview, Duryea explained that, during the show's first season, they had little more than a day to film a script. The second season, the schedule was upped to a day and a half. The shows were filmed back-to-back, unless they were using a prop such as a pagoda temple. Then, all the scenes of upcoming shows that involved a temple were shot simultaneously.

"This can foul you up", he said in the interview. "I had no idea that we had this kind of schedule. We took three days on the pilot. My contract said each segment couldn't take more than three days. I thought that meant the schedule would be three days shooting, but we never reached this in 62 episodes. There wasn't the money. We had a budget of $17,500 a picture."

He noted that, in 1952, he filmed 18 episodes in 21 days. Duryea maintained that they did a good job considering the budgetary constraints.

"It was too hurried a process to get anything satisfying. Most of today's TV stars couldn't operate under that pressure and speed." He also added, "There is not enough work done on the part of the actor at night, studying his work for the next day. I might be over trained from too much work, but I do feel more homework is needed at night."[5]

It was well known that Dan Duryea was an actor who burned the midnight oil when he was preparing for a part. It was not unusual for him to be up most of the night preparing his lines.

The show did run afoul of the Screen Actors guild when reruns were shown in syndication. Tableau Television, Ltd., run by producer Bernard Tabakin, saw its contract cancelled by SAG. The union charged that the production company "had fallen behind by about $10,000 in making royalty payment to performers who took part in twenty of the adventure films." This excluded the six episodes that were filmed in Mexico because they were not affected by Guild regulations. The series was in its fourth run in Los Angeles and the actors only received partial payment for four of the shows they appeared in. This caused a temporary shutdown of the show, but it would be revamped with new adventures after the legal mess was solved.[6]

China Smith was basically a waterfront gumshoe willing to solve any problem or find the missing pieces to his client's puzzle if the incentive appealed to his shady sense of ethics. Many of these problems dealt with murder. *The Corpse with the Purple Ear* was China Smith's first murder mystery case. He had to solve the murder of a British rubber planter. Colonialism was part of the show's makeup and it was implied that the royal kingdom had rightful ownership of foreign natural resources. China Smith was sometimes hired to assist these companies, usually in cases of blackmail, sabotage or theft. In this case, it was murder and it involved a wife, a doctor-boyfriend and complaints about a perpetual earache.

In *Devil-in-the-Godown*, China Smith uses the services of a brotherhood of assassins to track the murderers of a Singapore newspaperman. He acquires their compliance even though they are curious why the marked man is the already slain newspaperman. It is China Smith's way to finding a clue to the killer's identity and motives. The trail leads to an arson-for-hire ring that was about to have its cover blown by the reporter.

The seedy Singapore waterfront is China Smith's beat in *Dynasty of the Dead*. It is also a scroll of murder victims that China Smith tries to avenge after the killing of a café singer named Orchid. He interrogates the usual suspects and shows no surprise when it turns out to be the one with the not-so-hidden grudge.

High Sea is about a staged murder at sea and a new identity scam. A Chinese gambler hires China Smith to clear his name after he has been accused of the killing. A sexy Spanish dancer and her jealous knife-throwing husband know more than they are telling Smith. He is posing as a photographer and it is obvious that he is a phony.

They tell him what he needs to know in round about ways. Teases, come-ons, death threats and marital woes supply the answers to the clues that China Smith seeks to solve. The murdered man and the man with the new face are one and the same. It does not matter because he is murdered in the episode's final showdown.

A pearl diver hires China Smith to protect a string of pearls in *Full Fathom Five*. A gang of swindlers are trying to steal them from him. When they murder the diver and steal the pearls, China Smith negotiates the Hong Kong waterfront to locate the killers and the pearls.

Madame Shari (Myrna Dell), also called The Empress, was the local crime maven during the first run of *The Affairs of China Smith*. 1952, National Telefilm Associates (NTA).

Kris of Death becomes China Smith's headache when he tries to solve the murder of a British colonel. The military man was under investigation for compromising national security. His investigation is complicated by a beautiful blonde and a deadly Malayan kris.

The Sign of the Scorpion is a baptism of death for Commodore Tilson (Richard Glyer). Was it because he defied the ominous prognostication of Aban (Keye Luke), the seer, or was he murdered by a greedy beneficiary? Seems like it is a little of both as China Smith is hired by Mrs. Tilson (Linda Sutherland) but to no avail. The astrologer is just a dupe but the same cannot be said of Carla (Priscilla Pointer), daddy's little girl.

Blackmail threats, double crosses and false identities sometimes made earning his fee difficult. China Smith traveled in circles before the obscure becomes the obvious and he succeeded in identifying all the important players. Sometimes the party was right under his nose and there were the instances when he had to travel high and low to uncover the mystery guess.

Port of Thieves has China Smith tracking down the kidnapped daughter of a San Francisco art dealer. He is aided by Jasmine, an exotic taxi-dancer in his quest to rescue the kidnap victim. His main problem is receiving more than one ransom note. He begins to suspect fakery in the woman's disappearance. It does not take long to uncover duplicity when he rescues the kidnapped daughter from not-so-pressing danger.

The Kapprielian Cipher is a taut thriller about lost identities and hidden intentions. China Smith is hired to piece together the puzzle that was Max Kaprielian (Nestor Paiva). There were conflicting descriptions of the murdered man. Some say that he was a humanitarian, an explorer and a man of mystery. Others claim that he was a master criminal who hid a fortune in gems.

The man who hired Smith turns out to be Kaprielian, who now suffers from amnesia and needs to put together his life so he can reclaim his fortune. He is not the only man who wants the fortune. Col. Joliffe (Ted Hecht), a one-armed historian and Napoleon Rivard (Clarence Rovar), Smith's unofficial chauffeur and squire-about-town, also want to be privy to the fortune.

The Phantom Sampan is another face behind the mask tale. Blackmail, missing persons, and false identities figure in the story. Wu Chin is the wealthy director of the South Asiatic Export Company. He is distraught over a blackmailer's attempt to bleed him dry. The mystery man calls himself the Collector and what he knows about the businessman's past can ruin him. It is natural that Wu Chin should be upset. He is really a former notorious pirate who disappeared from the crime scene decades earlier. Now, the crime legend has come back to haunt the respected businessman.

The Tanaka Archive is a diary of a soldier that was left in the care of an ex-boxer turned soul saving preacher. His congregation is the waterfront and he is one of the people who figures in China Smith's adventure. The strange diary puts him in contact with a motley group, including a mystery woman named Sago and a rug merchant.

Black Wings of the Firebird has China Smith safeguarding a mute man whose only means of communication is drawing pictograms. He knows the secret location of a gold fortune and this marks him for kidnapping and death. A young woman named Moonflower hires Smith to protect the man but it proves to be a difficult task. Moonflower is kidnapped and the mute man is murdered during her rescue. His last pictogram was of the Firebird, a symbol that portends death.

China Smith becomes an *Escort to Saigon* for a diplomatic courier. He becomes suspicious of the man but before he can justify his suspicions

A press release for the slightly revamped show, *The New Adventures of China Smith*. 1954, National Telefilm Associates (NTA).

the man disappears. Was he kidnapped or was he a spy who defected to the Reds with his privileged information?

Being a sentimental Irishman, China Smith found it hard to resist assisting in the finding of lost loves. This brought him into contact with a series of intriguing women and frustrating circumstances. False clues and mysterious identities often complicated things for China Smith but he sorted things out even if that meant a broken heart or a little disappointment along the way.

In *Cruise to Columbo*, China Smith helps a forlorn visitor to Singapore disappear so he can start a new life. A promise turns into a double cross on top of a double cross. The dilemma of *Jungle Dragon* is a young woman's distress about her British fiancé's ostracism from his family. He is sent to Malaysia as a disciplinary measure and it is China Smith's job to locate him and reunite him with his lover.

Year of the Phoenix involves finding a missing husband and father who turns out to be a ringer in an inheritance money scam. A second wife and her step-daughter (Claudia Barrett) have their own reasons for China Smith to relocate the key to their fortunes. Love has nothing to do with it; still, the big-hearted Smith is glad to oblige and try to smoke out the missing man of the house. Only one of them knows that he is a phantom used to create an identity that will give the stamp of approval to her avowal of the inheritance money. A cruel twist of fate laced with China Smith's acerbic wit turns a fortune into dross for a scheming stepmother stranded at sea.

China Smith often found himself in absurd situations. One is the case of *The Emperor's Teapot*. A seemingly simple job of delivering a teapot becomes a complicated mystery when Smith finds out that the teapot is actually a dangerous weapon that figures big in a planned murder and the forced wedding of an unwilling bride.

A blind man hires China Smith to find his missing love in *Ferry to Kowloon*. He enlists the unwilling help of a playgirl and a purser who fleece passengers with a romantic version of the shell game. It seems that Renee (Maxine Cooper) is also a bait-and-switch girl and this causes her great embarrassment. It does not matter to her old lover. China Smith uses deception and avarice to reunite them.

Reuniting lost lovers is China Smith's gambit in *The Traveler from Tsintao*. This time around it is not so easy for Smith because the missing woman is a phantom who exists in the memories of the people he questions to ascertain her whereabouts.

China Smith may have been a maverick who helped the downtrodden but he also sold his services to corporations. There was always a colonial outfit that was being blackmailed, robbed or embezzled.

The Bamboo Coffin was the show's premiere episode. It introduced the underlying British colonial occupation theme of the show. The kingdom is represented by the rubber planter and the British inspector. Their nemesis is an escaped convict who vowed to steal from the rubber plantation.

China Smith gets his signals crossed when he mistakes the planter for the thief and the young woman (Rita Moreno) in his life as a hired hand. He is surprised when the planter becomes a revered martyr and the woman is his mournful daughter. The thefts were an inside job but Smith clears his vision when he apprehends the real thief and expresses honest condolences to the grieving daughter.

Shanghai Clipper finds China Smith in the employment of a mining company. They want him to locate a map of a fabulous oil discovery. It vanished when a geologist mysteriously disappeared from a plane in midflight. Did he bail out so he could disappear with the map and use it for his own enrichment or was he robbed and murdered? It is China Smith's job to search Singapore for the missing map.

China Smith agrees to help the fiancé (Marjorie Lord) of a murdered newspaper man to find his killers in *Devil in The Go-Down*. 1952, National Telefilm Associates (NTA).

A pilot accused of absconding with a payroll is the suspected *Bandit of Malaya*. He claims to have made the drop at the designated drop-off point but the planter said he never received the money. China Smith is instructed to parachute into the jungle and find the missing payroll. Things are complicated by a jungle bandit named Aslug (David Renard) and a duplicitous wife-mistress named Krisiva (Michi Kobi) who holds the answer to the mystery.

The Paper Dragon is the Communist menace that tries to discredit an American sugar warehouse by framing them for dope smuggling. That is the conclusion that China Smith comes to when he is hired by the firm to find out why thieves broke into the warehouse and stole nothing. Gretchen (Marian Carr), a sultry German croupier who works in a seedy bar, helps China Smith expose a Communist newspaper publisher as the mastermind behind the dope smuggling frame.

Several gold shipments have been hijacked from a bank in *The Yellow Jade Lion*. China Smith is hired by the bank to trap the thieves. His involvement in the case leads him to become captivated by a Chinese painting. The painting starts him on a trail that leads him to a notorious river pirate.

No old time mystery or adventure show would be complete without the charms of an array of women who needed the help of the dissipated but stalwart hero. They could be the innocents in the lost love adventures or the hard-tempered temptresses for whom lost love means nothing. Both types of women motivate China Smith to go out on a limb for them.

China Smith may have exasperated the Countess Von Idyll (Regina Gleason) but that did not stop her from procuring his services when she was desperate for help. In *The Tidewalker*, she hires Smith to discover who planted contraband on her tramp steamer, The Mokahana. The ship is impounded by the authorities and will be auctioned, which befits the plans of Mr. Norodami (Mark Sheeler), a Eurasian shipping magnate who uses underhanded methods to add ships to his fleet.

This time around, Mr. Norodami bribes the first mate, Mr. Shell (Ted Hecht), to do the dirty work. Smith pretends to be Morodami's non-existent partner to bail the crew out of her jail in an attempt to find the captain. Instead, he has a crew and a shaky plan to hijack The Mokahana from dry dock. His only mistake is to trust First Mate Shell, not realizing that he has no plans to testify against the shipping plan. It does not matter because Shell is no match for China Smith and cannot prevent him from discovering the captain's log, which incriminates the first mate. The title

A self-centered actress badgers China Smith into finding the stolen Manchu Emeralds. 1954, National Telefilm Associates (NTA).

refers to a beachcomber and is the way he describes himself to Mr. Norodami when he vows to brings the crooked businessman to justice.

A beautiful and mysterious nightclub singer named Mala intrigues China Smith in a *Wreath of Poppies*. He is hired to find out what happened to a briefcase containing $125,000 that went missing after its owner was found murdered. His investigation involves Smith, with a series of deaths caused by the use of Tiger Tonic herbs, a narcotic tincture that has deadly consequences.

Zorana the Destroyer is a phony fortune teller who extracts large sums of money from wealthy dowagers. China Smith is hired by the niece of one victim to expose the seer and recover the lost money. Zorana has more than fakery on his mind as his crystal ball portends murder. Phonies have never been much of a problem for China Smith. They have often been the butt of his sarcastic barbs. Zorana the psychic is no exception, something that his crystal ball did not tell him.

The Broken Rice Bowl of Chen Lo is not as mystic as Zorana's crystal ball but it contains secrets just as ominous. Instead of stolen money it is a seeing-eye dog that China Smith is tracking down. It is to provide relief for Precious Star (Frances Fong), a beautiful blind woman, who is lost without her aide.

The Sea Coffin involves an odd job where China Smith has to haul a coffin to sea for a watery burial. Smith hires a female tug boat captain to use her craft for the transport. His only problem is that the corpse turns out to be alive.

Double Crosswinds is the double cross that almost cancels out China Smith's passport when he tries to assist a beautiful young woman in searching for a sunken ship laden with treasure. She is a young American who wants to carry on the business of her deceased uncle. Murder also joins the salvage party in the form of a hard-hat diver who wants the treasure for himself.

My Ship has a Golden Keel is so absurd and impractical that it works. China Smith is hired by a nightclub singer to retrieve her wardrobe from a ship anchored at sea. In order to pose as a ritzy guest he becomes a card dealer for Julio Fortano and gets to wear the boss' tux on a dinner break that is really his chance to run away at sea.

He enlists the aid of a deck hand and finds out that the wardrobe is really gold bars and her husband is the jealous type. He is played by Phillip van Zandt in an over-the-top ham-of-the year performance.

This episode has a tough guy club owner who gives commands and always pays people through his secretary. He does not like the singer, only the gold she brings with her. First, he has to have it brought ashore. That is why China Smith is on the job.

Loose lips sink ships is the old WWII adage and in this case it applies to gold caches on a millionaire's yacht as well. The burnt-out piano player regains his verve when he storms the boat with a gang of silent but deadly Mandarins. They make off with the suitcases after the piano player gives a tough guy speech. It does not matter because he remains a loser in the end when his suitcases are weighed down with lead chains and ankle bracelets. No gold and no deal for a nightclub owner stuck with a blonde he doesn't want.

General Yang was once the governor of a Chinese province before he was disposed of and held captive in Singapore. His house arrest is so tight that his daughter cannot visit him. Distraught, the young woman hires China Smith to liberate her father.

Rare gem smuggling capers never tire because they involve the ingredients that make the other crime themes popular. Exotic locales, desperate power brokers, beautiful manipulative women, shady lowlifes all mixed with the allure of illegal riches.

My Ship has a Golden Keel that puts China Smith in the middle of a race to claim a fortune in gold. 1952, National Telefilm Associates (NTA).

A train ride to meet an intelligence agent involves China Smith with gold smuggling and
international espionage in *Espionage Express*. He befriends a small boy who does not understand English and they form an unlikely pair of crime busters in dealing with murderous turncoat gold smugglers.

Celestial Pebbles are the beaded connections to a backwards blackmail scheme. China Smith is hired to buy back a stolen necklace for an insurance company. The hitch is that he learns that the necklace has not been stolen. In *The Proverbs of Shen-Ze*, China Smith's race in time is to save his own life. He has to play fortune hunter for a notorious gangster. If he does not find a fortune in missing gold, he will forfeit his life to the crime lord. China Smith's next turn with commodities is turning jewel thief to steal a necklace that will clear his friend of a murder charge in *Jade Trap*.

Diamond smuggling and parrot ringers are the keys to *The Talons of Tong King*, a case where China Smith is hired by a nightclub entertainer to find a missing bird. Outwitting a dimwitted sailor is no problem for China Smith as he wrangles the bird from the salty sea dog. Returning the parrot becomes the problem when he sees that the show goes on with another sidekick.

China Smith's clever use of lipstick marks the spot where a courier becomes a prized sidekick and its double is demoted to a poison pen pal. Smith switches birds on his benefactor and uses the confusion to solve a diamond smuggling racket in *The Talons of Tong King*.

China Smith is hired by Tony Wong (Keye Luke) to find Babykins, a parrot that is essential to a nightclub act he has with Ming Toy, a burlesque dancer. The urgency of finding the bird arouses Smith's suspicions, especially after Ming Toy tells him that the parrots are easily replaceable because of the high mortality rate of traveling the circuit.

The Manchu Emeralds were stolen from a conceited American actress who hires China Smith to search high and low for them. She is apprehensive because of his dubious character but soon learns to appreciate his methods when she realizes that if anyone can find the emeralds, it is China Smith. Her confidence is not to be equated with admiration.

The show had an opportunity to switch gears by including a couple of jungle adventures. The Korean War had just ended but the Communist takeover in Asia was still continuing. China Smith worked his way through the elephant grass and the uncharted islands with the same ease and aplomb he had on the Singapore waterfronts or in the Macao nightclubs.

China Smith has a unique jungle adventure when he is hired to negotiate a truce with Kai Lee, reputed to be the most vicious bandit in Malaya. Much to China Smith's surprise, the notorious bandit is exceptionally beautiful. Despite his life being on the line, China Smith does not rue the encounter in *Killer in the Kampong*.

China Smith may have been excited by his dealings with Kai Lee but he is humbled by his encounter with Chang Po, a Buddhist monk in *Pagoda in the Jungle*. He is hired to find a lost Buddhist shrine so the monk can restore it to its former glory. What they don't know is that smugglers have used the shrine to store gasoline that they plan to use for illicit means. The monk has a moral decision to make regarding his pagoda in the jungle. His decision humbles China Smith in a rare instance when he does not have a wisecrack or a sarcastic retort as a rejoinder.

Forbidden Atoll is the domain of Marakow (Nestor Paiva), a self-styled king who jealousy guards his cache of useless currency. Anastasia (Geraldine Farmer) hires Smith to locate her missing husband but the peculiarities of the case lead him to believe that she has ulterior motives. What he finds is a demented expatriate lording it over a handful of mindless zombies who hail him as king.

China Smith finds himself in another jungle adventure in *Grave in Sumatra*. His benefactor is a scurrilous reprobate who wants to find the grave of an English war hero. Imagine China Smith's surprise when he learns that his guide is the man who is supposed to be buried in the hero's grave. In *Straight Settlement*, China Smith will be buried in a hero's grave if he cannot reason with a jungle bandit.

If the case involved a beautiful woman then China Smith would risk life and limb to please her. *The Tai-Ling Glaze* is a valuable piece of pottery that has to be found by China Smith. If he fails in his quest, a young girl will be burned alive.

The Communists popped up here and there in episodes but there were four episodes where they were front and center.

The Communists attempt to take over a small Thai province in *The Spectacles of Heaven*. Their first attempt is to assassinate the kindly ruler. When he is injured in a bomb blast, the ruler's #1 wife hires China Smith to investigate.

China Smith engages in another battle for survival in *Nightmare in the Green*. Members of the Nationalist Chinese underground kidnap him and conscript him in their cause. His mission is to go to Singapore, his old locale, to find a general who has plans of the Communists' latest campaign. His payment is his well-being, as in staying alive.

China Smith is hired to go behind enemy lines of red Indo-China to find *The Bible of Mr. Quaile*. It is a rare Gutenberg Bible worth half a million dollars. Mr. Quaile is not the only person after his Bible. An American woman and her boyfriend also embark on the perilous journey to reclaim the Bible for themselves.

In *Plane to Taiwan*, China Smith is hired to mingle with the passengers of a plane embarked for Nationalist China. Trouble ensues when George Loo (Victor Sen Young) tries to divert the plane to Red China. He does so under duress and it is China Smith's intention to find out which passenger blackmailed him into hijacking the plane. Was it Chen Yu (Conrad Yama), a non-English speaking mandarin, Wong (Keye Luke), his dour companion or Malfy (Werner Klemperer), a rich European who likes to harass his nurse, Iris Clark (Priscilla Pointer)?

A couple of episodes were humorous ones where China Smith became a guardian to some lost soul. He saves an old man from drowning in *Curse of the River Gods*. An ancient Chinese superstition requires him to become the man's guardian. It is with trepidation and dour spirits that China Smith accepts the dubious honor. Smith has his own superstitions

China Smith weathered four years of working in the perilous war torn Far East of the early Communist takeover years. 1954, National Telefilm Associates (NTA).

to deal with and it is not long before he obtains a reprieve from the river gods.

Moon Flower is an unexpected dividend on a loan when China Smith gives his old friend Kwong money to pay his bills and is forced to accept his young daughter, Moon Flower, as a token of gratitude. A comedy of errors turns into a kidnapping case and gratitude becomes its own reward when the plot is thwarted by the show's hero.

China Smith becomes the unofficial guardian to a mute refugee boy in *The Devil Chaser*. The boy's father is a servant named Lim (Larry Chan) who ran away from his master, Bergdhal (Jack Retzen). Murder stains the search for a fortune but China Smith tilts the odds in favor of his own friend, the Empress Steffi.

The Night the Dragon Walked is when China Smith agreed to be a guardian. It was obligation and not superstition that made him put someone else's life in his care. The son of a murdered Englishman feels that he, too, will be stabbed to death. It is China Smith's responsibility to see that it does not happen.

Dangerous assailants included the band of assassins in *Devil-In-The-Godown*, the beautiful blonde and the Malay death *kris* in *Kris of Death*, the island slaves in *Forbidden Atoll*, the underworld syndicate of *The Jade Trap* and the notorious pirate of *The Yellow Jade Lion*.

Spice was provided by the sultry Spanish dancer and her older jealous knife-wielding husband in *High Sea*, Kai Yee, the revolutionary jungle bandit in *Killer in Kampong*, the soul-saving ex-boxer, a secretive rug merchant and the woman named Sago in *The Tanaka Archive*.

Even humility was served by the Buddhist monk in *Pagoda in the Jungle*, the mute pictogram man of *The Black Wings of the Firebird*, the beautiful young blind woman in search of her lost seeing-eye dog in *The Broken Rice Bowl of Chen Lo*, and the mystery woman of The *Traveller from Tsing Ta*.

After China Smith wrapped in 1956 the residuals and benefits began to come in. Dan Duryea earned more than $25,000 for the original 26 China Smith episodes made four years before. NTA began to syndicate the series and local stations got a package that included the fourth-run rights to the original 26 half hours and second run rights on the revived series. Las Vegas also offered Dan Duryea $12,600 a week for an act based on his China Smith character.[7]

Dan Duryea formed a partnership with Alvin Ganzer, one of the show's directors. They had planned to produce *Lights Up*, a melodrama with a European background. Cuba Richardson was hired to write a screenplay based on her short story.

TV Anthologies, On the Big Screen, and the Old West

50's Television

Television anthology series were as popular as their radio forbearers. Many of the new television shows were adaptations of shows that originated in radio. It was mainly the sponsors' doing because they held sway over what was broadcast on the airwaves. That is what makes the television anthologies from the 50's such curious oddities. They produced some of the best television viewing during that decade despite having been carefully monitored by their sponsors.

Many anthologies had a former Hollywood star as a host while some had rotating actors and actresses doing the hosting chores. It was their role to say something about the forthcoming presentation and its players. They also shilled for the sponsors' products and closed the show with a warm goodnight or a sneak peak at the following week's fare.

When China Smith was on hiatus, Dan Duryea continued his television appearances with two anthology series, Ford Television Theatre and Lux Video Theatre. A newsroom comedy and a southern Gothic family drama by William Faulkner has Dan Duryea playing straight man to nerdy Marvin Kaplan and playing a son dominated by a mother played by Mildred Natwick.

Ford Television Theater was adapted from a successful radio predecessor. It was just as successful on television and ran from 1948 to 1957. That was 445 shows with running times of 24-26 minutes. The presentations played like abridged movies and that kept the pace moving.

Double Exposure is a newsroom comedy with Duryea playing a senior press photographer who contends with a nerdy copyboy with an amazing propensity for taking newsworthy photos. The romantic subplot has the nerd trying to use his charm on Jean Willes, a reporter who apparently is the apple of Duryea's eye. George Brent is Devlin, the harried editor of The Bulletin and he, too, is exasperated by the nerd's awkward manner.

Marvin (Marvin Kaplan) is an annoying adenoidal farm boy who works as a copy boy around The Bulletin's office. He annoys the editor with his clumsiness and space-headedness. If it were not for the stolid support of Red Findlay (Dan Duryea), Marvin would be back on the farm. As it stands, he is The Bulletin's fair-haired boy when he inadvertently snaps incriminating pictures of a couple of City Hall officials at a raid at the local gambling joint.

The Mayor (Pierre Watkin) insists that the photos are fakes and that The Bulletin is trying to smear his reputation. The newspaper claims that the mayor has the most corrupt administration since Boss Tweed. It is a game of legal tug-of-war between the newspaper and the mayor.

The comedy centers on Marvin's propensity for taking hot photos in spite of himself. His fame is short-lived when he is fired for incompetence. However, Devlin is forced to rehire him when he photographs the mayor's car accident which happened to occur down the road from his farm. This time around, the mayor's cohort is a gambler who is led to safety by the police. Red renegotiates Marvin's new long term contract and becomes The Bulletin's fair-haired boy again when the mayor resigns due to ill health.

Double Exposure is a tame comedy that has pleasant side effects. Marvin Kaplan parlayed his nerd character into a successful career, retuning the image for subsequent generations. Dan Duryea is the wise guy veteran who steers Marvin straight and does his best to teach him the business even though it's Marvin's naiveté that is the basis of his success.

Jean Willes plays the supportive reporter who sends Marvin into overdrive when she kisses him as thanks for the pictures that lend a punch to her gambling article. George Brent is fine as the harried editor, a throwback to the Hildy Johnson era in Chicago. Veteran director Lew Landers keeps the action going at a steady tempo and packs a lot of exposition in the 24 minute time span of the story.

Dan Duryea's next role is anything but mirthful. He has the opportunity to act with Mildred Natwick again and they star in a teleplay written by William Faulkner. It was on *Lux Video Theatre*, another television adaptation of a radio program. It had three hosts and ran from 1950 to 1959. *The Brooch* was based on a William Faulkner short story and the

Double Exposure is a pleasant comedy about a big city newspaper exposing corruption in City Hall. Pictured are (l-r) Robert B. Williams, Pierre Watkin, Marvin Kaplan, Jean Willes, George Brent and Dan Duryea. 1953, Ford Motor Company, Screen Gems Television.

Nobel Prize winning author wrote the original teleplay. Ed Rice and Robert McDonagh revised the teleplay and the result is a bowdlerization of a Southern Gothic Oedipal drama tempered by momism and censorship.

Mrs. Boyd is a bedridden matriarch who no longer has a family that she can dominate. All that remains is her obedient son, Howard (Dan Duryea), whose prime concern in life is to dote on his mother. What makes the situation problematic is that he is married to Amy (Sally Forrest), a young woman who is tired of being the second woman in her husband's life.

The original story is dark and has a tragic ending – the son's marriage falls apart when his wife takes to whoring around town and he responds by putting a gun in his mouth and pulling the trigger. This being 50's television assures us a happy and sanitized ending thanks to the writers who were brought in to temper the action.

Like her character in the short story, Mrs. Boyd uses her convalescence to maintain a vise grip on her son. It does not help matters that he has married a train conductor's daughter. Mrs. Boyd still maintains the pretensions of the South's glory years and to have a commoner in the family goes beyond the pale of southern etiquette. The conflict arises when Amy can no longer tolerate her stifling domestic existence. She finds freedom by going out every Saturday to the Country Club while her husband stays home and dotes on his mother.

The implication is that Amy is cheating on Howard and one expects a tawdry denouement but is pleasantly surprised to learn that Amy has been spending her Saturday nights alone reading novels in a neighborhood rooming house. Mother's suspicions are enough to rile the docile Howard to break the silver cord by berating his mother and telling her about what it means to be married and have responsibilities to a wife. Surprisingly, the mother from hell understands this and acquiesces by handing over the family brooch to Amy, who now becomes the new lady of the house. We are led to believe that they lived happily ever after.

The critics raked Faulkner over the coals for his teleplay. They noted that the newspaper exploitation ballyhooed the fact that this was William Faulkner's first foray into television and that the reality was much less than the expectations. At the time, there was no knowledge that the teleplay was revised by two writers who were brought in. That's not to say that things would have been that different if Faulkner's original treatment was used. This was 50's television and there was no way that such a delicate topic and tragic ending would have been fodder for prime time television. Still, the critics praised Mildred Natwick, Dan Duryea and Sally Forrest for their spirited performances.

The premise of *The Star and the Story* was to have the weekly guest select a short story and appear in the introduction to tell the audience what they have chosen. Dan Duryea selected *Sinners* by Kathleen Norris. Retooled into *The Lie*, it is the story of Jim Ripley, a man who was unjustly

Jim Ripley tempers his gratitude with spiteful vengeance in *The Lie*. 1955, Four Star Productions.

convicted and sentenced to serve time in a sanitarium for a murder he did not commit. He was convicted on the fabricated testimony of a girl who made the whole thing up to get attention.

Ripley has spent fifteen years behind bars and this has made him bitter, caustic and hopeless. Years later, Laura Kent (Beverly Garland) has regrets and feels an oppressive guilt that impels her to visit the man and ask his forgiveness. She promises to right her grievous deed but he is too eaten up by bitterness to appreciate a possible way out of the house of madness. He has his doubts but goes along with the plan because he has some things that he has to clear up himself.

He is liberated from the sanitarium by her confession. Her guilt is so strong that she lets him convalesce at her farm. Things are still tense between them, so much so that the only recourse is a bold hug and a kiss to ease the tension. After contemplating the changes in his life, Ripley's heart turns cold

Dan Duryea plays Sam Ireland, a federal undercover agent tracking a counterfeiting ring in *O'Brien*. 1955, Meridian Productions.

and he wants to shoot her but her attraction is too strong. He relents, drops the gun and accepts another hug and a kiss. There could have been more unsettling endings for this drama but closure seems to be the only way to keep things neat and tidy. Radical forgiveness is on everyone's mind, not only when dealing with each other but for confronting the demons within.

After *The Lie* it was back to *The Schlitz Playhouse of Stars* for *O'Brien*. Dan Duryea gets to polish his image with a federal badge in *O'Brien*. He is Sam Ireland, a federal agent hot on the trial of a fugitive and the operation that engineered his illegal entry across the border. The case will send him to a boarding house full of shady characters. He will have a chance to confront two of the female prototypes exemplified by *Too Late for Tears* and *Black Angel*. There he will unknowingly become involved with the lady gangster who is running things. She has a bit of Lizabeth Scott in her as she gives him a mickey. There is a touch of June Vincent in the housemaid who saves his life. She also turns out to be an undercover agent.

The action becomes hectic when the house is swarming with one type of cop or another. The closing joke is that it's a wonder they didn't arrest each other. It does not matter because O'Brien not only got his man, he also nabbed the woman behind the operation.

It was 1955 and Dan Duryea could very well spoof his tough guy image. He does just that on *The Jack Benny Show* and *December Bride*. Jack Benny had honed his craft in vaudeville and had a hit radio comedy show that started in 1932. He crafted a persona of the miser and many of his routines were based on his penchant for being a skinflint. He was supported by Eddie 'Rochester' Anderson, a wise cracking major domo, Dennis Day, a soprano and comic foil, Don Wilson, his rotund announcer, and Mary Livingstone, his wife.

He gradually moved into television where he continued his premise with many of his supporting players along for the show. He was part of an old school of comics that started out in vaudeville and were the pioneers of television comedy. The show's structure was a monologue followed by the story of the week.

The Duryea show started out with a Benny monologue that was interrupted by Dennis Day, who complained about losing his dressing room to Dan Duryea. This is solved when Day's mother throws Duryea out of the dressing room in an offstage confrontation. There is a brief banter between Benny and Day's mother. Don Wilson, the show's corpulent announcer appears and introduces the skit as "Death Across the Lunch Counter or He Died Sunnyside Up."

Jack Benny plays a luncheonette owner named Charleston T. Gunglefinger. He has a self serving cash register that relies on the honor system. A customer is impressed with the trust until he learns that the drawer opens and closes so fast that he can't retrieve his change. This flusters the patron but pleases Benny to no end, an example of his skinflint mentality and love of money. The joke is compounded when he cleans out the register and finds a hand among the money.

"He wasn't fast enough," he says and tosses the hand into the money bag.

Later, he wishes he was fast enough in closing up when he is terrorized by a belligerent mobster (Dan Duryea) and his henchman (Dennis Day) and a third figure in the shadows. Benny and Duryea basically go at it with non-stop one-liners. They are joined by Dennis Day as Duryea's henchman. The same sound effects used in radio are employed here for laughs. Duryea is served a can of sardines and slaps it between two pieces of bread. When he bites into it there is the crunching sound of pulverized metal. The same thing happens when Dennis Day eats a piece of cake because it is marble cake.

The laughs come when Duryea slaps Jack Benny across the face for suggesting salad.

"I don't like salad," snarls the gangster.

There are also extended laughs when Duryea plays the jukebox and performs a Tango with Dennis Day. Another laugh getter is the prolonged and exaggerated death scene for Dan Duryea. Not to be outdone, Dennis Day exclaims, "You ham!" and goes into his death throes after he is shot by the luncheonette owner. Duryea and Dennis Day stretch it for laughs and the audience appreciates it.

As Duryea and Day lie prone on the floor the third character steps up and reveals himself with a prolonged, "Yessssss!?!?", the signature quip of Frank Nelson. His routine was showing his face out of nowhere and saying, "Yes?', or something to that effect in a long drawn out way while flashing a maniacal grin with a demented look in his eyes. He closes the skit by introducing himself as the interior decorator and suggesting how they can incorporate the blood stains into the luncheonette's new motif.

The show's humor may be simplistic by today's standards but it had a refreshing novelty because it was done in good fun and performed live. That is true for the crude special effects. The self-serving cash register, having Duryea's gangster make his call by firing at rotary dial to make it move

The Gangster in Black harasses Charleston T. Gungelfinger on *The Jack Benny Show*.

or hearing the metal crunch of the sardine sandwich added to the silliness of the skit.

Dan Duryea spoofs his tough guy image once again in the situation comedy, *December Bride*. It was an early comedy that lasted from 1954 to 1961. Filmed in front of a live audience, the laughs were real and not canned. Spring Byington played Lily Ruskin, a spry mature woman who still had spunk and was always being lined up for a marriage proposal by her daughter and son-in-law.

Lily has her Dan Duryea encounter when she and best friend Hilda Crocker (Verna Felton) go camping in the Sierras and run into the actor with his agent while they are on vacation. Duryea is tired of people mistaking him for Richard Widmark and asking him for an autograph. His agent agrees and they look forward to a vacation of hunting and camping.

Imagine their elation when Lily and Hilda show up at the doorstep asking for directions. They can't believe that they have run into Richard Widmark. Duryea corrects them but they are still star struck. Duryea deduces that the only way to get rid of them is to pretend to be hardened criminals and intimidate the women into leaving. The plan backfires and the marshal is brought in to rescue the women who outfoxed the convicts by alerting the police.

They promise to drop the matter if Dan Duryea agrees to do an interview with Lily, who is a reporter on the local community paper. The show ends when Duryea shows up at the doorstep of Lily and the family. He confesses that he gave her Richard Widmark's biography when she

Dan Duryea enhanced his image change with a cheery beer ad. 1952

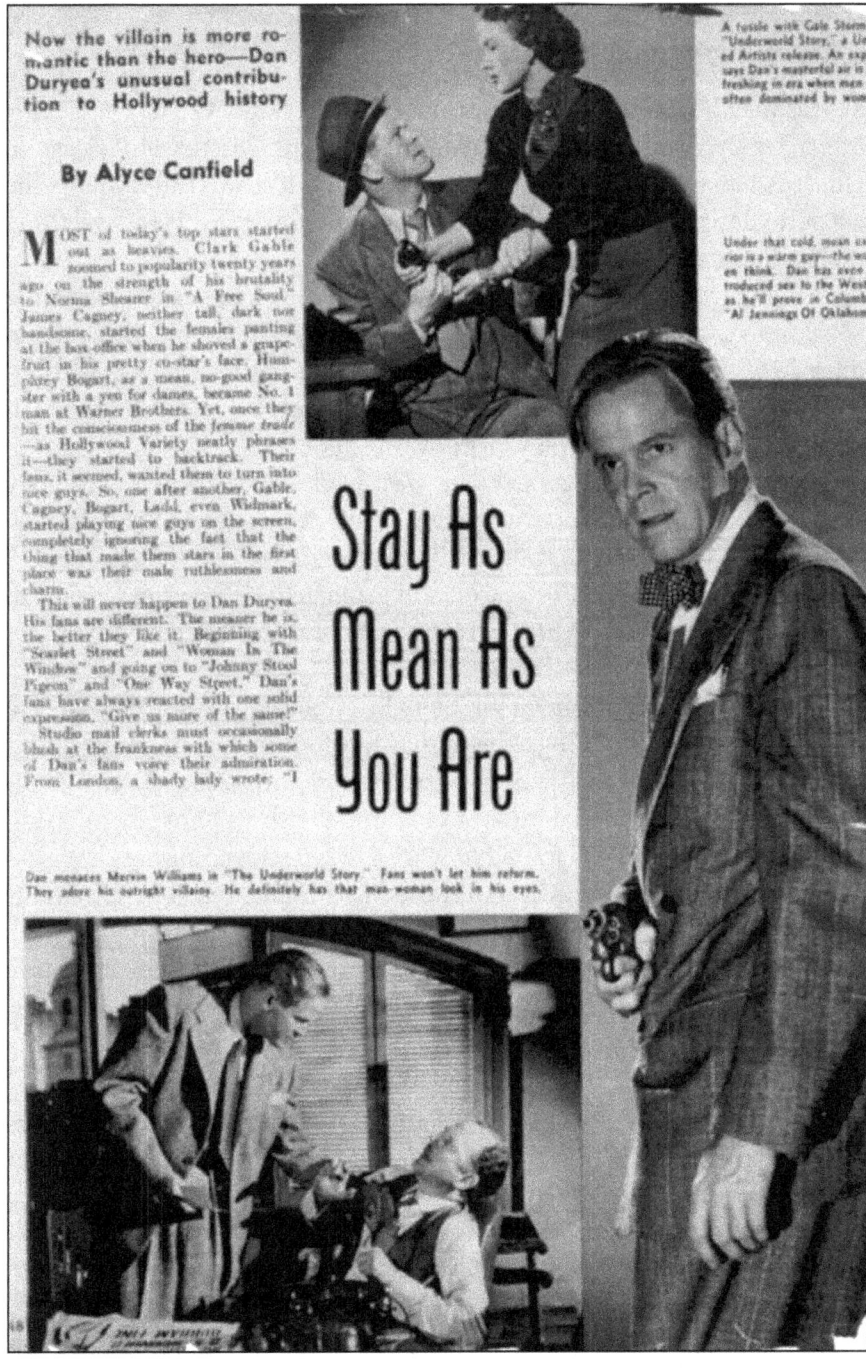

A fan magazine article begs Dan Duryea to return to his villainous past. 1950

interviewed him in the mountains. He sits down and gives Lily the real deal.

The episode is done with good humor. Lily and Hilda hiking in the Sierras may be reminiscent of any hare-brained skit with Lucy and Ethel Mertz but they still get laughs by working well with Duryea and his agent. Duryea's Duke Mantee impression is funny and it scares the women. The cigarette dangling from his lip is a nice comic touch. So is the watching the women terrified out of their wits.

The tables are turned and that's what gets the laughs along with the allusion to the Richard Widmark comparisons. Dan Duryea once had an interview with Hedda Hopper where Dan Duryea referenced Richard Widmark as an actor who made a successful career of playing bad guys. It figured in his decision to play criminal misfits.

Dan Duryea's next appearance was on the little known anthology show, *Chevron Hall of Stars*, an anthology series produced by Four Star Productions, which also produced *The Star and The Story* and *Four Star Playhouse*. It only lasted one season and produced 45 shows in 1956. Dan Duryea appeared in *A Matter of Nerve* with Myron Healey, Leo Gordon, James Parnell and Tracey Roberts.

Obscurity was not a factor of G.E. (General Electric) Theater, a popular half hour anthology series that ran for ten years and produced 209 shows. It started as a radio program before it made its television debut on Feb. 1, 1953. Ronald Reagan became the show's host in 1953 and continued until the show folded in 1962. He introduced stories that were adapted from various sources and starred names that read like the credits from golden age pictures.

Dan Duryea and Edgar Buchanan share the benefit of their experience with Piper Laurie, a bold newcomer, in the *The Road That Led Afar*. It is a tale about the death of a loved one and the promise of a new beginning for the bereaved. The strange moral emphasizes the way natural law was observed in the wilderness. *The Road That Led Afar* comes off like a creepy ghost tale more suited for *The Twilight Zone* or *Alfred Hitchcock Presents* than *General Electric Theater*.

It is introduced by the show's host, Ronald Reagan. He tells the audience that America is filled with different types of roads. By the end of the drama, we find that the road that led afar is anything but a happy road. It is a place that is morbid, macabre and depressing. A choir sings haunting harmonies that underline the sadness of the circumstances where the players move in slow motion as if their energy has been stifled by pain and depression.

Brad Lawson (Dan Duryea) is a somber mountain man whose responsibility is finding a new mother for his four children. His bereavement hasn't blunted his determination to accomplish this in an old-fashioned countrified way of courting. Only necessity has made the social amenities he has been paying over the years his courtship ceremony.

Phoebe Durkin (Piper Laurie) is a country waif who has just become a young woman. She relates her change by way of the wayfaring stranger that has greeted her over the years. Years of "Howdy, girl" finally became "Howdy, ma'am." Little did she realize that it was her courtship until the stranger came knocking at the door. She shyly greets him and apologizes for the way she looks.

"I ain't exactly stoppin' by. I take it you be single. I come a courtin.'"

He tells her that he hasn't been a widow long and he needs a wife to take care of his kids.

The bereaved stranger is a mystery man but, according to the ways of the hill folk, there is no second guessing when he proposes. She accepts and leaves on a moment's notice. Paw can't read and she does not know how to write so she tells a neighbor to tell her father that she's "gone a-marryin.'"

It is a strange opening to a disturbing tale of loss and gain. Phoebe's adventure is traveling to the other side of the mountain. It fills her with awe and she eloquently describes the landscape. Red tells her that she makes it sound like God is a woman because of the handiwork. He does agree that God has done much embroidering around these parts.

The sunshine that awakens the forest and the mountains is swallowed by the bitter darkness that awaits Phoebe when she arrives at her new home. Red's children sit like puppets on a shelf and their pain seems muffled and choked by tears. Eloise (Beverly Washburn) is the eldest and the circles under her eyes belie her tender years. Her little sister Sally (Cheryl Callaway) is as silent and motionless as her brothers, Trap (Gary Hunley) and Hutch (Don Wittenberg). They are stirred to life by their father's command to greet their new mother.

Preacher Bailey (Edgar Buchanan) is there in a dual capacity. One is to marry Brad and Phoebe and the other is to accompany Brad and the deceased on the road of the title. He is a somnambulant vision like an oak gnome with a long beard, a black frock and the croaking voice of a bull frog. Preacher Bailey is otherworldly and dispenses homilies and blessings from a rocking chair. He has an ounce of energy to keep him going and does everything in slow motion. The preacher still has his wits but

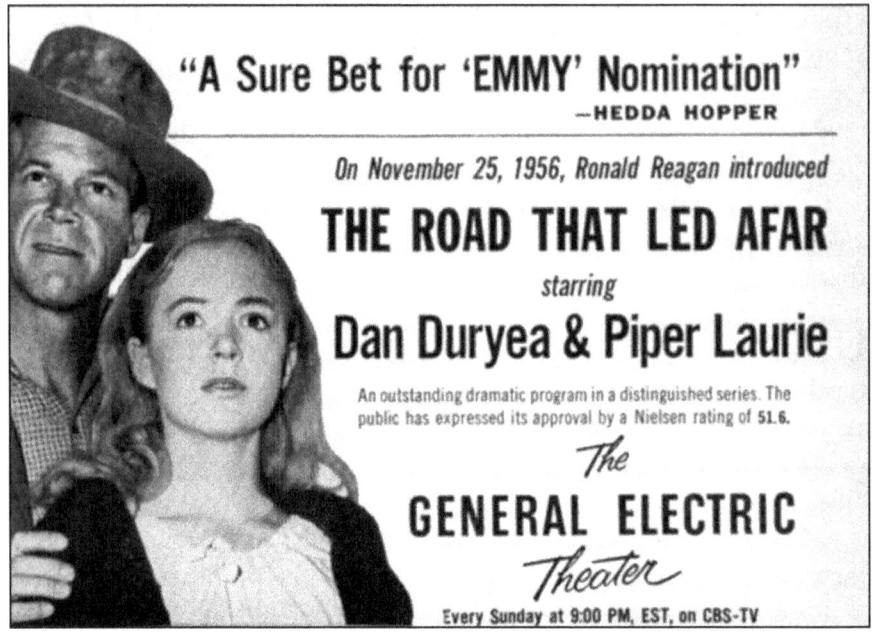

A television ad for G.E. Theatre's *The Road that Led Afar*, starring Dan Duryea and Piper Laurie. 1956, MCA Television, Revue Studios.

not much else. He tells Phoebe, "Brad here is in sore need of you" and his wedding ceremony steals the show for its eloquence and strangeness.

All live on the edge of a catatonia that becomes the mystery that captivates them. It is the death of the loved, the reason for the quick marriage. Normalcy under duress, there is a promise to be made. When the dawn arrives, Brad and the preacher leave to take a long and winding road beyond the other side of the mountain. The bereaved children become a healthy family again when Phoebe tells them that they play until their father and the preacher return.

Dan Duryea earned an Emmy nomination for his role as Brad Lawson. His next role is another character whose life is the forest. Cliff Mason is the leader of a troop of smoke jumpers and supervises them during blazes that threaten to destroy the flora and fauna.

The 20th Century Fox Hour presented new and abridged versions of movies from their studio vault. *Smoke Jumpers* was based on the 1952 movie, *Red Skies of Montana*. The Smoke Jumpers are the paratrooper fire fighters who combat forest fires. The drama incorporates actual footage of forest fires, paratroopers making their jumps and training exercises. It is done in such a way to enhance the story rather than pad it. There is a lot of action for a small screen presentation.

Cliff Mason is the hero of the drama although he is viewed through most of the story as a coward. The crew foreman was the only survivor of a catastrophic fire that had claimed the lives of his crew. Amnesia is something most of the smoke jumpers don't want to hear about. It's what happened on the ridge that concerns them. Did Cliff Mason desert his crew?

Chief of the accusers is Ed (Richard Jaeckel), younger brother of Mike (Robert Bray), one of the vets who perished in the inferno. He knew that there was bad blood between his brother and the foreman. Mike wants to make inroads on Cliff's girl, Peg (Joan Leslie) and that earned him a punch in the jaw at the canteen. That is where Peg works with her father, Pops (Robert Armstrong), the retired fire fighter who is unofficially one of the guys, if only in moral support and free coffee.

Mason was cleared by a board of inquiry but Ed has his own brand of justice when they square off with each other during the next forest fire. It's ax to ax and fist to fist as the men battle each other against the spreading flames. Mason subdues Ed and brings him back to the urgency of their mission.

Fires that jump from treetop to treetop are called crown fires and they are spreading. That means that atmospheric pressure will create an explosion. The men panic and want to make a run for it but Mason deters him with his fierce resistance. That's when it all comes back to him.

The same thing happened on the ridge. The crown fires were building to a crescendo when the men bolted rather than dig in and wet down so that the fire would sweep over them. That's what happens this time when the men maintain their nerve and take preventive measures against the oncoming inferno.

The next scene is the morning after and the forlorn blitz that reduced a forest to charring and burning embers. A helicopter beats its propellers and a voice calls Cliff Mason's name through a megaphone. It is a sad mechanized voice and seems to be calling out to no one. That's not the case when Cliff and his men come back to life and take a roll call. Even Ed is one of the guys, having realized that what it takes to be the boss includes perseverance under pressure and the need to know how to handle a frightened crew. Tough guy Cliff returns a conquering hero and that includes a radio message to the girl he loves, the goddess of the smoke jumpers' canteen.

In *Smoke Jumpers*, Cliff Mason is the foreman of a crew that faces a rampaging wildfire in the mountains of Montana. 1956, 20th Century Fox Television.

Dan Duryea made his fourth appearance on *Schlitz Playhouse of Stars* as Pete Richards, an intrepid reporter whose allegiance to the truth has made him amoral. Blinders prevent him from considering the negative repercussions of a follow up story to a gambling raid that shut down a crime syndicate operation. He has a change of heart when tips and leads point him towards his own doorstep.

Richards is continuing his gambling story because of its connection to the son of the rival news editor. Pleas and bribes will not deter him until he is told about his wife's peripheral connection to the mob. He is told by the editor of the rival newspaper that if he continues to dig into the editor's son's involvement there will be repercussions. They were not meant to be threats; just a heads-up into a little information that involves Richards' wife and the gambling ring that his son is being linked to. She was a friend of his rival's son and it happened when she first came to town many years ago. The newspaper photo of them being led out of the gambling joint is straight and to the point.

Is this the reason that Pete Richards drops the story or is it because it is old news or not worth holding up to a new light? His valor has turned into self-righteousness over the years. It does not matter that reputations may be destroyed by reportage of illicit activities that occurred more than five years ago. After relentlessly digging for facts, Richards is bothered by his conscience. It happens because his wife Jeanne (Marcia Henderson) is peripherally involved with his new gambling story.

Jeanne is a beautiful blonde who is tired of his long hours and dedication to his profession. Her way of compensating for no vacation is to decorate the apartment in a Hawaiian island motif. She plays steel guitar music and does a hula when her husband returns. He plays along by pretending that he has walked into the wrong apartment and wound up on a fantasy island. They play their parts well because they are in love.

Even the strongest love can be tested and it happens when Duryea finds out that his wife is tangentially involved in the gambling story. She was the companion of his subject and they were caught in a news wire photo of the gambling syndicate bust.

The reverberations upset the reporter's bearings and he is as confused as he is angry. He assumes she is guilty and questions her as if is a suspect. She says that she never told him about that part of her life because she did not want to jeopardize their marriage.

He thinks that he is being big-hearted when he forgives her but she is miffed because of his temporary lack of trust. She tries to hightail it out of town and even an attempt at reconciliation is quashed at the bus station. Only a bus ticket to the same destination will put him on the right track with her.

The drama examines the responsibility of a reporter and questions the momentum of zeal and dedication. Is there a fine line between honesty and the truth? Can the two be separated? Does personal ambition en-

Pete Richards is a hard-nosed investigative reporter who has a conflict of interest in a story that may damage his married life in *Repercussion*. 1956, Meridian Productions.

ter into the equation? If so, where do ethics fit? Did Pete Richards change his mind because he was convinced that he had an ethical duty or did he compromise his principles for personal reasons?

Sidekicks, Ciphers, Heroes and Bums

Dan Duryea starred in the China Smith series from 1952 to 1956 with a brief break in 1954. Due to the hectic filming schedule Dan Duryea was able to film an astonishing amount of shows in a short period of time. He made a total of 52 China Smith video flicks in four years. Due to the speedy shooting schedules, there was time in Dan Duryea's schedule to participate in other projects. There were the movies made for Universal and the shows produced by its television arm, Revue Studios. Independent projects were always being arranged and there was a slow expansion into the television market.

Like some noted actors of his day, James Stewart was partaking in the profit-sharing arrangements that became popular in the late 40's. He had a lucrative participation deal with producer Aaron Rosenberg and director Anthony Mann. The trio had previously scored big with *Winchester '73* and *Bend of the River*. *Thunder Bay* was the third picture that they undertook.

Taking over someone else's sovereign domain in the name of offshore drilling and becoming wealthy in spite of it is the story of Steve Martin (James Stewart), a two-fisted man who wants to rule the world and get something better. *Thunder Bay* is a passion play that serves as an apologia for the cherished myth of the individual with a vision that creates a new source of life while sacrificing the needs of a precious few for the even-more-precious many.

Martin and Gambi drill for oil and eventually find it, but not without cutting off the manhood of Teche (Gilbert Roland), the formerly respected resident male tough guy, and Phillipe (Robert Monet), the adoring sycophant who is swept away by a tumultuous sea that disagreed with their plans of sabotage.

Teche is an honest, hard-working man whose life is the sea. He belongs to a Louisiana fishing community that depends on the shrimp beds for its livelihood. He gambles, drinks, holds court, and wrestles at a sleepy, seafront club where the guitar player sings sad songs as drinkers argue with each other. His pleasant nature changes from tropical verve to a raging tempest when he leads the fight against the outsiders who introduce progress at the expense of tradition.

The ultimate insult comes from squiring the daughters of Dominique (Antonio Moreno), the inn keeper and town elder. He has resigned himself to losing Stella (Joanne Dru), his oldest daughter, to the snobbish

Macho man Teche (Gilbert Roland) orders a round of drinks to start a man-boasting contest between Johnny Gambi (Dan Duryea) and himself. 1953, Universal Pictures Company, Inc.

expectations of a college education, but to lose his younger girl to Johnny Gambi (Dan Duryea) in a sweep-me-off-my-feet deal is an ignoble insult. It results in the final rebellion of the male villagers against the oil rig.

It's too bad it happens when Steve, Johnny, and Macdonald (Jay C. Flippen), their benefactor, hit pay dirt when the black gold explodes. The geyser terrifies the village's men and they revert to their primordial instincts and flee. Their ancestors may have been intimidated by volcanoes and hurricanes, but they have to contend with a new aspect of nature.

The bulk of the spoilers' rewards belong to Steve Martin, who is unwavering in his insistence at sticking to the drilling target and getting the hostile residents to see things his way. Martin is there when the black gold changes the color of his life and the world of everyone around him. What saves Martin's hide is his accidentally coming across the revered beds of the golden shrimp.

Teche is led on to believe that he has discovered the coveted harvest, a ruse by Martin to let the man still think that he has primacy of his domain, never mind that Phillipe, his protégé, was swept away with the dynamite in a storm and that his former fiancé wed the impetuous Johnny Gambi, or that the college-educated bayou girl awards herself with the

Johnny Gambi (Dan Duryea) and Steve Martin (James Stewart) fight over different opinions regarding work habits. 1953, Universal Pictures Company, Inc.

man of the hour. Macdonald gets a taste of his former greatness and a percentage of being a maverick who still knows how to gamble.

What made *Thunder Bay* unique is the star-director-producer's habit of making actors out of the local populace when they filmed on location. *Winchester '73* had the benefit of employing many locals from Tucson and Tombstone, Arizona for extra work. They did the same by using the citizenry of Portland, Oregon when they filmed *Bend of the River*. Over 100 local people from and around Morgan City, LA, were hired to round out the cast of *Thunder Bay*. They included "shrimp fisherman, oil well riggers, waitresses, bartenders, and even the haute monde at City Hall." One of the locals, a part-time sports announcer at a local radio station, played a bit part where he got to do a love scene with Joanne Dru.

The comingling of the visiting Hollywood colony and the townspeople led to a fraternization as many actors and crew people had their room and board provided by the local denizens. James Stewart quipped, "It wasn't too long ago when actors with a show troupe hit town they would find signs tacked up on the local boarding houses reading, 'No actors or dogs allowed.' They began taking in dogs a few years ago-and now they're even taking the actors."[1]

Dan Duryea only spent four months filming his scenes before he returned to his *China Smith* series. It was probably a lot safer as he had suffered a broken rib and contusions when he fell from the roof of a tugboat wheelhouse during a fight scene in *Thunder Bay*.

Sky Commando was another film made during Dan Duryea's downtime from the China Smith series. The war movie was an independent production about an aerial photographic squadron during the Korean War (with flashbacks to World War II). The picture was made by the Sam Katzman producing unit and released by Columbia Pictures. A Sam Katzman production meant a bare-bones-slap-and-dash picture. He was prolific and highly successful and produced a strong body of grade-z movies.

Two bombers head home after a successful combat mission when they receive orders to take two enemy bunkers with machine guns. It seems like a simple mission until they encounter four enemy MiGS. They radio headquarters to tell them that they don't have enough fuel to take out the bunkers and take on the MiGS. They will have to deal with the MiGS. Colonel Wyatt commandeers the mike and orders them to complete the original mission. Over and out!

Only one of the flyers returns to base. The other flyer ejected from his hit aircraft and parachuted behind enemy lines. This eats away at the survivor because the downed pilot was his brother. He is hospitalized and vents his spleen to Ol' Poppy, a beloved vet. Ol' Poppy has heard accusations about the Colonel before and he does not hesitate to defend his old friend. This includes the story that becomes the crux of the movie.

It seems that Wyatt had always had to contend with animosity because of his unpopular life-and-death decisions during combat. During WWII, his main detractor was Hobbie (Mike "Touch" Connors), a junior officer who hated Wyatt because of something he did during a flying mission.

TV Anthologies, On the Big Screen, and the Old West • 207

Pressbook cover for *Sky Commando*, a modest movie about a clash of strong personalities during wartime. 1953, National Screen Service Corp.

After a raid, Wyatt realizes that they don't have enough fuel to make it back to the base. The only dead weights that can be jettisoned are literally two dead soldiers. They were along for the ride so they could receive a proper funeral and burial. It is when Wyatt gives the orders to dump the dead pilots that the survivors become enraged with a seething hatred for their commanding officer.

Colonel Wyatt (Dan Duryea) and Jo McWathy (Frances Gifford) have a rocky airborne romance in *Sky Commando*. 1953, National Screen Service Corp.

Hobbie is one of them and he spends the rest of the movie trying to bust Wyatt. It takes a long, hard lesson of keeping a clear head during combat to make Hobbie realize that Wyatt is truly an honorable man. He realizes the guilt and pain that Wyatt has to deal with and knows that his soul is made of scar tissue.

The bedridden soldier takes the story in stride and becomes relieved when he discovers that his brother survived the bailout. The young pilot is added to the list of soldiers who learned to respect the veteran for the stalwart leader that he is.

Sky Commando may be a low-budget cheapie that is over shortly after it begins, but it is worthwhile because of the principal actors. Dan Duryea and Frances Gifford were veterans by the fifties and Touch Connors had yet to become a television star, so their presence gives the film

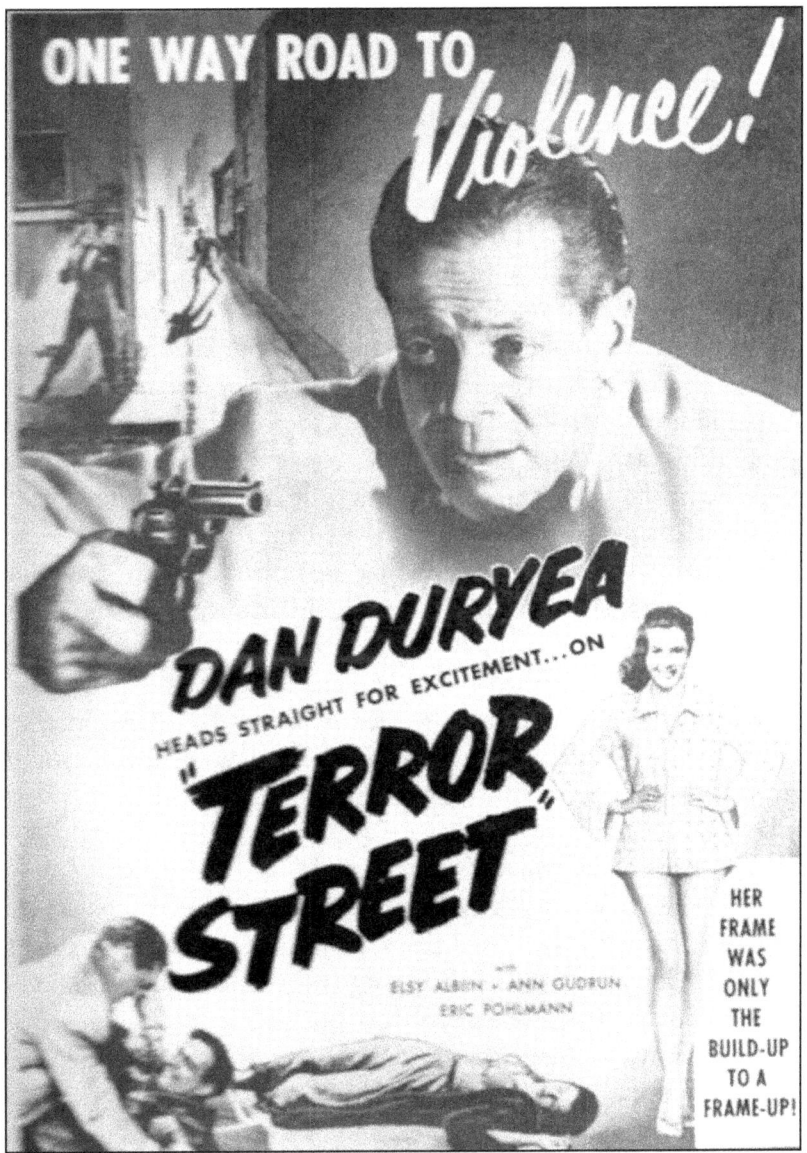

Press Book cover for *Terror Street*. 1953, National Screen Service Corp.

its interest. Add to that two vets like Selmer Jackson and Morris Ankrum as two generals and you have a curiosity piece, a movie that is not great shakes, but has redeeming value to keep it off the junk heap.

Robert L. Lippert was an independent international producer. He interested Dan Duryea into flying to England to make a movie.

In *Terror Street*, serendipity is the wall that Major Bill Rogers gets to bang his head against. Who says that all serendipity is the cause of good things and merits outbursts of song and merriment? Sometimes the smooth flow of events adds up to something painful with a message so deep that it takes a heavy loss to understand its meaning.

The original title of *Terror Street* was *36 Hours*, a title better suited for an understated film about a unique murder investigation. The movie is a British crime drama about lost love and smuggling that packs a punch and has plenty of spice. Duryea finds himself in the strangest situation when his military leave loses its hopeful impetus and turns into a countdown to a rope fitted around his neck.

He plays Major Bill Rogers, the main suspect in the shooting death of his wife, a woman he hasn't seen in a year because of a snafu. It was a snag that cost him his marriage and now robs the couple of a future. Major Rogers easily tracks down his wife, but is unsettled by her posh circumstances. Before he can get an explanation from her, Rogers is knocked out and his wife is shot dead by an unseen assailant. His furtive hookup with his estranged wife becomes a demented detour into a bum murder rap and a police dragnet out for him. He is the main suspect because he was seen fleeing the scene.

The plot hinges on the police's pursuit of Major Rogers and his attempts to crack the number-one suspect in his own investigation, a smug customs agent who had a closer-than-normal relationship with his wife. The dislike is mutual until fortune changes and power plays succeed before fading away.

Duryea becomes a man on the run who is aided by Sister Jenny, a trusting soul who works at a local goodwill mission and ministers to his wounds when she finds him hiding in her apartment. She is trusting and not fearful, even allowing herself to forge his wife's signature to find out what is inside the mysterious safety deposit box.

Sister Jenny's assistance earns her a spot in the intrigue and she becomes pawn of the murderer, a smuggler with an urge to kill anyone who gets in his way. The smuggler is effete and obscene, a smug huckster hiding behind the clever front of customs agent.

Slossen ([l] Eric Pohlmann) is a smuggler who has the goods on Col. Rogers (Dan Duryea) and a black market dealer. 1953, National Screen Service Corp.

The diamond smuggler is even seedier than the crooked customs officer. He speaks with a languid accent and fits in comfortably with the shadows of his forbidden basement, the oriental underbelly of his antique shop. The cartoonish menace adds spice to the finale as Major Rogers takes down the customs agent and the smuggler thanks to the misguided love of the lovelorn, psychopathic son of the customs man.

Smuggling is the crime that causes so much pain to the peripheral characters, including the major's wife. Her ill-fated heroics are not revealed until the end. It appears that she left him to live the high-life of a sophisticated escort. The truth is that she was hoodwinked into doing phony government work for the crooked customs agent, who used her and then neutralized her. The news offers closure for Rogers, who catches up with his other buddy on the tarmac to take off after their thirty-six hour leave has ended.

Terror Street is told in the typical understated British manner, but it moves well and reaches a satisfying conclusion with the clichéd smuggling den confrontation. The tear jerker finale is a mystery solved with old tears. It may seem cornball, but fits in comfortably with this small film.

After the maiden run of *China Smith* was stalled because of union problems, producer Bernard Tabakin announced that he was going to produce a big screen romance adventure loosely based on the series. It was called *World for Ransom* and would be directed by Robert Aldrich, who had recently wrapped up *The Big Leaguer*, his first film as a director. Lindsay Harding provided the script. Filming was scheduled to start on April 13, 1953 at the Motion Picture Center Studio.

It would be fair to say that *World for Ransom* is really a re-worked China Smith premise even though the main character's alias is Mike Callahan. It's B-movie madness and mayhem with a ne'er-do-well who has the same look, dress, and mannerisms of China Smith because that's who he started out as before legal entanglements changed things.

A direct reference to China Smith was avoided, but many things remained the same. The theme music was the same, as was the exotic Singapore locale. We have the same producer, Bernard Tabakin, of the television show and Robert Aldrich, who directed a couple of episodes. Douglas Dumbrelle was on hand as the dogged British colonial who had his suspicions about the legitimacy of the main player.

And then, of course, there is Dan Duryea. He dresses in white with an occasional matching fedora and is tagged as a soldier of fortune, smuggler, and beachcomber. The similarities end there because Callahan is an Irishman who does not speak with a brogue and he is droll and humorless not flippant and quick with a quip. This tide walker does not believe in the little people.

In *World for Ransom*, the colonials want to add charges of treason and murder to his files when he becomes involved with the killing of a British officer and the kidnapping of a nuclear scientist. The culprit is really Callahan's dubious friend, the erudite Julian March (Patric Knowles), an ex-British intelligence officer now in the employment of a nefarious nuclear saboteur, Alex Paderas (Gene Lockhart).

March is married to Frennesy (Marian Carr), Callahan's ex-sweetheart. Frennesy is the romantic mystery that gives *World for Ransom* one of its interesting angles. The adventurer tags after her like a wounded lover. She acts concerned about their past love, but is really full of spite. Callahan is still in love with Frennesy and tolerates March only because he is the only link to his old flame. There is no hope for a reunion but Callahan is led along by Frennesy's mock interest in him. He sees a chance of reconciliation when he discovers that March in involved in the treasonous plot.

Mike Callahan (Dan Duryea) confronts Frennesy (Marian Carr) about the disguise used for her husband's masquerade. 1954, Allied Artists.

Alex Paderas is a saboteur and blackmailer. He plans to auction the kidnapped scientist (Arthur Shields) to the highest bidder between Allied and Communist concerns. Nigel Bruce plays the colonial governor who gets to have a parley with Paderas, who drops by in an arrogant encounter with the colonials to deliver his demands. A monstrous nuclear weapon in the hands of the Communists makes the colonial governor quake, as do his subordinates. Somehow, Callahan becomes a prime suspect because of his friendship with March.

Only Callahan finds the courage to face the kidnappers, saboteurs, and traitors in an assault on their headquarters. Explosives and gunfire clean out the nest and the scientist is rescued. Did Callahan do it to clear his name? No. Was it because of loyalty to the freedom of the Western world? No. Maybe it was because he was inspired by love. Not only that but it was for the cause of liberating the captive girl of his imagination.

Callahan exposes his long-time rival as a fake and tries to reclaim the love of his former sweetheart. It backfires and the captive girl remains enslaved. Her destruction is also due to love. The traitor was also the only man who accepted her as she was. In the end, Callahan destroys her when he thinks that he has freed her.

In *World for Ransom*, Mike Callahan is a waterfront hustler like China Smith who tries to rekindle an old romance by destroying a subversive international nuclear espionage gang. He is also a noble scoundrel because he peddles his style in Singapore, where post-war etiquette rates him as above-board and honorable. The earthy adventurer is more serious and plays for bigger stakes than his television counterpart. Mike Callahan is playing a game where the fate of the free world is at stake.

Duryea is more serious in this role on film than on television. He is more tormented, but that's because he is dealing with his life's love, Frennesy. He is caught in a strange world where she weaves gossamer dreams to give him hope. He is a third wheel, one that is more pitied than appreciated by March and Frennesy.

This odd relationship bears on the violent climax, when Callahan storms the compound and wreaks havoc with his grenades. He has liberated the kidnapped nuclear scientist and believes that he has freed Frennesy from the evil March. His heroic status is negated when he destroys

Callahan (Dan Duryea) is surrounded by the traitorous March (Patric Knowles) and his saboteurs when he infiltrates the traitors' hideout. 1954, Allied Artists.

Frennesy's world by killing her husband, whom she had loved more than him. There was never a past to return to and this stuns Callahan. It should have happened to China Smith.

By the mid-50's, Dan Duryea settled into a pattern that he would adhere to for the rest of his career. He had a renewable contract with Universal-International which gave him the freedom to work outside of the studio. He also began to expand his involvement in television. It became part of his work schedule and he would gradually spend more time on the small screen than he would playing in the movie houses.

Many independent producers would make a film and then have it distributed by a major studio. It was not unusual for Dan Duryea to star in these minor vehicles. The actor was committed to working the independent market where he could try new character types on for size and also experiment with the profit sharing deals that many show people were getting involved in. They add subtlety and character to his resume. Some are pointed dramas and others are cloying soap operas.

This Is My Love is the story of how a typewriter and a wheelchair serve as crutches for two bitter dreamers who hate yet need each other for support in a world where they are secondary players. Vi (Linda Darnell) is a frustrated novelist on the verge of spinsterhood and Murray (Dan Duryea) is a vindictive former dancer who is confined to a wheelchair. They are in-laws whose common bond is Evelyn (Faith Domergue), Vi's sister and Murray's wife.

Their lives revolve around a diner that is the rock of their survival. Vi is a nanny and home attendant when she is not working the counter at the diner. She listens to Murray's put-downs and the children's inane chatter in between periods of writing her novel. She has a calm demeanor that is akin to that of a Buddhist monk, but beneath the peaceful surface is an active volcano about to erupt. When she finally erupts, Murray is dead and Evelyn is accused of murdering him with a lethal injection, the result of Vi spiking his medicine with poison.

This Is My Love is a turgid soap opera, a depressing descent into a whirlpool of passion, hatred, resentment, and frustration. There have been many lovers' triangles, but rarely has a volatile rectangle been explored in a cheap and tawdry way like love at the seaside café and hatred on the home front.

The female animal is represented by a waitress and an aspiring novelist and the man-beast is split into two species: the virile and the impotent. Faith Domergue supplies the fireworks, Linda Darnell applies the resent-

In *This Is My Love*, a bitter rivalry between sisters (Linda Darnell and Faith Domergue) threatens the well-being of wheelchair bound Murray Myer (Dan Duryea), a bitter ex-dancer who is married to one of the women. 1954, RKO Pictures, Inc.

ment, Rick Jason is the strong man, and Dan Duryea is the weakling in a wheelchair.

The haranguing is hair-raising at times and the romantic interludes are steamy because of Evelyn. Her wheelchair-bound husband screams, moans, and exacts guilt trips from his wife, a waitress who is bitter and frustrated until a male drifter steals her attention.

Vida (Linda Darnell), Evelyn's sister, and Eddie (Hal Baylor), her boyfriend, listen to Murray (Dan Duryea) make a frantic phone call to locate his missing wife. 1954, RKO Pictures, Inc.

The real rivalry is between Vi and Evelyn. Murray is bitter and gripes, but he is powerless because he cannot move beyond his confines. Vi desires Glenn, the gas station attendant with the steamy lines and dreamy eyes. He, in turn, desires of Evelyn. Vi's jealousy inspires her to conspire against Evelyn by poisoning Murray and framing her for it.

The frame is successful in all ways but one and that is Vi's attempt to have Glenn to herself. He sees through her scheme and deplores her for it. It is his confrontational and condemnatory affront with her that causes her to break down and confess her guilt. It is an interesting resolution to a soap-opera dilemma. The useless husband and the unwanted admirer are eliminated, and all that remains are the couple in love.

Western Gold, Steel Rails and Brass Bells

Dan Duryea had made two Westerns—*Along Came Jones* and *Winchester '73*—and his parts as gunslingers were memorable. It wasn't until 1954 that he began working in the field earnestly. He starred in three movies that set a pace that the actor would match for the rest of his career. The hero in the first movie was played by Audie Murphy, the most-decorated soldier in military history. He became a successful Hollywood actor and *Ride Clear of Diablo* would be the first of three Westerns Duryea would make with the iconic Murphy.

Ride Clear of Diablo stars Audie Murphy as Clay O'Mara, a Denver railroad surveyor who returns to town to avenge the murders of his father and brother by cattle rustlers. This is not an unusual theme for a Western, but it is certain plot oddities that make this movie unique. The viewer is aware from the get-go that the sheriff and his father's lawyer are the culprits. They are also the men who offer guidance to Clay O'Mara while actually trying to set him up for the kill.

It is their plotting against O'Mara that creates the drama because their efforts are turned against them. O'Mara convinces the sheriff to deputize him so he can investigate the murders. Meredith tells the sheriff in private that a way to throw O'Mara off their track is to send him on a bounty hunt for a notorious killer. They tell O'Mara that he was involved in the murders and can give him additional information.

Title card for *Ride Clear of Diablo*. 1954, Universal Pictures Company, Inc.

It is a mistake to hire O'Mara to track down Whitey Kincaide, an outlaw wanted for murder. What they didn't bargain for is that the gunslinger would bond with O'Mara and help him with his mission. That is what makes the movie unique: the strange detours, alliances, and frictions.

O'Mara confounds his benefactors by apprehending Kincaide and bringing him back alive. Along the way, the reluctant lawman and amoral gunman bond in a strange and uneasy alliance. This happens because Duryea's mercurial mad man is the Joker without makeup.

Whitey Kincaide is constantly laughing, snarling, scheming, and causing mayhem. He actually becomes the sidekick of the lawman who was ordered to bring him in dead or alive. They complement each other. Whitey Kincaide is won over by Murphy's honesty, but still does not grant him a free pass.

"I don't know where you was brought up, kid, but wherever it was, you were brought up wrong."

O'Mara still plays by Kincaide's rules. This is what earns him the criminal's respect. Kincaide also hates the crooked town officials. He is really setting them up. It is a case of the sober and the straight arrow contrasted with the amoral and impulsive.

Kincaide is impish in the way he strings O'Mara along and then leaves him alone to fend off a jam. This haphazard shooting gallery is how they wind up in a final shootout that starts in town and ends up in the mines. It's the sheriff, the lawyer and the cattle rustler versus the lawman and the gunslinger.

Kincaide's genius is to control the rivalries and direct them to a final standoff. Unfortunately, it is a warped Mexican standoff and the last laugh again is on him. Nevertheless, the crooked sheriff and lawyer are brought down and O'Mara is victorious.

Clay O'Mara is the only one who gets to go home as the winner. He has got it all, including Laurie Kenyon (Susan Cabot), the sheriff's niece and former fiancé of the lawyer. She is an odd love interest for O'Mara. There is something somber in the way she moves and speaks. She plays the sheriff's niece and fiancée of the lawyer.

Laurie is clueless to the dirty deeds that the dirty dogs in her life have been committing. Her only emotional moment is falling in love with O'Mara from the beginning. Laurie falls for O'Mara like a ton of bricks, but is calm and reserved when told of the circumstances of her uncle's and fiancée's deaths.

Whitey Kincaide (Dan Duryea) warns Kate (Abbe Lane), the dance hall queen, about giving away his whereabouts. 1954, Universal Pictures Company, Inc.

Susan Cabot plays her role with a somnolent nonchalance. Still, Susan Cabot on any level is still mystical and she lends a dark, almost sad tone to her scenes.

Duryea gives Whitey Kincaide some admirable traits, but only so in respect to the rules of the outlaw. His philosophy is, "There's only one law around here: get yours while the getting's good. There ain't no other law." He still likes to pit parties against each other in life and death situations. Kincaide also alters the odds by aiding Clay O'Mara.

By doing so, he cancelled out the policies of the assured lawyer, the nervous and guilt-ridden sheriff, and Jack Elam and Russell Johnson as vicious gunmen. Abbe Lane plays a sultry saloon singer who steams things up with two songs and some attitude.

Whitey Kincaide may be Dan Duryea's most endearing gunslinger even if he is delirious and psychotic. He has a devil-may-care attitude that borders on the lackadaisical. Maybe it is supreme self-confidence or carelessness; perhaps, he no longer cares about living and is looking for a bloody way out of life. Everything is a punch line to Whitey Kincaide. Laughing is the next best thing to shooting a man in the back.

No one makes him laugh harder than Clay O'Mara, a greenhorn deputy sent to Diablo to arrest Whitey for murder. Just the thought of being arrested is enough to keep Whitey in stitches. That the arrest is being made by a baby-faced law man sends him into hysterics. The humor is tempted by sobriety when O'Mara is quicker on the draw than Whitey and shoots the gun out of his hand when he tries to sneak a shot at the deputy.

Kincaide develops a grudging respect for O'Mara and tells him that he has decided to keep him around to see what makes him work. Earning Whitey's respect means being led into a couple of confrontations with outlaws. Whitey's admiration means leading O'Mara into one jam after another. It entertains him to see O'Mara fight his way out of an altercation. Whitey thrives on causing misery for others. The only thing better than shooting a man in the back is laughing about it. The gunslinger gets a dose of his own sardonic humor when he is accidentally shot during a showdown between O'Mara and a man he suspects of killing his father and brother. It happens in a mine and it boggles Whitey's mind to know that he may die as an innocent bystander.

O'Mara once suggested to Whitey that the reason the gunman won't kill him is that he is turning soft and becoming a human being. Whitey snarls, "If I ever feel that coming on, I'll shoot myself." The next best thing is sacrificing his life when he draws fire away from Clay O'Mara in the deputy's final confrontation with the men who actually murdered his father and brother.

Shortly after completing *Ride Clear of Diablo*, Dan Duryea signed a two-year picture deal with Universal-International. The first picture under his new contract was *Fort Laramie* with John Payne and Mari Blanchard. The title was changed to *Rails into Laramie*.

In *Rails into Laramie*, Duryea gets to play the gunman who makes it all the way up to being town boss. This time around he does not have to deal with a church bell but with railroad steel, instead. A certain somebody is still a headache. What makes this different is that somebody is a friend from the past who is currently working for the U.S. Cavalry. The movie is a take on how railroad justice trumps town-boss politics in the new West. Duryea's town boss still comes out on the short end of things.

Rails into Laramie is a short, quick-paced Western that illustrates the importance of the railroads in building the post-Civil War United States.

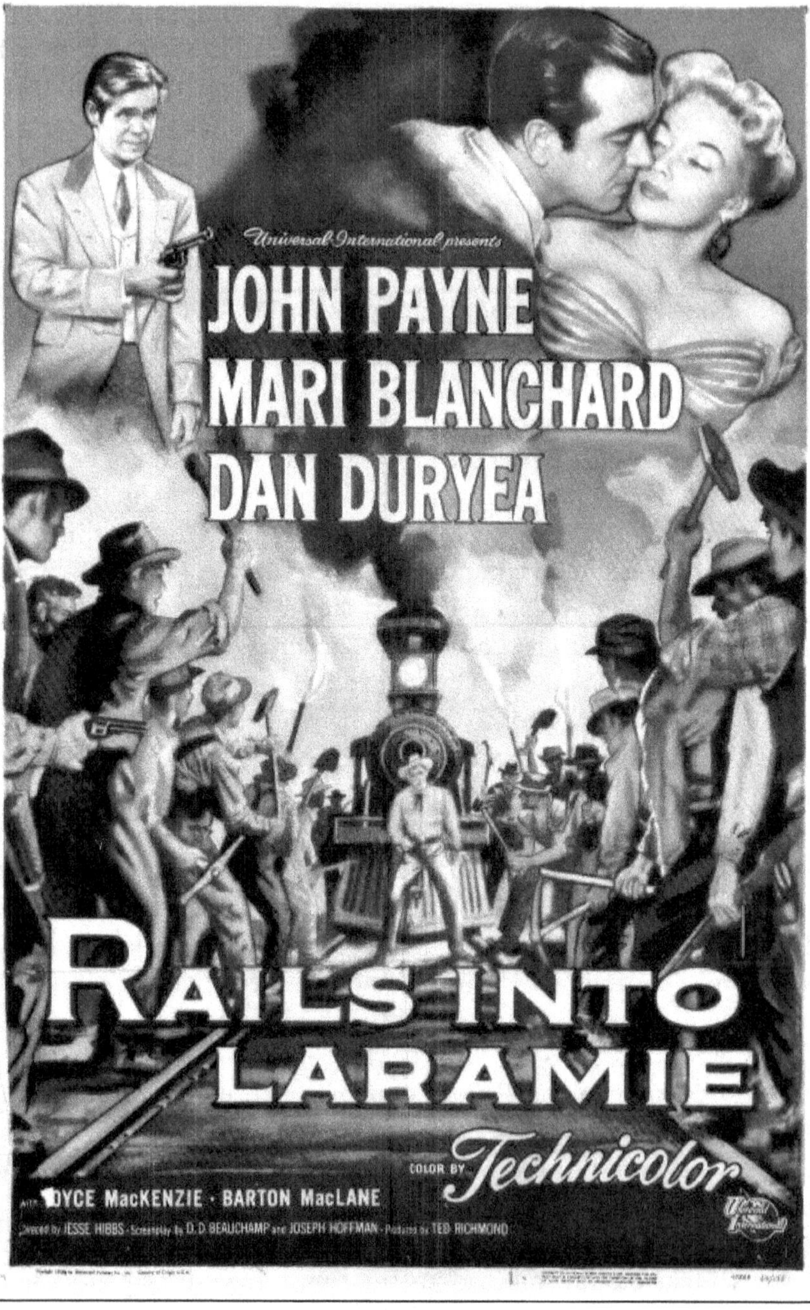

Poster for *Rails into Laramie*. 1953, Universal Pictures Company, Inc.

The railroads were not only a way of linking remote regions but in building commerce, the backbone of the nation. That's why the federal government is perturbed when there's trouble in laying rails down in Laramie.

The President orders a general to send in his top sergeant to clear up the trouble. The trouble is that Sgt. Harder (John Payne) is reluctant to go because efficiency and mobility are not his strong suits unless he's motivated. He likes to drink, fight, and frolic like a private, but orders are orders and the brig is still the brig. That much is a sobering thought and that is his motivation. Another incentive is receiving a captain's commission after spending several years traveling up and down the non-commission chain of command because of busts and infractions.

Sgt. Harder arrives in Laramie and finds that an unofficial work strike has halted the progress on laying the rails. There is no particular reason why the men won't work, but pretty soon it becomes apparent that Jim Shanessy (Dan Duryea), the unofficial town boss, is behind the work stoppage. Harder and Shanessy are old war buddies and this tickles the town boss pink because he thinks that his old buddy will throw in with him. It soon becomes obvious that their attitudes and philosophy are just as divergent as the paths their lives have taken.

Shanessy has married Helen (Joyce MacKenzie), Harding's ex-sweetheart, but there are no hard feelings. She is just window dressing for Shanessy's real hanky-panky, and that's keeping the rails out of Laramie. Helen uses her old charm to sway her former lover from pressing her husband. Her wiles soon wear thin and are not enough to prevent Harder from turning the heat up on Shanessy.

Lou (Mari Blanchard), the dance hall queen, is Shanessy's business partner. They rule the town and keep themselves free of law and order because they foot the bill for it. Everything changes with the arrival of Sgt. Harder. Lou is one of the dominoes that falls in the wake of the sergeant's two-fisted approach to solving the government's problem. She is impressed with his integrity, and how he can't be bought, intimidated with force, or seduced through temptation.

Shanessy is aided by two ornery henchman, Con Winton (Myron Healey), a smooth talking dandy and Ace (Lee Van Cleef), a sadistic, trigger-happy gunslinger. They assist the boys in subverting the rail splitters who have been fired by the new marshal in town. They plot against the government agent by wreaking havoc. They dynamite mountains to block rail travel in and out of Laramie, cut the telegraph lines to break down communication, and destroy the work camp to prevent new laborers from moving in. The insurrection comes to a head when Ace murders the marshal (James Griffith) as he rides to Colorado to deliver a message to the General.

The murder causes Lou to throw in with Harder and Shanessy is arrested. The townspeople are cynical because arrests and trials have meant nothing in the past because of rigged juries. Lou's brainstorm is using the newly framed suffragette laws to empanel an all-female jury, which enrages the men folk.

Shanessy is tried, convicted, sentenced, and imprisoned, mainly due to Lou's vote on the jury. Helen helps Shanessy escape by smuggling a gun into the jail when she has a last meeting with her husband. Shanessy escapes, exacts his revenge on his former partner, and confronts what he tried to avoid through the whole movie: a serious showdown with his former buddy.

He makes a break for it by hijacking the railroad and high tailing it out of town. What good can that do when he is not the hero of the movie? Harder rides his horse and catches up with the train in an old-fashioned Western style. He and Shanessy engage in a fist fight as a train approaches from the other direction.

Harder emerges victorious, not only because he subdues Shanessy and resumes the building of the railroad; he also becomes betrothed to the wounded Lou, promising to return to Laramie when his hitch in the Army is up.

Rails into Laramie is an enjoyable program. It is entertaining because everyone, from the players to the technical crew, performs their jobs well. It is an assembly-line film, but one that is done properly and that is why it is enjoyable. Jess Hibbs was a prolific director at Universal-International and was adept at directing in various styles, including costume dramas, film *noirs* and Westerns.

John Payne was a strong leading man, but he never achieved the popularity that he deserved. He handled himself well and created sympathetic roles out of flawed characters. Payne's Sergeant Harder is a good-time Charley with a strict code of honor. He may be a bar scrapper, but he is not corrupt.

Dan Duryea is slick as ever as Shanessy. He is smooth-talking, well-dressed, and oily in his machinations. Shanessy is married to Harder's ex-paramour and is partners with his future lover.

Mari Blanchard is a dance hall queen who plays the godmother to Duryea's godfather. Payne splits them apart and town politics changes when she throws her lot in with Payne. Blanchard had a sultry voice that

It was not beneath the scruple for a Duryea scoundrel to shoot someone in the back, even a woman. Luckily, Mari Blanchard is not only tough enough to get a guilty verdict against him but survive reprisal by gunfire. 1953, Universal Pictures Company, Inc.

matched her come-hither look. She pretends to be intimidated by the film's villain, but she pulls her own weight when push comes to shove. That includes not being intimidated serving on the jury or surviving being shot in the back by the cowardly Shanessy.

Joyce Mackenzie is the opposite as the good-girl gone bad through association. She is like the crime boss's moll who ignores the source of her wealth. Her corruption is laid bare when she smuggles the gun to her husband in prison.

Myron Healy and Lee Van Cleef play their usual, shifty, knuckle-busting sidekicks. Harry Shannon, Ralph Dunke, and Barton MacClane are three power brokers who are flustered by the new marshal's methods. James Griffith plays a marshal who is a heroic wimp who finds courage and is shot dead because of it. Charles Horvath has a colorful part as Pike Murphy, the blustery railroad foreman and Shanessy stooge.

The happiest day in a man's life is his wedding day. Imagine having it turned into a funeral march seconds before the nuptials start. In *Silver*

Poster for *Silver Lode*. 1954, RKO Pictures, Inc.

Lode, this is Hank Ballard's (John Payne) dilemma when he becomes the victim of a phony Federal Marshal's clever plan to have him arrested and extradited for a crime he did not commit.

In the course of this fateful day, Ballard sees all of his friends and would-be in-laws turn against him and he has to outgun a whole town turned insane by mob justice. It takes the love of two women: his former flame and his would-be bride, to save him.

Hank Ballard has his world turned topsy-turvy when McCarty (Dan Duryea) rides into town accompanied by his gunmen. He is a marshal with a warrant for the arrest of Payne, who is accused of shooting a man in the back and absconding with $20,000.

Duryea interrupts the wedding ceremony when he arrives with his men, setting off a wave of indignation. Most of the townsfolk cannot believe that such a popular and law-abiding citizen could be guilty of murder. There is a small group of dissenters who have blind faith in the federal agent and have their doubts about Ballard's integrity. Before the movie is finished, the whole town tries to hunt him down to kill him.

The mass lunacy is caused by a series of circumstantial evidence that builds until everyone is armed and taking aim at Ballard. This is because McCarty is a masterful instigator. He knows how to play the townsfolk and does a masterful job in subverting their opinion by rallying their support.

First there is the marshal's arrest warrant, something that the local judge validates when it is brought before him for authentication. The second is the sheriff's murder and Ballard holding the smoking gun for all to see. The third is Ballard's mad attempt to bolt for his life and the last is his brazen attempt to engage his former friends, family, and colleagues in armed shootouts.

Silver Lode has textured layers that have logical buildups to the final confrontation in the bell tower of a church. It ends with the marshal being shot through the heart when his bullet ricochets off the bell. Profuse apologies from his hunters are rebuffed by Ballard, who reminds everyone that they spent the whole afternoon trying to kill him.

John Payne should be given a lot of credit for successfully portraying this type of hero. He is a swashbuckler in reverse, an anti-hero who is fighting his pursuers by trying to elude them. The life he is trying to save is his own and that is the chivalry of self-preservation.

Payne successfully shows the transformation of a respected town figure into wily prey using his primitive wits to survive. He shows the gradual breakdown of the civilized man into a cornered animal. It is the saving grace of the church that restores the humanity to the animal, not only the one that was hunted, but the ones below who conducted the hunt.

Lizabeth Scott is the faithful bride-to-be whose conviction is shaken only when she sees her man holding two six guns with the dead sheriff lying at his feet after the townsmen break down the barn door. They refuse

McCarty (Dan Duryea), flanked by Mitch (John Hudson) and Kane (Alan Hale, Jr.), warns Hank Ballard (John Payne) about the perils of resisting arrest. 1954, RKO Pictures, Inc.

to believe that the marshal killed the sheriff. It is at this juncture that the crowd turns on Ballard and he becomes a hunted man, especially after he uses the murder weapon to make a quick getaway.

Dan Duryea is ambivalent as the lawman trying to bring in his man. He has hatched the perfect scheme, but the only drawback is the mark, who is an innocent man with a strong moral character.

Ned McCarty hides behind this veneer in *Silver Lode*. His character arrives in a cloud of prairie dust, a lawman appearing out of nowhere. He has two deputies to enforce his flowery speeches about justice, and one can believe that he might be breaking the commandment about telling the truth. He also has the strangest timing of any lawman trying to bring in a fugitive.

Duryea gains the town's support only after the sheriff is killed and it appears that Ballard shot him. He has their support until the end, when a wire from San Francisco exposes the marshal as a murderer and a rustler. This becomes apparent after one of his henchmen tells Ballard that Duryea killed the man who forged the arrest papers. It is also oblivious after Ballard tries to barter his life for his property.

Dolores Moran is Dooly, the bitter saloon girl who harbors a grudge against Ballard because he dumped her for the richest girl in town. Her anger isn't strong enough to make her turn her back on her ex-lover. She is the one who forces the telegrapher to forge the first letter that states what the real telegraph corroborates when it finally gets through.

Emile Meyer is the sheriff who believes in Ballard's innocence, but has to obey the warrant. Before he dies, he points to Ballard with his eyes bulging and gasps for air, making the townsfolk believe that he was identifying his killer. They can't imagine that he was trying to declare Ballard's innocence.

Morris Ankrum is the supportive future father-in-law who turns into a vicious hunter after he sees the sheriff die in front of him. His apology is rebuffed by Ballard when he climbs down from the bell tower.

The Old Standby System

More of the Same

Dan Duryea's renewable contract with Universal-International still served him well. It also came in handy when it came to appearing on shows that ran under the studio's television banner, Revue Studios. His next role for the studio is another sidekick, a doctor in a mid-Western coal mining town. The hero is played by Jeff Chandler and the female lead goes to Jane Russell.

Foxfire is the eerie phosphorescent glow of a gold prospector's dream. It becomes the name of a mining company by the end of the film. The story line is a boy-meets-girl soap opera set in the desert. Jeff Chandler and Jane Russell are U.I.'s answer to Adam and Eve. They are as primal as the sunsets and rocky plains that make up the environment.

Jonathan Dartland is a mining engineer whose claim to fame is that he believed in what the foxfire told him, and Amanda is the insane society dame who falls in love with him. They marry on a whim and it is a bumpy ride once they leave the altar.

It is a clash of cultures that causes the friction. He is a Boston blue-blood Apache and she is a spoiled eastern society girl who is used to getting what she wants. That makes him independent and emotionless, which conflicts with Russell's sentimental and romantic ways of doing things. Changes teach the couple things about each other and they reconcile just as he hits pay dirt.

It started when Dartland gave Amanda a lift after she was stranded in the desert when her car had a flat tire. He was returning from town where he picked up Doc after his friend had been out on a three-day bender. Seeing Amanda's bob cut, buxom manner, swivel-hipped capris, and high

Jonathan Dartland (Jeff Chandler) is a blue blood Apache who thinks that it is bad luck for his wife Amanda (Jane Russell) to visit the mine in *Foxfire*. 1955, Universal Pictures Company, Inc.

heels didn't hurt his incentive to be chivalrous. It is something that lights a spark in both men. Amanda invites the men to a party that her mother is giving that evening, setting the stage for a romance where the third wheel keeps spinning without even knowing why.

Amanda learns about racism when one of the town gossips visits and gives her the lowdown on Jonathan Dartland's quirks. The meddler assumes that there is a bond between the women because they are white. Comments like, "Once an Indian, always an Indian" or "they can never rise above their nature," peeve Amanda, who politely tells her guest that she would like to find out about her husband for herself.

Amanda gains further insight when she visits the reservation where her husband's mother lives. It is not only the squalor that affects her, she is also saddened by the listlessness and soulless existence of the people who once populated Colorado. Amanda's talk with Dartland's mother helps her to understand the Apache way of life, especially their ideal of manhood.

Independence is a crucial trait in an Apache man. To be self-sufficient is the fulfillment of an Apache man's development. This helps Amanda to understand her husband's aloofness; now he has to understand her sense of independence because she refuses to be relegated to the background. It is their cougar fight, everything else is incidental.

Dan Duryea is Chandler's inebriated buddy, the mining town's doctor who likes to do things with a slurred affect. He is adored by his beautiful nurse, played by Mara Corday, but he is oblivious to her charms. His daydreams are about Andrea. He thinks he has more finesse than the masterful Dartland.

Dan Duryea is there for comedic effect. He is annoying when drunk and cynical when sober. Too cockeyed to appreciate what he has in Corday, Duryea fakes himself out when he thinks he can take Andrea away from Chandler.

Mara Corday lives a hellish life in the mining community. She is still referred to as a half-breed, and this is cause for ostracism. It seems insane because she is beautiful and intelligent; even a buffoonish doc like Duryea thinks he is too good for her.

Frieda Inscourt is the befuddled mother, a society doyenne who is opposed to the strange marriage. Never mind that it starts with a gold

Hugh Slater (Dan Duryea) satisfies his desire with Maria (Mara Corday), but does not appreciate her love for him. 1955, Universal Pictures Company, Inc.

mine and ends in a new town, she opposes the introduction of Mayflower blood to the lineage of the original Americans.

Barton Maclane is still playing the obstinate stick-in-the-mud, the business Philistine who can't see innovation even when it stares him in the eye. He is oblivious to the old myth about Indian gold and that is why he becomes a phantom by the end of the movie. He does not need to be drilled by a gangster to be removed from the scene. All he has to do is exit the screen gracefully with egg on his face.

Dan Duryea's method of combining his steady studio work with independent productions occasionally produced an unexpected surprise. *The Marauders* is one such instance. Dan Duryea returned to the Metro lot for the first time since he filmed the retakes for *Valley of Decision* in 1944. The production was supervised by Arthur Loew, Jr. and was set in post-Civil War Arizona. Dan Duryea gives an over-the-top but compelling performance as Avery, a timid book keeper who morphs into the power hungry General during a range war when the land baron is killed and he takes over.

In *The Marauders*, Corey Everett (Jeff Richards) is a mysterious stranger who strikes a rock in the desert and finds water. He digs a well and this doesn't sit too well with John Rutherford (Harry Shannon), the

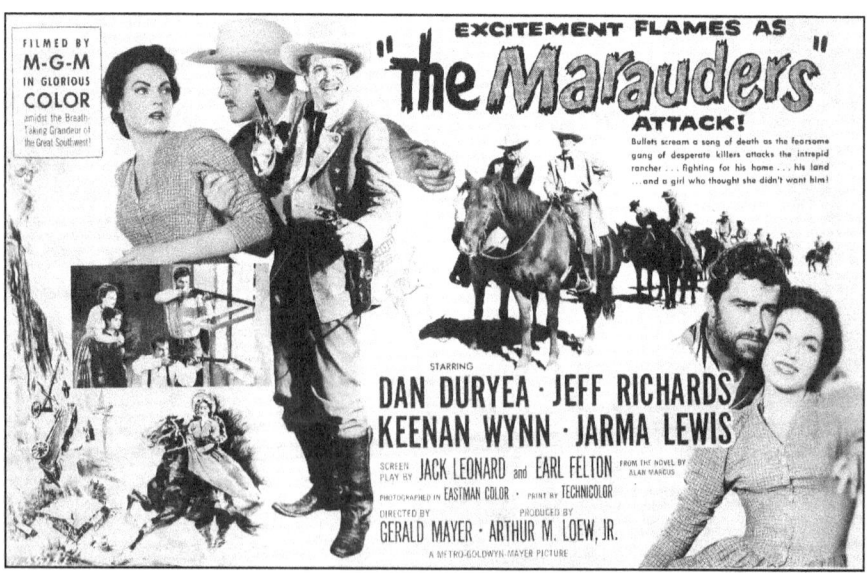

Poster for *The Marauders*, an unusual and intriguing Western about Mr. Avery (Dan Duryea), a timid book keeper who becomes The General, a maniacal land grabber. 1955, Loew's Inc.

land baron who wants it all. Now that a well exists amid the rocks, Rutherford is upset with the squatter so he organizes a band of mercenaries to displace the man and lay claim to the whole canyon.

Rutherford believes that the squatter has a small army aiding his occupation. The cause for alarm is ill-founded because Everett has cleverly placed rifles at windows and ridges that make his cabin seem like a garrison. This starts a range war that will end long after the land baron and his pacifist son are killed in the first encounter with the bearded stranger.

Mr. Avery (Dan Duryea) is the catalyst of the violent campaign that follows. He is a numbers man who gets his hands dirty. Avery is Rutherford's sickly book keeper, a timid man who was prevented from serving the South in the Civil War because of respiratory problems. Guilt inspires him to wear the Confederate uniform of his fallen brother as he serves at Rutherford's right hand. It is Mr. Avery who keeps the quest alive when he morphs into the mission's leader when Rutherford is felled in the first battle with the stranger.

Mr. Avery becomes The General and he is ruthless in his battle with the bearded outsider. Reckless ambition blinds him to the enormity of the task. Anyone who crosses him dies. A steady gun hand rules the ragamuffin regiment led by the pointed Hook (Keenan Wynn). He has tamed the band of outlaws that once worked for Shannon and has Hook under his thumb to keep the others in tow. Occasionally the mercenaries try to overcome Avery, but he rebuffs them and they eventually get the picture as they decline in number because of failed assassination attempts.

The General has dreams of taking over Rutherford's spread. He uses greed to keep his mercenaries in line. All he has to do is smoke out the stranger and his army. It's this mistaken belief in the phantom army that defeats the General. There is only one man, and he is aided by a wife and son abandoned by a well-meaning husband who sought the General's aid. The man winds up being tortured to death by the General for telling the truth that it is only Richards and his wife and son.

The battle commences and the General and his army are outwitted by the stranger, the woman, and the boy. Booby traps and vantage points decimate Hook and the mercenaries. The General without his army is nothing more than a book keeper with a mean temper. There is a final flare-up in the desert between the stranger and the General, who dies in the dust still applauding his plan with his dying breath.

Dan Duryea pulls out all stops as the timid book keeper turned megalomaniac commander-in-chief. His confederate uniform is no longer a

Hannah Farber (Jarma Lewis) watches as The General (Dan Duryea) asserts his authority over The Hook (Keenan Wynn) and Ramos (Peter Mamakos). 1955, Loew's Inc.

pathetic affection, but a bold statement. He is as adept with a gun as he is with a ledger. Hook and his platoon are stared down every time they try to take him on. Duryea effectively becomes tough enough to boss around a gang of thugs and make them risk their lives in a final assault on the stranger.

Grant Richards is the bearded stranger, a brilliant military strategist who takes on the General and his army. He is the one who ambushes them when they mount their last attack. Richards' well is the base of power that cost Rutherford and the General their lives. Jarma Lewis is stern prairie righteousness. She has contempt for her husband and the stranger when they battle Rutherford and the mercenaries. They are effective in changing the odds because Rutherford and his peaceful son are killed. The General takes over, but he and the mercenaries lose their licenses to kill in the second attack on the outpost.

Keenan Wynn is the Hook, the foreman of the killer roustabouts. He likes to confront the General and make power grabs but is always defeated and put back in his place. Being punked-out by the General makes it easy for Hook to keep his sidekicks in line. Wynn is vicious and mean and takes down everyone except the General.

Dan Duryea's next role is the other side of bombastic and shows a quiet courage that is maintained by steel resolve. Fred may huff and puff in *Storm Fear* but he has gumption behind the whining and reprisals. He is bitter about his ill health and how the remote mountain air is the only cure for weak lungs. He still has a private valor and outward resistance that makes him a whiner with a backbone. He knows chivalrous behavior is providing respectability for a Nordic queen; not his own but one who will send her knight on a quest that will claim his life.

Storm Fear was an independent production by actor-director-producer Cornel Wilde. Wilde had started as an actor during the 40's and gradually branched out into writing, producing and directing. He formed Theodora Productions and its first project was *Storm Fear*. He would produce, star and direct the movie, which would be distributed by United Artists. He had already signed Jean Wallace (his wife) and Lee Grant when he landed Dan Duryea for a co-starring role. Three days later, Steven Hill was added to the cast. The movie was filmed in Sun Valley, Idaho.

Storm Fear is a delirious, paranoid nightmare set in a snowy mountain retreat. Elmer Bernstein's haunting score includes disturbing harmonica solos that add a wistful sadness to the snowstorm that hems everyone in. Fred (Dan Duryea) lives in isolation with Elizabeth (Jean Wallace), his frustrated Nordic wife and David (David Stollery), his pre-pubescent son. He needs the seclusion to write novels that no one will read.

Fred is a bitter and sickly man whose sense of honor is outdated and unappreciated. He married his hoodlum brother's lover after she gave birth to a child out of wedlock. His chivalry imbues her with respect she does not appreciate as she still harbors a secret love for her bandit lover, Charlie (Cornel Wilde).

Repressed desire turns into unbridled passion when Charlie shows up with his holdup gang. They seek the solace of the mountaintop retreat as a temporary hideout after a bank holdup goes wrong. One of the gang had been shot and captured while Charlie has been wounded and needs a day to gather his senses. It is a day that will turn into an eternity as tempers flare, old wounds are opened, and allegiances turn into betrayals.

The sickly Fred is pushed into the background as Charlie recuperates after his former lover removes the bullet. His gang: crazed gunman Benjie (Steven Hill) and dissolute showgirl Edna (Lee Grant) dominate the household with their drinking and arguing. The person caught in the

A young boy (David Stollery) undergoes an identity crisis when there is a power struggle between virile Uncle Charlie (Cornel Wilde) and his weak father (Dan Duryea). Lee Grant, Jean Wallace and Steven Hill play different shades of gray. 1955, United Artists Corp.

middle of this madness is David, a young boy who is on the verge of an early entrance into manhood.

The boy is going through adolescent changes and his only guide to maturity is Hank (Dennis Weaver), the understanding ranch hand who harbors a secret love for his mother. The ranch hand takes the child hunting and teaches him survival in the wilderness. It is the ranch hand who changes everyone's lives when he becomes the conquering hero by the film's end.

Uncle Charlie is a father figure to the child, a former shadow that gains substance as he learns more about him. The boy does not know that he is his real father and prefers his manliness to Fred's.

By the film's close, it is obvious that the sickly Fred is more of a man than any of the other male figures in the drama. He appears weak because the weight of his torment bogs him down. His physical sickness makes him less appealing than the ranch hand and his shabby appearance is no match for the unbridled sexuality of the gangster on the run. Added to Wilde's attraction is his dominance of the crazed gunman and the hare-brained showgirl. They are lunatics who set things on fire, a whirlwind duo who would have taken down the family if not for the power of Uncle Charlie.

Lee Grant is brilliant as the brash, drunk ex-singer. Her fur coat and the bottle are the things she relies on to get her through the botched robbery. Steven Hill is pushy and always wants to knock somebody around or snuff someone out. The boss keeps him in line until the odds change during the failed getaway attempt through the snowy countryside. A triple cross cancels out the trio and leaves two of them dying in the snow and the third a crippled convict in a hospital death bed.

Cornel Wilde gives an intense performance as Uncle Charlie, but his real accomplishment is his direction of the movie. Wilde's direction creates electricity out of the isolation by squeezing the characters until they pop.

Horton Foote wrote a screenplay based on a novel by Clinton Seeley. It is a nerve-wracking group torture session where Fred's frustration turns into martyrdom, Elizabeth becomes an earthy, closet gun-moll within the cabin configuration, Benjie is an arsenal about to explode, and Edna is the

A confrontation of emotions between former lovers played by Cornel Wilde and Jean Wallace. 1955, United Artists Corp.

expendable dupe who becomes the fizzling fuse when she has served her purpose. She winds up with her fur coat and a fist full of cash but spending it on her back in the snow banks does not do her a whole bunch of good.

The hero of the movie is Hank, the honest ranch hand who observes the rules of social etiquette. He was always a surrogate father to the boy, teaching him about the great outdoors. The hero is the one who tracks down the convicts and rescues the boy from their clutches.

David Stollery is effective as the kid who gets to play the sensitive observer. He is held in check by the changes he goes through as he learns the lessons of manhood from his dad and Uncle Charlie. He is badgered by the gunman and intrigued by the bleached-blond nightclub singer who is fond of drinking and doing bits of her showbiz act to entertain him.

In the film's turbulent finale, his world is broken into many fragments, but when it is put back together again, it is rebuilt into a picture to his liking. Faux paw has been claimed by the snow when he tried to take a hike into the elements to find help to fight the gangsters. Uncle Charlie has been emasculated in the boy's eyes as he watches bio-dad die an ignominious death in a county hospital bed. The gun moll goes back to being Elizabeth, the Nordic queen, when she is rescued and freed by the new paw in town, Hank the heroic handyman, a safe and agreeable synthesis of Fred and Uncle Charlie.

The Underbelly of the Golden Years

1957 was one of those tell-tale years that punctuated Dan Duryea's career. They showed the fruition of previous career changes and the beginning of new directions. His overall career maintained the same kind of continuity that he established on his arrival in Hollywood. Instead of a contract with MGM, Dan Duryea had an open contract with Universal-International that included work in its television division, Revue Studios. He also continued to star in low-budget independent films that offered cogent perspectives missing from the popular mainstream market.

By now, Dan Duryea was a seasoned veteran of his profession. It showed in his face and that was an attribute for him because it enabled him to put variations and twists on previous characterizations. The maturity also gave Dan Duryea a chance to play stalwart television heroes, the patriarchal types that were role models during the Eisenhower years.

That meant that he also played the dark angels that were the antithesis of this bright period of domestic bliss and crass consumerism. Another constant is the variety in similar character types, whether it is shared fates or deferred dreams.

In 1957, Dan Duryea revisited familiar terrain to add new twists to old themes. He made three movies for Universal-International. He had to argue with the studio brass to get to play the role of Sgt. Herman in *Battle Hymn*. He is the good-natured supply sergeant who is the buddy of Col. Hess, a minister turned bombardier, played by Rock Hudson. In *Night Passage*, Whitey Harbin snarls and terrorizes as many people as he can while fending off encroachments to his authority from within his ranks. In *Slaughter on 10th Avenue* he plays John Masters Tipton, a former DA who is now a mob attorney. Charming and hospitable when he is jawboning with old cronies he turns carnivorous when there is someone on the witness chair in front of him. It's expected of him because he works for the Mob.

Battle Hymn is the screen story of Dean Hess, a combat flyer who became a minister after he accidentally bombed a German orphanage during World War II. The twist to the saga is that he leaves his Ohio church to return to active duty in Korea so he can teach a squadron of flyers how to fly combat missions. It is a tale of redemption, Hollywood style!—which means that it has its mawkish moments as well as courageous scenes.

Minister Hess is a man plagued by doubt, one who bogs down his sermons with guilt instead of hope. He is haunted by the thirty-seven orphans he unintentionally killed and believed that being a minister would alleviate the guilt. The film loses no time in touching on the tragedy with a powerful flashback. The accident was due to a faulty trigger mechanism that released the bomb once the original target was past. Informed of the bombing by a propaganda broadcast, 'Killer' Hess visits the site and is devastated by the destruction. What makes the situation more difficult is that it took place in his grandmother's hometown.

Five years after the war, doubt still clouds his judgment so he takes advantage of an Army recall program and volunteers for active duty as a senior USAF advisor/instructor pilot. His mission is to train the ROK (Republic of Korea) Army to fly F-51D Mustangs, nothing more. This is the irony that creates the conflict in the story when the enemy soldiers begin to broach the airfield and threaten the village.

Hess arrives in Korea and finds that his airbase is a rundown strip that was built by the Japanese during World War II. The American troops are rag bags who are killing time by doing nothing because they are sepa-

En Soon Yang (Anna Kashi) explains social conditions to Sgt. Herman (Dan Duryea) and Col. Hess (Rock Hudson). 1956, Universal Pictures Company, Inc.

rated from the action. Hess changes this by imposing strict military discipline, a step that is necessary in cleaning up the base to make it acceptable for the planes that will shortly arrive. This does not sit too well with Captain Skidmore (Don DeFore), his old battle buddy from the previous war.

Training turns into actual combat when the flyers spot a convoy of enemy soldiers and obliterate them. There appears to be one fleeing vehicle that is neutralized, but it is discovered to be full of refugees. This opens up old wounds for Hess, who berates Skidmore for disobeying orders by engaging in combat. Skidmore does not want to hear about guilt because he accepts accidents as being a part of war.

From that point onward, the challenges mount for Hess. He has to find a humanitarian solution to the orphans who have been flooding the base for meals. His authority is undermined when it is discovered that he is a minister. Things look bleak when enemy troops move closer to the encampment.

His solution to the orphan problem is to convert a bombed out Buddhist temple into an orphanage. He regains the men's trust by proving that he can still engage with the enemy. Hess felt comfortable being a trainer, not realizing that he would have to engage in combat. The rest of the movie shows just how wrong he is. His biggest challenge is to safely move over four-hundred orphans after the base is bombed and the orphanage threatened. He accomplishes this with the last-minute aid of a group of cargo planes who airlift the orphans to the island of Cheju.

Battle Hymn is a departure for director Douglas Sirk and producer Ross Hunter. They usually helmed glossy soap operas for the studio. This

Col. Hess (Rock Hudson) heroically transports an orphanage to safe passage during a bombing raid. 1956, Universal Pictures Company, Inc.

film breaks away from the heavy dramatics and improbable plot twists, possibly because it is based on a true story. There were deviations in the script. For instance, the real model for Kaskfi's character was older and did not die in the war, and the strafed refugees were fleeing on a boat rather than a truck. Otherwise, it is an uplifting and engaging film, truly inspiring and emotional.

Russell Metty's cinematography is breathtaking, which was the case with all of his films because of the mastery of his craft. The dogfights are impressive and powerful. The music is a variation of Japanese martial music mixed with American folk tunes, such as "The Battle Hymn of the Republic."

Rock Hudson is perfect as the square-jawed, broad-shouldered leader of men. He successfully portrays the conflicts Hess must have felt as a minister turned warrior. Hudson shows the subtle changes in his thinking as his challenges help mold him and give him back his confidence.

Anna Kashfi has a quiet reserve as the woman who is the mother spirit to the orphans. She carries on her charitable work until her heroic death during the air raid that caps the film's drama.

Dan Duryea is wonderful as the wily, cigar-chomping Supply Sergeant Herman. He is able to secure any ration or supply under the most arduous conditions. The sergeant is always cheerful and supplies a sorely needed sense of humor. Sgt. Herman in *Battle Hymn* is a laid back cigar-chomping supply sergeant during the Korean War. He is as resourceful as he is cheerful.

Dan DeFore plays Hess' old war buddy, someone who offers the audience a glimpse of Hess during the previous war, when he was known as 'Killer' Hess. He is at odds with Hess throughout the whole movie until he is mortally wounded during a heroic two- man mission towards the end of the film. His deathbed revelation is a touching moment and is not overdone or mawkish.

Philip Ahn plays Lun Wa, an elderly ivory carver who is a font of wisdom for Hess. He stays on to aid the orphans because he is needed. He seems to have all of the answers to Hess' questions and appears to be an angel whose wisdom is a salve for the wounds suffered in war.

James Edwards is Lt. Maples, a flyer who unintentionally strafes a truckload of orphans. He is an impressive character, one of the few African-Americans shown in war movies of the fifties. His only stereotypical moment is singing "Swing Low, Sweet Chariot" when trying to comfort the orphans after a devastating air raid.

Poster for *Night Passage*, with James Stewart and Audie Murphy starring as brothers who live on opposite sides of the law. 1957, Universal Pictures Company, Inc.

Martha Hyer plays his faithful wife, who remains steadfast in her love for him as he confronts his inner demons in Korea. Alan Hale, Jr. plays a garrulous mess sergeant and Jock Mahoney is a major who adds his farmland charm to a couple of scenes.

Lieutenant Colonel Hess was the technical adviser to the film. Hudson wore Hess' Navy-issued gold flying helmet with the United Nations emblem. Hess got it from a downed Navy pilot who crash landed at the Korean airfield. He donated his profits from the film to help the orphanage that he helped found in Korea.

In *Night Passage*, a single bloodline with mixed alliances provides the conflict for Grant McLaine (James Stewart), a soft spoken accordion man with the eye of an eagle. He has been hired by the railroad bosses to safeguard a payroll shipment from Whitey Harbin's gang. The robbers have been targeting the railroad as of late and the lack of funds is causing unrest among the rail splitters.

The Utica Kid (Audie Murphy) rides with the Harbin Gang, making things difficult for McClaine because the gun man is his kid brother. The disgraced railroad man was fired for allegedly colluding with The Utica Kid on a previous robbery. The railroad is desperate and needs McLaine's services once more when Harbin pulls three successful robberies of payload runs.

Night Passage is a lyrical Western because it shows the West at a time when it was about to be transformed into an urban empire. The movie shows the way the railroads changed how business was conducted and

Grant McLaine (James Stewart) is a lanky accordion man whose music enlivens a mining camp that has not been paid in weeks. 1957, Universal Pictures Company, Inc.

how the mining towns were taken over by the new conglomerates, namely the banking system.

However, the film's final confrontation takes place in an empty mining camp and it's an old-fashioned showdown between good and evil. It is a unique place to have the final confrontation and provides for an exciting finale. The sprawling canyon and the empty coal chutes dwarf the men shooting it out with each other. There is death and redemption, but not without losses. Reputations are restored and new alliances are made, all signed with outlaw blood and sealed with the sweet music of an accordion that went up in smoke.

Night Passage is entertaining and awesome in its portrayal of the great outdoors. The empty mining camps are like wounded giant canyons and the fertile prairie countryside are the new points of interest staked out by the new invaders. Its ledger sheet and bank balances dictate the law of the new West, and the old frontier vets are now hired guns and ranchers.

James Stewart is fantastic as the lanky accordion man with the lightning draw from the hip. Audie Murphy is charming and upright as the Utica Kid, a man caught in the middle of alliance and allegiance. Dan Duryea is slovenly and brazen as Whitey Harbin. He has a hair-trigger temper and it works against him in the final showdown. Dianne Foster is energetic as the woman who loves the Utica Kid. She is as tough as the merchants she sells her boxed lunches to, and she rides across hostile territory to see the Kid.

Elaine Stewart is the ice block that makes men sweat, whether it is in a sumptuous railroad car or a grimy bandit hangout in an abandoned mining camp. She plays the odds with her high-minded temperament and almost loses more than her cool in the final match between hero and villain.

Jay C. Flippen is railroad power, a fading field man who was kicked upstairs and fears that he is losing his grip on power. This is his last chance to show that he can supervise a successful payload run. Hugh Beaumont is an aggressive assistant to Flippen, a sidekick who is not above seeing things the way he thinks they should turn out. He has visions of being top man because he thinks that Flippen is soft and Stewart villainous. Herbert Anderson is a traitorous underling. His duplicity comes as a surprise and he pays dearly for being untrustworthy. Brandon de Wilde is a young boy caught up in the bandit life. He is mentored by Murphy, but rescued by Stewart. Jack Elam is one of the outlaws whose draw can't match his mouth when he challenges Stewart to a face off.

Whitey Herbin (Dan Duryea) is a sarcastic, trigger happy gunslinger who feels threatened by the presence of the Utica Kid (Audie Murphy) in his gang. 1957, Universal Pictures Company, Inc.

Two good examples of how Dan Duryea's movie and television roles complement each other are the *Slaughter on 10th Avenue/The Frightened Witness* and *The Burglar/Doomsday* combinations. John Tipton Masters is a former District Attorney turned effete mob lawyer in *Slaughter on 10th Avenue*. He defends a mob figure (Joe Downing) accused of staging a waterfront hit and his adversary works for the office he once ran. While playing a smooth talking and manipulative mouthpiece on the movie screen he put in an appearance of a different kind as an average Joe threatened by the small town mob in Cavalcade of Star's, *The Frightened Witness*. He is the owner of a small butcher shop who witnessed a mob hit-and-run execution. Several attempts to intimidate him into maintaining silence make him come forth and bring down the mobsters.

Corrupt labor-union movies became Hollywood fodder after the Kefauver Hearings in 1951. *On the Waterfront* is the most prominent example of the genre, chiefly because of Elia Kazan's artful direction, Budd Shulberg's vivid screenplay, and Marlon Brando's passionate characterization of the washed-up pug who brings down a union boss.

The film unfairly overshadows other movies on the same subject. One neglected movie is *Slaughter on 10th Avenue*, starring Richard Egan, Julie Adams, Jan Sterling, Dan Duryea, Walther Matthau, and Mickey Shaughnessy. It ranks high among producer Albert J. Zugsmith's achievements and tells the true-life story of fledgling ADA William Keating's attempt to bring justice to the docks when he handles the case of an honest pier boss' shooting.

Solly Pitts (Mickey Shaughnessy) is a rebellious longshoreman whose outspoken views about the union infuriate Al Dahlke (Walter Matthau), the union boss. The film opens with a meticulously-planned shooting of Pitts on the stairway outside his apartment. His wife, Madge (Jan Sterling), cradles him in her arms as he tells her that, "Cockeye did it! Cockeye Cook and two of his meatballs!" It is a declaration that will rock the waterfront world of corrupt unions, silent dockworkers, and impotent law enforcement.

Poster for *Slaughter on 10th Avenue*, an effective labor rackets movie. 1957, Universal Pictures Company, Inc.

The only man strong enough to challenge the corrupt system is a green Assistant District Attorney named Kenneth Keating (Richard Egan). It is his strong moral conviction and naïve inexperience that make him take on the case of the people versus Al Dahlke.

Keating is new to the job and this is his first contact with the waterfront culture. He is confused and angered by his initial impression of the clique mentality even though he belongs to the kindred world of the coal miners. His father was a union man who would have cringed at a man like Eddie Cook (Joe Downing) and dealt with him much like Solly Pitts did, with venom and violent counter-gambits.

The layers of corruption and the people who operate on each level fill the movie with distinctive characters and interesting situations. Sgt. Varsnick (Charles McGraw), a hard-nosed, gravel-voiced detective turned gray-haired before his time, is Keating's guide through the underworld. He educates the ADA on the code of the dock people, but Keating ultimately has to find out for himself. It's not until he puts his life on the line that Solly's intimates begin to trust him.

Solly Pitts is as tough as he is honest, and tenacious enough to stave off death for a couple of days. He still subscribes to the code of silence that he reluctantly breaks after he is told that he will not live. He names his shooters, but rues that he will die a rat to his friends although Keating remarks, "not your friends."

Madge is just as rough as her husband, standing by his side and staring down her intimidators. She once dug a slug out of his leg with a kitchen knife and washed the wound with iodine. Nothing can sway her, from midnight peepers, shadowy tails on the street, or threatening phone calls. Not even being badgered on the witness stand can break Madge's spirit. She is determined to find justice for her fallen husband.

Benjy (Harry Bellaver) is Solly's best friend and saw one of the assassins leave the Pitts' apartment building after the shooting but he won't cooperate with Keating. He metes out justice his own way, with two fists and a blackjack. Midget (Nick Dennis) is a militant dock worker whom Dahlke calls "five foot nothing and all of it mouth." He tries to incite the longshoremen with a litany of honest dock workers who were murdered by Dahlke's men. Nothing can quell his anger, not even a beating and a dunk in the ocean by Dahlke's henchmen.

He despises law enforcement as much as he hates the union bosses. It is because he once spilled his guts to a crime commission in vain and was rewarded with a broken back. Keating stinks, according to Midget,

A.D.A. Keating (Richard Egan) tries to talk Midget (Nick Dennis) into convincing Benjy (Harry Bellaver) to testify before the Grand Jury. 1957, Universal Pictures Company, Inc.

who ultimately gives the ADA the ultimate show of respect in the film's final shot.

Unique characters, vicious shootings, and difficult investigations are part and parcel of every crime drama but the setting is what gives *Slaughter on 10th Avenue* its extra charm and grit. The waterfront world of this movie is fascinating, from the supporting characters to the cityscape itself.

The hardscrabble environment is what makes the dock people unique. They have a code of honor forged by the will to survive. They not only have to deal with the natural element of the ocean but with the pier bosses and oppression by the dock union. Solly and Madge Pitts are the bedrock couple harassed by union thugs. Solly is shot and Madge is threatened by intimidation.

The buildings and the piers are characters in this waterfront drama, too, as are the lighting and shadows of the bricks and pipes, along with the breathtaking panoramas of the Brooklyn Bridge and the Atlantic Ocean.

Richard Egan is grim-faced and even-toned in his pronouncements. He can also fight, as he is from a coal mining town where many argu-

Former D.A. John Jacob Masters (Dan Duryea) taunts his former protégé Howard Rysdale (Sam Levene) and the green A.D.A. Keating (Richard Egan) about the lucrative benefits of private practice. 1957, Universal Pictures Company, Inc.

John Jacob Masters (Dan Duryea) pokes holes in Lt. Varsnick's (Charles McGraw) account. 1957, Universal Pictures Company, Inc.

ments were settled by bare knuckles. He is called to use his fighting prowess in the finale, when the film has the requisite labor riot scene with the protesters battling the head-busters brought in on the backs of trucks.

Julie Adams is the picture of smoldering sophistication. She is genteel and erudite yet supports the roughneck side of her husband's personality. Jan Sterling is the rough-and-tumble opposite; she has to be that way in order to survive the working class environment. Madge is honest and straightforward, a rock of support for her wounded husband.

Mickey Shaughnessy is magnificent as Solly Pitts. He is a stocky man shot down by garlic-laced bullets and holds on to life while dying in a hospital ward. Walther Matthau is a highlight as a slimy rackets man whose protégée, Eddie "Cockeye" Cook, supervised the shooting.

Dan Duryea plays John Masters Tipton, a former DA who became a successful defense attorney. He is smooth on the outside and merciless inside a courtroom. He is representing the crooked union boss accused of murder and graft.

Charles McGraw is the tough-guy detective who knows all about the dock people. Midget is a pint-sized firecracker played by Nick Dennis. Tom Kennedy and Mickey Hargitay work the waterfront, as does Jack LaRue as Father Paul, who supplies the soul for the dock workers.

Organized crime spread its influence beyond urban boundaries and intimidated and extorted small town America, too. *The Frightened Witness* is a short twenty minute drama about an organized crime syndicate menacing a small American town. It boils down to the individual versus the mob.

Joe Kohler owns Kohler's Meat Market, a butcher shop in a small town. He has just finished the books and is satisfied that business is okay. A call from his wife reminds him that it is past eight and he promises to close the store and head home. It is part of a weekly routine but Joe does not mind because life is good. He is his own boss and he has a loving wife and two charming kids to make up his family.

Kohler's life is turned upside down when he witnesses a hit and run accident outside of his store. His sharp eye-witness account becomes blurred when a helpful stranger assists him in calling the police before advising him to play dumb with the cops. The stranger is smooth and forceful; even insisting on walking Kohler home and coming in to meet the wife and kids. They think that he is an insurance salesman and that is the stranger's little joke. He is actually a mob goon trying to dissuade Kohler from cooperating with the police.

At home, Joe Kohler enjoys the American Dream with his loving family. 1957, Desilu Productions.

At work, Joe Kohler is pressured by a mob goon (Harold Stone) to keep quiet about a hit and run accident that he witnessed a few moments earlier. 1957, Desilu Productions.

It turns out to be a mob hit when it is announced that the victim was the chairman of a committee that was battling the infiltration of organized crime into their community. The syndicate tries to bribe Kohler by ordering the cuts for their high end night clubs from his store. He finally regains his courage when he sees the chairman's wife on television. She says that she is taking over the reins of the committee and is confident that she will get the support of the people.

Kohler gets tough and then calls the detective on the case to turn in the two goons that have been harassing him. Duryea is in fine form as he stands up to Harold Stone and Lewis Charles, two well known heavies of the time. He is the classic 50's TV dad and to prove the point his wife is played by Barbara Billingsly, June Cleaver of *Leave it to Beaver* fame.

Not everyone enjoyed the privileges of the new suburban middle class. There were still the underdogs and guys from the wrong side of the tracks. Nat Harbin seems to be a product of circumstance while Sam Mc-Dillard reaps the fickle rewards of free will. They are both master thieves who are defeated by the success of their capers.

The most compelling connection between a movie role and a television character is *The Burglar* and *Suspense: Doomsday*. Nat Harbin is a down-on-his luck sneak thief who plans and executes a daring jewel necklace robbery in *The Burglar*. Sam Shumacher goes by the name of McDillard, the Red Pepper bandit who robs banks when he is not tending to his cattle ranch in *Suspicion: Doomsday*. They may be from different social rungs and their reasons for stealing may differ, but they share a unique genius and similar dreadful fates.

Dan Duryea huddled with indie producer Louis Kellman for a starring role in *The Burglar* as early as 1955. The movie was shot in Philadelphia and Atlantic City by Samson Prod. and it sat on the shelf for almost two years before Columbia Pictures purchased it. *The Burglar* was the first movie to be shot in Philadelphia since Sigmund Lubin's movies in the early 1900's. Duryea had an extended shooting schedule due to inclement weather. Duryea and co-star Martha Vickers were relocated along with 46 members of the crew and three truckloads of equipment. He donated his extra salary to the hurricane victims' fund.

Nat Harbin is *The Burglar*, a crime master done in by his own ingenuity. He was an orphan asylum escapee adopted by a burglar who gave him a conscience when it came to keeping a promise. It is this iron-clad adherence to a rule that makes Harbin plan and pull off a jewelry heist with a built-in escape clause that guarantees failure.

Nat Herbin (Dan Duryea) has conflicted emotions about his ersatz kid sister, Gladden (Jayne Mansfield). 1957, Columbia Pictures Corp.

Before network news and cable television, newsreels were a way of conveying news, trivia, and the esoteric to the public. The newsreels were a dose of reality before the escapist fare of the main attraction. They were also a way for crooks like Nat Harbin to hatch their next heist.

Harbin is part of a movie theatre audience that enjoys the segment on Sister Sara, a fraudulent spiritualist who has swung a lucrative real estate deal from an eccentric millionaire. It is newsworthy because the miser did not believe in charity because he was a business man. The gimmick to the story is that Sister Sara bought the estate for less than two dollars, along with a diamond necklace for sixty cents. The necklace is the focus of Harbin's next job.

He uses his half-sister, Gladden (Jayne Mansfield), to case the mansion when she takes Sister Sara in her confidence after she travels miles to offer a fifty-cent donation. This impels the spiritualist to invite Gladden in for lunch and supper, which includes a guided tour of the palatial estate. Gladden later returns to the thieves' den with a carefully drawn layout of the house. All Harbin has to do is to plan the heist down to the split second because of inherent limitations in the set-up.

The heist is successful, but the necklace is so hot that they can't fence it. They have to lay low, which creates too much tension for them to handle. They begin to grate on each others' nerves, making them prey to an outside peeper. The point that connects them to each other is Gladden. She is an immature but sexually charged waif who grew up in

Tension mounts among the burglary team (Mickey Shaughnessy, Peter Capell, Dan Duryea and Jayne Mansfield. [l - r]). 1957, Columbia Pictures Corp.

a lair of male predators and is the cause of the sexual frustration among the men.

Nat Harbin is ambivalent about his feelings towards her. He has a love/hate relationship with Gladden that dates back to their childhood. He desires her, but cannot consummate his lust because of a promise made to the man who raised him. This confusion is what destroys him.

A nasty guilt eats away at his insides and clouds his judgment because of Gladden. He is the genius that pulls off the plan and the fool that turns it into a failure. Harbin is steely resolve held together by weak rivets. It is not something that is lost on his anxious sidekicks, Baylock (Peter Capell) and Dohmer (Mickey Shaughnessy), two stooges with a weary sense of fatalism. They claim to have a need for money and success, but they are losers waiting to cash in on their failure.

Baylock is a bundle of nerves, a neurotic chatterbox. He is the ice expert, a ruined jeweler who can still price a load through a worn-out loupe. Bitchy and somewhat jealous of Gladden, he is puzzled by her presence in the group.

The petty thief has big dreams of retiring to South America. He is a three-time loser who can't wait to fence the necklace so he can fly away from a lifetime sentence. He even recites his dreams to the fantasy strains of samba music.

Dohmer, a lascivious pig who likes to torment Baylock, can't take his eyes off of Gladden. He eats in his undershirt and moves his lips when he reads the comics. Brutal and gross, the ape-man underlies the sickness of the team. He thumbs a ride on the death express when he winds up stranded in a car dumped in the Jersey swamps.

Charlie (Stuart Bradley) is a crooked cop, the peeper who upsets the balance that sets the table for justice to be served on the Atlantic City boardwalk. He is more venal than the crooks that he exploits, if only because he has crossed the line that he is paid to obey. He is just as wily and careless as Harbin when he muscles his way into the gang and winds up accused of killing the mastermind.

Charlie romances Gladden and has his paramour, Della (Martha Vickers), hook Harbin. Della is the odd woman out, a cliché on paper, but made believable by Vickers. Her hard-luck story is convincing, even when accentuated by the strains of the depression era. Della is drained of everything except her last ounce of decency. She puts all the pieces together in the stadium hall after Harbin pays dearly for the necklace.

In the end, Nat Herbin (Dan Duryea) becomes the fall guy in his burglary heist. Gladden (Jayne Mansfield) and the police chief (Wendell K. Phillips) ponder the irony. 1957, Columbia Pictures Corp.

Paul Wendkos directed and edited *The Burglar* in a bleak, freakish, baroque style. The visual composition of his shots is perfectly balanced, gaining an extra dimension from the clever editing that keeps the action movie's pulse beat strong. The oboe concerto and a passage that becomes the leitmotif are cloying, but add to the characters' desperation. It is mood music for depression and despair.

Everything about the movie is low-rent, from the dreary settings to the spent characters. The look of the film is dark, even during the daytime scenes. It is an oppressive *noir*, one where the seagulls have the final say. Atlantic City is the perfect place for the plan to unravel. The beachfront standoff, the house of horror music-box tip off, and the carnival act showdown are masterfully handled.

"We the dead welcome you," is the greeting of the keeper of the dead as he welcomes Nat, Gladden, and Charlie the cop into his Atlantic City labyrinth at the end of the movie. The scene is spooky, chilling, and unnerving because it is Nat's big payoff.

Nat Harbin, the man with the patent leather name and gelatin heart, winds up in a real-life newsreel viewed by a curious crowd of Atlantic City revelers as they gawk at a pair of anonymous shoe soles in a police meat wagon.

It all happened because of a necklace that had been bought for sixty cents. It was a piece of jewelry that inspired dreams in people who hated their lives. Belief in what the necklace represented was what doomed the players. Its origin was false and tainted by the pretensions of a phony spiritualist. Everything about the necklace is cursed because Sister Sara is a fake who lives in the world of the dead.

It's a straight line from the world of the dead to doomsday. It's a path that Mr. Schumacher will travel and it will take him to the same place as Nat Harbin. Mr. Schumacher is a Texas rancher who considers cattle to be his hobby in *Suspicion: Doomsday*. He may have flown his private plane into town to attend the cattle show but once he shaves his mustache and discards the ten gallon hat he becomes Sam McDilliard, The Red Pepper Bandit.

McDillard is compelled to rob banks. He does not have to in order to survive; it is something that he does when the urge moves him. It is his vocation. He plans and executes bank robberies only when the urge inspires him and the jobs are sure things. He earned his nickname because his gang of thieves uses packets of red pepper instead of fire arms.

The Red Pepper Bandit is a crime master with a precise style and technique that demands professionalism from his recruits. As a precaution, he never uses the same gang twice and his only constant is his contact man, Sam Banton (Robert Middleton). It is Banton's responsibility to make the arrangements and assembles the team before he becomes a hands-on player during the robbery.

This time, it is a small town bank and his team of experts has to be synchronized, from the jackhammers tearing up the cement, the prospective customer filling out a deposit slip and the casual bystander talking to the cop on the beat. They know the deal. That is why they are professionals.

McDillard's plans are foolproof blueprints because they were created by the legendary Red Pepper Bandit.   He is calm and steady, proceeding with his orchestration of the robbery with a low key effectiveness. It is a credit to his discipline considering the bad feelings he has about the job once it is set in motion. First, the mechanic who owned the seaside gas station that they are using for a rendezvous passes out because of whiskey guzzling over marital woes. Then the bank manager, a photography buff, takes a candid of McDillard when he poses as an inspector during a trial run of the robbery. The worst omen is being recognized as Schumacher, or Shoes, by an old Army buddy.

Sam McDillard vowed to kill any man who betrayed his secret identity. The odds are slim that he would be discovered but it happens when Perry Slavins (Edward Binns), one of the recruits, recognizes him from the old Army days in Hawaii. McDilliard takes him for a ride to a se-

Dapper cattle man Sam Schumacher is pictured before he transforms himself into McDillard, the Red Pepper Bandit, in *Doomsday*. 1957, Shamley Productions.

cluded cliff where the surf pounds against the rocky coastline below. He gives his Army buddy a chance to live if he forgets that he ever saw Shoes and looks at his old friend as McDillard. The jinx's inability to keep his promise of banishing Shoes to the past earns him a bullet in the gut and a tumble off the cliff into the ocean.

The master bandit who used red pepper as a getaway plan breaks his own murder code when an old acquaintance chooses death over silence because of a leaky mouth. His genius may have enabled McDillard to overcome other obstacles with furtive ease but too many bad omens are jinxing this operation.

The bank robbery is executed with minute precision and borders on perfection. Each player has performed his task well and all that is left is the getaway. The nagging anxiety achieves a perfection that makes the job a success but it is cruel fate that turns the reward into a death penalty. A mystery bullet fells McDillard during the getaway and he winds up in the back of a meat wagon that was supposed to be his failsafe device.

A private ambulance becomes his hearse and he is to be disposed of by Banton, his identity rendered untraceable thanks to the acid remedy. That was the extreme agreement between the partners should he die during a heist. With no red pepper to get him out of this jam, McDillard has to settle for Banton's account of the radio's recognition of the brilliance of his plan.

The bulletin also announces the capture of the other robbers and tells about a seemingly unrelated incident about two Portuguese fishermen arguing over a boat and a shotgun wedding. McDillard unwittingly caught one of the errant bullets fired during the argument. It was an argument he spent the previous day listening to in the hotel room that he booked so he could monitor the activities of the bank across the street.

The ambulance veers off to an isolated stretch of beach and the camera focuses on a proverb etched into the rock. It tells about the futility of reaching for a dream that is out of arm's length. It recapitulates McDillard's far reaching ambition and his failure to reap the success of his plan.

Doomsday is an excellent melodrama deftly directed by Bernard Girard. His work is given a steady beat by the alert editing of Bill Mosher. Bud Thackery was the director of photography and his brooding vision lends a sense of doomed urgency to the drama. Sy Bartlett's tight screenplay is brought to life by a cast of expert players. The gang is made up of familiar faces that include Charles Bronson (Cal), Paul Birch (Big George) and Robert Cornthwaite (Fitzgerald).

1 **Dan Nixon and Jasmine Lee** are completely engrossed in one another. They pass two neighbors without speaking. "Well, you can see how infatuated they are," one says to the other. "But what I can't figure out is why her husband don't do somethin' about it. He must know. The way it is, she's makin' a fool of both of them. Everybody's talkin', you know."

Life Magazine ran small photo-plays with a melodramatic slant to them. In one of them, Dan Duryea plays a husband who appears to be wearing the cuckold's horns... on the other hand. 1957, Life Magazine.

2 **But Les Lee** seems unaware of the gossip. The next day he helps Dan get ready for an extended business trip. That afternoon his wife disappears. Neighbors say she has run away with Dan, but Les refuses to believe it. "Only foul-minded fools'd believe a thing like that," he says. "I trust my wife, and Dan is my best friend. I know she'll come back."

The New Marquee Economics

Towards the end of the 50's, Dan Duryea worked primarily in television. He only made three films from 1958 to 1962. *Kathy O, Platinum High School* and *Six Black Horses* are a diverse lot: a domestic comedy, a military academy terror ride and a lyrical Western that still makes a stand as a pleasant anachronism.

Hollywood exposés tend to be dark shockers filled with terse comments on illusion, subservience, egotism, and blind ambition. The players are often repugnant characters, the antithesis of how they are perceived by an adoring public. *Kathy O* is an expose, but it is tame and without casualties. A moral lesson is played out but it is sugary and not mocking.

Kathy O'Roarke (Patty McCormick) is a cumbersome, pig-tailed child star. She is distraught and becomes involved in an unwitting kidnapping plot when she runs away from the studio and holes up with the family of Harry Johnson (Dan Duryea), a Hollywood press agent. It is family fun and a useful ethics lessons for eight-year-olds.

She is an attitudinal child star who irritates everyone who has to deal with her, whether it is her co-star, press agent, or guardian. We get the impression that she is spoiled and hard to handle but by the end of the film we find out that she is stressed out because she is exploited by her surrogate stage mother Aunt Harriet (Mary Jane Croft) and the profit-minded studio.

The drama unfolds at the expense of Harry Johnson. It begins when he tells the child star to pour on the charm for Celeste Saunders (Jan Sterling), a journalist who is writing a profile of the girl for her magazine. It does not help matters that the writer is Duryea's ex-wife, who develops a rapport with the actress after they spend a day on a chartered fishing boat.

Kathy O and the writer realize that they fill the void in each other's lives and begin to resent how showbiz politics are keeping them apart. Accordingly, they need each other to survive: the star needs favorable publicity and the writer needs interesting subjects. Both are being manipulated by the studio for the cause of a favorable public profile.

It all comes to a boil when Kathy O decides to run away. Harry spots her on the street and squires her to his home, promising to contact Celeste, with whom the girl wants to live. She is distrustful of Harry because he represents studio politics. He is also leery of her because she is an accomplished actress who is rarely sincere. The common ground is Harry's home life, which is a fascinating and enjoyable mystery to Kathy O.

Harry's wife Helen (Mary Fickett) and their two sons are the ones who break the plastic bubble that the child star lives in. All it takes is a home-cooked dinner, pillow fights, and sage advice from mom to turn Kathy O into an average American kid. The only trouble is that Kathy O's disappearance is being treated like a kidnapping by the studio, police, and the news.

The situation is tenuous for Harry because he has to act normal with his co-workers, be level-headed with the police and rational with his wife. His resolution is to sneak the girl onto the studio lot at night and let the guards discover her. It is a successful plan until she is returned to her aunt and the intruding reporter begins to unravel the scheme.

All ends well, with Kathy O beaming for the camera.

Kathy O is *Father Knows Best* meets a heavily-censored *Bad Seed*. In fact, the deadening pace of the movie could have benefited from Kathy O striking out at the adults in a psychotic frenzy. There are no peaks and valleys to the movie so the viewer does not feel compelled about the plot or characters.

Harry Johnson (Dan Duryea) is a Hollywood press agent who explains an ad campaign to the unappreciative Kathy O'Roarke (Patty McCormick). 1958, Universal Pictures Company, Inc.

The sub-plot between revived feelings with the reporter and his ex-wife and how it affects his present marriage is more interesting than Kathy O's dilemma. Because of this tangent, Helen Johnson becomes the most interesting character in the movie.

She has a good life in Hollywood with a husband who has a seemingly glamorous occupation and two sons whom she adores. The stability of her world is threatened by the arrival of Sterling, who is still single and somewhat unhappy.

It's not just their time spent together because of Kathy O that upsets Helen; it is Celeste Saunders' job offer to her husband to work on her magazine in New York that pushes her buttons. Despite the threat to her home, Helen seeks a solution that will bring happiness to Kathy O and exonerate her husband of any wrongdoing.

Dan Duryea does not have much to do in *Kathy O*. He is nervous and flustered most of the time, having the manic energy of a pinball in

Lt. Chavez (Ainslie Pryor) suspects Harry Johnson (Dan Duryea) of having something to do with the child star's disappearance and wife Helen (Mary Frickett) hopes the cop does not find out that they are providing sanctuary for the weary star. 1958, Universal Pictures Company, Inc.

motion. He is perceived as part of the problem, another studio flack who looks at Kathy O as little more than studio property. It is his wife who changes his perspective and the incentives to change are the possible loss of his job and impending kidnapping charges.

Kathy O hates him from the start because he represents the studio's tyrannical control over her life. He only gets her seal of approval because he provides her with a window of opportunity when she is introduced to the wonderful world of his intimates, which not only includes his family but Celeste Saunders, as well.

In 1958, Dan Duryea had signed a contract to star with William Bishop in the Malvin Wald-produced *Seven is for Sinners*. The press releases stressed the novelty of teen singing sensation Jimmie Rodgers getting 1% of the profits for singing the title tune. There was nothing beyond the press release; another deal gone sour in Hollywood.

In 1960, Dan Duryea was offered a straw hat tour in *The Little Foxes*. It had been eighteen years since he came to Hollywood to film the play for Sam Goldwyn. Now, he was primarily a television actor who occasionally made a picture. It was not for lack of work or any missed opportunities. Duryea chose to make the television rounds because that was where the work was. He had an open-ended contract so he would work on the programs from Universal's television division, Revue. For instance, in 1960 he starred in *Mystery at Malibu*, a pilot for a Revue series about a newspaperman. His name was Barnaby Hooke and he was a crusader for justice.

It had been two years since he made a movie and that was *Kathy O*. It was time to return to the big screen. Dan Duryea's next movie would make him part of the cult universe of Albert J. Zugsmith.

Platinum High School is another study in terror through intimidation. This time, the setting is a military academy on a remote island called Saber Island. The boss is a retired Marine officer named Major Redfern Kelly (Dan Duryea), and his henchmen are two ex-Marines who commandeer a squadron of maladjusted teenage misfits.

Major Kelly is a cool, calculating, and malicious headmaster whose motivation is greed. His academy is a high-priced reform school for rich juvenile delinquents. Twenty-four students at an annual tuition of $15,000 a year are enough to make him cover up a lethal hazing.

Part of the curriculum is intimidating the locals, including a handful of civilians who run businesses on the island where the academy is situated. Saber Island may as well be Hell because it is an isle of the damned. Redemption comes in the form of Steven Conway (Mickey Rooney).

Maj. Redfern Kelly (Dan Duryea) is the power hungry headmaster of *Platinum High School*. 1961, Cinema Associates, Inc.

Conway is the father of a boy who died under suspicious circumstances at the military academy. The official explanation of the younger Conway's death is that it was due to his falling off a dormitory roof. Conway visits the school to get some insight and answers as to his son's untimely death. Evasive answers and hostile cynicism are what the father receives, and it's enough to embroil him in a life-and-death struggle with the commander of the military academy.

In *Platinum High School*, the Major is the mania-driven headmaster at a boys' academy where everyone, from the staff to the distaff boating people, is cowered into silence. It all unravels when the boy's father comes to investigate his son's death. Major Kelly oversees a cover-up of the death of Conway's son.

His students are a brown-shirt committee who protect their fearless leader. The main heavy is Hank Marlow (Richard Jaeckal), who supervises a group of thugs that includes Conway Twitty, Jimmy Boyd, and Harold Lloyd, Jr. The odd man out is "Crip" Hastings (Warren Berlinger), the object of ridicule, abuse, and ostracism.

Hastings is befriended by Conway. Together, Conway and Crip crack the academy's criminal code. Along the way, Conway has to pass several macho rites of passage to broach the mystery that smells of murder. It does not matter to him because he is a Marine. He first shows this in a bayonet confrontation with a henchman in Joe Nesbit's (Elisha Cook) luncheonette.

He also has to deal with Jennifer Evans (Terry Moore), the Major's torrid secretary, information gatherer, and compliant slave. She wavers in her loyalty as the facts bear against her boss/lover. Evans pays the price of betrayal when she swims with a different kind of shark in the film's final showdown.

One of Conway's strange allies is Lorinda Nibley (Yvette Mimieux), a mute country girl with the classic Daisy Mae look: blonde pigtails, revealing blouse, cut-off off jeans and bare feet. She runs the bait shop with her pa, a fat, bearded, dim-witted slob. It is a strange image of mute beauty and dumb beast, a perverse variation of the backwoods, country-bumpkin style of living.

She and her father suffer intimidation from the brown-shirts, who are led by Richard Jaeckal and Christopher Dark at their sinister best as cadets/teachers who inflict pain to ensure dedication to the school code. The code is broken in a final battle at sea between Conway and the Major in a yacht-versus-motorboat demolition race that nets the officer his *Gotterdammerung* chops.

Mickey Rooney and Dan Duryea play well off each other. They are two pros making the most of their pulp roles. Each character has the tenacious attitude earned by their respective stints in the Marine Corps. However, they are complete opposites not only in stature and demeanor, but in moral character, too. Each man is determined to get what he wants, but since this is impossible, confrontation means victory for one and total ruination of the other.

Major Kelly (Dan Duryea), Steven Conway (Mickey Rooney) and Jennifer Evans (Terry Moore) enjoy a tense lunch with the academy faculty. 1961, Cinema Associates, Inc.

Warren Berlinger plays Crip Hastings, the witness to Conway's son's death by baseball bat in a hazing gone bad. He is threatened by a trio of thugs who only befriend him when Conway comes to the island. They turn on him again when they suspect that he is aiding the murder victim's father in bringing them to justice. His reward is being adopted by Conway at the end of the movie.

Elisha Cook, Jr. has a small role as the proprietor of a luncheonette that is a hangout for the major and his goon squad. It is a change of pace for Cook to be cowered into silence. Usually, he played the macabre creep who did the intimidating; now, he gets a taste of his own medicine.

Terry Moore and Yvette Mimieux play the only two women on the island. They, too, are opposites. Moore plays a school teacher whose reason for staying is a higher-than-average salary at her teaching position. She winds up as the major's secretary and scheming ally. Yvette Mimieux is the abused blonde beauty. In one scene, the sergeant tells the major that it would be wise to get her off the island. He cites that the recruits are tense enough as it is. She only turns them into tomcats sitting on a fence.

The major replies that "They're being trained for manhood. Where there's manhood, there's women."

This becomes evident when Conway stops two recruits from molesting her. She returns the favor by aiding him in his one-man assault on the major and his crooked recruits.

Van Alexander's military march theme music was the reverse of his big-band rock-and-roll soundtracks, but it still had the cadence of a juvenile delinquent's score. This film still had the requisite quota of sex and violence, even though drill and ceremony replaced stompin' the boards.

Some examples of the Zugsmith touch are the ambiguous death of a cadet, a one-on-one bayonet confrontation between Rooney and an officer, Daisy Mae's assault during her heroic scene at the end of the film, the secretary's swimming with the shark scene, and Duryea's explosive histrionics as he sails into the sunset. In this movie, murder and intimidation are the choice of decision makers as has always been the case with Zugsmith's sleaziest productions.

Harry Nesbit (Elisha Cook, Jr.) is an intimidated luncheonette owner who watches Vince Perley (Christopher Dark) combat ex-Marine Steve Conway (Mickey Rooney). 1961, Cinema Associates, Inc.

In 1962, Dan Duryea had the opportunity to add a third movie to his Audey Murphy collaborations. In *Six Black Horses*, Ben Lane (Audie Murphy) and Frank Jesse (Dan Duryea) trade away pieces of their destinies when they cross paths on a fateful day in the desert. Jesse prevents a band of mustangers from lynching Lane, whom they mistake for a horse thief. They ride into town and are later offered a dangerous job that will be a way for them to abandon their dreadful pasts and start fresh lives… if they survive the mission.

Ben Lane (Audie Murphey) and Frank Jesse (Dan Duryea) are two diverse personalities whose destinies cross paths in *Six Black Horses*. 1962, Universal Pictures Company, Inc.

Ben Lane can stop being a cow-poking drifter when he buys a spread to call his own. Frank Jesse can stop killing for a living when he hangs up his gun belt and finds a place to spread out with a woman to keep him warm. All they have to do is to escort Kelly (Joan O'Brien), a wealthy enigmatic woman, across Indian Territory to reunite her with her husband.

Kelly is bitter and angry, which has made her a reckless benefactor. The deal she makes with Lane and Jesse is fraught with danger and there is no guarantee that it won't be a suicide pact with three scalps hanging on a Coyotero lance.

Kelly may have persuaded the men to escort her to DelCobray so she could be reunited with her husband, but it is really a ruse to kill Jesse. She holds him responsible for murdering her greenhorn husband in a gunfight. She wants Frank Jesse to be killed on the desert trek.

Along the way they are stalked by hostile Indians and confronted by a gang of ornery scalp-hunting pale faces. There is a gun fight at a mission and face-to-face encounters with angry Coyoteros. The men turn on each other when the stakes change because of Kelly's hidden intentions.

The real terms of Kelly's deal become irrelevant because killing Frank Jesse is not an option. Lane knows that he and Jesse have been deceived, but it does not matter to him because he has found someone to share his life with. Ben and Frank are no longer partners when Ben tries to call the deal off. He wants to find a safe passage for Kelly, but Jesse is intent on escorting her to the original destination and collecting his fee. This leads to a final showdown and a new beginning for Ben Lane and Kelly.

Audie Murphy re-channels his man-of-few-words cowpoke for Ben Lane. He tames a wild buck, saves a dog from a crooked fight, calls an Indian's bluff, and is quick on the draw when his life depends on it. It is Lane who becomes unhinged when he falls in love with Kelly.

Joan O'Brien is the stunning if inscrutable beauty that has a tantalizing mission for them. Frank Jesse deflates her bravado when he shows her that they are two of a kind. She slept with men for money during bleak times and he killed for money as a matter of course. He didn't remember the faces of the men he killed and he asks Kelly if she could remember the faces of the men she slept with.

Her silence is a negative and Jesse tells her that is the reason that she is no better than him because "that's how we made our way." Kelly is manipulative and self-hating in the end. It takes a sincere cowpoke to melt her heart and the betrayal of his friend to turn it into love.

Ben Lane (Audie Murphy) and his best friend share a meal while Frank Jesse (Dan Duryea) wishes he can share Charlita's dance moves. 1962, Universal Pictures Company, Inc.

Dan Duryea's eloquent portrayal of an aging gunslinger at the end of his line prevents the movie from being a routine Western. Duryea had the Western heavy down pat by now, but he still found a way to create a unique character with nuances that created a gray area out of stark good and evil.

In *Six Black Horses*, Frank Jesse is a seasoned gunslinger, one who lives by collecting silver for shootings that he deals with in escapes into whiskey terrain. Frank Jesse is a blend of noble and venal traits. He has an iron-clad rule to never do an honest day's work unless it is absolutely necessary. Jesse became a hired killer by choice, not chance. It was an easy way to earn money, something that is not as clean-cut as it seems because of his conscience. He drinks away much of his pay trying to forget the men he has killed. Still, he swears by the profession as evidenced when he tries to persuade Ben Lane to earn a living by the gun.

Jesse is a hired gun with a sense of righteousness that does him no good in the end. Jesse saves the life that will take his and his road to riches

Frank Jesse (Dan Duryea) takes great amusement in telling Kelly (Joan O'Brien) that they are two of a kind although Ben Lane (Audie Murphy) disagrees. 1962, Universal Pictures Company, Inc.

is mined by a golden-haired assassin whom he calls Ma'am. He hedges his bets on mortality and delivers an elegant treatise on the art of dying. It includes how a man ought to have a proper funeral procession with six black horses drawing a black, spangled hearse. It is something that he gets in the long run and it is a powerful epitaph to his unique character.

Harry Keller's direction is adequate and Burt Kennedy has written a script full of great lines, even if he has pilfered his script for *Ride Lonesome*. George Wallace (Commander Cody) is the ill-fated leader of a pack of scalp hunters, and Charlita still has her fire in a small role as a cantina dancer.

The Golden Age of TV Westerns

Wagon Train

There was hardly a time when Westerns were not the boon of kiddie matinees and serial buffs. The Westerns' movie heyday was during the 1930's and 1940's. The Westerns popularity spilled over into radio and the pulps so it was only natural that the adolescent rite of passage should adapt and dominate television in the 50's and early 60's. The Hollywood version of how the West was won has produced a staggering saga even if most of it was myth and legend. The mania that once consumed the kids of the Depression and World War II years continued during the nuclear age of the 50's. Television Westerns were a gold mine and they ranged from cheap video versions of dime store thrillers to well-written and acted dramas.

If the old West could be recorded on newsreels and picture books, then edited for a mass consumptive mentality, then *Wagon Train* would be the chronicle of that cataclysmic era. A new frontier was being carved out of an old one and new meanings were given to the old world by the heroes and villains from both sides of the realm. There are many characters and stories in the Western saga.

Wagon Train lasted nine seasons and went through many changes. It started as a half-hour show that was expanded to seventy minutes before turning to color for a season. The show also shifted from ABC to NBC. *Wagon Train* also had two wagon masters: Ward Bond and John McIntire. Bond played Maj. Adams, a gruff and paunchy Civil War vet who was tougher than the terrain and the adversaries that challenged his payload of greenhorns each week. McIntire took over the reins after Bond died in 1961. He played Major Christopher Hale, another Civil War officer, whose even-handed temper was tempered by Biblical wisdom.

Robert Horton played Flint McCullough, the head scout during the Ward Bond years. Terry McGrath moved up in rank and created a space for Scott (Denny) Miller as Duke Shannon. The only original member of the cast who made it to the last Western trek was Frank McGrath as Charlie, the irascible cook and all-around-trooper.

The strength of *Wagon Train* lay in the stories, situations and characters the regulars encountered each week. The stories complimented the week's star, usually someone who had star power in the old Hollywood. Dan Duryea appeared in seven episodes; two with Ward Bond and five with John McIntire as the wagon master. All of Duryea's guest turns on the show were from the black and white era.

The first time the wagon train encounters him is as the lone rider on the open prairie who fires his rifle in the air. That is how *The Cliff Grundy Story* begins. Thinking that it is a distress signal, Clint McCullough rushes to the stranger's aid only to find out that the shot was the man's way of getting the wagon train's attention. Stranger still is finding out that the eccentric rider is Flint's old buddy, Cliff Grundy.

If ever there was a good-natured teller of tall tales that glorified his own myth, it was Cliff Grundy. After he joins the train and they set up camp, his braggadocio entertains the men, especially his claim of owning a gold mine. Major Adams likes to rib Grundy and Charlie; the cook eggs him on. Cliff Grundy's tall tales amuse everyone except Craig Manson (Russell Johnson), a morose black clad traveler who feigns respect for Grundy but is inwardly greedy for his wealth.

The next morning, the major decides that a small party should go on a buffalo hunt to shore up provisions. When Grundy is seriously injured in a stampede Maj. Adams advises McCullough to stay with his dying friend. He can catch up to the train after he buries Grundy. Manson offers to stay with the scout to tend to the injured man. It is merely a ruse to endear himself to the dying man and become his heir.

Every time McCullough is out of bounds Manson tries to get Grundy to reveal the whereabouts of the gold mine. He is even so brazen as to tell Grundy that the mine is useless to him and might as well benefit someone else. McCullough discovers Manson trying to sweat his old friend and they fight. The scout is knocked unconscious and Manson tips over the water barrel and takes off, leaving the men to die in the wilderness.

Cliff Grundy is resilient and refuses to die. He recovers from his wounds and gains his strength only to find himself seriously injured in a

Cliff Grundy is Dan Duryea's most upbeat character. A part of his legend is told in *The Cliff Grundy Story*. 1957, Revue Studios, Universal Television.

fight with a marauding bear. He grappled with the beast after it attacked him. He and McCullough overcame the bear but not without Gundy suffering from serious lacerations.

His super-human strength keeps him alive but the ill effects of no water and food almost turn him and Flint into a meal for the vultures. A desert rainfall revives them and they make it to town. Grundy and McCullough enter the local saloon and inquire about Manson, claiming that he is a friend who wandered off by himself in the desert. The bartender admonishes them for being foolish enough to let their friend wander off alone in Indian territory. He points to the backroom, where they find Manson dead, an arrow in his back.

Before they part ways, Grundy and McCullough share a drink and the teller of tall tales reveals that his gold mine is really a wealthy widow waiting for him out West. The men part company and McCullough returns to the wagon train. Maj. Adams scolds him for the length of his absence, not realizing that the wagon train journey has just become another story added to the saga of Cliff Grundy.

The episode is good-natured and incorporates drama and suspense in the action. The buffalo stampede and bear attack are handled well. So is Russell Johnson's portrayal of the greedy Samaritan. He is defeated by his own smallness, which he reveals through his underhanded means to steal Grundy's secret.

Cliff Grundy is Dan Duryea's most cheerful role. Grundy is a good-natured braggart who is distinctive because there is no embroidery to his tall tales. They are all true and that is what makes him a Western legend, one that only Flint McCullough and the four elements know about. Proof of the episode's optimistic tone is its Christmas broadcast date.

Evidently, Cliff Grundy never managed to marry his gold mine because he was back for a brief appearance in *The Sacramento Story*. It is Robert Horton's farewell to *Wagon Train* so a couple of characters show up from past shows to give the episode an extra jolt. At one point of the adventure, Cliff Grundy saves Flint McCullough from being shanghaied to China to be sold as a slave.

The man who was intent on retiring rich was working as a deck hand on a ship when he noticed two scalawags dragging his unconscious friend to a cabin. That's when he intervened and a full-blown fight breaks out. Grundy rescues his friend after he ran afoul of a swindler's henchmen. McCullough was tracking down a swamp salesman posing as a realtor. He sold a dying member of the wagon train worthless land and Flint had to take him to a lush alternative so he could believe that he finally had something of value to leave to his daughter.

In his next *Wagon Train* appearance, Dan Duryea gets to play a man whose sense of guilt is compounded by a false identity. His mind is trapped into the Limbo of amnesia but his conscience insists that he has committed a grave crime. A diary found at the site of a wagon train calamity suggests that he is a parasitic murderer who made sure that he was the lone survivor in *The Last Man*.

The wagon train is threatened by rapidly falling temperatures that predict snow. Maj. Adams sends Flint McCullough out to scout for a quicker passage to their destination. His search leads him to the grim remains of a wagon train. That is when he is confronted by a wild man who attacks him for invading his territory. The last man is a cagey mountain man, a bearded coot driven insane by isolation. He is the only survivor of a stranded wagon train decimated by a cruel winter. Scruffy, bearded and shaggy, he is a feral man unaware of his true identity. It takes the fear of the travelers to give him a name that begs for lynching.

Maj. Adams and Flint search the camp for other survivors but all they find is a grim diary by a man named Danton. It is a moribund account of how he staved off starvation and death by stealing rations and taking advantage of the weaker members of the train. The travelers assume that the mountain man is Danton and he accepts the identity, not knowing that it will create a lynch mob mentality. The travelers want frontier justice but are kept in check by the major and his scout. It is a good thing that their efforts were circumvented because the stranger turns out to be the man who killed Danton.

Duryea goes through a range of primal emotions before he becomes aware of the circumstances of his final fight with his conscience. He is one of three survivors who are about to shorten the ranks through attrition. He is cagey and vicious as the lone survivor whose territory has been trespassed upon. There is a taming of the senses after the wagon train has christened him the name of the notorious scourge of the doomed wagon train. He reverts to introspection when he reveals his murder of Danton. Duryea describes the horrible thing that he has done and it is not the betrayal of his fellow travelers. It is as if he was making a death bed confession that absolves the settlers' guilty intentions of executing him.

Dan Duryea went from playing an unhinged feral man caught between natural savagery and domesticated compliance to a prairie gentleman whose predatory nature is more barbaric than anything naturally savage.

Joshua Gilliam becomes the newest addition to the wagon train when Bill and Duke find him sprawled on his back in a ravine. He was horsewhipped and left to die in the wilderness when the scouts spot him. The stranger is brought back to camp where he is nursed and asked questions about his wounds. His story is that he is a school teacher who was punished by a father and his friends for disciplining the man's affluent child with a switch. His even-tempered and forgiving attitude impresses

Joshua Gilliam is an Ivy League wit whose hypnotic charm envelops an heiress' good fortune until her mother breaks his spell with a hysterical plea for deliverance. 1960, Revue Studios, Universal Television.

the travelers, especially Major Adams, who asks Gilliam if he would like to aid Miss Halstead with teaching the children as a way of paying for his room and board.

The new teacher has a winning way with the children. His soft-spoken manner is peppered with positive aphorisms and he charms the kids with his magic tricks. He also charms Miss Halstead with his upright manner and valiant philosophy.

Actually, he is a liar and deception is the guiding rule to his life. He is really a sharpie with an eye on Miss Halstead's inheritance of 5,000 acres of land. His only impediment is Miss Halstead's mother, a dour overprotective woman who suspects that any man who shows an interest in her daughter is a gold digger.

Things come to a head between Gilliam and the mother when he sees him in intimate conversation with her daughter. He was using his watch as a pendulum to hypnotize the woman. It was the soothing speech patterns and intense glare that alerted the mother to imminent danger. His solution to the problem is to use his young students to drive Mrs. Halstead out of her mind. His method is to teach them about the 1691 Salem witch trials.

Joshua Gilliam excels at enrapturing his students with his enthralling lessons. He has a field day explaining the characteristics of witchery to the children. Being coy and clever, he uses descriptions that fit the old lady to a tee. This includes having bellicose attitudes against children, using a broom and a cauldron plus having stringy hair and a haggard expression. The children put it together when she uses her broom to chase them away from her wagon or when they see her using a paddle to stir the clothes in a cauldron of boiling water.

It is natural for the children to tease and bully the woman and it turns her into a nervous wreck. Her behavior becomes a problem when she is ostracized by the other travelers for being eccentric. It does not help her disposition when Joshua Gilliam uses a little hypnosis to drive the old woman over the edge. Gilliam also plays both sides against the middle when he gives periodic reports about her deteriorating mental state to Maj. Adams.

Hypnotic suggestion impels her to seek a doctor's assistance in the nearest town, which happens to be a ghost town. That is where Joshua Gilliam intends to settle their dispute once and for all. His treachery backfires when he falls into an abandoned shaft that has been flooded. He can't swim and spends his last moments begging Mrs. Halstead to save him. The confused woman is rescued by the scouts who find Gilliam's body in the shaft. The gold watch finally ran out of time for its owner. The wagon train moves on.

Time will eventually run out for those who do not heed the signs! Or so says Samuel Bleymeir, a belligerent traveler who dominates a sheltered daughter. When the rains turn into a raging storm, a splinter group of the wagon train decides to take a shortcut through Sioux burial grounds. That may have its own consequences but what about nature's signs?

Bleymier is a man bent out of shape by anger and despair at not being taken seriously. He became embittered when his wife was struck and killed by a bolt of lightning. He has learned to fight the elements by reading nature's signs and omens. It has turned him into the wagon train's Farmer's Almanac, a soothsayer that serves as the equivalent of the fire and brimstone preacher. He renders vindictive conclusions based on cloud formations, bird flights and colors in the sky.

He and his daughter Belle are part of the wagon train's splinter group headed by Flint McCullough. Bleymier reads the sky and warns McCullough that their trail is doomed. Many reject him as an angry and overprotective father. His daughter, Belle, is a nature sprite and attempts

Samuel Bleymeir is a naturalist who heeds nature's signs as a way of exacting revenge against his antagonists. 1960, Revue Studios, Universal Television.

to control her cause his collapse. e commands her to stay in the wagon and accuses her of "flaunting yourself before men…like a scarlet woman."

A storm hampers the trail and makes using the usual route unwise. They have to travel through Sioux territory and this tactic gains the approval of the wagon train with the exception of Bleymeir. He warns them that no good will come of it but no one heeds his warnings. They consider him a bellicose crackpot.

Bleymeir takes his feud with nature personally. After his warnings are blown off, he confronts the brewing tempest and declares, "You won't whip me this time. I know all of your tricks and how to turn every one of them against you. You ain't never gonna beat me down again."

Thunder and lightning heed his message and accept his challenge. The elements curse his journey by breaking a wheel on his wagon. Being left behind with a scout to replace the wheel leads Bleymeir on an ill-fated adventure that ends with a face-to-face encounter with a twister. Mr. Bleymeir invents the twist and winds up a lifeless mannequin heeding the signs.

In his next *Wagon Train* role, Dan Duryea may not wind up entangled in an uprooted tree but he gets to breathe in the wagon train prison wagon. He is arrested for *The Wagon Train Mutiny*, a powerful episode that belongs to Jane Wyman who all but steals the show with her sensitive and far-reaching performance.

Settlers and immigrants caught up in the Western migration make the transition from greenhorns to seasoned travelers when rampaging Commancheros put the wagon train on alert to possible attack. The scouts see the renegades decimating the smaller train that preceded their train.

Wagon Master Hale believes they are next because of the testimony of a wounded commanchero boy, the only survivor of the wagon train's advance party raid on the outlaws. The wagon train believes that they boy is lying because they consider him a savage unable to tell the truth. Maj. Hale does not take a chance and gathers a small invasion force to kill the commancheros in their sleep. This will weaken the marauders when the returning half of the band come back to a dissipated ambush squad.

It is a risk either way. Hale believes the boy but Bill does not; neither do most of the members of the wagon train. The opposition does not matter to Hale. He has a responsibility that is backed up by the law so there is no hesitation on his hand when he demands a roster of men aged 18 to 40.

Hannah (Jane Wyman) does not want her son to go. He has just turned 18, but she still considers him a boy. Amos (Dan Duryea) steps in to tell Hale that there is no conclusive proof. It does not matter to Hale.

They have to make a preemptive strike. During the battle, the settlers listen to the gun fire. There is a rifle shot and Hannah screams. She felt the bullet that killed her boy.

The tension builds as the settlers try to give Hale the benefit of the doubt. The expeditionary force is victorious but not without casualties. The deaths of young sons and the fathers that tried to rescue them divide the wagon train in their opinion of retaliation by the second train of Commancheros.

The Wagon Train Mutiny boasts an exceptional performance by Jane Wyman and a sly turn by Dan Duryea as a malcontent stirring up a mutiny. 1962, Revue Studios, Universal Television.

Amos instigates a mutiny after there is no Commanchero raid on the third day. The insurgents are about to take over when they hear hoofbeats. It's the Calvary who have arrived to thank Hale and his men for decimating half of the Commanchero brigade. The soldiers are in pursuit of the second half. The Calvary officer commends Hale on his courage and salutes him. Peace is restored to the wagon train. Hannah has a change of heart and tends to the wounded while Amos is led away to the prison wagon.

Dan Duryea's part is relatively small but he is still a force to be reckoned with as he gets the settlers to back him up as the new wagon master. He looks pretty silly being led away under arrest when the smoke clears. It is Jane Wyman who gives the most spirited performance of the drama. The emotional changes she experiences vary from blind hatred to maternal devotion.

Dan Duryea's last appearance on *Wagon Train* was in *The Race Town Story*, made in 1964. Barnaby (Michael Burns), the newest addition to the show, has a rite of passage when he encounters the evils of the world in *The Race Town Story*. Barnaby, the young pup and Bill, the seasoned vet, are assigned to accompany two showgirls to Race Town, a tent city-carnival. Barnaby is enamored of the women and acts chivalrous towards them. It is Barnaby's infatuation with the two showgirls that gets him into trouble at Race Town, a mobile den of iniquity run by Sam Race, an affable jackal.

The night after they escort the women to Race Town, Barnaby accompanies Bill to the fare when the scout decides that he needs a night away from the wagons so he can blow off steam. The excitement of the sawdust boardwalk intoxicates the teenager. The barkers, their games and the dancing girls thrill him. Unfortunately, his honesty ruins many of the set-ups when he points out what he deems are honest mistakes.

Barnaby may be able to handle the responsibilities of trail-blazing like a man but he is still a boy at heart. He is righteous and caring, always looking out for the welfare of others. Race Town does not meet the women's standards. This is as true for the two showgirls that he and Bill Hawkins squire to Race Town as it is for the patrons he sees being cheated in Race Town. This honesty sets him up for a lesson in maturity and humiliation when he tangles with the denizens of Race Town.

No one belittles Sam Race and gets away with it. He has an iron-clad attitude about the business of making money. This is apparent when Annabelle wants to buy her way out of her contract. She thinks that $40.00 will get her off the hook and is flabbergasted when Digger tells her that she owes the company $300.00. She didn't figure on the costs of the costume and overhead.

The miners tie Barnaby's hands behind his back and send him on his way along with an unconscious Bill. Their horses carry them back to camp. It is a matter for Barnaby to avenge his humiliation. He is confronted by conscience and liability when he is humiliated in what was supposed to be a night of fun and games. Although Bill and Wagon Master Hale insist that he accept evil, the young man does not agree with him. He rides alone to square off with Sam Race. Bill follows him and backs up Barnaby when the teenager is jostled by the trinket seller and strong arm man. He dispatches them with ease and calls out Race.

Sam Race is a dirty fighter. When he is not distracting Bill with homey threats, he snaps a bull whip, swaps with a hatchet and a swings a lit torch for defense. It does him no good because the scout wears him down a flurry of punches and knockdowns. What is sad about Race's beating is that it does not diminish him in the eyes of his workers. Instead of using his defeat by cutting themselves free, they help him to his feet and go on with the business of Race Town.

Barnaby has avenged his humiliation by confronting his tormentor and calling him out face-to-face. He can ride back to the wagon train as a young man who stood his ground and fought for his principles. The irony of the ideal is that when Bill lends Barnaby the money to buy out Annabelle's contract she is amused by his offer. She has come to like Race Town and is pleased with the money she is making. Annabelle has decided to stay and wishes him good luck. Barnaby has had his rite of passage.

Dan Duryea hones his skill as a mobile town boss. It is funny because that is what he is even though Race Town is a traveling saloon and carnival. He has no set boundaries and the prairie is his domain. It is a place where miners and cowboys blow off steam and the air of cruelty only aids their need for satisfaction. They relinquish everything and are thrilled by the debauchery.

His smile is a lure for willing victims and desperate job opportunists. His business has a fly paper quality to it because the workers and patrons can't free themselves from Race's terms of employment. Sam Race is a larcenous rascal with a perpetual smile and an endless line of compliments. He will look you in the eye and compliment you while sizing you up for one of his humiliating schemes. He is not shy about his brusque behavior. It is something that he is proud of because it is strengthened by the fear it has instilled in his workers. They all worship him and feed off of his evil. It gives them strength. They return the favor by surrendering their souls to him.

Like most tyrants, Sam Race provides security and comfort for society's outcasts. He gives them a home and, in return, they give him the backup that he needs to stave off any outsiders' challenges to their boss' authority. He runs a crooked business and he is proud of it. He affirms his corruption by adamantly denying its existence. Sam Race insists that he runs a clean business. If anyone catches a card dealer cheater, he is awarded one hundred dollars.

The traveling con man has a clear conscience because no one forces his customers to patronize his business. They come of their own free will, surrendering their humanity for a night of bawdy entertainment, even if it means that they lose their hard-earned pay. They don't mind because it fills their emptiness.

Sam Race is the carnival barker who hit pay dirt with a traveling troupe of his own. His set up is unique because it is a portable Western town. That is why he calls his camp Race Town. He is phony to a tee and his charm is really bravado thrown in your face.

He does not hesitate to break bones or whip people into shape when he has to. Nobody interferes with his demonstration of principles. The only ayes are the cries of the defeated. In Race Town, people gamble on corruption, hoping to get more than they give out. Sam Race is their king.

Laramie, Rawhide and Bonanza

Dan Duryea guest starred on *Laramie* for three episodes and played memorable characters who believed in their own sense of justice. Bud Carlin, Luke Gregg and John Sanford are three different studies in honor that run counter to the rule of law. Bud Carlin is a notorious outlaw who uses intimidation to get things done. He aims to cuckold the judge who sent two of his gang to the gallows and plans to do the same with a third cohort. Luke Gregg knows his way around a ranch but he has all of the earmarks of a gunslinger. Is it just part of his history or is he an assassin sent to Laramie to lay claim to Slim and the sheriff for their vigilante days? Ben Sanford aims to avenge his son's murder by overruling the court's decision to sentence his killer to prison. He and his two sons aim to lynch the prisoner. All of the stories involve a wish to swap a stagecoach passenger for personal vendettas. Each scenario has the regulars being held hostage at the stage stop.

Stage Stop was the show's premiere episode and establishes the setup to *Laramie*, an engaging Western that eventually became a showcase for co-star Robert Fuller. John Smith gets star billing and gives an excellent reading as Slim Sherman. He inherited a ranch and a stage stop when his parents died. Slim splits the chores with his younger brother Andy (Robert Crawford) and an old pal, Jonesy (Hoagy Carmichael).

The trio is augmented by the addition of the wistful stranger, Jess Harper (Robert Harper). Jess is passing through Slim's territory and the two clash over squatter's rights. Andy takes a shine to the stranger and Jonesy keeps his distance. It's not until the stranger aids them in their struggle against Carlin that he earns their respect and a spot on the show.

Bud Carlin begins his plan when he forces a typesetter to reset the type to a story dictated by Coleman. It is a bold promise to shoot up the town to liberate one of his imprisoned men. He uses psychology to instill fear and give him leverage in what most people think is a jailbreak attempt. Even the law is fearful of tangling with Carlin.

His gang has grown smaller through attrition. Two men were hanged and a third is the one to be transported for trial. The law may suspect violence but Carlin's scheme is to impersonate the judge and peacefully move the prisoner himself. Peace and tranquility are the furthest things from Slim and Jess' minds when Carlin and two of his goons show up at the stage stop. It is where they plan to make the first switch: Carlin for Judge Thomas A. Wilkens (Everett Sloane).

Judge Wilkens is the man who sentenced Carlin's men to death and will preside over the next trial. Coleman does not have any intention of physically harming the judge. He will humiliate the man and take away his dignity before stealing his identity.

The gang leader has a cavalier attitude towards violence. It is something that amuses him because he is a self-described watcher. Carlin's muscle is Clint (Gordon Jones), a gun-toting slob. It is Clint's job to spread the pain and keep order. That includes keeping everyone at the stage stop in his cross-hairs while enjoying stew heavy on the pepper. Carlin also enjoys his pie. He plots and counts the minutes while enjoying his pastry.

He also instigates a sadistic beating of Slim by Jess. Carlin wants to see the effects of the perfect punch on Slim's jaw. It is a way to pass the time until the stage arrives. Jess will find out for himself. Jones shows him his idea of the perfect punch.

What follows is a scene that shows the Duryea touch of using charm as a disarming maneuver to strip someone of every ounce of dignity. The travel-weary judge arrives and is greeted by Carlin, who politely invites him in for a cup of coffee. Carlin introduces himself and lets the indignant judge give a little speech about justice and the validity of capital punishment. The judge maintains that he will not be bribed or coerced into throwing the case and killing him would not be a viable option because there are other judges to preside over the case.

That is when Carlin makes the judge eat his words. He commands the judge to remove his coat. It takes him three attempts to make the judge do so. The first order was met with righteous resistance. The second request got more blather that was cut in half by full-lunged command and a shove to the floor. The pliant judge surrendered his top hat and coat. Carlin was still not satisfied with his appearance because his boots were dirty. It was the judge's duty to shine Carlin's boots. He had to do it on his knees. The judge spent the rest of the episode sitting at the table covering half his face with his hand and shamefully moaning, "I am a coward."

Carlin's plan to impersonate the judge and transport the prisoner to a new venue for trial worked but he can't make the final getaway because he is flanked on both sides by Slim and Jess. His gang is cut down and his life is spared but he gets a chance to play the perfect punch game with Slim,

Bud Carlin is a gang leader who looks out for his men when they are in trouble. Clint (Gordon Jones) is his bloodthirsty enforcer. 1959, Revue Studios.

only this time he is not the observer. Coward is the final epitaph for Carlin when he becomes a defenseless weakling without his gang. Slim and Jess play the beat down game with the dethroned gang leader, who is advised not to roll with the punches.

The Lone Riders are the land baron Ed Mckeever's (John Anderson) hired guns. They are in Laramie to settle the Adobe Wells Massacre. What makes this group of avengers unique is that the leader of the killers is the land baron. He has an unquenchable thirst for revenge against the vigilantes who defeated him at a standoff that curtailed his land grabbing agenda at Adobe Wells. All but two are dead and both of them live in Laramie. One is the sheriff and the other is Slim Sherman.

Luke Gregg (Dan Duryea) is the land baron's advance man. He makes himself known to Slim and Jess when they spot him fleeing a band of angry Indians. The Indians have him in the sites but turn tail and retreat when Slim and Jess fire on them. They meet the stranger and introductions are made with the stranger possessing a personable personality with a charming humor.

Slim and Andy welcome Luke into the fold but Jess is suspicious and rebuffs Luke's courtesy with his own brand of cold hostility. They square off with each other in an attempt to make each other see things differently. Odds are against Jess because Slim and Andy need Luke because he knows his way around the range. So what if he may have been a gunslinger in the past? That includes teaching Andy to draw from the hip, something that rattles Jess but gains Slim's approval because he believes that the boy is old enough to learn how to defend himself.

Luke Gregg is a charmer and he easily wins over Andy. Slim is impressed by his good humor and is pleased that Gregg is practical around a ranch. He had piqued Jess' interest when he asked Slim about the Adobe Wells Massacre. Not too many people knew the identities of the vigilantes hired to battle with McKeever. When pressed for an explanation of how he knew about something so obscure, Luke Gregg laughs it off and says that it's a legend where he comes from.

Where he comes from means only one thing to Jess: that McKeever sent Gregg. This suspicion does not sit well with Slim. He thinks that Jess is jealous of the inroads Luke has made with Andy. He greets the stranger with a friendly familiarity that creates a bond of trust. Jess has become the odd man out and he does not let this dampen his hunches about Luke Gregg. It's when the sheriff is shot that it becomes apparent that McKeever is behind this and that can only mean that Slim is next.

Luke Gregg turns out to be the odd man out when he stalls McKeever when the boss wants to exact his revenge. It does not take McKeever long to realize that Gregg is trying to weasel out of their deal. McKeever has tied up Jonesy and Andy to get them out of the way. He does the same with Gregg when he realizes that he is about to be betrayed. It's not the double cross that disturbs McKeever; he is incensed because Gregg has lost his edge. This is tantamount to cowardice.

McKeever and one of his men guard the stage stop and keep an eye on their captives while a couple of bushwackers wait for Sherman. It only hastens their deaths because Slim already knew there would be an ambush waiting for him after he found out that the sheriff had been shot. He did not die and told Slim that McKeever and his gang did it and they were gunning for Slim. While Slim is dealing with the bushwackers, Gregg is cutting himself lose with an Indian flint. He tries to fight Mckeever but is shot before the land baron, in turn, is shot. McKeever curses Slim with his dying breath and wishes that he had another chance to kill him but there won't be a next time.

Luke Gregg is an advance man hunting down the enemies of a land baron who felt he was wronged by them. He has a change of heart when he bonds with one of his marks, Slim Sherman. 1960, Revue Studios.

Luke Gregg is one of Duryea's conflicted bad men. He has been hired as a scout for McKeever. His stalling and resistance to the lone riders' wish to dispense their revenge delay the death sentence until help arrives. It's the change-of-heart scenario that makes him a martyr. Luke is redeemed and dies with a good reputation.

In *Mountain Men*, Ben Sanford, a proud mountain man, and his sons take over the stage stop just like Bud Carlin and Luke Gregg's boss did in their episodes. The contrast is the mountain man's motives and delivery. Sanford wants to ambush the stage and liberate the prisoner so he can hang him for the murder of his son.

Sanford is a simple mountain man with his own brand of justice. Calm and subdued, he is given to brief speeches about the natural way of living. He gets angry when he has to, like keeping his eldest son Carl in line. The young man lives to inflict harm and it is his impulsive bloodlust counteracted by his timid younger brother's sense of justice that derails the plan.

He disciplines his older son to teach him about a code of honor. Like the other characters who took over the stage, the Sanfords have an amazing sense of timing their capers. It is something that seems common to many of Duryea's portrayals. Losing control of the situation may destroy them but it was impeccable timing that made the jobs a smooth success. However, if outcome were factored into the equation, then not many of Duryea's masterminds ever grabbed the brass ring and lived to enjoy it.

So much is learned about Ben Sanford's personality in the scene where Daisy (Spring Byington) tries to reason with him about carrying out the hanging. She wants to soften him up and asks him about how it felt to be the first white settlers on the mountain. He waxes reminiscent when he speaks about felling the first log of the cabin that he was building for his 17-year-old bride and himself. He spoke of the wilderness back then and there is a romantic lilt to his memory.

He believes that there is nothing wrong with his intention of lynching the man who killed his son. It is the natural law that he has abided by since he became a mountain man. She begs to differ, quoting passages from the Bible but the only biblical justice Sanford is concerned with is the "eye for an eye" philosophy. One has to admire Ben Sanford's belief in frontier justice because it is part of the natural order of things.

Primal survival instincts delineate Carl from his father. He is an impulsive hot head who would solve most problems with shooting or fighting. It is his belief that the witnesses should be killed that causes dissension between father and son. That gives the timid one the time to take a shot at the stagecoach to scare it off.

Sanford is not defeated by his sons' betrayal so much as he is by changing times. Civilization, as unnatural as it may be, is too powerful to overcome. He may have avoided it for the rest of his life had he been able to escape to Canada. The same could not be said of his sons. They had to make their peace with the modern world. Of the two sons, only the timid sees the value of accepting change. He shows his father a different type of courage when he prevents the lynching.

Rawhide was a popular Western that starred Eric Fleming as trail boss Gil Favor and Clint Eastwood as Rowdy Yates, his ram rod. Paul Brinegar was Wishbone, the cook and jack-of-all-trades. Like *Wagon Train*, the show had a variety of plots and themes because of its episodic nature. The regulars faced an eclectic assortment of heroes and villains and among the villains three were played by Dan Duryea. He was Jardin, a laconic love scarred executioner, Cannon, an elemental prairie dog who is a wolf exterminator, and Brother William, a zealous religious fanatic whose words do kill.

Each man is just as unsavory as the other, with the distinction being their styles of killing. Bullets, poison and fire and brimstone achieve the same result. So does the ironic outcome of becoming the final victim of their own peculiar maniacal hatred. They are characters who leave a bad impression once they've stated their case, which includes bowing out in humiliation.

The executioner is a silent killer until circumstances reduce him to a jilted husband. The hunter's poison has warped his family and they turn on him after they kill a pack of marauding wolves that have been threatening the cattle drive. The lay preacher uses ironic biblical logic to pinpoint the guilt of others and sets himself up for judgment by his own measure.

Incident with an Executioner is a cautionary tale about conscience and the consequence of trying to avoid the inevitability of fate. Gil Favor and Rowdy Yates have become escorts for the survivors of a stagecoach mishap after it capsized at top speed trying to make a turn in the road. The drivers appeared to be fleeing an unknown assailant when they lost control and the accident happened. The passengers are a bank president from back east, a blacksmith who has inherited a farm and plans to become a man of the land, a woman who owns a popular saloon in Arizona, her new singer, a nervous spindly traveling salesman and a boastful gunslinger. They are shaken up except for the gunman. He is quick to assert the speed of his draw and casually challenges anyone to question his claim.

A lone rider marks their trail with his mystery ride. His black satchel holds the secret to his bloodlust and its mystery lends an aura to his mystique. It also impels the passengers to question their lives and suspect their fellow riders. The specter of death has put the motley group of passengers on the defensive as their consciences begin to ask why someone would hire a gunslinger to execute them.

The executioner is named Jardin and he is silent and pensive. He only speaks when it is necessary; otherwise, withering looks and deliberate hand gestures communicate his point. That is when he is invited into camp for dinner and can face his prey. When Jardin is not up front and personal, he is stalking the cattle drive from a distance. It could be an open prairie, the rim of a ridge or the top of a hill, Jardin conducts a silent vigil from his saddle and appears to be a silhouette on the horizon.

The gunslinger is the only passenger who claims not to be afraid of the shadowy stranger. Neither is Gil Favor when he invites the stalker into the camp for dinner. It is also a way to keep an eye on him and ascertain his target. The camera pans across the nervous stagecoach passengers

Jardin is a meditative executioner who expresses himself through silence and killing. 1959, Columbia Broadcasting System (CBS).

when Favor asks Jardin if he knows anybody. The executioner maintains his poker face and eats his dinner. The stagecoach passengers stare at him with fearful visages as the music is reduced to a steady pulse. Everyone has their Jardin moment.

The cowardly salesman would rather ride into the night, without concern for what lies out in front of him, than be near Jardin. The salesman recounts a frightening memory to Gil Favor before bolting camp on his horse.

"I saw a town once when Jardin rode in. It was like the wind stood still. People hid out. Stores closed, everybody afraid. And he came into town like a ghost. A man died. Shot by that death rider."

It was something the others would be saying about the bragging gunslinger a second later. The young gunslinger displays his fear through a boastful display of speed and dexterity when he shoots a bulls-eye through a coin dropped at will by the farmer. Not everyone is dazzled by his precision shooting and the gunslinger pays the price of empty boasting when he mistakes Jardin for a coin.

Favor returns to camp and asks Rowdy Yates if the killing was justified and he is told that the gunslinger drew first. Jardin slowly looks up from his plate, removes his gun from the holster and holds it up, all without taking his eyes off Favor.

He displays the same sardonic style when the saloon keeper is in hysterics and tries to bribe him into telling her who his target is. He lights his slim cigar and stares into space while she blubbers about promises of not revealing their secret. Jardin's answer is looking at her and walking away without saying a word. It was as if she wasn't there and he was listening to the wind.

Jardin acts the same way when Gil Favor prevents the banker from shooting him in the back. He, too, has a guilty conscience and believes that one of the victims of his failed financial institutions may have hired Jardin to kill him. The gun man was lighting his stogie when Favor grabs the banker's wrist, removes the gun and lectures him about honor on the open range and the cowardice of shooting a man in the back. It's just more whispering wind to Jardin's ears.

Even Rowdy Yates has his moment of doubt when he breaks away from the cattle drive to ride up in the hills to confront Jardin. In a one-on-one confrontation, a bold Rowdy Yates wants to know if it is him that he has been sent to kill. A cool-headed Jardin says that they should not send a boy to do a man's job before telling Rowdy that he is not the target.

He is laid back and self-assured because his languid manner is the method to the madness he instills in others. Jardin has led the riders to the site of his choice and when they set up camp he welcomes them and explains how and why he lured them into his trap. It was to reveal the great mystery that had been haunting everyone since they became aware of him. His mark is the farmer and it has something to do with what turned him into a hired killer. Now he wants to close the circle.

Gil Favor shows why he is the trail boss and steps in between Jardin and his mark. He performs what amounts to a voodoo ritual that divests Jardin of his mojo. He does not realize that he has lost his power because Gil Favor knows what was inside the black satchel. They are power charms to Jardin, something that reminds him of the horror that has warped his soul. His wife's photo, a child's rag doll and a lock of hair are the totems that neutralize the memory of familial betrayal. A wife and a child plus a secret lover set Jardin up in the business of killing. The charms are the mementoes of his first execution.

Jardin's future is used up when favor orders Yates to throw the charms into the camp fire, one memory at a time. A will to die is what Favor said was one requirement of a gun man. Jardin fulfils his fate by losing a draw with Favor, something owing more to the will to die than superior shooting skills of the trail boss.

In *Incident of the Wolves*, Cannon is a man numbed by the use of poison to kill varmints that plague the prairie. He is a wolf exterminator and his method is feeding them meat tainted with strychnine. Cannon is rude and uncouth, a slovenly blackheart with bad manners and a vile attitude. Clad in animal skins, he is more savage than the beasts he traps and kills.

Cannon rejects civility and invites disparagement with his depraved manners. He goes about his business and does not want to have anything to do with anyone except his family. He wants 50 head of cattle for exterminating the wolf pack. He plans to barter them with the Indians for beaver pelts. Cannon knows how to wheel and deal. It is easier to transport pelts than cattle and just as lucrative. It will be a good payoff for a grisly mission.

His is a brutal job and it takes a beast to get it done, from slaughtering a cow and boiling its pieces in strychnine treated water to tossing the meat to the ravenous wolves. Cannon blows on his duck waddle and a strange quacking like demented drakes excites the wolves and draws them toward the hunters and their poisoned meat.

Cannon is a varmint exterminator who is more bestial than the animals he kills. 1962, Columbia Broadcasting System (CBS).

Cannon and his sons may be effective in their dirty vocation but it is the odd dominance of Cannon over his family that unsettles the trail hands. He dominates his family with unquestioned filial devotion expected in return. His two sons assist him in his work and he jealously guards his daughter and stunts her growth into womanhood. He forbids his daughter to speak with anyone outside the family. He once bullwhipped a salesman for glancing at his daughter.

The family revolution erupts when his daughter bluffs her father into believing that Rowdy Yates read her mother's farewell letter to him. It sets him off in a rage and he threatens to shoot Yates. The ram rod has to ignore the rifle trained on him and moves away. Cannon takes aim and is shot by his daughter. It's the end of a nightmare for the kids.

Incident of the Prophecy is about the ominous death threat of Brother William, a self-styled preacher who holds Rowdy Yates and Rabbit responsible for the freak shooting death of his brother. The raucous trail blazers arrived in a sleepy town and started firing their guns at a brass bell in an abandoned schoolyard bell tower. They wanted to alert the town's bartender after they found the saloon closed. Brother William rushes out of the building, screaming "Sacrilege!" and pointing out that the building is a house of God.

His anger rises to righteous indignation when it appears that one of the bullets ricocheted off the bell and killed an innocent bystander—his brother. Brother William swears that they will suffer the wrath of God, who will make crooked things straight. He tells them that they are all guilty because no one interceded to stop the shooting. As they ride away he reminds them that death will be riding with them all of the way.

"Nobody can outrun death if he deserves it," he intones. "And you deserve to die."

The trail blazers take their grief back to camp. They believe the curse and this baffles Gil Favor, the trail boss. He can't believe that his men are so superstitious that they let the preacher's ranting upset their equilibrium. Rowdy and Rabbit are the ones affected most by the death sentence. Rowdy tries to quell his fear but Rabbit sincerely believes that he is destined to die on the trail. First, his horse loses control of its senses as if it had eaten loco weed. The colt throws Rabbit off the saddle and tries to stomp him to death. His next test is an intense encounter with a mountain lion.

What compounds the guilt is the ubiquitous Brother William. He ambles into camp one night playing his harmonica. The only thing he tells Gil Favor is that he is there to prevent his three brothers from killing Rowdy and Rabbit once they arrive. This confuses favor. He tells Brother William, "You tell my men that they will die before their time, now you tell me you aim to prevent it."

"No man can prevent it," replies Brother William in his bellicose style. "Therefore why should I let my brothers commit a pointless sin? The sin of revenge, leave that to the Lord."

Gil points out that the Christian God is one of love and mercy but Brother William will hear none of it: "When the Lord is angry, He wields a sword—they will be cut down."

The self-styled preacher borrows the stalking technique of Jardin and compounds his hex by following the cattle drive's trail. Brother William cuts a menacing figure sitting on his horse playing a harmonica. A long shot of him in dusky shadows portends death dressed like an undertaker. He sets up camp with them and plays melancholy harmonica music that has an un-

Brother William is a gunslinger turned vengeful preacher who incriminates himself according to the outline of his biblical law. 1963, Columbia Broadcasting System (CBS).

settling effect on the men. No matter where they go, they hear the sad music in the night, even when the camp is stalked by a wild cat. He tells them that the cat is death and that he has nothing to fear because it is not after him.

Brother William is tough with his act but it comes apart when his brothers arrive to avenge the death of their sibling. They have a low opinion of Brother William and enjoy ridiculing him as a retort to his biblical intonations. They remember when he was a gunslinger in the family tradition. His conversion also fails to impress them because it was caused by a guilty conscience.

Brother William harbors a guilty secret that is as overwhelming as his malediction. Like many judgmental fundamentalists, he is as guilty as those he accuses of being sinners. It is his inability to deal with his own iniquity that has turned Brother William into a holier-than-thou lay preacher. It is his way of wearing blinders to ease his conscience. Brother William, too, is guilty of accidental death by association. It happened when he and his brother, Judd, rode through a town wreaking havoc with wild gunshots. His brother's wanton shooting resulted in the shooting death of a woman. It happens that she was Rabbit's young wife. It also turns out that Rabbit took the trail blazers into town so he could shoot Judd while the others were watching the bell dance to the tune of gunfire.

Rabbit's death bed confession actually satisfies the brothers, who realize that he was justified in his revenge killing. They now turn their brother William's twisted logic against him. If the cow herds were guilty of Judd's shooting death then Brother William is responsible for Rabbit's wife's death. The validity of this logic settles in and Brother William's face turns from stone to abject shock and surprise. It is done slowly to build up to the final look of acknowledgement of self-incrimination. The effect is superbly pulled off by Dan Duryea in a masterful portrayal of a fall from grace.

Bonanza was once a Sunday night staple during a time when family viewing was common. The Sunday lineups included revered classics like *Lassie, Walt Disney Presents*, and *The Ed Sullivan Show*. Every television era has a handful of shows that have clicked with the public and the Cartwright clan from the Ponderosa was once a part of the American psyche.

Lorne Greene as patriarch Ben Cartwright sired his minions from three different wives. His sons were a mercurial lot. Adam (Pernell Roberts) was the firstborn, a serious and pensive man who dressed in black. Hoss (Dan Blocker) was a giant who would have been at home as a blacksmith. Instead a ten gallon hat was his moniker. Little Joe (Michael Landon) was the youngest and most popular of the lot.

In *Badge without Honor*, Dep. Marshall Gerald Eskith's shooting prowess earns him the gratitude of Ben Cartwright, owner of the Ponderosa. The heartfelt thanks are for shooting two highwaymen who fired at his son Adam and did not get a second chance to hit their mark. Adam is apprehensive about acknowledging the favor, feeling that there was something impulsive about the killings.

Ben Cartwright does not want to hear anything from his eldest son and tells him that he is indebted to the marshal. Adam does not feel that way but amends his suspicious behavior. The deputy marshal is Ben Cartwright's guest and he thrills his hosts with his fencing skills and erudite story telling. That is why they don't question his intention to take back Jason Blaine, one of their friends, to testify in a statewide crime ring trial.

Blaine is fearful and apprehensive but Eskith has little regard for his protests. When they are alone, Eskith tells Blaine that he is marked for death and tells him when he will die. To add insult to injury the renegade lawman makes romantic overtures to Blaine's wife, Mariette (Christine White). She plays along biding her time because she knows that he wants to kill her husband. It takes time for the Cartwrights to see through his scheme. There is a final showdown in a silver mine that is colorful and tense. It is where the marshal pays for his insolence.

Badge without Honor may bring to mind *Silver Lode* because both villains create a disguise to exact revenge that is sanctified by the rule of law even though that code may be warped. What separates U.S. Dep. Marshall Gerald Eskith from Ned McCarty is his education and defensive skills of fencing and shooting.

The deputy marshal is a smooth-talking charmer. Cultured, witty and possessing a quick prairie sense to keep it real, he bluffs his way into people's confidences by pretending to be a diligent federal marshal. The clever twist is that he is the Dude Butcher Boy, the hired killer of the Murdock Mob and he hides behind the power of a badge when it comes to enforcing the law. He is sent to Virginia City to eliminate a renegade member of the Murdock Mob: Jason Blaine. Official papers are death sentence affidavits delivered by hand.

Eskith is well-educated and possesses a rapier logic that matches his fencing skills. He is an adept swordsman and displays his skill in a friendly match with Little Joe. The sheriff almost loses himself and pins Little Joe to the wall and is about to move in for the kill when he is reminded that it is just a jesting match. The killer look in Eskith's eyes shows that he disagrees.

Deputy Marshal Eskith is a hired gun who becomes enraptured by his mark's wife. 1960, National Broadcasting Network (NBC).

The scoundrel also has an unabashed infatuation with Mariette, the wife of his mark. He touches her in the way of a forward gentleman and eventually announces his intentions of having her run away with him. Emotions are what make people weak, he once reasoned, and losing his heart caused his downfall. That is what softens him up for the kill in the shootout in the silver mine. He was in love with himself.

Dan Duryea returned to *Bonanza* in 1964 for a role that is an appropriate contrast to Dep. Sheriff Askith. Sam Logan is a burnt-out bank robber released from prison after a 20 year hitch. He is quiet and unassuming. Ben Cartwright's charity is not lost on him. He appreciates his old friend's hospitality. Cartwright is the only man who believes Logan's claim that he does not know where the stolen gold is buried. He claims that his partner hid it before the posse caught up with him and lynched him. This means that he will be dogged by several ghosts from the past and wants to be around when he digs up the money.

They include Frank Reed (John Kellogg), a bounty hunter; Angie Malone (Virginia Gregg), an over-the-hill saloon girl; and Mike Crawford (Tim McIntire), his ex-partner's son. The only thing that protects him from their prying eyes is Ben Cartwright's trust in him. Cartwright is the only one who believes Logan does not know anything about the gold.

Frank Reed worked for Wells Fargo and was fired after he failed to retrieve the stolen gold. Humiliation turned him into a vengeful man and his hatred was so strong that he bribed the prison guards to torture and starve Logan into telling them where he hid the gold. Reed is bent on finding the gold so he can throw it on the desk of the man who fired him. He also wants to spit in his face.

Angie Malone is along for the ride. She pretends to be tenderhearted but Sam sees through her façade. Her attempt to cozy up to Sam earns her an old-fashioned slap in the kisser al la the 40's heel. That only makes her fall back on a note she has that can place Sam near the assassination of a federal officer.

Mike Crawford is won over by Sam's attempt to mollify him about his mother's jaundiced view of him. The young man is full of hate and is apprehensive about trusting Logan until he hears the positive things that are said about his father.

In the end, Ben Cartwright is wrong because Logan was the robber who hid it. He knows exactly where it is buried and could find it with blinders on. He agrees to split the gold with the son of his late partner. Mike accuses Logan of selling out his father and the old man tells him that he's got it all wrong. The boy's mind has been poisoned by his mother, who accuses Logan of betraying her husband so he could have the gold to himself. Logan can't show enough admiration for his ex-partner and to show the boy that his intentions are good, he promises to split the gold with him.

They find the booty but run into the bounty hunter. He is intent on grabbing the gold and breaking in Logan, dead or alive. There is a standoff that is mediated by Ben Cartwright. Reed is told to vamoose and Logan has to give up the gold to insure a free future. He agrees and starts a new life with his ex-partner's son. Ben Cartwright wishes his old friend good luck and Sam and Mike ride off together, sort of surrogate father and son bonding.

Logan is one of Duryea's latter day characterizations. That means that he is a man who is running on fumes given strength by memories of the past. He is quiet and soft-spoken, totally humbled by Ben Cartwright's charity. His old self surfaces when he is hounded by the bounty hunter

Ben Cartwright (Lorne Greene) is the only support Sam Logan (Dan Duryea) has after the outlaw has served a prison sentence for robbing a gold shipment he claims not to have buried. 1964, National Broadcasting Network (NBC).

and the ex-saloon girl. He even reverts to type by slapping her, a nod to Duryea's former reputation as a big screen heel. That happens after she tells him that the only reason she tracked him down was that she loved him. The gold was incidental.

Prairie Shadows

Not all television Westerns hit pay dirt. The network schedule had its share of fool's gold. It also had good shows that never caught on. Still, quality stars appeared on these programs and some of the stories rose above the mediocrity of the shows. Then there were the programs that occasionally veered into Western territory, like the anthologies. It is in this area of obscure shows and forgotten players that you will encounter an actor or actress' minor gems. That includes an appearance on an honorable classic like *The Twilight Zone.*

Dan Duryea's first television Western was *The Jane Wyman Theater: Nailed Down.* He played Doc Munday, a notorious bank robber whose humanitarian instincts unwittingly make him trade his life for a new born child's chance to survive.

Lucas (Gene Barry) is a man who is stretched between two histories. One is his time riding with the notorious outlaw Doc Munday. The other is his life as a rancher with a wife who is about to go into labor. The sheriff will be the arbiter of conscience when the drama is finished. He is the one who will disconnect the past to insure a future for Lucas and his family.

For Lucas, things are not so easily defined when Doc Munday rides onto his ranch in the night. Armed with a shotgun, Lucas is prepared to shoot whoever is rustling his horses. He is shocked to see his old boss, Doc Lucas, has no problem lending Doc and his outlaws fresh horses.

Doc and his gang had pulled a bank robbery and were being pursued by the sheriff and his posse. Doc Munday's decision changes the course of the escape when he trades his life for the hope of Lucas' newborn son. The time it took to deliver the baby was long enough for Doc and Lucas to settle matters regarding the stolen money. Consciences remain intact as the men part ways. The sheriff is a common link to both men who takes care of the Munday legend and reaffirms Lucas' place in the community.

Doc Munday is a phalanx of emotional dispositions. He bosses around his gang and faces Lucas toe to toe but also maintains the humanitarian principles of the medical profession. He is dedicated to Lucas and his men. That's what claims his life. It was not a surprise ambush by the sheriff and his posse. It was a surprise attack on the law as his men were being ambushed.

Dan Duryea went from one side of the law to the other in *The Marshal and the Mob* for *Campbell's Star Stage.* He is a marshal who is faced with the threat of mob violence. He has the herculean task of providing

Doc Munday is a bank robber whose predatory survival instincts are compromised by his vow as a healer and preserver of life. 1955, Dumont Television Network.

the law that prevents convicted criminal Ward Bond from being lynched. Barbara Eiler also starred and it was directed by Sidney Lanfield and told the story about a lynching in the old West.

It is Dan Duryea's small roles that lend support and variety to his better known characters. It was true in the movies and also applied to television. Duryea played two polar opposites who shared the same sense of honor in *Dick Powell's Zane Grey Theatre: This Man Must Die* and *Knight of the Sun*. The first presentation is an intense drama and the second one is a comedy.

Kirk Joiner and George Hanlin are two different types of heroes. Joiner is an honest businessman framed and sentenced to death for a murder he did not commit. He has to elude a posse to prove his innocence and

Dan Duryea uses his authority to prevent the lynching of a convicted criminal played by Ward Bond in his pre-Major Adams days in The Marshal and the Mob. 1956, Revue Productions.

in defying great odds he triumphs. Hanlin is a dissipated desert rat who rides a burro into an abandoned Confederate fort. Heaven is solitude and a cask of whiskey. Nothing lasts forever and he is forced to assist a southern belle who appears out of nowhere with a mission to be fulfilled.

In *This Man Must Die*, Kirk Joiner escapes from prison two days before he is to hang for a crime he did not commit. He aims to kill the man who bore false witness against him. Hunted by a posse and forced into hiding, the fugitive enlists the aid of Lil (Carole Mathews), his girlfriend and his business partner to track down the witness. Little does he realize that he will need the man alive so he can testify about his false testimony. The real murderer turns out to be his former partner, a false friend who framed him so he could control the mining business.

Kirk Joiner certainly has his work cut out for him. He is attuned to his surroundings, keenly aware of the world closing in on him. His time is limited and he has to accomplish his mission as quickly as possible. What changes the dynamics is Joiner's realization that he has to keep the snitch alive because he may have been someone else's paid dupe. The unfolding of possibilities alters Joiner's plans and he is lucky to use up his spare time

Kirk Joiner is the classic innocent man on-the-run. He even finds sanctuary with his own dance hall queen, Lil (Carole Mathews). 1958, Four Star Productions.

George Hanlin, a whiskey loving desert rat, is a southern belles' (Constance Towers) *Knight of the Sun*. 1961, Four Star Productions.

wisely. Everything falls into place, including being led to the sheriff's office with the lying witness who will testify that the real murderer lies dead in the cabin.

Bo Svenson is the ex-partner, a smiling snake who welcomes the fugitive with a phony welcome. He wants Joiner and Grusz to cancel out each other. Instead, he is forced to kill them and fake the evidence. It didn't work when he was shot dead by Joiner in a plan gone awry.

Throughout the ordeal, Joiner is aided by Lil (Carole Matthews), the dance hall queen who loves him and gives him support in his plan.

The original title of *Knight of the Sun* was *A Cause for Dying*, and it is the light-hearted tale of George Hanlin, a desert rat who is promoted to knight by a southern belle (Constance Towers) in distress. His idea of heaven is being the only living man in a ghost fort whose main amenity is a cask of southern whiskey. He even gets to wear the captain's coat and hat. His fantasy life is cut short when a covered wagon arrives, driven by a beautiful woman. Inside the wagon is the remains of her father, a fallen Confederate officer. It is the other occupant of the wagon that provides the basis for the action. It is the newly invented Gatling gun.

Hanlin is unimpressed by the woman's insistence of transporting the gun to Mexico where rebels will use it against Yankee troops. He is coerced into helping the woman transport the gun after she shoots a hole in the whiskey barrel. Luckily, Hanlin has managed to fill a canteen and that will fortify him for the knightly mission.

Their main obstacles are the desert, Apaches and Union patrols. He avoids the Yankees and mows down an Apache war party with the automatic weapon with the revolving barrels. Hanlin is a hero to the lady and is a tall order in her eyes when he completes his desert quest to uphold the honor of a lady and the southern cause.

In the *Schlitz Playhouse* production, *Kinsman*, Dan Duryea plays a star-crossed family man whose life is destroyed by a crime of passion that backfired on him. He is a cuckolded husband convicted of manslaughter when he shot an innocent bystander instead of the homewrecker who was fleeing with his wife. Fellow movie tough guy Anthony Caruso plays the louse and the unfaithful spouse is played by Edith Barrett. Duryea's character loses his wife and ten years of his life behind bars.

His only desire is to be reunited with the son he never knew and he is given false tips on his whereabouts by his former wife. She was abandoned by Caruso but it is not long before they are reunited in a scheme to fleece Duryea of his new found fortune. It sounds like a reversal of his role in *Scarlet Street*.

Duryea finds his son and takes him back to the ranch, where gold is discovered. It seems that a lost decade has turned into a pot at the end of the rainbow. Things are not as idyllic as they seem because the scheming couple reveal that the boy is not really his son and they will reveal the whereabouts of his real son for a tidy sum.

There is no deal and a gun duel ends with Caruso on the losing end of a sweet dream turned sour reality. Duryea is told that his real son died long ago but it does not change the affection he has for the waif he picked up on his journey to locate his son. They return to the ranch, where a new life awaits them. Jules Bricken has written a tight teleplay that is well rounded for a half hour drama, which he also directed and produced.

A holster and a gun also fortifies Jim Budinger and Al Denton at one point or another in their criminal careers. Because of the gun, they are two characters who live in a private Hell. In one instance, it was the perplexing side of everyday life that created anguish out of normalcy. The second case took place in *The Twilight Zone*, the fourth dimension where normalcy was created out of perplexity. One character finds what he is looking for and the other loses everything he holds dear.

Jim Budinger lords it over captive wayfarers who mine his underground lead mine in *Cimmaron City: Terror Town*. Al Denton's inebriated vanity is tempted by a fate that restores lost gun fighting skills at a dear cost in *The Twilight Zone: Doomsday for Mr. Denton*.

Cimmaron City was a boom town that was growing into an Oklahoma territory. Matt Rockford (George Montgomery) was the son of the town's founder and he was a cattle rancher elected mayor. He is a hands-on man and supervises his own cattle drives. That is how he became a prisoner working a lead mine for Jim Budinger, a deranged retired bank robber who heads a gang of miscreant half-brothers in *Cimarron City: Terror Town*.

Roy Budinger is the educated head of a misfit gang that consists of his brothers, three cretins of varying degrees. They have the same mother and she had four husbands. This accounts for their various degrees of intelligence or lack thereof. Budinger's wife is an alcoholic shadow that serves him under a burden of abuse and humiliation. She is a tender soul ruined by her love for an abusive man. Her brothers-in-law are sub-human and the only one who keeps them in line is their brainy half-brother.

Their domain is Lead City, a ghost town with an active lead mine. The town was abandoned when the people realized that there was no future in mining lead. Like the alchemists of the Middle Ages, Budinger found a way of transforming lead into silver. To make it profitable, he needed plenty of time and cheap labor. There was plenty of time in a ghost town and enough cheap labor supplied by the curious ranchers, cow herds and mountain people who came to investigate the smoke coming out of the mountain. Now, the latest addition to the underground chain gang is Matt Rockford and he uses it as leverage to keep Jess, his wounded rod, alive.

The miners mine the lead, fill the ore cars and boil the alchemist mix in a giant cauldron. They skim the silver and cool it in molds. The mine is a horror cavern with the ghosts of former humans eking out a miserable existence. It is a sweet deal for Budunger except for one incontrovertible detail. His stained reputation makes it impossible for him to deposit the silver banks in any bank. Matt Rockford and his sterling reputation may be the perfect front for his enterprise. Instead, Budinger's empire is challenged by Rockford and it proves to be his undoing.

Budinger is one of Duryea's sadistic town bosses. He is a sharp-witted bookworm who is always reading, even at the dinner table. He delights in ridiculing his dim-witted half-brothers for their lack of intelligence and

Ghost town boss Jim Budinger loses his empire in a tug of war with Matt Rockford (George Montgomery), mayor, cattle baron and the show's star. 1958, Mont Productions, National Broadcasting Network (NBC).

social graces. They have no choice but to deal with his abuse because he has stored the gold bars in a place they would never dream of looking—hollowed-out books in his library.

The brothers provide him with the power of coercion that a tyrant needs to achieve maximum production under the least desirable conditions. Judd (Jonathan Haze) is a short, attitudinal punk with an itchy trigger finger. Grant (Don Megowan) is a muscular giant who uses anything as a reason for beating someone up. Carl (Dan Blocker) is the bearded and soiled behemoth who delights in his job as the subterranean turnkey and sadistic overseer of the underground chain gang.

Forget that Lead City is a ghost town, it's the fortune in silver that will build Budinger's power base. He does not intend to split the profits with his half-brothers and may leave his wife behind in the dust. All he has to do is convert the silver into money.

He thinks that he is a step ahead of Rockford in their cagey negotiations. Budinger believes that he can use the rancher's life as a bargaining tool, not realizing that time is on Rockford's side or that his disappearance will alert his ranch hands and neighbors to possible danger. Threats and counter-bluffs don't faze Rockford. They only bolster his confidence.

It is Matt Rockford's value to Budinger that gives him the leverage to foment a revolt. Careful planning and strict timing enable the enslaved miners to kill the half-brothers during the revolt. All that remains is a dejected Budinger and his supportive wife and they are vulnerable to the hangman's noose.

The Twilight Zone was the brainchild of Rod Serling. It was a groundbreaking show that used the fantasy genre as a social critique format. It was done within the boundaries of drama so that messages and points were not obvious or self-indulgent. The show still stands up today. Dan Duryea takes a trip to the fourth dimension in *Mr. Denton on Doomsday*.

Al Denton rises from the ashes with the help of a guardian angel in black. A little hocus-pocus and two bottles of elixir help him resolve a paralyzing guilt that has reduced the former gunfighter to the town drunk. He goes from singing three bars of "How Dry I Am" to squaring off with a gunfighter who took up the cause of challenging the best gun in the region. It is because the man in black is an angel that the shooting match is blessed with redemption for the faded master and the green challenger. He is a traveling salesman and his route is *The Twilight Zone*.

The joke behind the town drunk is that he was once a notorious gunslinger. Not even the modern duelists show him respect because of his

Al Denton ponders a question whose answer will change his life in Mr. Denton on *Doomsday*. 1959, Cayuga Productions, Columbia Broadcasting System (CBS).

reputation. The classic man in black makes him sing three bars of "How Dry I Am" before he will buy a drink for him. The gunslinger will be singing a different tune when Denton miraculously recovers his speed and mental acuity after he finds a gun in the dust.

Denton humiliates his bully and amazes the people in the bar. They call him 'mister' and want to buy him drinks but he refuses. He says that he is through with drinking and goes to the barbershop for a makeover. The reborn Al Denton is not intent on seeing if he can still win a showdown because he outdrew the man in black. It is fate that makes him strap on a gun when a new fresh faced kid comes into town to issue a challenge.

The torment of carrying the heavy load of a dangerous reputation once drove Al Denton to drink. Now, he sits in a hotel room and ponders his options. It is the traveling salesman beneath his window that draws his curiosity into accepting a vial that contains a potion that will give his gun hand a temporary jolt. It is something that the traveling salesman has given his opponent because the showdown ends in a draw when both men damage each other's gun hand with their aim. It was fate that gave Denton the potion and it was part of a lesson in personal ambition. He thanks the heavenly emissary with a knowing look as the salesman passes with his wagon.

Dan Duryea was able to return to his town boss character with Dan Trask in Walt Disney's *The Legend of Texas John Slaughter*. It was one of the mini-series that the program ran during its run although the term was not used to describe the shows during their original run. Texas John Slaughter was able to confront and defeat a series of Western bad men and women during his stint for Walt Disney. Along the way, Slaughter would encounter crime boss Dan Trask when he and the Texas Rangers pursue the Bardo gang into Mexico where they planned to take refuge in the secret town run by the overlord.

As Texas John Slaughter, Tom Tryon is cut from the Charlton Heston cloth of heroism. He is tall, broad-shouldered, and square-jawed, with few words to spare and a clear-cut sense of right and wrong. That is why he makes the perfect Texas Ranger.

His Ranger skills are admired by his cohorts, but not by his fiancé. She fears that the violent lifestyle will claim her husband-to-be. Slaughter believes in the ideals of law and order, knowing very well that blood may be required to make things work.

The conflict between Slaughter and his woman is one of the things that occupy the Ranger's time. Another growing point of his interest is to avenge the shooting death of his buddy during a bank robbery by the Bardo gang. Slaughter miraculously avoided being shot when a quick getaway was required by the gang.

The bulk of the movie deals with the Bardo Gang's reign of terror. They are run by a married couple, the twist being that the wife (Beverly Garland) is the brains of the outfit. That is the only unique point of the movie. Beverly Garland gives a good performance as Addy. Lyle Bettger hides behind his trademark pearly whites and the gang is the generic group of outlaws along for the excitement and money.

They rob banks that run in a pattern that will take them to the Mexican border. It is when a captured gang member spills the beans that the Texas Rangers realize that they are heading towards Sandoval, a safe haven for outlaws.

The outlaw town is run by Dan Trask, a debonair leader. The Texas Rangers will impersonate the Bardo Gang. Slaughter's fiancé will play Mrs. Bardo, much to the consternation of the Texas Ranger.

Texas John Slaughter (Tom Tryon) confers with fellow Rangers on how to bring down the Bardo Gang. 1954, 1959, Walt Disney Prod.

Trask entertains the false Mr. and Mrs. Bardo with a charm that nets him more than he bargained for. It costs him a duel at dawn and this coincides with the masqueraded Rangers taking over the town before destroying it with dynamite booby traps.

Trask becomes a memory as his army of outlaws is blown to kingdom come by Ranger Slaughter and his wife, plus the Ranger recruits who posed as the Bardo Gang. It was a fast paycheck for Trask, who got to throw a fancy silver cup at the mariachi band in his hacienda after his come-on was rebuffed and he was challenged to a duel.

It is more than can be said for Trask in *Sundown in Sandoval*. He is the town boss who does not get to give a death speech when he is gunned down by the hero. He already gave his speech the night before when he tried to bewitch the hero's wife at dinner.

Dan Duryea plays Dan Trask, a debonair outlaw who runs Sandoval, a safe haven for outlaws south of the border. Trask, for all his charm and tall talk, is taken down by Texas John Slaughter in an old-fashioned gun duel. It happens at the end of the movie, which centers on a Texas Ranger's hunt for a murderous band of outlaws called The Bardo Gang.

Trask owns an outlaw town south of the border in *Texas John Slaughter: Gundown at Sandoval*. The town boss makes his appearance during the second half of this Disney outlaw tale. Beverly Garland and Lyle Bettger dominate the first half as the Bardo gang, vicious bank robbers. They are chased to Sandoval by the Texas Rangers. The outlaw town is run by the charming but reptilian Trask.

Dan Duryea stepped in as temporary captain of The Enterprise for two episodes of *Riverboat*. No, this was not the member of the Starfleet, but a riverboat piloted by *Kolchak, the Night Stalker* and the star of *Smokey and the Bandit*, that is, Darren McGavin and Burt Reynolds.

The show was riding some rough waters and it was understood that star Darren McGavin wanted out. Dan Duryea was signed to play the part for two shows and he turned down an offer from executive producer Richard Lewis to become the skipper of the Enterprise. The show was

Trask (Dan Duryea) romances Texas John's sweetheart Adeline Harris (Norma Moore), who is posing as an outlaw along with her fiancé. 1959, Walt Disney Prod.

faltering because its hour format was not suitable for sponsors' investments. It was the general consensus that viewers are fidgety with one hour programs and often change channels, thereby missing the commercials.

Two half hour programs would command the viewers' attention and subject them to the commercial indoctrination. This was the administrative logic behind network scheduling and it was an obstacle for *Riverboat*, as was the fact that it was boring. It had a curiosity value because of Darren McGavin and Burt Reynolds, although Jack Lambert's role was noteworthy and well-played.

Wichita Arrows and *Fort Epitaph* are stories with warring Indians, although things turn out differently than they appear in both cases. No one is safe from marauding Indians; neither the vulnerable settlers nor a fort full of soldiers can keep the body count from mounting when they come under fire. The only difference is the Wichita Arrows are really a white man's desperate cover for a series of robberies and Fort Epitaph is a lesson in mutual respect taught by an Indian chief who teaches a Calvary martinet that inciting a war as a way to advance one's career can only lead to a dead end conclusion.

The *Wichita Arrows* that were left behind in deadly raids indict the tribe, but the captain's keen logic deduces fraudulent setups. He's really a ruthless and psychotic businessman who preys on people who have cash or valuables in hand. He leaves as a seller and returns as a rampaging Indian.

It is Captain's Dan alertness that makes him realize that the peaceful Wichitas would not risk war for these senseless crimes. It seems more like a white man's ploy to assign blame to someone else for his own crimes. There is a genuine sense of shock when the steadfast businessman turns out to be a murdering psychotic.

Captain Dan returns for a second episode at the behest of Captain Holding. This adventure puts the lives of the captain and his crew at risk. *Fort Epitaph* is a soldier's moniker for the desert fort under siege from warring Indians. It is the despotic major that instigated the war by humiliating two Indian maidens. He did it for war glory. This is a portrait of a man who seeks immortality through myth instead of a sound bloodline. Plagued by the barren womb of his wife, Major Luke seeks to fight and defeat the local Indians to create a legend around his shadow life.

Major Luke is a by-the-book commanding officer. He is familiar with every comma, period and footnote of Army rules and regulations. It is his unholy ambition that enables him to bend the law to fit his ambition. It would have been easier if he didn't have a formidable foe like Captain Dan.

Captain Dan examines a war mongering officer's mark of shame in *Fort Epitaph*. 1960, Revue Studios.

The captain and his men are conscripted by the major after they deliver four cannons to the besieged fort. Only fifteen of the original fifty troops are still alive. The captain and his men will help to defend the fort until reinforcements arrive. They eventually relieve Captain Luke of his command when they believe that he is unfit to lead.

Captain Dan's understanding of tribal customs saves the men and sets the stage for a strange court-martial. The riverboat captain also assumes command of the fort when he resolves to ease the tension and move the survivors to safety. He accomplishes this with the protection of the Indian chief, whose only concern is that the white renegade major is punished for his heinous crimes.

Heinous crimes and justice are the occupational hazards of *Shadow of a Pale Horse*. The judicial process in bush country consists of a kangaroo court with a lynchpin mentality. Dan Duryea is called on to defend the accused murderer of his son. The accused's prosecutor is played by Frank Lovejoy, once a longtime friend and employer of the man on trial for his life. The case rests on the spooky testimony of the suspect, who swears that he saw a man on a pale horse highlighted by the moonlight. He slowly lolled by the spot where the young victim was beaten to death with a club.

The jury returns a guilty verdict and the accused is hung. A pale horse with a dead rider tied to the saddle strolls into town. He bears a message about death in the saddle from the Book of Revelation. It condemns the jury for executing an innocent man and declares them guilty of committing vengeance not justice.

Expressionist sets highlight *Shadow of a Pale Horse*, a haunting lynch mob drama set in the Australian outback. 1960, Theatre Guild.

Dan Duryea plays a man bent on revenge in *Frontier Circus: The Shaggy Kings*. He is Terrance Tiber, a rancher who became an itinerant mountain man. Bearded and bedraggled, he wears a coonskin cap and is clad in fur. Tiber is fixated on the shooting death of his son, a young man who was on the losing end of a gun duel with a professional gunslinger. He has stalked the killer, Tom Jace, for five years and plans to settle the score on a buffalo hunt.

Frontier Circus was a chronicle of the T&T Circus, a wagon show that traveled the southwest during the era that followed the Civil War. Col. Casey Thompson (Chill Wills) and Ben Travis (John Derek) were partners who were aided by Tony Gentry (Richard Jaeckal), a scout who scoured the countryside for suitable sites to showcase the little Big Show. For the T&T Circus, the circuit lasted one season before folding the tents for good.

The Shaggy Kings refers to the buffaloes that once filled the Western plains of the United States. The circus folk are on the verge of hunger when they are reduced to poisoned salt pork and beans. Casey's dream of taking the circus west of the Mississippi has hit a dead end and tension mounts between him and his partner. They are at loggerheads about whether or not they should turn back. Travis thinks it was a foolish idea to entertain the miners but Casey bristles at the idea of turning back.

They think that their prayers have been answered when Michael Smith (Michael Pate), a mixed-blooded Comanche, enters the camp and offers his services as a guide in a buffalo hunt. The circus men don't realize that Smith is responsible for tainting the grub with pot ash so that Col. Thompson and Ben Travis will accept his offer. His intention is to start a war between the whites and a Comanche tribe.

Smith instructs the partners and their guide to meet him at Murphy's Trading Post, where he and his men will guide them to Adobe Wells where the hunt will take place. The hunting party consists of four disparate men. Terence Tiber (Dan Duryea) is a weather-beaten mountain man who likes to talk. Karl Maynard (Frank De Kova) is a dissolute gambler with an air of desperation about him. Jeb Randall (Dick York) is a fresh-faced youth with a secret that is tearing him apart. Art Baker (Jack Lambert) is a sour-faced cipher who rarely speaks.

Tiber is the most talkative man in the sullen bunch. He makes the introductions and tells Travis that he shot the last man who appropriated his name. Tiber is also the one who asks Travis to show them the money to bolster their confidence. There seems to be a mysterious and abrasive connection between Tiber and Randall. The mountain man constantly needles Randall as if he is trying to spark a confrontation.

"He gets around as much as I do," Tiber says as he eyeballs Randall, "but I reckon for a different reason."

After the men track the buffalo herd to Adobe Wells, they set up camp, where Tiber regales them with tales of the old days. His first buffalo hunt was thirty years ago when the west was a different place, with real men to tame the wild frontier. He talks about the buffalo hunts and waxes nostalgic, telling the party that the herd they spotted was small compared to the numbers that roamed the plains before the buffaloes were decimated. Back then, it would take a medium herd three days to pass and the dust they kicked up would block the sunlight and darken the sky.

Terrance Tiber is a mountain man who plans to use a buffalo hunt to confront a gunslinger about the shooting death of his son in *The Shaggy Kings*. 1961, Revue Studios.

He mentions Western legends like Kit Carson and Davey Crockett and reviles the fresh-faced killers of modern times. Tom Jace is the name that unnerves Randall because he is the former gunslinger that has earned Tiber's enmity. This unsettles Randall and he confronts Tiber, telling him that he knows that the mountain man has been dogging him over the years. Tiber tells him why.

Tiber is obsessed with the shooting death of his son, a righteous youth whose pride and joy was a perpetual grin. The bereaved father refuses to believe that his son wanted to establish a gunslinger's reputation by challenging Jace. He also disbelieves that his son shot Jace in the back when he refused to duel and walked away from the confrontation. Randall/Jace gives an honest account on how he left that life behind and why he had to put up with it for so long.

"Five years I've waited, Jace. Now it ends," warns Tiber.

Before the men can square off they are attacked by the Comanches, who have been agitated by Smith's insistence that the buffalo treaty has been broken by white hunters. The gambler and the cipher are killed and Jace is wounded. In a change of heart, Tiber nurses him back to health. He now realizes that his hard-nosed discipline turned his son against him and the boy took out his hatred on everyone he met, including Tom Jace.

The survivors engage in another battle but are saved when the frontier circus comes to their rescue. They have enough buffalo meat to feed the circus folk and the animals. Travis invites Tiber and Jace to stay with them until the ex-gunslinger recuperates from his wounds. Tiber says that it is not necessary because he will be riding with the man to tend to his wounds.

"Now it ends for both of us," says the repentant Tiber, who has vanquished his vengeance-filled desire to kill the man who shot his son in self-defense. They ride off together, having bonded as surrogate father and son.

There are other dramas along the way, like the gambler trying to steal the money and ride by himself or the Comanches attacking the hunters before fleeing when the circus arrives.

It is the premise and the colorful characters that make the story work. A frontier circus seems like an anachronism but Chill Will's desire to make his big top a success is admirable. John Derek is his partner and has doubts about the operation. Richard Jaeckal is the young but seasoned scout who deals with Derek's barbs. They act well together, mainly because Chill Will's gravel-voiced oldster offers ballast to their young blood characters.

The hunters are comprised of actors known to Baby Boomer television fans. Dan Duryea, Frank De Kova, Dick York and Jack Lambert are the ornery quartet. Dan Duryea's Tiber is a bereaved father who wants justice from his son. Seeking revenge has made him irascible and quick to judge. He does not believe Jace's story until after it finally sinks in that his son was not the man he thought he was.

Tales of Wells Fargo was the five year saga of Jim Hardie (Dale Robertson). He was a troubleshooter for the company and his job took him across the country for a series of frontier adventures. His job takes him into some spooky terrain in *Winter Storm*, a story that has an *Old Dark House* feel to it. It is the premise of having disparate strangers trapped in an eerie setting that is dogged by a psycho. In this case it is a derelict hotel in a ghost town. The hotel has been booby-trapped by the owners. They appear to be expecting unwelcome company.

Jim Hardy (Dale Robertson) arrives with his party: Tina (Lory Patrick), a young woman, Jeb Gaine (William Demerest), his old codger buddy, and Tom (Boyd Stockman), his driver, who is injured by one of the traps. The beauty has land to claim, Pop has to get his teeth fixed, and Hardy has to testify at a trial. The driver was injured by one of the booby-traps and needs the attention of a doctor. Later guests include Eddy Pierce (Jim Beck), a one-armed trapper and an Indian woman named Ruth (Gale Garnett), plus the U.S. marshal (Dan Duryea) they rescued from a snow drift. His name is Blake and he is on the trail of an escaped killer.

The owners of the hotel are an odd couple. Hanson (R.G. Armstrong) is a bulwark of stoicism and his partner Kelly (Eddie Firestone) is a bundle of nerves. They tote rifles and are suspicious of the strangers but feel a sense of relief with their company. Still, everyone is one edge because fear permeates the hotel.

Hanson and Kelly are expecting an escaped convict, someone they help render useless with their store-bought vigilantes. His name is Jennings and he has escaped from prison to exact revenge on the only living members of town businessmen who hired vigilantes to kill the marauders who were harassing the town. Jennings was the only survivor and he has put the fear of the law into the men, who no longer have a thriving town to defend or a band of mercenaries to protect them.

The tell tale sign of his defeat is a chest wound, the reminder of the assassination attempt on his life. This piece of identification will come in handy when fate steps in to even a score. The old dark house theme includes having the murderer among the guests. In this case, it's the stern marshal, who happens to be Jennings in disguise.

Jennings is a master manipulator, an outlaw posing as a federal marshal who turns out to be the devious intruder within. He has lent a semblance of security to the fright fest but it is just to lower the guards of the two men he plans to kill. They are an odd duo and a study in contrasts. Hanson is quick to point out that he is not afraid of anything. He claims that he has not been afraid a day in his life. The same cannot be said of Kelly, a small man who is a bundle of nerves. He runs around the hotel pointing his rifle in every direction because he expects to finds Jennings lurking in a shadow.

The drama also serves as a character study. The one-armed trapper and his squaw are going through personal changes. It is the drama that helps the trapper expect sudden changes in his life, like the loss of his arm. She finally becomes his woman when he overcomes his shame and accepts her love.

Jim Hardy and his party are just there to spend the night. They have business to tend to. It is basically Hanson and Kelly's show until the marshal shows up. He is the consummate professional. Serious about his duties, he claims to be hunting Jennings and claims that he is outside stalking him. No one realizes that the marshal is Jennings because there is no need to doubt him. It is not until they are fired upon that his plan moves towards closure. Jennings forgets that there is a real law man among them and is shot dead before he can realize the second half of his bloodlust. The ordeal is over when morning arrives and the guests can leave the old, dark house.

TV: 1958-1963

The All American Role Models

Dan Duryea only made three movies—*Kathy O, Platinum High School* and *Six Black Horses*—from 1958 to 1962 and worked almost exclusively in television. He alternated his character types with each successive role and in doing so never wore out his welcome. Duryea may be noted for certain characterizations when pigeonholed or chronicled for a profile. His hard-edged roles get most of the attention and for a good reason. They were performed with verve and conviction and created performances that made indelible impressions. His television roles created a subdivision that includes the characters who embodied the change in character type he had hoped to achieve in the late 40's.

There may have been movie stars who considered their participation in the new medium a descent in their careers, but for Dan Duryea it meant another extensive outlet for his talents. He definitely added to his villains and Western range resume but also built a new reputation as a hero without ulterior motives. *China Smith* and a *Zane Grey Theater* scoundrel may have been the best of his lovable rogues but Duryea also played upright All American men of law and order, the type that were the role models celebrated on 50's television.

The late 50's was a time when the post-war opportunities created a prosperous lifestyle that was characterized by the nuclear family. It was portrayed and legitimatized on television, in the movies and in the print media. The nuclear family was basically a family headed by a mother and father with two children. They lived in an American small town, an anti-urban Utopia where nothing bad happened. The daring writing of the better anthologies began to question the placid attitudes of the time and the small Utopia was now confronted with the threat of an outside enemy.

It may be hard to imagine Dan Duryea in characters suited for *Leave to Beaver* or *The Andy Griffith Show* but it becomes comprehensible because his small town Americana is threatened by the bad guys and it takes more than pithy aphorisms and canned laughter to take them down. He is a small town butcher who balances his family's safety against testifying to witnessing a mob execution in *The Frightened Witness*.

His wife is played by Barbara Billingsley, who would later gain fame as June Cleaver in the warmly regarded *Leave it To Beaver*. In *The Vengeance*, he is Marc Johnson, a small town Justice of the Peace hunted by a psycho on the eve of the Strawberry Festival. He, too, has a loving wife and son and it is his decision to get them out of harm's way when he acts as bait for the escaped murderer.

But when it comes to valiant symbols of community pride, none of his characters come close to Dr. Sullivan. When has a medical show not been on the television schedule? The nature of the medical profession and its players has always been the subject of many fine dramas and comedies. Dr. Sullivan gets it all done because the Chief of Nurses is his wife and she is his chief bedrock. Reminders of postponed holiday weekends at the beach keep him longing for sandbox memories as he struggles with a stormy night of grave decisions.

Also living life on the larger than life circuit there is Cliff Mason in *Smoke Jumpers*. His girl is the waitress at the local canteen where the firefighters chow down. She belongs to the top dog and he has her unconditional support when he is suspected of deserting his men during a forest fire that killed everyone on the team except him. New heroics reinstate him to his tin god status.

Dan Duryea had turned down eleven *Climax* scripts when something about *Four Hours in White* caught his attention. He accepted the role of Dr. Sullivan, the chief of surgeons at Yakima Medical Hospital. Among his travails are fighting the odds in a kidney transplant operation, balancing the lives of the twins involved in the new procedure, dealing with a guilt-ridden absentee father and an over-anxious fiancée opposed to the operation, and battling the hospital administration's conflicted views of his decision. He also has to prevent the downslide of a capable surgeon whose confidence has been shattered by the loss of a third patient during surgery. Not to mention the three weeks since he spent a weekend with his wife at their beach retreat. It is something that he is aware of because she is the chief of nurses and they constantly remind each other of it.

Dr. Sullivan is stretched in all directions by the wide array of people and problems he has to deal with. One twin has lacerations of the scalp and the other is in shock with a weak pulse. The artificial kidney machine has to be flown in from Frisco on a stormy night. It might be possible to

Dr. Sullivan outlines the pros and cons of a kidney transplant with one of the twins (Steve McQueen) involved in the new medical procedure. 1958, CBS Television City.

Dr. Sullivan uses tough love to snap a dejected doctor out of a self-afflicted collapse after he has lost a third patient during surgery. 1958, CBS Television City.

perform a kidney transplant operation although Dr. Skinner, the hospital's assistant administrator, is adamantly opposed to it. The doctor's other dilemma is saving Dr. Whitaker, a surgeon who has lost three patients, from destroying himself through self-pity and failed nerves. There are also the intimate and awkward personal reality checks and the across-the-board administrative challenges and ultimatums.

It becomes evident that the heir-apparent to the administration chair would rather work the wards. Maybe one day he would like to serve as a hospital administrator, but now he is content with the life and death responsibilities of being chief of surgeons.

Dr. Sullivan proceeds with the operation with Dr. Whitaker as his assistant. The transplant is a success and it has earned the chief of surgeons and the head of the night nursing a little barefoot time in the sandbox on the children's floor.

Buzz Kulik was a veteran at directing live television, having worked on the major anthology shows like *Desilu Playhouse, Lux Video Theatre, Climax, Studio One Playhouse* and *Playhouse 90*. He also directed several episodes of hit programs like *Perry Mason, Rawhide, Gunsmoke, Naked City, The Twilight Zone* and *The Defenders*. He also directed feature films and television movies, including *Brian's Song*.

Baseball is considered America's pastime and has been the springboard of much fiction. There are all sorts of plot devices that give the story its meaning and momentum with the love of baseball as its underlying theme. *The Comeback* is a drama about a baseball player whose big league career is ruined by alcoholism. He hits rock bottom after he is drummed out of the Major Leagues and winds up bumming from town to town like a hobo riding the rails. Every town is the same to him because he has not changed. Thompson is the drunk who came to visit and was shown the door after one too many Happy Hours. By the time he arrives in New Bolton he is reveling in drunken self-pity.

New Bolton is a small town whose thrills are provided by little league baseball. The citizens treat the youngsters like big leaguers when they compare stats and performances. For Thompson, the town's enthusiasm for the national pastime opens old wounds for him and reminds him of his tenure in the big leagues.

Thompson's tenure in the big leagues is also on the mind of Joe Grady (William Frawley) when he recognizes the itinerant wreck as the once-famous Cal Thompson. Grady coaches the kids and is about to bridge two worlds when he asks Thompson to manage the little leaguers. Thompson is reluctant because he has lost his confidence. His insecurity is wrapped in self-pity and this annoys Grady because he will not sympathize with a man who threw away a successful career.

The usual pep talks and tough love inspire Thompson to rehabilitate his life against all odds. Dealing with a team of attitudinal munchkins is not Thompson's idea of a good time. He'd rather be locked up in a fleabag hotel drinking his time away. There is no room for hooch in the dugout and the field of dreams sparkles with the resurrection principal. Thomp-

The cast of *Tiger on a Bicycle*. 1958, CBS Television City.

son and the kids encourage each other to the point that the drunkard is rehabilitated and the team of losers wins twenty games in a row.

This makes Thompson a hero with the kids and their parents but puts him in the dog house with Grady, who has become jealous of the ballplayer's new found popularity. Grady tries to take much of the credit for Thompson's reversal of fortune but his protégé will have none of it. They have a war of words that leads to a peace offering. Grady's feelings about him don't faze Thompson. He is having the time of his life becoming the small town hero and this includes winning the affection of Beth Jones (Maggie [Margaret] Hayes), the mother of the sarcastic and leery-of-adults moppet Duff Jones (Stephen Wooten). It's when he wins the trust of Duff that Thompson finally finds love with Beth.

Dan Duryea gives it his utmost in playing the clichéd character of Thompson. The same can be said about William Frawley, Maggie Hayes and Stephen Wooten. The drama plays like an abbreviated Frank Capra-inspired movie. Usually, the tragic outsider who affects the lives of a sleepy town is the basis for hard-hitting dramas. *The Comeback* is supposed to be a drama about personal salvation but it is too cloying and obvious to provide inspiration for the hopeless. Veteran film director Arthur Lubin helmed the production, which was filmed by Carl Guthrie.

Mark Johnson is the beloved Justice of the Peace of Aston. It is a peaceful setting in a story with the violent title of *The Vengeance*, an episode of an anthology hosted by David Niven. A small town banner reads Aston Welcomes You to the 15th Annual Strawberry Festival. 5,000 people are expected, including an escaped murderer who vowed to return to kill the man who convinced himself to surrender to the police. Mark Johnson is the marked man, the Justice of the Peace who has earned the enmity of George Hilton, a former farm hand who murdered a family after he accused his employer of trying to kill him with black magic to avoid paying him his salary.

The tension of monitoring the killer's approach to town contrasts with the sedate tone of the town preparing to celebrate. 5,000 people are expected and it's a foregone conclusion that Hilton will be one of them. The killer appropriates a pickup truck through murder, a bicycle through bludgeoning and uses suspense as his wife as he closes in for the kill.

Johnson is cool as he evacuates his family so that he can bait Hilton into confronting him alone. Things get out of hand when Hilton uses a loaded gun to threaten Johnson. It takes a friendly knock at the door to rattle Hilton's nerves and it ends with his dive through the window.

Crashing glass is followed by the sheriff doing his duty with dead-aim accuracy. Hilton is shot to death by the sheriff after he crashes through a window after his plan is thwarted. The knock at the door was an invitation to have a drink at the party next door. Johnson has no qualms about accepting the offer.

Dan Duryea signed for a role on *Pursuit*. The signing was on Oct. 20, 1958 with a broadcast date of Nov. 2. Jonathan Latimer wrote the teleplay, Charles Russell produced it and Paul Nickell directed it. Dan Duryea's next valiant character is also in law enforcement. He is a big city detective named Matt Shaw and he has to find a delicate way to break the testimony of a boy who may be an unknowing part of an armored car heist.

The armored car scenario makes for interesting drama because of the "against-the-odds" factor of the caper. It is rare that such robberies are successful and it is generally conceded that it can't be done. That was the assessment of Slim Dundee, Dan Duryea's crime boss in *Criss Cross*. It took him almost twenty years to get to the other side of the law and have a chance to crack such a case. That is the challenge of *Tiger on a Bicycle*.

The robbery in *Criss Cross* was successful because of an inside man. It is almost the same in *Tiger on a Bicycle*, only it's a boy that's on the inside even if he does not know it. He is the crime brain's son and he is persuaded to cross the path of the armored car. This would distract the guards and make the robbery possible. It takes the careful scrutiny of a cynical cop to suspect the boy was part of the robbery. The only way to find out is to find a delicate way to question the boy without traumatizing him.

The child's mother is not pleased with Shaw's suspicions and voices her concern. She maintains that the boy is innocent but this is a technicality because he was still used by his father for the $600,000 robbery. That much comes out in the interrogation. The pinch is made and the boy is off the hook.

Dan Duryea gets to play it clean and smooth as Matt Shaw. He has to use discretion in questioning the boy. Psychology and kid gloves are a good combination to break the boy without harming him. David Ladd (son of Alan Ladd) gives a savvy performance as the boy who broke the law to please his father. He maintains a steadfast demeanor during the interrogation until he slips and breaks down with the truth.

Neville Brand is sinister in his role as the law breaker. Brand has no sense of decency to his character and a big cash payoff is worth more to him than the soul of his son. He is a braggart who still likes to drop in on his ex-wife to annoy her. Lorraine Day plays the wife and mother and

In *The Vengeance*, Marc Johnson is the much loved and admired justice of the peace of Aston. Too bad he is marked for murder by an escaped psychopath who holds him responsible for his incarceration. 1959, Four Star Productions.

she gives a textured performance as a woman caught in the crossfire. She also asserts her maternal instincts when protecting her son against the detective's investigation. Director Paul Nickel keeps the action moving at a steady clip. The script is credible and was written by Joanne Court and based on a short story by Jonathan Latimer.

Dan Duryea plays a British man who returns to his days as a Japanese P.O.W. in *The United States Steel Hour: Hour of the Rat*. *The Hour of the Rat* is midnight and that is when the bell tolls for Sakamura, a man who has lived with a dirty secret that is about to become common knowledge.

John Woodruffe is a man who still carries the mental scars of World War II. It is impossible for him to forget the torture and deprivation he experienced while imprisoned in a Japanese prisoner of war camp. It has instilled in him a deep seated hatred of the Japanese.

Now a successful civil servant who needs a cane for support, Mr. Woodruffe relives his war horrors when he swears that he has seen Sakamura (Khigh Dhiegh), the commandant of the prisoner of camp, at a business meeting. His friends try to dissuade him from pursuing his own brand of justice but their warnings remain unheeded. Duryea is intent on exposing the war criminal and will stop at nothing, including harassment and stalking his prey. He turns out to be right.

Arthur Hailey has a written a tight script where everything seems to fall into place. The emotional denouement makes it worthwhile. The use of flashbacks recreates the hell of the prison camp and gives Woodruffe a chance to recollect his nightmare. Ronald Long, Arthur Mallet and John

John Woodruffe confronts his wartime jailer and tormentor with exposing his war crimes. 1958, Theatre Guild.

McLiam play former British officers. They appear in the flashbacks and are on hand for present day commentary meant to diffuse his attempt to exact recompense for something they prefer to forget.

Sakamura, the sadistic Japanese soldier, is played by Khigh Dhiegh, whose claim to fame was playing Wo-Fat on the original *Hawaii 5-0*. Another connection to *Hawaii 5-0* is the plot of *Hour of the Rat*, which was used for *Reunion*. Simon Oakland played the former P.O.W., a bitter man who can't walk without the use of crutches. At a reunion of Army buddies, he swears that he sees the man who tormented him during WW II. After discouragement from his Army buddies and repeated warning from Steve McGarrett and 5-0 he proves his case and wins justice after a lifetime of living in a mental prison.

In 1961, Dan Duryea was supposed to star with Margaret Hayes in a television series, *The Holidays Abroad*. The pilot was to be done at Desilu-Gower. Jack Sher was to direct a script written by Bill Manhoff. The show was created by Josef Shaftel and Stanley Adams.

The Dysfunctional Relative

Dan Duryea's first television role of 1960 was portraying Muff Potter in *Shirley Temple's Storybook: Tom and Huck*. The former child star hosted this anthology of classic children's stories and American folk tales. It ran from 1958 to 1962 and was a precursor to *Shelly Duval's Tall Tales and Legends*. There were 41 stories to *Shirley Temple's Storybook*.

Tom and Huck is based on Mark Twain's book, *The Adventures of Tom Sawyer*. David Ladd and Teddy Rooney play Tom and Huck respectively. The drama was directed by Paul Nickel. The last time that Dan Duryea worked with Paul Nickell and David Ladd was a couple of years previously in *Pursuit: Tiger on a Bicycle*.

Muff Potter is a fisherman with a fondness for drinking. He is also fond of children and often goes fishing with them and mends their kites when they are in need of fixing. Muff is accused of killing Dr. Robinson after he is convinced by the evil Injun Joe (the real killer) that he did it. The dissolute drunkard is put on trial but saved by Tom Sawyer's testimony.

The role of Muff Potter is a natural for Dan Duryea. It is basically a "scalawag with a heart of gold" role. Poignant and moving, he is a lonely man who recreates his lost world with booze. The children remind him of an innocent past that no longer exists. He is a downtrodden soul who still ha s spiritual beauty to heal his inner pain.

Existential grief has no place at *Checkmate*, an exclusive and expensive investigative agency located in San Francisco. The elite detectives that comprise the agency are Don Corey (Anthony George), Jed Sills (Doug McClure) and Prof. Carl Hyatt (Sebastian Cabot).

Tight as a Drum starts out as a strange mystery that baffles then intrigues Prof. Hyatt. He has to devise a plan to spy on Maj. Sam Wilson, the commandant of a military academy. Two junior cadets suspect him of foul play in the death of their gym instructor and they accuse Maj. Wilson, if only in hushed whispers. A cryptic message to Checkmate's Maj. Carl Hyatt ought to clear things up. Its urgency causes Maj. Hyatt to abruptly cancel a lecture as he is about to take the stage. He is mortified when his clients turn out to be boys and their cloak and dagger ritual leads him to believe that they have over-active imaginations.

A meeting in the bushes, a secret pathway through the grounds and an unauthorized visit to the gym stretches the detective's credulity even before the boys present their evidence. By the time they tell him about the black-clad motorcycle rider he feels like he's been had. It's not until he explains the episode to his partners, Don Corey and Jed Sills (Doug McClure), that little pieces begin to cling to each other and the men realize that they might have a case.

Maj. Wilson presents a dignified front and is the figure of respect and admiration among the cadets. It is a false façade and something that has made him the stooge of a greedy smuggler of Asian scrolls. Henry Creasy (Dabbs Greer) is the black-clad motorcycle rider and he is also the mastermind behind the black market scheme. Creasy uses the major's guilty secret to force the commandant into using his international and influential connections to sell the smuggled art objects. The gym teacher was the weak link in the chain and was accidentally killed in a fight with the major.

The secret that made the major a dupe and an accomplice was cowardice in battle during the Korean War. It is a sad fact that mars the myth of the warhorse who is teaching military discipline to rambunctious youngsters.

The young cadets pierced together little incongruities that are corroborated by Checkmate's investigation when Jed Sills is hired as the new gym instructor, Don Corey acts like a courier with a stewardess (Tita Marsell) and Maj. Hyatt arrives in time to prevent the young cadets from being neutralized by Creasy. It is Maj. Wilson's heroic body exchange with Creasy that makes him a martyr and hero for sacrificing his life for the kids in the gym.

Maj. Wilson may have been a fake, but so are Pierre the fortune teller and Bennet Lorrigan the medical charlatan. Pierre is a spiritualist who knows all of the tricks that make lonely women part with their money. He offers them hope and blesses them with soothing compliments. Bennet Lorrigan is also a dealer in spirits. He is an unlicensed hypno-therapist posing as a psychiatrist. He instills false confidence in a frigid woman who hates men.

In *The Sign of the Zodiac*, Pierre sees more twists and turns in the life of Helene (Joan Blondell), a woman who pretends to be helping her widowed sister-in-law when she is actually trying to frame her for her husband's murder. 1961, ESW Productions.

Pierre uses his fakery to right a wrong and turn the tables on the woman who hired him into pressuring another woman to confess to a murder she didn't commit. Lorrigan betrays his patient's trust in him when he becomes everything she loathes in a man. Both men determine their fates with a single decision. Only one of them gets to light up a smoke and stare at the night tide.

The Barbara Stanwyck Show was hosted by the noted actress, who also starred in a couple of episodes. In *Sign of the Zodiac*, she plays Madge. a woman who is being set up into confessing that she killed her husband. Madge's husband recently died and it has put her in a fragile state of mind. Helene's idea of getting her back on track is a psychic reading with Pierre, the waterfront psychic. Madge is edgy and belligerent, but Pierre is good at cold readings and helps to steady her. He uses his clients' hints and suggestions as a way of discovering more about her. He becomes alarmingly convincing when he reveals her innermost secrets.

Is Pierre a fake spiritualist? If so, how did he know so much about Madge's life without having met her before her first reading? Did the crystal ball tell him anything or did he make up things based on the formation of the cloudy chaos within the globe? Why is Madge so hostile against him? Is it personal or unfathomable or does she sense his pretentious charade? And why is her friend Helene so obliging? Did she coach Pierre to unhinge Madge because she believes that her sister-in-law killed her brother? There are so many questions and one answer when it seems that it was the latter.

Pierre has been a part of the sting since the beginning. The success of the setup depends on his convincing Madge of his power to transcend time and comprehend action. His clairvoyance and mental images are based on information supplied by Helene. That includes the contents of her purse and the significance of her late husband's watch. He tells Madge that her husband is alive spiritually so long as the watch is ticking.

She is driven over the edge and believes that he knows that she killed her husband. It is something that she firmly believes even though there was no proof. Pierre was hired by Helene to expose Madge as a murderess; now he is not so sure that she is guilty. He vows to Helene that he will set things straight even if it means implicating Helene.

Helene is the catalyst of the scheme, but will her past become Madge's present? Is that what will happen? Is it in the crystal ball? It is a reversal of fortune for Sagittarius the archer? The bow she shot is actually a boomerang. She switches from Pierre's employer to the subject of his investigation. He relinquishes his fee for a promise of helping Madge recover the breakdown and prove Helene's complicity in setting up her sister-in-law.

Pierre is affable and seems to have a perfect memory. He remembers Helene and the reading he gave her. Pierre exudes an artificial warmth. His gestures accentuate his sentences to produce an hypnotic effect on his clients. He never misses a beat and proceeds at a steady pace.

He is as solitary as his beachfront parlor. The loneliness of the beachfront cabana gives the impression of the boardwalk during the off-season. The only signs of life are the seagulls that hover in mid-air. Pierre believes that they are the souls of the departed and wonders what they are thinking about?

That is what Madge asks the police when they arrest her for trying to shoot Pierre after she already shot him dead to prevent him from exposing her. She is driven over the edge when she returns to the room and finds the body gone. When she goes to his house, she is alarmed when he greets her. She tries to shoot him again but the police prevent her. They were in on the scheme from the start. The only problem is that Pierre believes that Helene was using suggestions to influence Madge's fragile mental state. That's why he pledges to solve the case and undo the outcome of the invitation.

Pierre may not have been a total fake, but the same cannot be said for Bennett Lorrigan of *The Eleventh Hour: Why am I Grown So Cold?* Wendell Cory starred as Dr. Theodore Bassett, an adviser to the Board of Corrections. Each week, he and his assistant, Dr. Paul Graham (Jack Ging) try to unlock the mysteries of the deranged mind in *The Eleventh Hour*.

Why am I Grown So Cold? is a diatribe against medical quackery. Dr. Bassett becomes a crusader against con artists after a court order puts Connie Folsom (Eleanor Parker), an unstable young woman with a drinking problem, in his care. She has a serious attitude problem regarding men and cannot deal with affection, especially if it comes from a man. Connie has a history of attacking men who made passes at her and she resists Dr. Bassett and his Freudian concepts.

The enabler of Ms. Folsom's convoluted anguish is Bennett Lorrigan, a hypno-therapist who does not have a license to practice medicine. He cuts a mysterious figure shrouded in the shadows of an office decorated with mystical figurines. He possesses a cool, deliberate manner with a voice that is soothing and somewhat patronizing. Being unrecognized by the medical profession has not made him bitter. The rejection and condescension makes him feel superior and he has developed an uncanny knack to put his accusers on the defensive.

His livelihood is threatened by Dr. Bassett when the medical man testifies at a city council's hearing on quackery. Bennet Lorrigan uses the open forum to challenge Dr. Bassett point-for-point. He even uses Connie Folsom's present mental state as a result of Dr. Bassett's interference in his therapy. She concurs.

The animus is made potent by the fact that both men knew each other in medical school. It was Bassett who encouraged Lorrigan not to

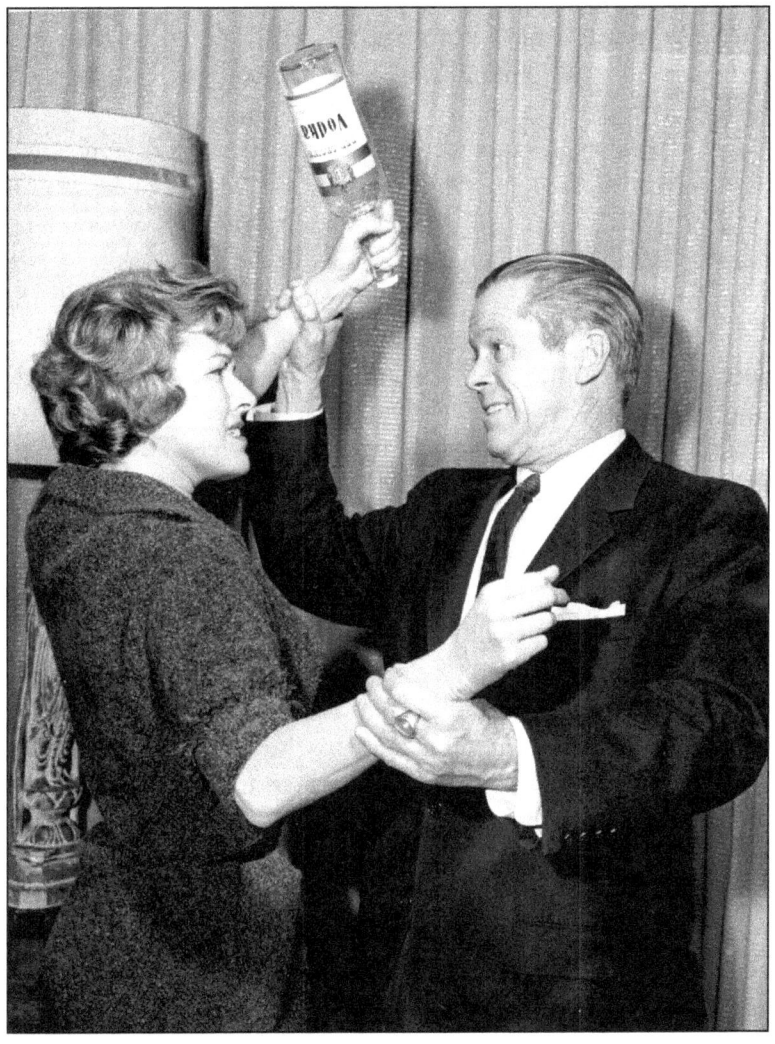

Bennett Lorrigan pushed his luck into unwelcome territory and suffers a form of regression therapy at the hands of his patient, the man-hating Connie Folsom (Eleanor Parker). 1963, Arena Productions, MGM television.

drop out of school. The faker's intentions become obvious when he takes Connie back to his office for a new type of therapy: drinking and hypnosis. He uses hypnotic suggestion to convince Connie that she loves him. Consuming liquor has made her susceptible to his advances until her subconscious fears kick in. She breaks the liquor bottle over his head and stabs him to death with the broken bottle neck.

Eleanor Parker gives a powerful performance as a woman tormented by child abuse. Connie Folsom is a beautiful woman with a damaged mind. Any attempt to appeal to her sexually provokes a violent outburst. There have been a few violent outbursts lately. The only man who rose about Connie Folsom's paranoia was Bennett Lorrigan and he violated her trust when he assumed the role of step-father.

Dan Duryea again channels his inner snake charmer to play the phony therapist. He is so smooth that it is eerie. There is a sense of nonchalant arrogance to him. He is too confident for his own good. He is a decadent psychic healer who has taken a short cut to ply his trade. There are no laws to force men like Lorrigan to hang up their shingle. That is the point of the story. Most businesses require regulations yet the medical profession is not one of them. Besides providing false hope for the hopeless, the quack also sets himself up for a nasty fall. Bennett Lorrigan is one of them, a faker whose happy hour beat the clock when it ran out of time.

Amidst the good deeds and derring-do, Dan Duryea also found time to make a guest appearance on a show called *Make Me Laugh*. The object of the show was for contestants to maintain a straight face while being subjected to a barrage of jokes from three comedians. The show lasted three months. He also appeared as a guest on *The Joe Franklin Show*, the longest running talk show ever.

The 1960's portended many changes for the movie industry and, consequently, television. Television's popularity cut into the movies' revenue and this caused the collapse of the studio system. Many old time stars were moving into television, some of them doubled as producers. Syndication was seen as a lucrative way for many producers to turn a profit. During the 60's, most of Duryea's time was spent playing parts on many of the popular shows of the era. It was the same thing as he had done during the 50's, when he first became familiar with the television audiences. His big-screen genres may have run the course of their popularity with the new young audiences, but the same crowd accepted him on the small screen.

Checkmate, Route 66, Kraft Suspense Theater, Alfred Hitchcock Presents, and *Burke's Law* are some of the crime dramas Duryea worked on, and *Bonanza, Wagon Train, Daniel Boone,* and *The Virginian* are some of the popular Western shows from his long list of credits. His prolific television output seemed to be ribbed in his consideration of narrating an LP called *Music for TV Haters*.

The 50's All American suburban family experienced changes with the new decade. Urban dramas showed the cracks in the traditional family with portraits that would nowadays be called dysfunctional. Back then, shame replaced rationalization and anything that went outside of the mother-father and small family mode was considered an unfortunate circumstance.

In the late 50's, Dan Duryea was able to play a string of American archetypes that were 50's role models of heroism. In the 60's, societal changes showed the imperfections and contradictions of the ideal 50's small town Utopia and the breakdown of the stalwart man of morals. In the late 1940's Dan Duryea established one character type in the dominant miscreant. Almost 20 years later he played a series of characters that were variations of the cruel lover. The deadbeat dad not only dramatized the conflicts of familial devotion and betrayal but mirrored the perils of losing a sense of purpose in an impersonal society. It was about alienation and the fine line between responsibility to the self and to others. In some cases, there was also the question of forgiveness and redemption.

Many of Dan Duryea's characters from this period still possessed the odd sense of responsibility or irresponsibility (depending on one's perspective) of their 50's forebears; only now they had children to contend with. It was no longer a matter of women with broken hearts on both sides of the looking glass. The offspring could be children or young adults. In the case of Duryea's parental sense from these shows, that meant that there would be grudges that had to be settled and unanswered questions that needed to be explained.

Adventures in Paradise was an exotic show starring Gardner McKay as the seafaring skipper of a quay, which he sails among pacific atolls in search of adventure. He finds more than he bargained for when he has to deliver a package of hi-fi tubes to Theodore Florian in *Judith*.

Skipper Troy and Oliver, his first mate, arrive on Boralap and are surprised to see Judith. They knew each other when she nursed Troy back to health in a Pearl Harbor hospital after he was wounded in Korea. The familiarity is not lost on Florian. He may have his hi-fi tubes, but being a spiteful man, he will soon have his twisted vengeance.

Florian does not have a life outside of his work and he makes demands on people without giving them anything in return. He is emotionally dead but tense with fierce eyes and a clenched jaw. His posture is rigid and he is a bundle of raw nerves kept in check by a deceptive outward calm. Florian needs his machines because they are the only things that he can control. They serve him but he is enslaved to them because the power that he derives from them makes him feel that he is superior to everyone on the atoll. What makes this especially sad is that his social circle consists of his wife and the Brody family.

Judith is a plain Jane who has found Hell in Paradise. She can't compete with the machines for her husband's affection nor does she want to anymore. Her love is unrequited and all she gets is little doses of sarcasm from her uncaring husband. The Brodys are a worn-out couple with four children. Mr. Brody is a bitter alcoholic beachcomber who is a self-declared enemy of Florian's. His wife is a long-suffering woman who is kind to everybody. Florian loathes their children, too, and has referred to them as 'cannibals.'

Despite this animosity, Florian invites them regularly for drinks and hi-fi concerts of classical music. This contentious situation is what Adam Troy contends with when he is invited over for drinks and music. The technological wizardry unnerves Brody, who feels that life was swell before the modern technological weather station was built. He hates the steel fortress with its humming air-conditioner, whirring machines and the hi-fi that blasts classical music.

What use are barometers, odometers and thermometers? He cannot comprehend that Florian's weather forecasts may warn the surrounding atolls and islands about inclement weather. During a tense exchange at an unfriendly get-together, Mrs. Brody eases the mounting hatred when she compliments Florian by telling him that, "I think your machines are nice." Nice? He wipes the vapid smile off her face when he dryly intones that her opinions are inconsequential.

Florian was going to entertain everyone with his news about the hurricane; instead, he will use it against Adam Troy and does so the next morning when he gives the sailor a forecast of sunny skies and smooth sailing. It does not take Adam and Oliver long to realize that a hurricane is brewing when they smell dry land and then see the white capped waves. They cannot believe that Florian would intentionally mislead them with a false and dangerous weather report.

The Tiki makes it back to Boralap and Troy makes his way through the raging winds and water to use Florian's transmitter to alert the sur-

Clyde Royd forces his daughter Helga (Barbara Harris) to get a makeover that will attract teenage wolves that he can take down with military style ju-jitsu. 1962, Shelle Productions, Screen Gems Television.

Clyde Royd tells Det. Flint (Paul Burke) everything that is wrong with parenting and policing before he is arrested for assault and battery. 1962, Shelle Productions, Screen Gems Television.

rounding area to the disaster. Florian, armed with a German luger, flies into a rage and fights with Troy because he won't allow anyone to touch his machines. Only one of them will enjoy the next day when the quiet morning makes everything seem normal, as if nothing happened. Troy and Oliver bid farewell to Judith and the Brodys. There will no longer be any need to deliver hi-fi tubes to Boralap. Judith will be returning to San Francisco.

Many of Dan Duryea's imperfect fathers attempt to undo years of neglect and bitterness, but there is one father who may not be an absentee father but should have been. Familial hell is a father who fights a war on two fronts in *Naked City: Daughter, Am I in Thy Father's House?* To the world at large, Clyde Royd is an aging war vet who no one cares about, and his need to play protective emissary for his little girl has made him combative and itching for a fight. His grip on his daughter is tight and is what convicts him in the sickness of this tenacious grip.

The retired officer is a frustrated insurance salesman. He conducts business by phone and wonders why people don't respond to his sales pitches. Royd has a chip on his shoulder that matches his belligerent attitude. Even a simple visit by the police to return his daughter's book and a present turns into a confrontation. It is as if he is blaming them for his inadequacies.

Royd is a former Major in the US paratroop corps in Japan. He still maintains his military bearing, from wearing combat boots underneath his dressing gown to displaying artifacts of WWII Japan in his apartment. He also uses ju-jitsu to bust the skulls and break bones of the teenage boys who flirt with his daughter.

He goes into combat mode when his daughter Helga (Barbara Harris) is harassed by a group of frisky teenage boys at the local theatre. They went over the line and offended her. Her father was enraged by her tears and vowed that the boys will pay.

He forces Helga to get a makeover and parade herself through the streets while he follows her, ready to pounce on the boys who consider her street bait. It is a disturbing scene where this deranged vet is actually stalking his own daughter. The police catch up with him as he breaks into a rant and beats up the kids.

At the station, Clyde Royd is hurt by his daughter's betrayal. Helga does not mind saving the teenager, who asks her out for a soda. Outside of the police station, Dom gives Helga a handkerchief to wipe off her lipstick.

Clyde Royd is the most intense of the modern relatives. The only comparison to him would be Westerners like Blaymeir or Cannon. Royd's lit fuse fizzles when he makes a jerk of himself. Luckily, Clyde Royd was in a world of his own. The rest of Duryea's irresponsible adults may have feet of clay, but none of them knew ju-jitsu.

Glimmers of Hope and Renewal

One of the traits of the 60's youth revolution was the search for identity and the meaning of life. This quest existed during the 50's with the Beat Generation, but it became more pronounced in the 60's because of the staggering number of Baby Boomers. Route 66 was part of the search that was initiated by Jack Kerouac's book, *On the Road*.

Route 66 was a real place, a stretch of highway that ran across America's mid-section. It has a rich history and exists as a real inspiration to songs, stories and anything related to adventure and wanderlust. The freedom of traveling Route 66 was an antidote to creeping uniformity and mechanization of American society.

Route 66 was also a fine television show that used the road as a premise for meeting interesting characters and facing unusual circumstances. It was a writer's dream in that the road story afforded a wealth of opportunities in creating characters and intriguing stories that could be seen as a portrait of a changing America. Nelson Riddle composed an up-tempo jazzy theme song for the show.

Buzz (George Maharis) and Tod (Martin Milner) drove their car in search of adventure and they found a trove of characters whose problems and puzzlements drew them into an emotional drama that ended with them hitting the road again. Dan Duryea starred in *Don't Count Stars* and *Cage in Search of a Bird*. He plays an uncle to two different kinds of nieces in the dramas. He is an unrepentant alcoholic who was appointed the guardian of his 11-year-old niece. She is now the executive of a large hotel that may not survive her uncle's spendthrift ways for him and his wayward friends. The other uncle is a man who robbed the U.S. mint 33 years before he decides to make his niece a legacy if she can confront a dubious proposition that spells tragedy for them.

Don't Count the Stars in the daylight is what Uncle Mike says. You have to see them at night before you can appreciate anything about them. Uncle Mike is a poetic visionary whose spirit comes out of a bottle and that's something a court wants to use against him in a custody battle.

Mike McKay is fished out of the bay by Buz and Tod when they are waterskiing with two women. He is drunk and caustic, slyly hinting that they ruined his business deal after he is drying out on the pier. They don't know it, but the artful drunkard is about to draw them into a strange custody battle.

The unstable wastrel is claimed by his 11-year-old niece and they leave after she thanks the men for saving her uncle. They tell her their names and say that they are workers at the missile plant. That is enough information for her when she needs them to safeguard her uncle until a custody hearing in a day. If they can keep him sober there may be a chance that she won't be separated from him.

Uncle Mike does not take kindly to the interest everyone is showing in him. He actually agrees with the stolid banker (Vaughn Taylor) that he is unfit as a guardian and a leach whose generosity is impacting the hotel's economics.

There are two ways that Tod and Buz try to salvage Uncle Mike's reputation. Buz keeps guard on him and engages Uncle Mike in arguments about responsibility. The old man tries to feel sorry for himself but Buz won't let him. While they are going through their torture therapy Tod and Eileen are rounding up Uncle Mike's parasitic friends at the racetrack. Tod has to give them a speech that makes them cough up the money they owe him for sponging at the hotel.

Things seem like a lock when Uncle Mike wants to run and not go to the hearing. They think that he is afraid but are stunned to find out that Uncle Mike is really Eileen's father. It is his lack of faith in himself that impelled him to ask his brother and sister-in-law to bring up his daughter in an affluent environment with all of the entitlements that she deserved. All this will come out at the hearing and that is what he is trying to avoid. Running away won't solve anything as he is shamed into accepting his responsibility as the child's father. They leave in a taxi to go to the hearing while Buz and Tod wrap up another adventure and hit the road.

Dan Duryea returned to *Route 66* two years later in *Cage in Search of a Bird*.

Uncle Jay is the con artist that she aspires to be even though he is at the end of the road. Jay Rigby's claim to fame is that he robbed the United States Mint over 33 years ago. Now that he has reached his golden years, Uncle Jay wants to make amends for his wanton ways. He tells his niece that he wants

Uncle Mike and Eileen are an odd couple in *Don't Count the Stars*. 1961, Lancer-Edding productions, Screen Gems Television.

to leave money to someone in the family and he has chosen her. No, it is not the money that is left over from the robbery. He spent that living the high life of a bachelor hell bent on riding in the fast lane. Now he has another scheme in mind that will pay off big for Julie if she wants to play.

"You're a little crook in big trouble. I'm going to leave you a legacy. I'm going to make a good woman out of you."

He shows her a scrapbook detailing the mint robbery and tells her to memorize the details because she is going to turn him in for the reward money. Julie is not impressed; in fact, she is livid and tells him, "I make my own rules and one of them is don't be a fink."

Uncle Jay explains the reasoning to his scheme and then tells her about his concept of connections. He believes that the only way people can define themselves is if they are connected to someone else. Julie replies that what is a connection to him means a cage to her. She is not the type of bird to live in a cage.

"You're stupid! You don't even know me! Leave me alone!" she blurts.

The intention is love and legacy but she can't cozy up to her Uncle Jay's idea of philanthropy. Julie does not buy his philosophy that people cannot reach their potential if they don't invest in someone else. She is sensitive and confused and seeks temporary respite from her identity crisis when she meets Tod and Linc after she escapes a crooked card party. Not only is Julie a card sharp but she's betrayed her partner when the game turned bad. She takes half the pot at gun point and leaves the rest to her sidekick who is now being held by one of the players.

Julie hides the money in the hub cap of Tod and Linc's car with the intention of hooking up with them later. They think that it's their well-deserved good fortune when she jumps in the car after being spotted by her betrayed partner.

Tod and Linc are enamored by the mystery beauty that jumps into her car with an angry man in hot pursuit. It was a strange way to start a friendship but that fits in with the show's premise. The accuser and the cops catch up to her later and she has some explaining to do about an alleged card party turned bad. That is when Uncle Jay steps in.

He claims that they were traveling cross country on a bus when she alighted and got in trouble. She tells the officer that she is only 19 years old and told the stranger that when he invited her up to his hotel room for dinner. Uncle Jay tells the officer that if he wants to file charges against Julie, he has a couple of charges to file himself.

Unfortunately, the charges are made against him when Julie's ex-partner uses the scrapbook to leverage revenge at the expense of Uncle Jay. It is all in vain because there no longer is any reward money to claim. The old man will wind up in a cage while the bird he tried to impress remains free to be dominated by fear and insecurity. Her only sense of closure is the afternoon of fun she had with Tod at a square dance. They find a false sense of security and forget the parts they are playing in the world of adults.

Dan Duryea's next con artist is a father who wants a chance to see his daughter get married. It is a role that has the flavor of an old movie, because of its star and because it is based on an old movie. In *Going*

My Way, Gene Kelly played Father O'Malley, the role created by Bing Crosby.

Mr. Second Chance is a story about redemption and the possibility of positive change in a crooked man's life. In this case, the crook is Harry the Horse, a suave racketeer who made a fortune from the numbers, bootlegging and loan sharking.

Harry the Horse is aware of good publicity and never passes on a photo op when making a sizeable donation to charity. It is no different when he writes a $250,000 check for the church. His ulterior motive is to create a favorable impression on his ex-wife and their daughter, who is about to be married. He is forbidden from attending the wedding and this causes distress for him.

Harry was not allowed to attend the state funeral for his son, a soldier who died a heroic death in Korea. Exclusion from his daughter's wedding would be too much of a strain for him. Father O'Malley is caught in the middle of the imbroglio, which becomes a crossfire when he does research on the man with the $250,000 contribution. What he discovers disturbs and the parish is forced to return the check.

The rejection causes Harry to vent his spleen on the hypocrisy of public persona in America. He compares himself to the robber barons who ultimately bought respect and good reputations through philanthropy. He makes one excuse after another, blaming his soiled reputation on the shortcomings of other people. This does not sway Father O'Malley but he is persuaded to see the ex-wife and daughter to plead Harry's case.

They are outraged and unrelenting. It is not until the priest learns about a local legend named Mr. Second Chance that he finds a way to change Harry and his daughter's mind. Mr. Second Chance was a reformed mobster who used his fortune to help ex-cons get back on their feet. He would pay their debts or finance their return to society.

Father O'Malley's friend informs the priest that Mr. Second Chance is dead and feels that it is a shame that no one can take his place. This gives the priest the challenge he needs to confront Harry the Horse about the power of redemption.

Harry is known for his charm and blarney, never hesitating to blame others for his shortcomings. Hypocrisy and anti-Semitism are some of the excuses he uses but Father O'Malley does not buy any of it. He uses the Mr. Second Chance angle to help one of his parishioners out of a bind. The man embezzled $1,000 from company funds and was caught before he could return it. He will not be prosecuted if he can return the

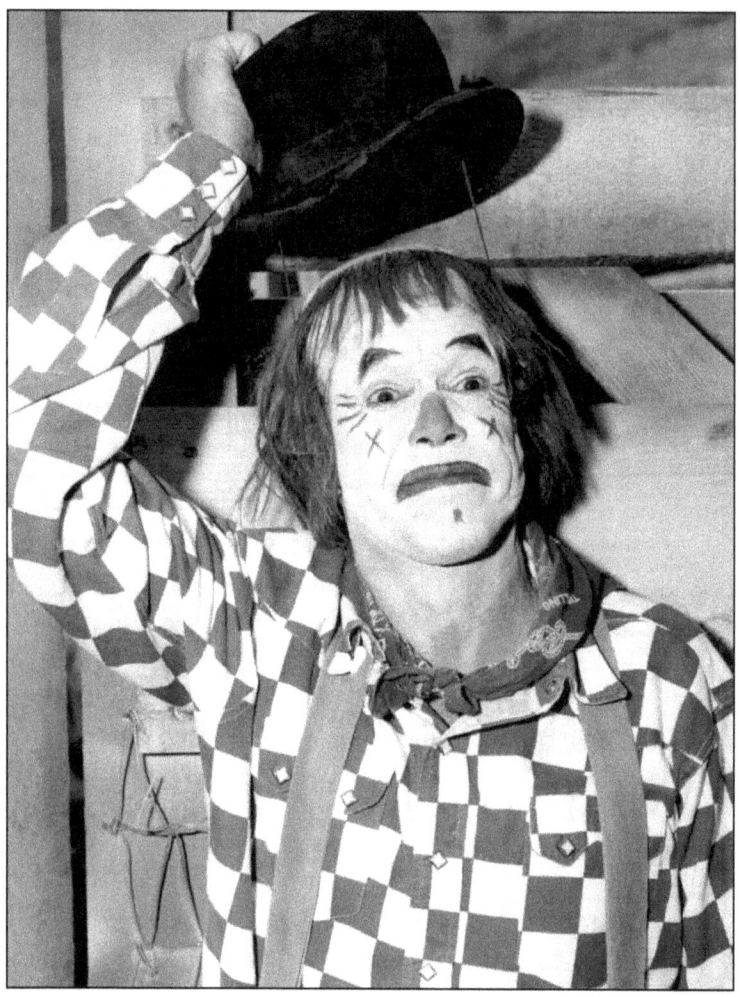

Willie Xeno is a fading rodeo clown who braves his decline to support his spoiled son's lifestyle in *Tears on a Painted Face*. 1962, Ralph Edwards Productions.

man within a week. Only Harry the Horse as Mr. Second Chance can help him out. Father O'Malley makes it clear that it is not a one time deal. Harry the Horse agrees and begins his new life as a benefactor to hapless cons.

Father O'Malley passes on the tale of the good deed to Harry's daughter and she is ultimately persuaded to let her father attend the marriage, only if he sits unobtrusively with the choir so her mother will not see him. She acknowledges his existence with a big smile when she leaves the church. Mr. Second Chance beams with pride.

Pride almost causes rodeo clown Willie Xeno's fall in *Wide Country: Tears on a Painted Face*. The show was an episodic study of human nature and the itinerant nature of the premise provided many storylines about interesting characters, good and bad. Mitch Guthrie (Earl Holliman) is a championship rodeo rider working the circuit during the waning days of his career. Andy (Andrew Prine) is his younger brother and tags along in hopes of becoming a rodeo rider, something that Mitch discourages as often as he can.

A father's blind devotion to his selfish son is what makes the *Tears on a Painted Face* real for Willy Xeno (Dan Duryea). He is a faded rodeo clown whose career is over and it is something that he does not want to face. His legs are weak and racked with pain so it is hard for him to entice the bulls away from fallen riders. The use of a cape does not fool any of the riders because they know that the newly added prop is a poor substitute for quick legs.

Pressure for him to retire makes him irritable; still, the riders are in agreement on banning Willy from the arena after he had a run-in with a bull that left him wounded in the dust. It is obvious that his legs are shot and this makes the riders uncomfortable. Even a negative prognosis from a doctor fails to deter Willy from facing the bulls. Being told that getting a second opinion will be futile falls on deaf ears.

Mitch does his best to be the peacemaker between Willy and the circuit riders. It does not help that Willy is not being honest with Mitch or that the rodeo clown becomes defensive every time they talk about his health. Another factor in the rodeo clown's decline is his slavish devotion to Chris (Charles Robinson), his only son. The young man is Willy's only reminder of a wife who died too soon and that is the reason why he spends his pay on the spendthrift. The young man is spoiled and self-centered, but his dependence is viewed as obligation by the old man. Chris is the reason why Willy continues to put on the greasepaint and baggy pants. It is something that will have to come to an end.

Willy also resents being told by outsiders that his son is a sponger but it also drives home the point that he might not be able to earn the money that he lavishes on the youngster. The end comes when Willy has a final close encounter and junior sees the error of his ways. Owning a hot rod was the pinnacle of success for the snobbish son. That was the latest present from his father. Now, Chris will forego the luxury of owning a symbol of juvenile delinquency and become a mechanic to earn a living to support his father in a reversal of fortune.

Wide Country successfully portrayed the sub-world of rodeo riders. They are a group unto themselves and appear to be anachronisms in the mechanized world. The rodeo riders are the last of the frontier individualists and they eke out a modest living working the rodeo circuit. Usually, the show dealt with outsiders who infiltrated the rodeo world for one reason or another. Willie is a man on the inside track who becomes an outsider when his pride jeopardizes the well-being of the riders. He suddenly becomes an outcast and it irks him that he can become an unwanted stranger all of a sudden.

Mitch is the only rider who shows him respect by giving him a benefit of the doubt. There is a heated exchange between the men when Mitch finds out the truth about Willie's health. The biggest exchange is when Chris finds out about his father's frail health. There is none of the self-pity one would expect from a spoiled brat who has just lost his ticket for the gravy train. It is Chris who shows the most honesty of anyone in the story when he decides not to buy the hot rod so he can use the money to start a new life for him and his father.

A minor aspect of the story is Holly (Carole Wells), a baton twirler who dreams of being an actress. Of course, she is misunderstood and will gladly discuss her dilemma with anyone involved with the rodeo, even a peripheral figure like Chris. Towards the end of the story, there is a telling close-up of her twirling the baton when the marching band takes to the arena to start the show. That's all she wants out of show business-a little close-up.

Harlan Tracey (Tommy Sands) is seeking a close-up of another kind but he does not have a father to finance his whims. All that is left of his dad is a tape recording of him playing a sad but powerful piano etude. Harlan's only way of bonding with his father is playing his trumpet to the taped music.

To the world that knew him, Joe Tracey is a stone marker that commemorates the plane crash that killed him 16 years prior to the action of *Alcoa Theater: Blow High, Blow Clear*. His wife is grateful that her second husband picked up the pieces of her shattered life and put them back together again. The same cannot be said of her son, Harlan, a conflicted and uncommunicative 19-year-old whose only solace is playing his trumpet to accompany a tape recording of his father performing a melancholy piano concerto.

Harlan is obsessed with a tape of his father playing a melancholy piano concerto. He plays along with his trumpet and this annoys his step-father, a good-natured and understanding man who has his limits. His mother must play along and discourage him from pursuing a dead man's memory but it is of no use. He even enlists the help of a sailor friend who uses port calls.

The monument is a hollow reminder of the follies of war. It is false and has no bearing on the blind piano player at Felipe's in the Latin Quarter. Harlan's dad may have left his remains behind in the Pacific hideaway but his soul pours out itself for the man with the shades that partially hide the scars that nobody wants to look at. All they want to remember is the solitary monument on the Pacific island.

Harlan is obsessed with visiting the stone marker and will do anything to travel to the shrine. His friend Jerry Doyle is a naval officer who promises to get him a berth on his ship, The Mandalay. This proves impossible when Harlan alienated everyone with his erratic behavior. His chip on his shoulder is too large to carry on the close quarters of the ship.

Harlan depends on Doyle for moral support. He knows the mobility of the Navy gives him a chance to visit the shrine. The stress takes its toll on Jerry and his work performance slips. This attracts the attention of his mentor.

It is Doyle's mentor who uses psychology and patient observance to understand why Doyle insists on helping Harlan. The commander listens to the tape and recognizes it as the playing of Charlie, the piano player at Pepe's, a run-down joint with a piano, four walls and eight bottles of tequila. Now, he realizes that Charlie is Joe Tracy, the memorial. This secret is something that the commander carries inside because he does not want to alter too many lives abruptly. He sets up a way to introduce Harlan and his mother to the father. It's at the club, where the social setting makes it impossible for awkward moments. Harlan does not mind. He grabs a trumpet from the bandstand and fulfills his dream, the one that conquers his guilt and birth pangs.

The coming-of-age saga is also a closure scenario for the father. He has spent 16 years of his life as a shadow that plays the piano in out-of-the way dives. His passionate music satisfies the lonely souls who find solace in his notes. His ability to read faces is his only connection to the modern world. Everything else is locked up in the overseas stone monument.

It is a strange reunion set to an impromptu jam session, the end of a long and strange journey that started with accompanying the tape recording of his father and finished with actually playing alongside him in a New Orleans bar.

Harlan (Tommy Sands) is reunited with his father, bringing to a close a coming-of-age drama of a young man in search of an identity. 1963, Avasta Productions.

Around this time, Norman Belton, executive producer for MGM-IV-Arena, approached Dan Duryea for a starring role in his pilot, Grand Slam, a television pilot for a sports-themed show.

Western Twilight

Retro Cowboys

The popularity of traditional Hollywood Westerns decreased as the 60's progressed. This was mainly due to the deconstruction of American history and the denunciation of the genre through the new counter-culture perspective. Still, old-fashioned Westerns were being made and there was a faithful audience even if it was shrinking. Network schedules held spots for old reliables like *Gunsmoke*, *The Virginian* and *Bonanza* but newer entries rarely lasted more than one season.

Isolating the films from the time they were made offers a better chance to appreciate them from a Western fan's perspective rather than through a cultural critique. Many of the retro-Westerns were below par but there were others that deserved praise. Ironically, the most popular Westerns of the time were the "spaghetti Westerns" of Europe made during the late 60's. They were brutal and fierce and dealt with the same themes as the Hollywood Westerns, only they had an honesty that resonated with the audience. It didn't hurt that many of the heroes and villains of the Euro-Westerns were expatriate Americans.

Universal Pictures was still making old time Westerns during the early 60's, a time when television was gaining popularity over a medium whose dwindling popularity saw the last of the 40's movie emporiums close or become sub-divided in a phase that preceded the creation of the multiplex theaters. Dan Duryea had his renewable contract with Universal, even though the studio had gone through a couple of its periodic changes since he first signed with it in 1945. The early 60's basically recycled the best of the decade that preceded it. There were still diehard fans out there but, overall, the times were changing and the Jet Set age dominated the industry. Still, cowpokes, showgirls, gunslingers, displaced

Native Americans and distaff European settlers still found a place on the playbills.

In the 60's, at a time when even the television Westerns that had supplanted big screen showdowns were also riding into the sunset, Universal pushed a new movie cowboy hero and he was played by Tony Young. Young was the star of *Gunslinger*, a television Western, when he was pegged to star in two movies for the studio. He had a firm speaking voice with precise diction and had good posture, bringing a soap opera actor's technique to the great outdoors.

Tony Young made a convincing lawman because he was made of righteousness and could outdraw any gun. Young starred in two Westerns for Universal: *He Rides Tall* and *Taggart*. Dan Duryea played his nemesis in both movies. Bart Thorne and Jayson are twin villains, split visions of Frank James, the philosophical villain in *Six Black Horses*, the first film in Duryea's twilight gunman phase.

Morg Rocklin (Tony Young) assures his wife Ellie (Madlyn Rhue) that nothing will go wrong on his last day as sheriff. 1963, Universal Pictures Company, Inc.

He Rides Tall is an apt title for a movie about a man who has to create order out of chaos and put his life on the line during a crisis that threatens the hopeful turn his life has taken. Morg Rocklin (Tony Young) is a marshal who will be turning in his badge and gun to get married to Ellie (Madlyn Rhue), his sweetheart. What should be his last day on the job turns into a nightmare when he winds up at odds with Josh McCloud (R.G. Armstrong), a powerful cattle baron and the man who raised him. The Marshal shot the cattle baron's son in self-defense in a saloon showdown. In doing so, the marshal also rekindles an old feud with Bart Thorne (Dan Duryea), McCloud's foreman, a man he once sent to prison.

Thorn is an arrogant opportunist. He doesn't care if people are aware that his smile is phony or that he grates on their nerves. His laughter is mocking and his speech is labored. He considers obnoxiousness to be a virtue and thinks that he is doing people a favor by paying attention to them. It is all a prelude to ruining his mark.

He talks a drunken cattle baron into ordering his doctor to perform surgery on the hero's gun hand, then rustles the baron's cattle, barters the baron's wife when an Indian brave declares that it is either his life or hers, and instigates a cattle stampede that kills the baron who pursues him. His *coup de grace* is taking over a town in a midnight siege. It all ends with him crawling on his belly like a dying snake as the hero rides tall.

He Rides Tall plays like a cowboy *noir* because it is dark, harsh, and dreary. The obvious example is the final showdown in the sparsely-lit town. The dark shadows and razor thin highlights are hallmarks of the film genre, but there are also other elements that form a kinship. The puritanical righteousness of the hero and the amoral sociopathic behavior of the villain are severe contradictions. Cruel deaths and ironic plot twists are the other touches that make this film a strange, deranged crime drama.

Tony Young is the stoical hard boiled lawman ready to turn his badge in for love. A crisis interferes with his plans and he has to deal with a life-and-death situation in a short amount of time. Young is a wax-figure cowboy who can withstand the heat of a high-noon showdown. He gets the job done during a time when movie Westerns hardly caused a ripple.

Madlyn Rhue was a distinguished television and movie veteran who gave many fine performances in Warner Bros. shows and many other comedies and dramas. She was married to Tony Young when they made the movie. She delivers a solid performance as the saloon owner and

Morg Rocklin (Tony Young) recuperates from an operation under the watchful eye of Dr. Sam (Joel Fluellen) as Bart Thorne (Dan Duryea) examines the gun hand rendered useless by a scalpel. 1963, Universal Pictures Company, Inc.

bride-to-be. She, too, is tough and made to last, as evidenced in the scene when Thorne takes over the town and temporarily has the upper hand in her business.

Duryea plays Thorn as an opportunist who only thinks of himself. His charm is a thin veneer for a strong ego. He is really flattering himself when he compliments others. He looks people in the eye, says something charming, and cancels it out with a mocking laugh. He intimidates the weak and grovels before anyone stronger than himself. In the movie, only two people dominate Thorn: Morg Rocklin, the hero, and the Indian who demands—and gets!—his purloined woman.

Jo Morrow is feisty, torrid, and restless. She can plan a get-rich scheme on paper, but does not have the wits to make it all happen. She becomes someone else's trophy in a hair-raising scene.

R.G. Armstrong gives a robust performance as a hard-edged cattle baron confined to a wheelchair. He is the backbone of the movie and his unraveling provides a storyline for the other characters to make their claims. Duryea and Morrow take him for all that he is worth. Rocklin gives him the respect due to a foster father and Dr. Sam keeps his conscience straight and that is a blessing to the doctor.

The surprise performance of the movie is Joel Fluellen's portrayal of Dr. Sam. He comes from a long line of faith healers. His grandfather was a witch doctor in the Congo, his father was a shaman on the plantation, and he was an assistant surgeon during the Civil War. The doctor is the voice of reason and supplies a conscience for the movie.

Taggart is a routine Western with some merit, namely a couple of nice bits by old vets such as Dan Duryea, Dick Foran, Emile Meyer, and Bob Steele. Tony Young is still deadpan, monotone, and stone-faced as the hero, but this time, he's in color. Jean Hale gives a strong performance of a pioneer woman, the daughter of a displaced rancher acted by Dick Foran. His scheming wife is played by Elsa Cardenas, a Latina vamp from old-school central casting. She uses her torrid charms to get what does not belong to her only to be destroyed when her warped desires exact a deadly price.

Bart Thorne (Dan Duryea) romances Kate McCloud (Jo Morrow), a rancher's wife, before he sells her out to an Indian brave. 1963, Universal Pictures Company, Inc.

The movie's theme is the quest for power and the people who work for it through sanctimony and sweat versus those who expand their bases through violence and intimidation. It is a tale of carving out a niche in a new country where the rules had more meaning than what was stated in books and declared in courts.

Taggart begins with a standoff between settlers and a land baron because of the difference between a court decree and the power of coercion. Ben Blazer (Emile Meyer) is a grumbling town boss who does not take kindly to squatters. Neither does his son, a hot head who raids a settlement camp with his father and kills the couple and their handyman, leaving the son with a head wound and a motive for revenge. Blazer is critically wounded and escorted back to town.

Tony Young plays Taggart, a young cowpoke out to avenge the murder of his parents. 1964, Universal Pictures Company, Inc.

The next scene is one of the highlights of the movie, because it is well done and sets up the premise for story of the hunt. It depicts the hero and villain in their defining moments, one achieving one-on-one justice for his parents' murders and the other exacting blood money from a dying man whose dreams of power will mean nothing before the day is over.

Ben Blazer lies dying while former silent screen comic Eddie Quillan ministers to him as a country doctor. The old man is comforted by his son when Taggart, the survivor of the raid, enters the room and challenges the young man to a duel. The kid is feeling his mettle, which becomes cold to the touch when he draws and loses.

His violent death agitates Blazer, who almost passes out but holds on until the sheriff comes to perform his duty. The doctor attests to the fairness of the draw when asked by the law man for an account of the shootout. The sheriff escorts Taggart out and lets him free when he finds out his family name. The corrupt law man sympathizes with the young man when he realizes that his parents were the settlers who were brutally murdered at the behest of Ben Blazer.

Taggart's departure is followed by the arrival of Jason (Dan Duryea) and two other hired guns played by Tom Reese and David Carradine. They have come to hear the dying man's terms of employment. A petulant Jason is told by Blazer that it will take three men to take down Taggart. That is why he is offering the men five thousand dollars apiece to kill Taggart.

Jason, ever the pragmatic gunman, seeks a guarantee of payment because he gets the dying man to realize that the deed will be accomplished after he has succumbed to his wounds. Blazer assures him that his promise is validated by documents held by his lawyer. Jason's nagging hastens Blazer's death and he is off to collect his fee, trying to outwit the two other hired guns.

After Carradine makes an early exit and Reese is put to sleep in the desert, it will be Jason versus Taggart in a game where the winning stakes are five thousand dollars or the freedom to live a normal life. Taggart becomes the mark of Jason, a hired killer who is also a philanderer, gold stealer, and leering panderer. They star in a chase that uses clichés, stock footage, and cardboard sets to make things exciting.

The usual things keep the action going: heroics, revenge, gold fever, duplicity, and Apache attacks. One thing that the movie relies on is stock footage of stunt men dressed as Indians careening off their horses after having been shot.

Like any chase movie, motives and momentum are gained by alternating between the scenes of hero and villain doing the things that help define their labels. In one scene, Taggart is kind and generous to a widow (Claudia Barrett) who reluctantly resorts to being a showgirl in a woebegone cantina run by veteran character actor Peter Mamakos. In another scene, Jason shoots Tom Reese's gunman to put him out of his misery after he is wounded in a showdown with Taggart. He rides away leaving the dead man at peace with the desert sun.

The movie goes from one type of survival movie to another when Taggart stumbles upon a strange type of squatter, Stark (Dick Foran), a displaced rancher living in an abandoned mission with his young wife

Jason (Dan Duryea) is a cynical saddle tramp who hires out his gun to hunt down Taggart. 1964, Universal Pictures Company, Inc.

Consuelo (Elsa Cardenas), and Miriam (Jean Hale), his slightly younger daughter.

The secret to his eccentricity is his discovery of gold in a nearby cave. Stark has mined sacks of it and is guarding his turf until the Apache uprisings die down and he can make a safe getaway with his family and fortune. Stranger still is the arrival of Jason, who claims to be a bounty hunter in search of Taggart. This does not sit too well with Stark and his daughter and the gunman is viewed and treated with suspicion by Stark.

Jason's response is to make a cuckold out of over-the-hill tough guy Stark by treating him like an impotent sugar daddy who lives in an abandoned mission divided by his colluding, insatiable young wife, and strong-willed independent daughter.

Jason would not be a bona fide Duryea villain if he didn't romance someone's wife (Elsa Cardenas). 1964, Universal Pictures Company, Inc.

Consuelo is the flame that will light Duryea's way through the desert, regardless of cattle stampedes or Indian uprisings. It is Consuelo and the gold that adds spice to this Western when she motivates Jason with promises of a promising cut of her fortune.

Elsa Cardenas plays the schemer two ways: as an over-the-hill beauty when filmed in bad lighting and breathtakingly beautiful in naturally lit sequences. Her voice goes from being strident and whiskey-coated to soothing and seductive. She is the movie's broad-stroked baddie because she is ready, willing, and able to collude with any man to double-cross her mature husband and rob him of his gold reserves.

It takes a bold and brazen nut like Jason to accept an offer of riches with a getaway that will inevitably include an encounter with marauding Apache warriors. Such a conclusion means more to Consuelo than it does to Jason until he is indirectly undone by an Indian raid in the grand finale.

Jason has faced Indians many times by the end of the film. The first time is in a chance encounter between him and Taggart when they inadvertently wind up aiding a pioneer couple in a mountain standoff with a war party. Jason also deserts an Army wagon train when he rides away with Consuelo's stolen gold and survives. His last stand with the gold is at an army fort where he is trapped because of an Indian raid. The end of the chase is a frantic shootout where a wounded Taggart shoots Jason to death. For all his bravado, the gunslinger throws up his arms and is done with everything as he hits the dust. No matter how hard he tried and how many people died because of it, Jason was still outmaneuvered by Taggart in the final showdown.

Sundown

Producer Alex Gordon acquired the rights to Rex Lake's Western novel, *Three Rode to the Rainbow's End* with the aim of starring Dan Duryea in the role of the bounty hunter. With a title change to emphasize the film's perspective, *The Bounty Killer* begins when city slicker Willie Duggan (Dan Duryea) is saved from barroom intimidation by Johnny Liam (Rod Cameron), a gunfighter who salvages Duggan's honor by shooting a loudmouth in a barroom confrontation. The haranguer is tough by the city slicker's standards, but he is a boorish loudmouth to others. This still does not sit well with Liam, who is having a drink to relax.

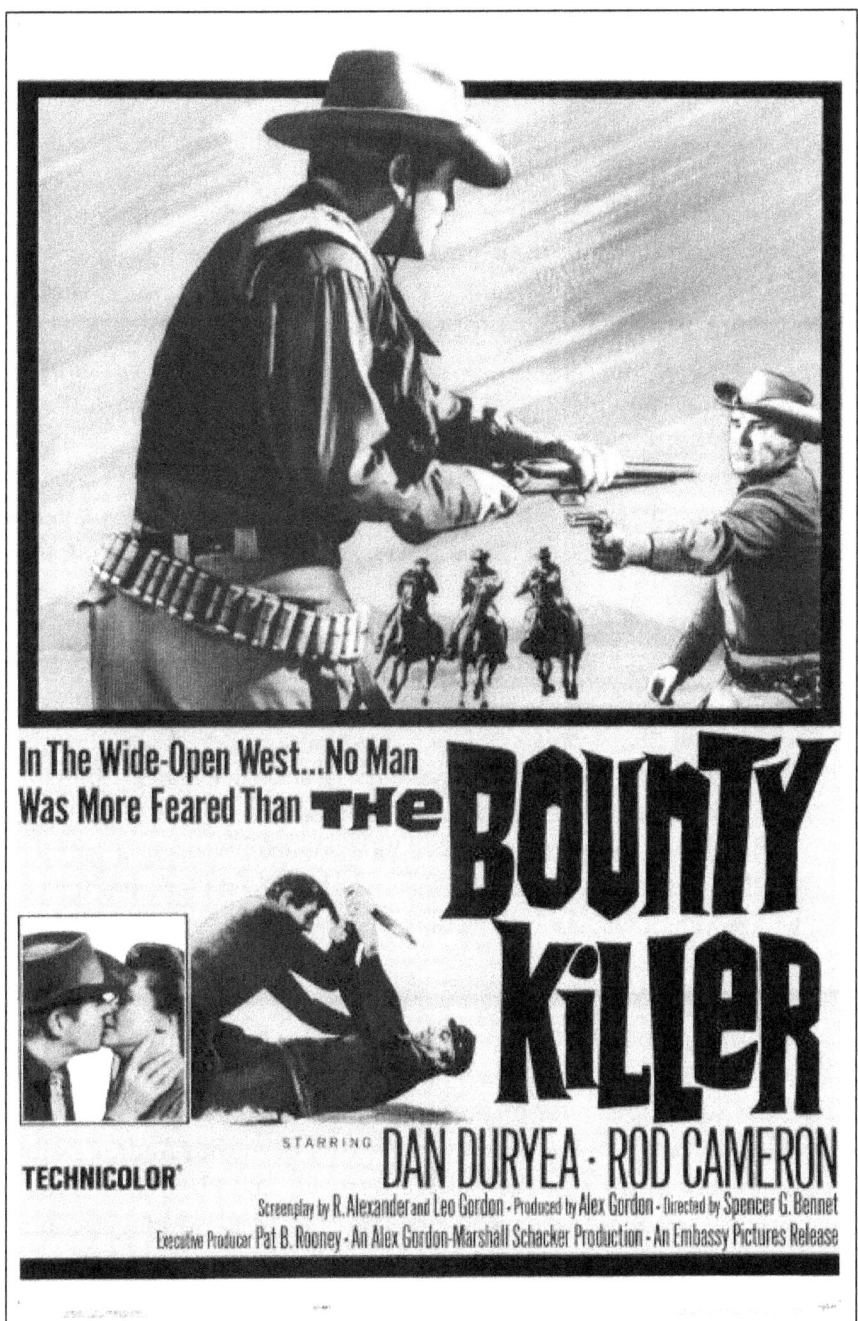

Poster for *The Bounty Killer*. 1965, Embassy Pictures Corp.

The gunslinger challenges the loudmouth to a draw and this petrifies the wise guy. He pleads for his life as Liam counts down from five after telling the man that he better draw when the countdown is complete. Willie Duggan watches in horror as Liam guns the man down.

A drink with his savior leads to a debate of principles between Duggan and Liam. Killing is a way of surviving says the gunslinger, but the city slicker remains undeterred or grateful for six-gun justice even though his life was saved by it. This is the beginning of the big change in Duggan's life.

Much of Duggan's change is motivated by meeting Carole (Audrey Dalton), the dance hall queen with the heart of gold and Luther (Fuzzy Knight), a jovial, land-bound sailor. She dreams of returning home to start a fresh life and he wants to build a wind ship, a Conestoga wagon with a sail for propulsion.

Their dreams inspire Duggan to become a bounty hunter. The mealy-mouthed nice guy turns into a hired gun after he and Luther survive a showdown with a gang of ruthless killers. After the shock wears off, they realize how easy it is to kill. This is the path Duggan decides to take to help finance the dreams of his friends.

It is ironic that his final bounty on-the-house is Johnny Liam, who is enraged when he discovers that Duggan has killed three of his buddies for the bounties on their heads.

This zany premise lays the framework to show Duggan's disintegration into a depraved maniac. Duryea is a fearsome hired gun until alcohol wears him down. He is reduced to a bitter drunk lecturing a group of townsfolk about the art of killing as he waves his gun at them. It is the gun that brings him down, not only because of what it has done to others, but because of what it has done to him.

A dissolute Duggan still retains enough social bearing to woo Carole, the only woman he has loved, when he runs into her again at the end of the film. It is all for nothing as he becomes a losing part of the vicious circle that he has drawn for himself.

The Bounty Killer may be a low budget Western with Audrey Dalton and a cast of mostly over-the-hill Western vets and cheap sets thrown in, but it has redeeming values in a couple of good performances, some clever lines and plot development, and an ironic twist ending that seems existential and sappy at the same time.

Dan Duryea is very good as Willie Duggan. His performance is what makes this film memorable. It is characteristic of Duryea to elevate an otherwise unmemorable film into something to watch because of his performance. Duryea has done this throughout his career and he gives an earnest account of a cultured Easterner's devolution into a Western-plains bounty killer.

Duggan is laughable at the beginning of the movie, when he is a teetotaling dude being harassed by a loudmouth in a cantina. By the end of the movie, he is a cold-hearted plains killer whose forgiveness comes from a whiskey bottle. The only people he cares for are the Captain and Carole. They are like his family and it is because of his dedication to their dreams that he becomes a bounty hunter. The Captain's wind wagon and Carole's dreams of going home are enough to make Duggan put himself in harm's way and tarnish his name with a repugnant reputation.

Audrey Dalton actually pulls off playing sexy and wholesome at the same time. She gives her cantina numbers the heat they need to get the drinks flowing and also lays on the cornpone when she expresses her desire to return to the open ranch. That is where Duggan sees her again at the film's end when he is on the lam from a posse pursuing him for the accidental shooting of a sheriff.

Fuzzy Knight returns from yesteryear's Saturday matinee to play Luther, a jovial, land-bound sailor whose dream is to build an airship. He is enthusiastic but also addled, so it is somewhat amusing to see him tied to a tree, being tormented by Mike Clayman (Buster Crabbe). The blade man throws his knives at Fuzzy, whose popeyed dismay adds more humor to the scene because the shots of the blades hitting the tree around his head have a weird, Claymation-like effect to them. It's too bad for Luther that Clayman's bullets are more to the point.

Buster Crabbe is to be commended for staying in great shape more than thirty years after he gained fame as the movie serial versions of comic strip heroes Flash Gordon and Buck Rogers. Mike Clayman is a tough posse boss who doesn't mind throwing torture and intimidation into his moments of rest and relaxation, but even his knives are no match for Duggan's draw.

Richard Arlen has a supporting role as Carole's father. He disapproves of her friendship with Duggan and chases him off the ranch after the gunman tries to find shelter there from being captured by the posse. Arlen earned his place in film history by starring in the first picture that won an Oscar, 1927's *Wings*, a silent movie directed by William Wellman.

Despite serious setbacks to his health and a film career that ended with appearances in the B-movies of the 40's, Arlen appears to be in great shape. It is plausible that he would chase away his daughter's shady suitor.

The Bounty Killer draws a bead on two members of the Clayman gang. 1965, Embassy Pictures Corp.

Excepting Dan Duryea, Buster Crabbe and Richard Arlen, *The Bounty Killer* is a mausoleum of forgotten Western heroes. Rod Cameron, Fuzzy Knight, Bob Steele, Red Morgan and Johnny Mack Brown are the matinee idols taking a final bow. Tom Kennedy, Grady Sutton and Eddie Quillan are former funny men blending in to give straight support.

When Dan Duryea started filming *The Bounty Killer*, an Alex Gordon indie made on the Paramount lot, the press pointed out the unusual point of featuring his son, Peter, as the young gun slinger who shoots the vet in the film's final showdown.

"It's a good, promotable angle that could stir comment and give the picture a boost", Duryea said. "Pete had a small part in *Taggart* but he doesn't want to be hooked to me, and I'll doubt if we'll have a father-and-son act going for us much longer. His ambitions are for legitimate stage."[1]

Straw Hat producer Richard Bloom met with the father and son to offer them the roles in *Why Do We Live?* But they were not interested. They did appear together one more time on a *Daniel Boone* episode in 1965.

In the same interview, he expressed no regret at being typecast as a villain and insisted that he did not have any ambitions to go behind the camera. He told a Variety reporter that he does not believe in actor-director combos.

"It takes a genius to wear those two hats at the same time," he said, before adding "I can't even watch my own rushes."

Dan Duryea was happy to stick to the routine he had developed when he got to Hollywood as it still worked for him. While he started filming *The Bounty Killer* audiences could see him on the big screen in *Taggart* and on television in *Wagon Train: The Race Town Story* and *Bonanza: Logan's Treasure*.

After Dan Duryea finished filming *The Bounty Killer*, Robert L. Lippert wanted him for the title role in *The Mesa Kid*, based on a short story by Randall Rood. Instead, he returned to Universal to star in *The Faceless Men* with Robert Fuller. The title was changed to *Incident at Phantom Hill*.

The ads declared that *Incident at Phantom Hill* was TV's famed frontier fighter Robert Fuller's first starring role. The star of *Wagon Train* and *Laramie* gets top billing in a revenge tale where "a woman's fury was deadlier than Apache arrows and a man's gold fever hotter than the desert sun!"

That woman was Jocelyn Lane, an English actress who made her American film debut in *The Sword of Ali Baba* and later appeared in *Tickle Me* with Elvis. She plays a dancehall girl of questionable moral character, forced to become the flame that lights the way for the ragtag band of suicide troops.

Incident at Phantom Hill is the story of the massacre of a cavalry troop and the theft of the gold bullion they were escorting. Captain Matt Martin (Robert Fuller) reluctantly accepts a suicide mission to retrieve the gold. He is duty-bound to do so because his brother was the commander of the massacred outfit. His other burden is using Joe Barlow (Dan Duryea), the convicted ring leader of the rebel marauders, as a guide through the desert.

He is aided by a motley trio of dubious qualifications traveling incognito. Adam Long (Tom Simcox) is a survivor of the raid and is driven by guilt; Dr. Hannaford (Linden Chiles) is a dazed Civil War surgeon who is along for the ride; Krausman (Claude Akins) is a quiet giant who carries a music box and likes to kill Indians; and O'Rourke (Noah Beery, Jr.) is a jaunty, whiskey-drinking bloke who wears a derby hat.

An Italian poster for *Incident at Phantom Hill*. 1965, Universal Pictures Company, Inc.

A dancehall queen with a Parisian motif named Memphis (Jocelyn Lane) becomes the mission's jeopardy factor. She is a hotter-than-the-sun type of stunner who is being kicked out of town for moral reasons by the sheriff. He insists that Captain Martin take her along for the ride as a way of ignoring the objectionable presence of the Confederate rebel Barlow.

The sheriff does not realize that the true nature of their mission is to go through Indian territory; neither does Memphis. This scenario is what gets the indentured servant Barlow to thinking and scheming to find a way out. Freedom is the promise of helping find the gold, but that is not enough for Barlow. He wants the gold and he will appeal to Memphis' bold sense of independence to help him get it.

She knows that he is a phony and will sell her out, but that is what she would do to him. They need each other to get the gold out of the desert. An even split would be for one of them to be eliminated. Neither can stand Captain Martin and they use each other to take him down.

Barlow almost succeeds in duplicating his success at Phantom Hill. He absconds with the gold a second time after he picks off the doctor and the Irishman. He escapes with Memphis, leaving Captain Martin and Krausman to fight a band of attacking Indians.

Krausman loses his music box and appetite for killing Indians and Captain Martin escapes with his life. He tracks Barlow, Memphis, and the gold to a cliff side hideaway. The requisite showdown occurs over Memphis and the gold. Barlow fights a mean battle, but loses his smirk when he is felled by a fatal bullet. Captain Martin avenges the *Incident at Phantom Hill*.

Duryea dusts off the vicious cowboy routine for this movie. He has a few original tricks left up his sleeve. His character is still odious and is not above trying any means necessary to thwart the soldier boy and make off with the gold a second time. His character is a sweet talker who makes big promises to Memphis, who is unimpressed by his shenanigans and double-dealing. He stills dies a gunman's violent prairie death.

Noah Beery plays O'Roarke, an Irishman with a merry disposition. It is the dreaded whiskey that is the death of him and he bites the dust without wetting his whiskers. Linden Chiles is a bitter doctor disillusioned by horrors of The Civil War. He is serious and wracked with so much guilt that his death in an Indian raid seems like a just penance for his self-induced loathing. Claude Akins is Krausman, a silent, Indian-hating brute who lets his music box do the talking for him. He pays a stiff price for all

Joe Barlow (Dan Duryea) taunts a doomed rooster with the money he plans to spend on getting blind drunk. 1965, Universal Pictures Company, Inc.

The poster for *The Hills Run Red*, a Spaghetti Western. 1967, United Artists Corp.

the Indians he has killed and part of it is never being able to be comforted by his music box again.

The American Western was revived by the Italian film industry. It has been written that the passion of the "Spaghetti Western" was an allegory for Italy's struggle for sovereignty after WWII. The aftermath of the Civil War, the time period of many Italian Westerns, was a parallel to Italy's fractious history and its own Civil War. It was Clint Eastwood's star turn in Sergio Leone's *The Good, the Bad, and the Ugly* that made the "Spaghetti Western" an international phenomenon.

Dan Duryea signed on with Thomas Hunter and Henry Silva to star in Dino DeLaurentis' *River of Dollars* and filming started in Rome on April 4. *The Hills Run Red* is one of the many prairie ghosts of a million desert revenge dramas. Duryea's ambiguous gunman and Henry Silva's villain in black breathe life into this choppy and violent shoot-'em-up tale of vengeance.

Dan Duryea and Henry Silva recreate their unique brand of villainy for *The Hills Run Red*, a Spaghetti Western that is dangerous to the palette. Duryea is Getz, the itinerant hired gun lending a hand to Jerry Brewster (Thomas Hunter), a righteous stranger who seeks revenge on a former partner for a double-cross. Henry Silva is Mendez, the marauding Mexican bandit in black whose scowls and laughter mean one thing: ornery sadism.

Nando Gazzolo is Seagall, the traitorous ex-partner who becomes a greedy land baron after he escapes with the loot from a botched robbery. It was mutually agreed upon that one of them would be bait for the posse while the other safeguarded the loser's share until he got out of prison.

Instead, Seagall uses the money to build a fiefdom, lets his ex-partner's wife die in penury and has allowed his only child to be raised as an orphan. Revenge is the theme and Brewster does what he can to eliminate a gaggle of minions before he gets to Seagall.

Nothing much goes on, except for a lot of mendacious laughter by Menzez and furrow-browed assistance from Getz. A couple of pop tunes about optimism do not add anything to the film; even a scenic prairie panorama is wasted. There are the usual Western elements, but they are used to no avail. The only redeeming value is Duryea and Silva walking through their parts.

Willie Getz is laconic, but always there to lend a helping hand to the hero. In the end, Getz twists his personality and bestows a gift on the hero that restores his public respect. Getz is a tough old bird who uses dynamite to fight rebels in the final's shoot-'em-up finale. He also turns solid citizen in a scene that shines the cavalry's brass, much to the advantage of Brewster, who starts a new life as a man with a star.

The star in the dust is Henry Silva, who milks his high-noon scene for all it's worth. He spits laughter throughout the whole movie, so it's not surprising that he bombards his nemesis with a gaggle of yuks every time he gets plugged and revs up for more misery. This scene was a dream for the editor, because he cut the different reactions from several angles before focusing on his death in the dust. The sombrero in black can trade so many laughs for his leaden pain before becoming another crazed marauder biting the dust.

Dan Duryea as Getz, the mysterious lone rider who aids Jerry Brewster (Thomas Hunter) in his quest for revenge. 1967, United Artists Corp.

Henry Silva plays Mendez, a sadistic high plains drifter. 1967, United Artists Corp.

Dan Duryea returned from his European sojourn with some financial advice for any Americans planning to work in the Italian film industry. Government red tape will tie up timely payment of salaries especially if there is a stipulation to be paid in dollars not *lira*. To be paid in *lira* means losing at least five per cent of its value if it is exchanged on the black market. If the actor wants to be paid in dollars, it may take up to six weeks to receive the salary. This reason, along with the irritatingly slow shooting schedules, is the reason why Duryea passed on three offers to star in other Spaghetti Westerns. He opted to return to the States for a role in Universal's television remake of *Winchester '73*, a movie the actor made in 1950.

He said that making Spaghetti Westerns could be lucrative for an American actor and pointed out that the biggest stars of this genre are Americans. Duryea explained that Clint Eastwood is Italy's second top draw, coming in behind Marcello Mastroianni.

Western TV Reprise

Old Western television standbys like *Gunsmoke*, *The Virginian* and *Bonanza* were still going strong in 1965. They were the exceptions to the rule. So were yesterday's heroes who returned to capture lightning in a bottle for the second time. Fess Parker had started a craze with his Walt Disney-produced Davy Crockett series in the 1950's. It started a merchandising boom that included coonskin caps, plastic muskets, puzzles and lunch pails. In 1964, Fess Parker returned to American folklore with *Daniel Boone* in a hit show that lasted from 1964 to 1970.

The Sound of Fear is very much like *The Desperate Hours* in a Western setting. Instead of Humphrey Bogart and Frederic March it is Dan Duryea and Daniel Boone. Simon Kilgore actually sells Indian scalps. He does this without apology and the same can be said for three of his gang members. The fourth is a member through blackmail and does not share his comrades' bloodthirsty enthusiasm for their vocation. He thinks that he has no choice, but it is his quick and devious maneuver that shifts the balance of power away from Kilgore.

Daniel Boone and Mingo are on their trail after they discover their handiwork, an Indian village massacred by the gang. The only survivor was an elderly woman who was spared because she was white and lacked market value. She becomes the sole witness against Kilgore and her eye witness testimony gets him arrested.

Too bad Mingo and the royal guard can't keep him in check. Kilgore's gang ambushes the patrol and a wounded Mingo secretly creeps into the forest while the guardsmen are scalped to make it look like they were murdered by Cherokees.

Kilgore and his gang hold Daniel Boone and his family hostage. They will die if Boone does not do Kilgore's bidding. When he does, Kilgore promises to lighten up on his family. Instead of having them killed, he will sell them into slavery among the Indians.

A renegade member of the gang, the one who is held in check by blackmail, turns the tables on Kilgore when he returns with his son. It is a mawkish turn as the fourth member uses Kilgore's son as blackmail. His naïve son does not know about his father's brutal reputation. The good and evil confrontation between father and son is a maudlin turn in the action and takes a bite out of the episode. Dan Duryea got a chance to act with his son Peter again in *Daniel Boone*.

The last time that Duryea worked with Rod Serling was in a 1959 Western episode of *The Twilight Zone*. *Doomsday for Mr. Denton* tells the story of a dissipated gunfighter who gets his gun hand back but relinquishes a chance to relive his glory days for something more practical and worthwhile: a healthy life. *A Little Stroll to the End of the Line* is the story

Simon Kilgore is a bloodthirsty scalp hunter who is unwittingly undermined by his own son, a naïve and wholesome city boy (Peter Duryea). 1965, 20th Century Fox Television.

of another dissipated gunfighter who uses his last standoff to negate his reputation and win despite dying in the showdown.

Rod Serling created *The Loner*, a series about William Colton (Lloyd Bridges), an ex-Union officer who develops a wanderlust that takes him on a cross-country trek that helps him understand the paradoxes of human nature. The premise was utilized by Rod Serling for his unique voice and perspective and his scripts gave the series a thoughtful slant. In *A Little Stroll to the End of the Line*, Dan Duryea plays Matthew Reynolds, a broken-down sickly old gunfighter recently released from prison. He aims for an unusual final showdown with Preacher Whatley (Robert Emherdt), the man he holds responsible for the death of his son.

Betrayal is all Reynolds can think of when he pictures the pudgy preacher in his mind. That's why the evangelist enlists the aid of Colton, who has been deputized to protect the preacher from the gunman's revenge. Colton is disgusted to find out that Whatley is a bogus preacher who uses his homilies to fleece innocent backwoods families. He wants to hire Colton's gun to settle the Preacher's score with Reynolds.

This causes Colton to keep an eye on Preacher Whatley, too, because he knows the hustler will hire a gun to do his bidding. When he does it is Colton's job to neutralize him by breaking his arm. This impresses Reynolds but depresses Preacher Whatley. He takes the law into his own hands by shooting Reynolds. He claims self-defense but lacks credibility because Reynolds was unarmed.

The irony of the shooting is pre-meditated although no lawyer could prove it. It was the dying gunslinger's intention to shoot him so he would be arrested and hanged, a just retribution for killing Reynolds' son.

At this point of his career, Dan Duryea was playing a couple of laid back characters here and there. It's not that he walked through the part but he conveyed an easygoing way, an adjustment to playing older characters. In *The Virginian: The Challenge*, Ben Crayton is a ranch owner who lets a mysterious stranger recuperate under his daughter's supervision. He becomes conflicted when he realizes that his guest may be part of a holdup gang responsible for a stagecoach robbery and massacre.

The Virginian was a popular Western that ran from 1962 to 1971. It was the first 90-minute Western and it made stars out of James Drury and Doug McClure. The Virginian and Trampas played the duration of the series that saw Lee J. Cobb (1962-1966), Charles Bickford (1966-1967), John McIntire (1967-1968) and Stewart Granger (1970-1971) as successive heads of the Shiloh Ranch, the stasis of power in an 1890's Wyoming territory.

The Challenge happens during Charles Bickford's turn in the cat bird seat. The Virginian is concerned about the lack of word from Trampas when the wild cowhand fails to telegraph his friends at Shiloh after a long stagecoach trip. Grainger promises the Virginian that he will stay on top of things while his best man tends to business in another territory.

Trampas has amnesia and wanders on to the ranch of Ben Crayton (Dan Duryea), where he collapses. Sarah, Ben's daughter, tends to his injuries but Ben is apprehensive about letting his daughter have any quality time with the stranger. He felt the same way about Jim Tyson, the ranch hand who was shown the road and became the deputy sheriff in town.

Now, Ben Crayton cannot help but wonder whether Trampas is one of the stagecoach holdup men? It is something that nags at the rancher after his son, Bobby, tells him about the ambush that left no witnesses or trace of the miners' payroll. A shooting iron with a nickel plated handle is a sign of one of the robbers and that's the gun that rests in Trampas' holster.

Ben Crayton tries to remain even-tempered, something that cannot be said of the Deputy Sheriff. He has his eye on the stranger after the news of the gun piques his interest; at least, that is what he wants Bobby to believe. It is necessary for the deputy sheriff to gain the boy's trust because he needs all the help he can get to subdue Trampas. He is the only survivor of the stagecoach ambush and he can identify the deputy sheriff as one of the real holdup men.

Tyson's brother, Sam Fuller (Bing Russell), was the ring leader of the gang and it's his nickel plated gun that's supplying the circumstantial evidence. Big brother's advice to the turncoat law man is to kill Trampas before his memory returns. It's not that easy and Tyson fumbles a moonlit showdown with Trampas.

Grainger catches up with the answer to a telegraph and it is revealed that the deputy sheriff was in on it after all. It does not matter to him because he dies rather than go to trial and Trampas gets his memory back.

Dan Duryea gives a subdued performance as Ben Crayton. He still has enough spit and polish to run things but he is not over-the-top. Things are tense for his kids because of the death of their mother but their experience with Trampas teaches them to be a family again.

The Challenge is a Trampas episode. The Virginian is off on a business trip for Grainger. The grand old man sits around worried until he receives a wire about a missing person. This time around, Trampas is nobody's sidekick. He gets to go through a few acting lessons. He stumbles

T.J. Elderbush is a poetic prospector who promises one of the Monroes a stake in a gold mine if he will finance the venture in *Gold Fever*. 1966, Qualis Productions, 20th Century Fox Television.

through the wilderness, dazed and confused as to why he is where he is. There is the drawing a series of disturbed blanks when asked about his identity and origin bit. He elicits cool determination when he fakes an identity and heads into town to find out who he is. During the proceedings, he is involved in two shootouts and survives both. The same would not have been said if the posse got hold of him before his boss arrived.

Then, he would not have gone that far if Ben Crayton did not back up his daughter against his practical judgment. Crayton's support helps Trampas stall for time while the sheriff and his posse ride through the hills. The real problem was the deputy sheriff. Everyone thought that he was an ally until they realize that he was a turncoat and a member of the gang.

The Monroes was a family of five orphans struggling to maintain a homestead on the Wyoming range during the 1870's. Clayt and Kathy (Barbara Hershey) head a family of twin brothers, Jefferson and Fennimore (Keith and Kevin Schultz) and a baby sister Amy (Tammy Locke). They are accompanied by a willowy Indian named Jim (Ron Soble) and their dog Snow.

Dan Duryea's last Western role was T.J. Elderbush, an impoverished mountain man obsessed with making one last strike in *Gold Fever*. T.J. is bearded and scraggly. He is reduced to raiding the Monroes' pantry and stealing their deer meat. The wily mountain man is protective of the land he has squatted on. A modest strike has given him gold fever and he senses that pay dirt is within his reach and all he needs is financing.

The only person naïve enough to take him seriously is Clayt, who is willing to take the family's life savings and invest it in the old codger's dream. It happens when Clayt confronts Elderbush about his trespassing and is regaled with stories of gold reserves waiting to be mined. He shows the young man a bag of gold nuggets as proof of his claims. Clayt is struck with gold fever and will temporarily abandon his family if it means striking it rich. Kate does everything she can to talk him out of it but the stranger's dreams are more realistic to Clayt than common sense and logic.

T.J. Elderbush has the soul of a poet and looks at prospecting the way an artist ponders nature. He is deep in his sentiments and can describe his fever in grandiose terms. His mountain is a woman whose color is her jewelry. She won't give it up to any man. He has to have a way about him that will allow him to walk away satisfied. But the discovery of gold is a temporary high. The need to sustain it becomes even greater and it takes more time and dedication to trap lightning in a bottle one more time.

Loneliness is referred to as a constant companion by T.J. as he describes how he withdrew from a normal life to chase his rainbows. It seems like a desolate life but it is worth it when the gold is weighed and it buys the respect of people who never knew you existed before you started spending money on them.

Elderbush mesmerizes the children with his gold mythology. He tells them that once upon a time there was an expanse of sky with a lone eagle and two suns. The eagle cut a hole in the sky and the sun fell through it. It crashed into the mountain and splintered into a million pieces of gold that scattered all over. That's why he and their eldest brother are heading to the mountain—to get their pocketful of sun.

Clayt and T.J. are not the only ones with gold fever. Two ominous horsemen want to bogart T.J.'s claim and they follow the duo into the hills where there is a final confrontation. T.J. is shot and realizes that he is dying. He reckons that he is through chasing rainbows and gives Clayt his gold nuggets before bidding adieu to the world after giving a brief but florid valedictorian speech.

Dan Duryea left for Europe after filming *The Monroes*. He starred in *The Hills Run Red* for Dino De Laurentiis. Duryea, dissatisfied with the economics of making Westerns in Italy, turned down an offer by De Laurentiis to appear in three Westerns. He chose to return to Universal for *Winchester '73*, one of the first hybrid movies known as TV-Movies.

Many critics dismissed the form as a crossbreed that has "the artistically recessive genes of both media" and did not accept the offerings as "pre-theatre showings of a motion picture" because they believed that the films were more like padded television shows. Needless to say, the TV Movie was still a movie and it came into its own during the 1970's, when the tube was saturated with them. In 1967, there was just the World Premiere series, and *Winchester '73* and *Stranger on the Run* were two of its movies.

Winchester '73 was remade nearly two decades later as a television movie by Universal when it was owned by MCI. Dan Duryea had a supporting role as the father of the villain, a part that was not in the original. In fact, very few elements from the original were in the remake, including the insightful character studies and artful direction.

In the remake, Tom Tryon plays the Jimmy Stewart role and John Saxon is the villain originally played by Stephen McNally. In this movie, they are cousins. Duryea has a supporting part as the villain's father. He is the one who starts the drama when he holds a public shooting contest with one of the original Winchester '73s as the prize. It comes down to blood kin, two cousins named McAdam. One is a sheriff and the other has been released from prison after serving a six-year sentence for bank robbery.

The unique rifle is the crossing point that tells the story of death on the open plains. The rifle keeps changing hands because its uniqueness causes a pattern of death that makes the action of the movie progress. The other motive is revenge for the murder of a loved one. It was all over the Winchester '73, which is how Saxon wrongfully gained possession of the rifle after he shot his uncle to wrest it from him. Paul Fix is the father of Lin. They have their ways of hunting down the killer. McAdam does it through the law, and Rawhide does it according to the bloodlust code.

Tom Tryon gives it his best shot as the sheriff. Tryon is a somewhat ragged version of his earlier, rugged tough-guy stuff. He is still broad-shouldered and lanky in the Gary Copper sense of style, but he appears ragged around the edges with a somewhat desperate look in his eyes. His voice is squeaky, but he is still tough enough to make everything turn out in the long run.

John Saxon is bitter and tries to spit venom as the villain. He mainly scowls and grimaces. He has an attitude of his own making, but still likes to blame everyone for his misery. He is a formidable villain but is ultimately defeated by the anger that has clouded his thinking.

Dan Duryea gives a sensitive performance as the villain's father. He does what he can to gain the respect of his son, even if it means losing the respect of others. Bart McAdam, Dan Duryea's character, is the most complicated character, mainly because of his unwavering love for his wastrel son.

His blind devotion makes him a weak man, but he is more three-dimensional than the other characters with the exception of Meridan, a cynical croupier played by Barbara Luna. Her sour disposition makes her an earthy character with plenty of sex appeal. It is a shame that she is kicked out of town when she pulls a derringer on a boisterous gambler. Luckily for the viewer, she joins the action later and goes along for the ride.

John Dehner is dry and wily as a card sharp and gun runner. He acquires the Winchester '73 by beating a desperate Dakin McAdam at a couple of hands of table-stakes poker. He is brusque and erudite, but those qualities are not enough to stay alive in a gun deal turned rotten. John Drew Barrymore is sharp and straight to the point as the Preacher. He was a cellmate of McAdam's for three years and has filled up on Bible

Lin McAdam (Tom Tryon), his Uncle Bart (Dan Duryea) and cousin Dakin (John Saxon) covet the cherished Winchester '73, the rifle that will change their lives. 1966, Universal Television.

quotations. He is droll with his wit and calculating with his decisions. The Preacher is also a cadaverous undertaker who thrives on the commission of crimes.

Jack Lambert is borderline insane as Scots. He is a heavy drinker and handy with a dagger. He speaks with a thick Scottish brogue and can square off with the best of them. He is headstrong, but not tough enough to butt a wagon wheel. John Doucette plays a tavern owner who keeps wise guys in tow with his rifle. Doucette was always the frog-voiced bulwark who played a brick wall you didn't want to run into.

John Hoyt plays an Indian brave who mistakenly believes that owning the Winchester '73 will make him immortal. He plans to achieve great things with the repeating rifle and stake a greater claim than that of Chief Crazy Horse. Joan Blondell has a small part as LaRouge, an over-the-hill dancehall queen who owns a saloon in some jerkwater town where McAdam and his gang plan to rob the local church of its gold and silver icons.

It's impossible to compare the remake from the original because many of the unique elements are missing in the updated version. Most of the characters are stock figures and it's impossible to care about them because they lack personality. The rifle also does not have the intense charmed quality about it, either. There is no sense of the foreboding and eerie luck that is associated with it.

There is little tension between the card-playing gun dealer and McAdam. The same goes for the confrontation between the gun dealer and the Indian brave. In the original, the Indian chief needed the repeating rifle to help his tribe fight a winning battle against the Cavalry. In the remake, the brave wants to advance his standing with his newfound shooting prowess.

Uncle Bart (Dan Duryea) supervises a shooting contest that pits Lin McAdam (Tom Tryon) against his outlaw cousin Dakin (John Saxon). 1966, Universal Television.

There is no interesting saloon singer like the part played by Shelley Winters. Meridan is interesting, but she does not have much to do. It is Barbara Luna's beauty and mystery that add an allure to the character, nothing that is written for her. She is still one of the film's highlights.

There is no climactic raid on a Cavalry encampment. Instead, the warrior just harasses a wagon of poor Mexicans making a pilgrimage to the shrine of St. Jude that McAdam and his gang plan to rob. There is no Waco Johnny Dean to speak of although we still have Dan Duryea, more mellow and obliging than ever.

The most noteworthy part of the film is the ending, when the gang robs the church. The robbery and the final shootout are impressive. The movie stands on its own as an entertaining Western, one of the early made-for-television films. It just can't compare with the original because the primary theme has been blurred and made secondary to wooden characters.

The Hunters was the original title for *Stranger on the Run*, a lyrical swan song to the turn-of-the-century West, an era when the railroad barons became the new conquerors of the West, wresting power from the cattlemen. The railroad town supplanted the cow town and the businessmen with derby hats gained the power to knock off a ten gallon hat and let it roast in the sun of a one-horse town.

That's how it plays in *Stranger on the Run*, an early made-for-television movie directed by Don Siegal. It is a survival drama between boots in the dust and steel wheels that cut through anything, a clash between individualism and the new conglomerate. Mr. Gorman (Lloyd Bochner) is the derby hat from the East with the talking briefcase that spells the law out for head law man, Vince McKay (Michael Parks) in the film's opening scene. The city slicker's credo will dictate everything that will happen in the movie.

McKay has been told by Mr. Gorman to govern the railroad town to the railroad's satisfaction because the railroad is the law that puts the authority in his badge and the badges worn by his men, a vicious crew of craven outlaws played by Sal Mineo, Tom Reese, Zalman King, and Rodolfo Acosta.

His right hand man is O.E. Hotchkiss (Dan Duryea), an over-the-hill gunslinger who uses his reputation to disguise the fact that he needs reading glasses. Without them, he is the gunslinger who can't shoot straight and this becomes apparent during a shootout between the law men and their prey, a stranger falsely accused of murder and the itinerant farmer who helps him through tough times in the desert.

It starts when the fiefdom of the railroad town is upset by the arrival of a drunkard (Henry Fonda), after he is tossed off the train when it makes its stop. He earns his whiskey by working for Berk (Michael Burke), the merchant. It is when he mentions the name of Alma Britton (Madlyn Rhue) that he becomes a marked man. This sends ripples through the chain of power in the town and it takes the good ol' deputy boys to straighten things out.

It is the residual heat of the beating of a saloon entertainer and her subsequent murder. Justice is the silence that absolves the railroad of any responsibility for the actions of the deputies who stepped over the line. Sequestering the victim (Madlyn Rhue) in a shack does not help because it becomes her tomb, something that turns into a murder charge for the stranger when the sheriff's posse tracks him down as he flees from the shack.

Protestations of innocence only buy him time in a game Hotchkiss calls 'Bear Dog'. It's a baiting game used to take the minds off of hard times to enjoy a good blood sport. It is a matter of time before the sheriff and his boys start tracking the stranger.

The sheriff will do anything to hold on to his job, trying to maintain control while dealing the board of directors' guidelines. He has to be tougher than his men and sometimes he needs to toss them a bone with some meat on it. The stranger is the bone that blesses them with absolution because they have found someone who has atoned for their sin of murder.

The killer deputies are a rambunctious gang: Tom Reese, Sal Mineo, Zalman King, and Rodolfo Acosta. Hotchkiss (Dan Duryea) is the faded gunman who plays it big for Matt Johnson (Michael Burns), his green, adolescent protégé, someone the old man can teach and show off to. This does not bode well with the boy's mother, a sexy prairie woman played by Anne Baxter. She is an independent-minded and hard-driven woman who is not impressed with the creed of the hired killers. She looks at them as being mercenaries of the railroad bosses. It is the new metal mule train that is throwing everything out of kilter in the West and the prairie dogs are feeling the heat of the bankers back East.

Michael Parks is atypical of the young gunmen of his era, young and toughened by the viciousness of the killers' circle. He is the captain of the killers who are paid to keep the railroad town a quiet and productive place. The sadistic attack on the woman is not deplored because of its brutality; it is condemned because it can bring an indictment down on the railroad.

O.E. Hotchkiss (Dan Duryea) teaches his shooting technique to a young admirer (Michael Burns). 1968, Universal Television.

Hotchkiss is considered a has-been by the railroad people. He keeps his job because the sheriff vouches for him. The other deputies fear his reputation, but still goad into showing off his stuff. Sal Mineo, Tom Reese, Zalman King, and Adolpho Avosta are also terrorists, bending the will of the power to obey their new masters. It is Mineo and Reese who are responsible for the beating and the murder, something they need to make the stranger pay for.

Henry Fonda plays the dissolute hobo as a drunkard with an inflexible will to do what is right. He is not swayed by a beating from a deputy or harassment by the deputies-formed posse. Henry Fonda is the odd man out, someone who crosses a line few people care to acknowledge.

The Cold War

Crime: Postscript

Dan Duryea returned to his roots when he gave a live recitation of Stephen Vincent Benet's Civil War poem, *John Brown's Body*. He planned to return to Broadway in 1963 when he signed a run-of-the-play contract to appear in *Libel and Slander*, a play written by Henry Denker and directed by Sam Wanamaker. The play was based on the first section of the Louis Nizer book, "My Life in Court."

The title eventually became *A Case of Libel*, a successful drama about the Westbrook Pegler-Quentin Reynolds libel suit. Duryea's role was Boyd Bendix, based on Pegler. A week after it was announced that Duryea had been added to the cast the trade papers reported that he had withdrawn from the play. A member of the cast said that Duryea was fired. "But being fired by Wanamaker was an honor. He was the worst director I've ever worked for."

Dan Duryea admitted that a return to Broadway would have given his career a boost.

"I suppose a lot of Broadway people will want to kill me for saying it… but I wanted to use Broadway so I could make more money in the movies. Some actors act for art's sake and starve. That's not for me. I can't afford it. My reputation as an actor is a good one, but I've no illusions about it being the world's greatest. A Broadway success would have given it a boost."[1]

Dan Duryea received a star on the Television Walk of Fame.

Dan Duryea may not have had a Broadway boost to his career, but he was still able to tread the boards when he became a part of the summer playbill for Canal Fulton straw hat theater. The tenth season offered a playbill that included Farley Granger in *Toys in the Attic*; George Montgomery in *King of Hearts*; Marjorie Lord in *Blithe Spirit*; Faye Emerson in *Witness for the Prosecution*; Pat O'Brien and his wife in *Holiday for Lovers*; Arnold Stang in *Three Men on a Horse*; Dan Duryea in *The Country Girl*; Monique Van Vooren in *A Shot in the Dark*; Edward Everett Horton in *Miss Pell is Missing*; Jack Kelly in *Come Blow Your Horn*; Ann Harding in *The Corn is Green*; Dody Goodman in *Sunday in New York*; Earl Holliman and Anthony George in *The Tender Trap*; MacDonald Carey in *Oh, Men! Oh, Women!* and *Love and Taxes* with Betty White.

After acting in summer stock the UCLA Theatre Group offered Dan Duryea the chance to participate in *Brecht on Brecht*. The two part program consisted of readings and excerpts from his plays, plus songs by Kurt Weill and Hanns Eisler that had lyrics written by Brecht. It ran from Oct. 25 to Dec. 1 at the Humanities Building Auditorium of the University of California Extension.

The Theatre Group Presentation was adapted by George Tahori and directed by William Allyn. Piano accompaniment was provided by Don Abeny. Besides Dan Duryea, the cast included Nina Foch, Kim Hamilton, Kevin McCarthy and Dolores Sutton. Dan Duryea only missed one performance for the limited engagement, and that was to film an appearance on *The Alfred Hitchcock Hour*.

The Variety review was mostly harsh although there was praise for some performers. Nina Foch seemed to have gotten the stamp of approval for her Dietrichesque vocals on *Ballad of the Nazi Soldier's Wife*, *Pirate Jenny* and *Barbara Bong*. She also received compliments on her readings, especially *The Ballad of Marie Farrar*. Kevin McCarthy was congratulated for his reading of *The Old Hat* but criticized for the exaggerated tones of his other pieces. Dan Duryea was on firm footing with his offering of *In Memory of Maria A* but was regarded to sound flat with his *Galileo* excerpt. *The Private Life of the Master Race* was Dolores Sutton's highlight.

On the movie making front, the old studio system had finally disintegrated in the 1960's as new trends and economic policies changed the dynamics of movie making. Dan Duryea's 60's movies were a strange blend of styles that included two British thrillers, a series of low budget Westerns, two made-for-television Westerns, a small part in a Hollywood desert survival opus, a low-budget Filipino spy flick and a Cold War science-fiction adventure.

Duryea had made a *Taggart*, a Western for Universal, when he sojourned to England for two downbeat and intriguing mid-60's sordid thrillers for Parroch-McCullum Productions. *Do You Know This Voice?* and *Walk a Tightrope* are bleak, black-and-white tabloid crime dramas. A child murderer and a paid assassin are Duryea's 60's Yanks in England. The lead characters are so loathsome that they are hypnotic in the way they draw you into their warped sensibilities.

In *Do You Know This Voice?* and *Walk a Tightrope*, one can sense the resentment toward the aging American in working class England. He was once part of the post-war effort but now is an unwelcome reminder of the Cold War. What makes matters worse is that both Americans are poison to British society, cold-blooded killers who learned their craft during the last big war and now ply it in the decaying rebirth of the last blitzkrieg.

Do You Know This Voice? is a grim and disturbing movie about John and Jackie Hopta (Dan Duryea and Gwen Watford), a couple of kidnappers who demand a ransom even though their victim, a boy, has died during the commission of the crime. A blown sting leads to a dragnet that tightens due to police procedure. A tape recording of a garbled and

Supt. Hume (Peter Madden) tries to jar Rosa Marotta's (Isa Miranda) memory for details about the kidnapper she unwittingly saw at the phone booth in a scene from *Do You Know This Voice?* 1964, Columbia Pictures.

eerie voice gives them a clue. The dragnet and a guilty conscience turn into a lasso and a catch. This time it is due to gum soles and a glass of poison.

Dan Duryea is droll and vicious as John Hopta, the inept kidnapper. It is bad enough that he pulled off a kidnapping, but unwittingly killing the victim puts him further in peril. As he pushes his luck and demands a ransom, banking on the authorities' ignorance of the accidental death, he leaves a trail of clues for the police to follow.

A simple trace on the ransom call turns into a police investigation thanks to Mrs. Maloota (Isa Miranda), an elderly woman who is apprehended by the cops at the scene of the call. It helps the course of action that the woman is the neighbor of the culprits. It is something that is not lost on the guilty couple, because their neighbor has attracted attention from having been drawn into things because of happenstance. Call it serendipity for the cops, but for the couple it is bad luck.

Superintendent Hume (Peter Madden) is the chief cop and he looks like a beanstalk with a large head. His prominent forehead, furrowed brow, thick eyeglasses, and droll speech give him an edge of authority. It is a change of pace from having a handsome leading man playing the head detective. His 'eureka!' moment comes when the cops sweep up an elderly woman who was using the telephone pinpointed by the trace. That meant that the previous user was one of the kidnappers and that the woman had to have seen him.

They use her as bait and plant Detective Sergeant Connor (Barry Warren), a boarder in the home. The couple next door is the guilty party, but knowing this does not ruin the suspense of the movie. This is due mainly to Dan Duryea's loathsome performance and the dry, matter-of-fact procedure of the British police. If you ever wondered what Johnny Prince would have become if he had escaped the death penalty, take a look at Hopta. He is a charmer in public, but abusive to his wife Jackie (Gwen Watford) in private. She was his mainstay, but has now become a liability because of her skittishness and his paranoia.

Hopta goes to extreme lengths to eliminate his other liability: Mrs. Maloota. He tries poison and garroting, but fails twice. He leaves his mark as a horrible looking man because of the stocking mask he wore during the attempted strangling. The attempted murder scenes are atmospheric and chilling.

Dan Duryea is truly tortured in this lurid thriller. He is repugnant and wicked, a bitter man who dominates his wife and forces her to be

John Hopta (Dan Duryea) confers with Jackie (Gwen Watford), his subservient wife, about how to handle Mrs. Marotta, the witness who lives next door to them. 1964, Columbia Pictures.

an accomplice in an unthinkable crime. Hopta is full of anger and rage, blaming others for his job as a hospital orderly. The kidnapping would net him some money, or so he thought. It did not occur to him that he may not handle success because it would make him the object of a manhunt.

Duryea's Hopta character is a low-class hustler with a small-time way of scheming. The accidental death and insistent ransom demands further prove the extent of his small-mindedness. What makes him seem big is the magnitude of his wife's fear and devotion. She suffers his abuse, and has sacrificed her life to make him happy. She complied with his scheme, but now criticizes him because he has botched everything. Hopta thinks that he has turned drawbacks into bigger grades of success. Paranoia derails his plans, and it all backfires during an ill-fated toast.

Gwen Watford as Jackie is a study in hysteria. She is critical of her husband yet dons a trench coat and men's clothes when she makes her disguised calls. Though fearful of his violent outbursts, she is not resistant to his occasional embraces.

Isa Miranda's Mrs. Maloota stands out as a foreigner in xenophobic England even though Duryea, as an American, does not. She is introduced on-screen as she is being harassed by her next-door neighbor, who torments her cats and suggests that she return to Capistrano. A kindly woman, her courage controls her fear as she is stalked and marked for death by the maniacal kidnappers after telling the press that she saw the culprit in the phone booth. It never dawned on her that they were her next-door neighbors.

Duryea's British follow-up to *Do You Know This Voice?* is less turgid although his character, Carl Lutcher, is just as sleazy and offensive as Hopta. *Walk a Tightrope* is a short movie, one that could pass as an hour-long cop show like *Law and Order*. There is the commission of the crime, the arrest, and the trial. Ellen Shepherd (Patricia Owens) is a woman madly in love with her second husband. Her ex-spouse proves to be a bothersome problem so she decides to have him killed by Carl Lutcher, an unscrupulous American. He murders the wrong husband and this leads to the complications of his arrest and trial.

The trial basically consists of Lutcher trying to prove Ellen Shepherd's duplicity in the crime. Her angle is that she performs as an innocent babe in arms. She claims that she is being implicated by the crazy American and gains sympathy from the judge and jury. The only wrinkle to her alibi is the foggy memory of Doug Randle (Richard Leech), a family friend who was knocked out by Lutcher and awoke from his stupor after the murder. He thought that he heard Ellen and Lutcher speaking with each other, but cannot swear to it because of his head trauma.

The mystery to *Walk a Tightrope* is the trust that a friend lends to the wife of a man killed by a hired assassin in front of his spouse's eyes. The friend was knocked out by the killer when he came downstairs to see what the commotion was about. He is semi-conscious when he hears the assassin and the wife talk business about the contract. However, the wife is a good actress and leads everyone to believe that Lutcher is delusional. That is the basis of her trial: insanity, but on behalf of the murderer.

This strange hook gives Duryea an opportunity to beg for his life in a court of law, much like he did in *Scarlet Street*. This is amusing because he still is odious and frightening, but now pays the price of his own expertise. He carried out the hit but killed the wrong husband. That is why this is a mistaken-identity movie combined with a courtroom procedural and a drama queen's desperate soliloquy.

Walk a Tightrope is a stiffly-acted film with the exception of Dan Duryea, whose portrayal of a hired killer blows away his fellow cast mem-

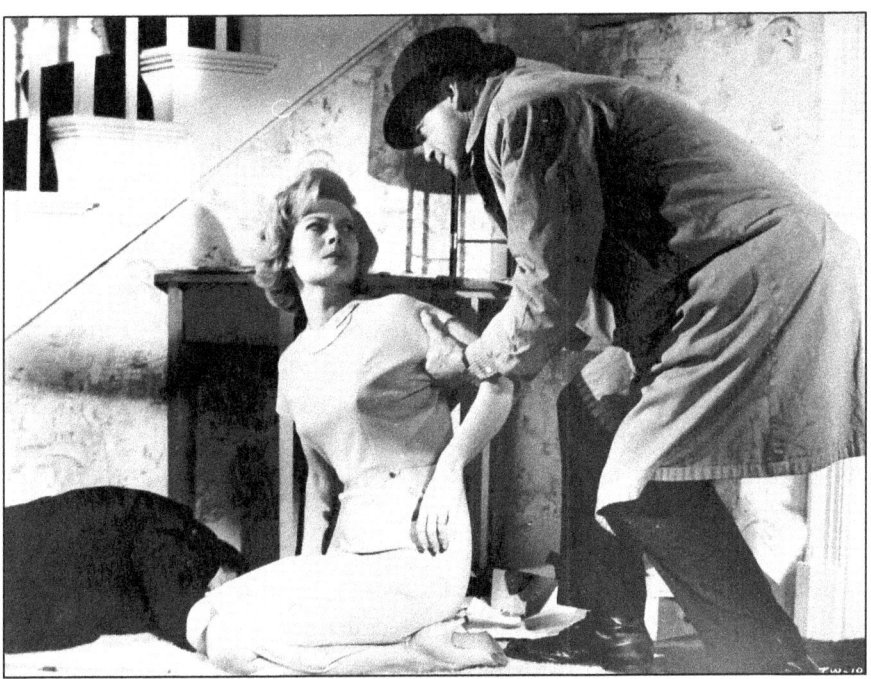

Ellen Shepherd (Patricia Owen) hires Carl Lutcher (Dan Duryea) to murder her intrusive first husband. 1963, Paramount Pictures Corp.

bers in multiple ways. His deranged personality makes all of the other performers seem like wooden dummies. They are stilted and constipated in comparison to Duryea's nihilistic killer.

He has been betrayed by the woman who hired him for a hit where the murder happened to be a case of mistaken identity. Collusion and an unusual eyewitness to the murder land the unlikely couple in court. A strident Patricia Owens elicits sympathy from everyone with her insistence that she is a random victim of a lunatic-at-large.

Other cast characters include a prim police inspector, a gregarious first husband who returns to haunt the widow, and a family friend who was semi-conscious when the murder occurred. He witnesses the exchange between the killer and the widow but is dissuaded from his suspicions when she insists on her innocence.

There is not much to the movie other than the actual hit, Duryea's home life, and his turn on the stand as a defendant and lawyer defending himself. Everybody else is cardboard. Duryea is cool and calculated when he bursts in on the couple and shoots the husband after he is identified. The short puffs of the silencer are brutal.

The killer is a pigeon in a coop when he is at home with his shrewish girlfriend. She is dim-witted, but her buxom charm is enough to satisfy our sly villain. He is crude and direct with his interrogation and rebuttals.

The murder, betrayal, and trial are crucial steps in the resolution of the murder. They are ways to persuade or dissuade the jury from believing in Duryea's guilt or innocence. A tangent comes in the form of indicting Patricia Owens due to incriminating suppositions.

Dan Duryea's stateside television roles were demure compared to his two British thrillers. There were always shows for Dan Duryea to appear on. His style had mellowed and it was a matter of finding something that he could walk through. Fits of rage are replaced with calm resolve on *The Alfred Hitchcock Hour*, an elongated version of *Alfred Hitchcock Presents*, the classic suspense anthology hosted by the legendary film director.

Many tales have been written and told about traveling salesmen, not to mention a canon of jokes. You can add *Three Wives Too Many* to the collection. Raymond Brown (Dan Duryea) is an affable salesman who is on the road a lot. Ordinarily, this would cause consternation and frustration in his wife but Mr. Brown's case is unusual. He has three wives and

Carl Lutcher (Dan Duryea) is the sole defendant in a murder trial when no one believes that he was hired by Ellen Shepherd. 1963, Paramount Pictures Corp.

one of his spouses thinks that he has two wives too many. By the end of the story, the meaning of the title becomes obvious.

It is Marion Brown's (Teresa Wright) plan to change the score in her favor. She accomplishes this by visiting each wife to break the news to them and poisoning them with cyanide when they need a drink to calm their nerves. Mr. Brown learns of their deaths when he makes his stops in New Jersey and Baltimore.

His bigamy is a solution to his gambling problem. His wives are affluent and he does not have a problem paying off his debts. He is such a big time bettor that he has a special bookie, Mr. Bleeker (Robert Cornthwaite) who meets him to accept a briefcase of money to gamble with. At one such meeting in the park, they get into a philosophical discussion about the motive for marrying. Is it for love or money? Mr. Brown replies that he believes that a man can marry for both reasons.

Love is an obsession for Marion Brown, the oldest of his three wives. She is insecure about her age and knows that she will not find another man if Raymond divorces her. The only way to have him all to herself is to murder her competition. That's when the curtain comes down on Lucille (Linda Lawson) and Bernice (Jean Hale). Raymond Brown tries to maintain a game face after he visits his wives and finds his apartments have become crime scene investigations.

It is a matter of time before he realizes that they have been murdered by Marion. This much becomes apparent when Marion gives Raymond an ultimatum: remain married to her or face the worst of two worlds: he can be tried for murder in the poisoning deaths of his wives or he can drink a poisoned cocktail when he least expects it. He thinks that he has a clever rejoinder when he tells her that he has been cleared by the cops. She reminds him that so much is true in his one-on-one encounters with the police in two cities but two murders would be too much to explain. There is a telling look between them and it becomes obvious that he is safe so long as he can be controlled by Marion.

Three Wives Too Many has the restrained black humor that has become the hallmark of Alfred Hitchcock's work. Although he hosts the episodes, the show has his macabre personality stamped all over it. The effect is emphasized by having former screen ingénue Teresa Wright play the murderess. Wright came to fame in the 40's as a bubbly fresh faced teenager from the Mid-West. Here she appears to be a middle-aged spinster even though she is married. There is a crass desperation to her character and her insecurity guides her every step.

Dan Duryea is very much in character as the genial bigamist but goes against type when he is trumped by his wife. There is a scene when they are in the basement to look at some repairs. The water heater is suspended over a pit and he slips and falls into it. His glazed-eyed wife has her hand on the lever that can drop the boiler in place. He cautions her to be aware of what she's doing and begs her to remove her hand to prevent an accident.

The scene is played for laughs even though it is ambiguous whether or not she plans to kill him. She definitely has him at a disadvantage and has established a bargaining point in the ultimatum she later gives him. Dan Duryea and Teresa Wright acted together for the first time since *Little Foxes*, their movie debuts. Their roles are the opposite from what they played in their first movie. Leo Hubbard, Dan Duryea's screen role, shocks Alexandra (Teresa Wright) with his wanton ways. Here, Duryea's character is cowed into submission by Wright's controlling wife.

It is with a laid back humor and a sly smile that belies close scrutiny that Dan Duryea played Lt. Boyd Manners, a homicide detective in a Car-

Teresa Wright plays against type as Marion Ross in *Three Wives Too Many*. 1964, Alfred J. Hitchcock Productions.

mel, California town. It is rumpled suits, teen spirit and a guilt-ridden widow suspected of murder in *Who is Jennifer?*

Kraft Suspense Theater was a well-made anthology show that only lasted two seasons. One of its notable features was an unsettling opening where strange and haunting animated figures twist and turn in a cubist landscape. The pulse-pounding theme by John Williams heightened the hysteria. Most of the stories lived up to the anxiety inspired by the opening credits and the show benefitted from well-known stars and professional writing and directing.

Who is Jennifer? is a strange murder-mystery that seems calm for this series. It is set in Carmel and the placid beachfront setting almost belies the tragedy and mystery that underlies the case. Lt. Boyd Manners (Dan Duryea) has an opportunity to solve an old missing persons case when he finds his hands full with a sarcastic runaway teenage orphan (Brenda Scott). A check into her background leads one detective to believe that she may be the missing daughter of a wealthy widow. The most plausible link is a rare AB blood-type.

When Lt. Boyd Manners (Dan Duryea) is informed of this theory, he recollects the original case. It involved the rich people by the seashore. He always had a sneaking suspicion that Mrs. Heaton (Gloria Swanson) murdered her daughter. His assumption is based on charges of child beating that were never brought against the woman.

He decides to use the runaway to uncork the suspect and has a chance to test his theory when he introduces the young woman to Mrs. Heaton. It is an awkward encounter based on mutual fear and loathing. Mrs. Heaton is obliging but apprehensive, but her attempts at bonding are met with hostility. Eventually, the couple begins to understand each other but not much is solved.

This is a low key performance for Dan Duryea. He does not have much to do and stays in the background to help connect the dots so that the drama continues at an even pace. It is basically a generation gap drama where the women get a chance to share little bits of their secrets with each other. The young girl finds freedom as she continues her identity quest and the mature woman opens the drapes to let in the sunshine for the first time since her daughter disappeared.

Beneath the contentment lies the twofold mystery of the drama. There is a scene when the teenager is walking down the stairway when the last step bends and creaks. There is a fast zoom before a cut establishes a new scene. Could there be something buried beneath the staircase? When she takes a bus ride out of Carmel she tells an inquisitive passenger that she has two sisters. The wistful look on her face seems to imply that she was Mrs. Heaton's daughter.

When she leaves the beachfront house, Mrs. Heaton is relieved to know that her daughter was not buried in a plot of earth on the beach where she thought her abusive husband killed her many years ago in a fit of rage.

Dan Duryea's next roles were guest spots in a glitzy police procedural named *Burke's Law*. Gene Barry starred as Amos Burke, a sophisticated *bon vivant* who rode in a Rolls Royce and courted beautiful women. It seemed incidental that he was a police captain. He was aided by two sidekicks: Tim Tilson (Gary Conway), a bright college graduate, and Sgt. Les Hart (Regis Toomey), an old-school seasoned vet.

The show was based on an episode of the *Dick Powell Theatre* and Powell played the role. After two seasons, the format of *Burke's Law* was revamped and Burke became a secret agent, presumably to cash in on what was left of the secret agent craze. The show was revived in the 1990's with Gene Barry now playing a chief of police. The glamour of Old Hollywood was an integral part of the show and this was a trademark of an Aaron Spelling production. A collection of old time stars (in alphabetical order) played the suspects in the murder of the week. Dan Duryea appeared in two episodes, *Who Killed 711?* and *Who Killed the Paper Dragon?*

711 is the room number of the murdered man found in the elevator. His name is Buddy Jack Cook and he is an unsavory character who was about to testify before the grand jury. The list of suspects is Tristram Corporal (Broderick Crawford), Sam Atherton (Dan Duryea), Clarissa Benton (Rhonda Fleming), Harold Harold (Burgess Meredith), Pepe Van Heller (Hans Conreid) and Aurora Knight (Mamie Van Doren).

Their star turns are the scenes where Burke questions them. Broderick Crawford plays a crusty business rival who spends his time in the hotel room taking dancing lessons from a couple of twisting beauties. Dan Duryea plays a shady lawyer whose midnight trysts are shifts at a local bakery where he can work out the kinks of the legal profession by making pastries. Rhonda Fleming is a hot-tempered business woman who'd like nothing better than to get Captain Burke under a ledger sheet. Burgess Meredith is the victim's bespectacled book keeper whose hobby is building useless contraptions that would make Rube Goldberg envious. Hans Conreid is the effete hotel manager who thinks everyone—especially cops—is beneath him. Mamie Van Doren is a kept woman who is looking for a well-heeled keeper now that she is unattended because of murder most foul.

Amos Burke goes undercover as a maître d' and his assistants play waiters. They get entangled in the affairs of the guests and generally get on their nerves. Although Harold Harold is arrested for the murder Captain Burke feels that the police evidence was planted by someone to make him look guilty. That someone is caught red handed in an old-fashioned sting, forcing the hotel to place a want ad for a new manager.

Dan Duryea's most unique role is Hop-Sing Kelly in *Burke's Law: Who Killed the Paper Dragon?* He is actually Irish-Chinese and seems to be a hybrid reject from the *China Smith* show. Hop-Sing can be seen as a flip Irishman or a tricky Mandarin or a combination of both. He owns a restaurant-night club where the mysterious Lotus Bud (Myoshi Umeki) dances.

She is the center of attention after she is seen fleeing a crime scene with a small girl. A ditzy tourist captures the couple on film and she becomes a temporary media subject. Burke identifies the murder victim found in the trunk of her car as a professor of oriental history at the university. In *Who Killed the Paper Dragon?*, Myoshi Umeki, Barbara Eden, Dan Duryea, Howard Duff and James Shigeta are the suspects.

Hop-Sing Kelly confuses police captain Amos Burke (Gene Barry) with his mixed heritage in *Who Killed the Paper Dragon?* 1964, Four Star Productions.

Lotus Bud (Myoshi Umeki) is a college professor who doubles as a traditional Chinese dancer. Sylvia Hanson (Barbara Eden) is the murder victim's uncaring wife. She is a space cadet and a pseudo-Buddhist. Sidney Yang (James Shigeta) is an unscrupulous hustler who makes a living supplying tourists with whatever they want from Chinatown. Charley January (Howard Duff) is a washed-up ventriloquist who does his act in bars for free drinks from the patrons. Hop-Sing Kelly (Dan Duryea) is the Irish-Chinese owner of the restaurant where Lotus Bud dances. He remains true to his roots by placing a noodle in each serving of Irish Stew.

Amos Burke surmises that the murdered professor was involved in a refugee smuggling ring. Lotus Bud's daughter is his latest human cargo. One of the suspects murdered the professor to eliminate from the profit sharing tips of the business. Who else could it be but an unscrupulous hustler who sells everything from cheap watches to hashish to the tourists?

Espionage: Adventures and Thrills

Dan Duryea had a couple of false starts with interesting projects before he was signed to do *Flight of the Phoenix*. Alex Gordon was preparing *War Against Crime* and he was negotiating to have Robert Sparr direct it. Gordon had written the script with his wife Mildred and secured the services of Dan Duryea as his star. *War Against Crime* was never made. The second project sounds tantalizing since it was based on Joseph Conrad's *Heart of Darkness*. Writer-Director Randall Hood was going to adapt the novel to a script where Dan Duryea would play Kurtz. That, too, fizzled out.

Flight of the Phoenix featured an all-star international cast in a desert survival drama directed by Robert Aldrich. James Stewart stars as a gruff pilot who crash lands in the Sahara Desert with a motley group of passengers.

Disaster movies are dystopian critiques of technologically-advanced societies. It is not only a question of survival through primitivism, but the question of identity and the authority or lack thereof it accords. Superior strength or ultra-intelligence is the edge, but the unknown odd factors are the things that wind up creating or taking away good fortune.

In *Flight of the Phoenix*, Capt. Frank Towns (James Stewart) and Heinrich Dorfmann (Hardy Kruger) vie for the leadership of a band of C-82 Packet plane crash survivors in an attempt to beat the odds of sur-

Poster for *The Flight of the Phoenix*, a plane crash in the desert survival drama. 1965, Twentieth Century Fox Corp.

viving the Sahara Desert. They consist of a strange assortment of personalities.

Capt. Harris (Peter Finch) and Sgt. Watson (Ronald Fraser) are a staid and brave British officer and his munitions sergeant, a resentful weakling about to commit three acts of cowardice as a way of proving his independence. Trucker Cobb (Ernest Borgnine) is a roughneck with a few loose screws, accompanied by Dr. Reneaud (Christian Marquand), a company doctor who is accompanying the stressed-out worker back to the States.

"Ratbags" Crow (Ian Bannen) is the cynical tough guy with the sarcastic mouth and jittery attitude. Standish (Dan Duryea) is a quiet, Sunday-school-teacher type whose meekness and love for figs keeps him going. Mike Bellamy (George Kennedy) is the tough guy with the muscles that never quit. Gabriel (Gabriele Tinti) is a wounded young man whose love for his wife keeps him alive.

They were off-course when they crash landed, and it seems hopeless to think that they will be rescued. Vain attempts to find a remedy claim the lives of a few survivors. The odds change when the model-airplane designer suggests that they can build a smaller plane from the wreckage of the larger one.

It seems implausible, and this is the basis for a clash between old-school attitudes and new-school styles. It is a case of the crusty veteran who insists it can't be done, and the man with the calculations and the power of certainty who says that it can be accomplished. The movie ends with a smaller plane flying back to the oil field. The story of the movie is what happens in between the announcement of the possibility of building a Phoenix and the actual moment it takes off on the last cylinder.

One thing that enlivens the possible boredom of survival flicks is the clash of personalities. Getting on each other's nerves hampers and hastens project survival. The one-time passengers are now players in a real-life game of survival, and a miscue can mean a meal for the vultures.

It is inevitable that there are casualties, either through missteps with nature or Neanderthal bloodletting. This aspect is somewhat amusing because the victims are either known actors in small parts or nobodies who remained that way after the film. One thing was for sure, and that was a forceful and victorious personality clash that would build a new plane and fly it out of the desert.

Disaster movies are adventure fantasies that jab at civilized mores and the false gravity of ranks and identities. Social standing and ultimately accepted authority are obliterated and everyone returns to the starting line in a primitive game of survival. A new social system arises, based on an individual's worth to the overall survival of the others.

In the case of *The Flight of the Phoenix*, it all comes down to the usual question of opposites. It's savvy hands-on experience versus cerebral cunning, with the outcome being the melding of the two. Frank Towns and Heinrich Dorfmann are the old-school pilot and the young aeronautics designer who are faced with finding a solution for the crash landing in the desert. It is the designer's belief that they can build a smaller plane from

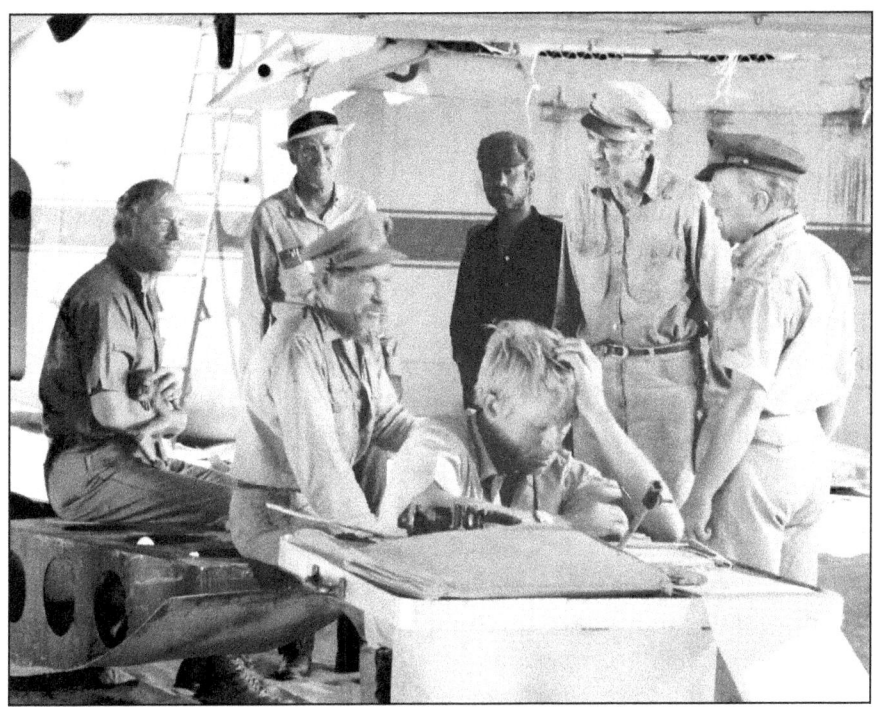

Frank Towns (James Stewart) berates Sergeant Watson (Ronald Fraser) while Heinrich Dorfman (Hardy Kruger) works on his blueprints. George Kennedy, Dan Duryea, Gabrielle Tinti and Richard Attenborough lend moral support (l-r). 1965, 20th Century Fox Corp.

the wreckage that sets off a bitter survival drama in which a disparate group of desperate people fight the slim to conquer death against slim odds of survival.

The filming was not without incident. Tragedy occurred during the filming of the Phoenix's flight to freedom. The plane crashed, killing the pilot and injuring a couple of the actors, Dan Duryea included. He suffered a contusion and broken ribs. On a calmer note, Dan Duryea also created three oil paintings while on location in Yuma. After recuperating from his experience in the desert and putting away his palette and brushes, Dan Duryea addressed the Cornell Dramatic Society on December 9.

Dan Duryea had a chance to try out a southern accent when he guest starred on *The Long Hot Summer*. The show was based on the movie and starred Edmond O'Brien as Will Varner, the part played by Orson Welles in the film. His autocratic rule of Frenchmen's Bend, a community in Mississippi, is challenged by the return of Ben Quick (Roy Thinnes). The loner with a purpose has returned to town to take back his father's property from the double-dealing power hungry town boss.

In *Return of the Quicks*, Dan Duryea is part of Ben's family. They have returned to Frenchmen's Bend to reclaim their heritage. The producers had planned to make Ben Quick a semi-regular but the show was not renewed for a second season. It was not hard to see why, as the show was broadcast against Dean Martin's long-running variety show.

War dramas were once as popular as Westerns. Discounting the movies made during WWII as part of the war effort, the war story was part of American mythology. Its biggest post-war influence was in the 1960's when the original movies had a rebirth, when they were sold to television to fit schedules that included afternoon matinees, late night television and weekend features.

WWII was part of the national psyche because of the decade's proximity to the actual war. It was a time that was molded by people who fought the war and it was a saga they passed down to their children. It was natural that movies and television perpetuated the legacy. Part of this mythology was the television shows that glamorized the war against the Axis powers. The most popular of these shows was *Combat*.

The stars of the show were a troop of American dogfaces led by Rick Jason and Vic Morrow as a lieutenant and sergeant, respectively. The unit was made up of a mix of characters so audiences could pick someone they could relate to. Dick Peabody was the popular Littlejohn who, like his namesake in Robin Hood, was a gentle giant until riled. Dan Duryea appeared in two episodes of *Combat*: *Dateline* and *A Little Jazz*, made two years later.

G2 has sent a captain on a clandestine mission to rescue Robert Barton (Dan Duryea), a war correspondent, from a German POW camp in *Dateline*. Sgt. Saunders and his men are assigned to accompany the intelligence officer to the perimeter where he will surrender to the Germans. The scuttlebutt is that there is an escape tunnel that was dug and will be used for the escape. The captain is killed when he steps on a land mine. The responsibility of the mission falls on Sgt. Saunders and his men.

Barton has sensitive information that the Germans can use to fight the Allies. That is why G2 wants to liberate him. First, Saunders and his men have to find the secret tunnel; then, they have to convince Barton to let them rescue him. They are secluded in an abandoned stable and they find Barton reclining in one of the stalls. He suffers from a leg wound and is in a foul temper. Being rescued does not interest him.

"No, thanks. Not interested," he mutters, adding that there is no tunnel.

He hops across the room and tells the men to look out the window at the spot he is pointing to. Pointing to a fresh mound of earth he says, "There's only one way out of here. He tried it last night."

The men are angry because of Barton's resistance. He believes that the war will eventually end and that he will be safe in the camp. The men realize that the Nazis will break him to get the information they need from him. He seems unfazed that an officer died for him and that they are putting their lives on the line, too. During a heated exchange, Sgt. Saunders accuses Barton of writing about the war, not soldiers.

They fail to change his mind and their mission seems impossible after the German C.O. promises Barton the comfort owed a non-combatant. It is to Barton's credit that he rejects the offer because he will not surrender vital information. However, it's the Nazi major's offer of a trip to a hospital safe haven that backs up his decision to stay.

The standoff between Barton and the soldiers, along with the CO's promise to relocate him to a safe haven, creates a tension that is heightened by the search for the tunnel. They find it by accident but it leads to a

In *Dateline*, a courageous battalion of G.I.'s rescues a reluctant P.O.W., a famous journalist who is reluctant about risking his neck over his own life. 1965, Selmar Productions.

stone bedrock dead end. Barton feels justified with his obstinate behavior but Saunders still believes that there is a functional tunnel to be found. He bases his conclusion on a rusty bolt that he found while exploring the tunnel with the dead end. The bolt was there too long for the tunnel to have been freshly dug. Saunders locates the tunnel when he sees the smoke from a soldier's cigarette drift through the cracks in two wall panels. He realizes that it is the draft caused by the tunnel.

The escape is fraught with danger because Barton has been anesthetized with morphine. They manage to escape when the ambulance arrives for Barton. He panics and wants to return to his stall so they can take him to the hospital but the men prevent him from turning back. The alarm is sounded when the Major finds the planks and the entrance to the tunnel. It is too late for the Germans because the Americans have escaped into the forest.

The last scene is in the rear when Barton speaks with his rescuers for the last time. He is wearing his dress greens and using a cane for support. The men are burnt out and grateful for having survived the ordeal. Mundane pleasantries are exchanged when Sgt. Saunders asks him what he is going to do.

Barton replies, "I have a story to write… about soldiers."

As Barton limps to the car that will take him to a safe zone, Sgt. Saunders and his men silently walk away. These anonymous soldiers are the real heroes of the war and the only glory they receive is a chance to survive another battle.

Barton is a complex character, one full of contradictory traits. He is a brave man for participating in the war armed only with a notepad. Fear also rules him because he is afraid to die. Sgt. Saunders tells him that he and his men are afraid to die, too. The men have to force him to make every step of the way. Even when they emerge from the tunnel, he wants to bolt back to the camp when he sees the ambulance arrive. But he summons his courage in the forest when a German sentry corners the soldiers and is distracted by the reporter so the Americans can bayonet him.

Dateline portrays the frustration and absurdity of war, albeit through a sanitized perspective. The challenges of uncertainty, the gravity of on-the-spot decisions, and the madness of surviving the odds are played out by the tug-of-war between Barton and the soldiers and the cat-and-mouse game between the Nazi commandant and the Allied soldiers. The existence of two tunnels also adds to the tension. The ending provides closure to the sobering thought that the real heroes of war rarely get their proper recognition. Even a famous war correspondent's glowing articles are not proper compensation for the personal sacrifices made by the troops. Without men like the G2 officer and Chip Saunders and his soldiers, Barton would not have the sterling reputation that he hides behind.

A sterling reputation is something that band leader Bernie Wallace (Dan Duryea) once enjoyed during the heyday of swing in *A Little Jazz*. He had a band with 45 musicians and was booked solid at the best jazz joints around. Now, he heads a five man Dixieland band touring Europe with the USO. A slight detour into enemy territory has the band attracting unwanted attention with their jamming while the truck driver changes a tire and the shot gun scouts the area. They needn't have bothered. Thanks to Wallace's arrogance the band's music attracts a platoon of German soldiers who don't plan on taking any prisoners.

Luckily for the band, Sgt. Chip Saunders and his men are also lured to the scene by the music. In wonderment, they engage in a firefight with the Germans while the spaced-out musicians rant and curse when their instruments are shot up in the exchange. Sgt. Saunders and his men will do the ranting for the two soldiers shot dead thanks to the musicians' lack of discretion. Bernie Wallace is not appreciative of the sacrifices made to save him and his men. He is outraged that they were led into a precarious situation in the first place. He grates on Sgt. Saunders' nerves until he is told to cool it. He obeys, if only temporarily.

Bernie's band is made up of familiar faces. Dennis Hopper plays Zack Fielder, the drummer. The bassist is Woody Jones, played by Robert Easton. Noah Beery and Joe Maross round out the musicians. They are wrapped up in their music. It is the only thing they think of. Enemy territory means nothing to them; neither does getting caught in the crossfire. Even when they are outflanked by the Germans, Bernie still tries to use his USO officer's rank to boss around the soldiers.

Later, they are pinned down in a farmhouse with limited ammunition and a promise of reinforcements. Bernie tries to end the standoff by crawling outside and waving a flag of surrender. The American soldiers have no intention of giving up and this sends mixed messages to the German patrol. The white flag at the end of a branch contradicts the shooting death of one of the enemy soldiers. To be killed when a flag of truce is being waved makes the Germans dig in, especially after their reinforcements arrive.

Things appear to be hopeless when the extra patrol of American soldiers arrives to change the tide of battle. This time around, it is Bernie who loses two men. His pigheaded interference finally sinks in as he holds

Bernie Wallace is a self-centered jazz musician who imperils his USO band in *A Little Jazz*. 1967, Selmar Productions.

the dead body of Woody, his bass player. His piano player lies dead in the field after he heard his dead G.I. son calling his name. Overcome by delirium he rushes out of the safety of the farmhouse, only to be cut down by a German officer who was sore about the false attempt to surrender that resulted in the death of one of his troops. The episode ends with Will playing a funeral oration on his clarinet.

Bernie Wallace gives Dan Duryea the chance to lather his role with arrogant obnoxiousness. He is totally out of his league when he tries to boss around the American soldiers. Even his loyal band mates have second thoughts about him when he waves the white flag. They know that he is used to having things his way and that he never got over losing his big band and the huge crowds they used to play for. He believes that he is above the fray because he is with the USO. Behind a jazz musician puts him in another universe.

The American soldiers have little use for him and his musicians after the driver and his shot gun were killed in their initial encounter with the Germans. His nagging turns a tense situation into an anxiety-filled experience. He tries to subvert his men every chance he can get by getting them to ignore orders but they eventually see the light, especially after two of them are killed. A trio does not seem plausible so it seems that their hillside jam was their last performance.

Despite having regular work in television, Dan Duryea still acted in films even though the quality of his films—*Flight of the Phoenix* being the exception—were low-budget. There were several deals, some at Dan Duryea's initiative, to make movies but either the deals fell through or they never made it beyond the planning stage. Robert L. Lippert wanted to engage Dan Duryea for *The Prairie*, a James Fenimore Cooper novel that was adapted for the screen by Dorothy Kamer Gray. Duryea bought the rights to Horace Jackson's Civil War novel *Benedict Borgeous* about Libby Prison, the notorious Confederate prison. In 1966, he bought the rights to Oswald Lawrence's psychological thriller, *The Mad Man of Muscle Beach* but it was not developed into a movie property. Two years later, Dan Duryea sought the rights to Niven Busch's *The Bradley Curse*, about San Francisco in 1916. In August of 1966, Dan Duryea conferred 20th Century Fox TV producer Richard Bluel for a part in a *Green Hornet* episode. He was also wooed by Japan's Toho to play a role in *The Yellow Grasshopper*.

Operation Blue Book was set in motion in October of 1966. It was supposed to start filming at Producers Studios but unnecessary costs and restrictions by some unions forced producer Jerry Fairbanks to relocate his production company to Spain. A company like this becomes a runaway production and Fairbanks explained why some unions insisted that he take up deadwood that increased production costs and slowed down production.

That policy was the impetus to become a runaway production. Fairbanks was able to reason with important unions and guilds and was able to hire the personnel that he needed so that he could afford to return to Producers Studio and make the film in four weeks instead of the ten weeks it would have taken in Spain. Fairbanks inked a deal where the movie would be distributed to theaters and television by National Telefilm Associates.

"I'm making a runaway feature in Hollywood. Depending on the cooperation of the few segments of the production economy that have not seen the light, I'll shoot my next four pictures here."[2]

Fairbanks signed Dan Duryea to star with John Ericson in *Project Saucer*, the new title for *Operation Blue Book* before *The Bamboo Saucer* became the final title. The cold war science fiction film started filming at Producers Studio and was put on the shelf when it wrapped because Fairbanks could not find a distributor for his movie.

In 1967, Jose Luis Calderon said that he would co-produce *Twist of the Knife* with Mark Cooper and Arthur Steloff of Gaumont for a budget of $450,000. Calderon announced that he had signed Dan Duryea, George Montgomery, Curt Jurgens and Tere Valazquez. *Twist of the Knife* had a seven week shooting schedule with six weeks in Mexico and one in the Sudan. Sam Fuller was the director.

Despite trade paper announcements about signings and shooting schedules *Twist of the Knife* remains a total mystery as to intent and pur-

Spanish poster for *Five Golden Dragons*, a Shaw Brothers spy comedy that plays like a weird spoof. 1965, Warner-Pathe Distributors Ltd.

pose. After that, there was nothing to be said about the project. Perhaps it would have been just as well for Dan Duryea with his next project. He had acted in a Spaghetti Western so now it was his turn to be in a British-Hong Kong-Filipino-made espionage movie; in other words, another James Bond knockoff and a bad one at that.

Harry Alan Summers was a successful British producer whose main achievements were the Fu Manchu films. In *Five Golden Dragons*, he capitalizes on the dying secret-agent film craze. He assembled many once-upon-a-time notable names for the film, which was made in conjunction with the Shaw Brothers, who would later be noted for their kung-fu exploitation flicks.

Bob Cummings is Bob Mitchell, the smiling, smug, ersatz secret-agent star of *Five Golden Dragons*, a Filipino movie that found its way into the endless loop of Bond imitators that flooded late-night television in the late 60's and early 70's. Cummings was a popular actor in 40's films and gained fame in three successful sit-coms, *Love That Bob*, *The Bob Cummings Show*, and *My Living Doll*.

The Five Golden Dragons are a secret society comprised of former American screen hard-boiled tough guys. Dan Duryea, George Raft, and Brian Donlevy don ceremonial costumes and plot crimes with a fourth member played by Christopher Lee. The fifth dragon is a mystery until his fatal recognition in the film's countdown.

The British cult icon and the former crime king icons wear Japanese ceremonial gowns and don ornate dragon masks before grumbling about how things aren't what they used to be. They look like ornaments at a Chinese New Year fireworks celebration. Fireworks are what one of the five dragons gets before the organization collapses in this bottom-of-the-barrel espionage spy film.

Five Golden Dragons is the nadir of the spy genre, a hodge-podge mess of feeble espionage with a cast that had seen better days. Bob Cummings virtually resurrects his television personalities for this comedic spy film. One can't help but think of *Love That Bob*; instead of Ann B. Davis as Schultzy, we have Klaus Kinski as a chain-smoking killer with twisted nerves.

Bob Mitchell is a conceited player whose perpetual smile and forced good humor help him to mug his way through this spy adventure. He somehow gets mixed up with the Five Golden Dragons and actually has a hand in their demise. They are trying for one last grand scheme and it involves doing business with a Mafia-type organization and a band of local thugs.

Bob Mitchell (Bob Cummings) is a suave American photographer who tries his charm on two sisters, Ingrid (Maria Rohm) and Margret (Maria Perschy). 1965, Warner-Pathe Distributors Ltd.

The action starts with a defenestrated tourist who passed a cryptic note to a taxi driver before being murdered. It reads, "Five Golden Dragons." The note winds up on the desk of Commander Sanders (Rupert Davies), who enlists the aid of his top cop, Inspector Chiao (Roy Chiao).

Bob Mitchell gets mixed up in the action when he flirts with Ingrid (Maria Rohm) and Margret (Maria Percy) at a resort. They are amused but unimpressed by his one-liners and annoying smile. It is when Margret is found dead in bed that Mitchell is implicated in the investigation.

The action is centered on the European cabaret run by the perpetually-smiling Peterson (Siegardt Rupp), who has a mysterious hold over his sexy chanteuse, Magda (Margaret Lee). She, too, brings Mitchell deeper into the mystery that also involves Girt (Klaus Kinski), a vicious enforcer, and The Five Golden Dragons.

Everyone bumbles around in this chaotic, badly-edited-and-dubbed fiasco until it builds up to a twist ending that wakes the viewer up with a bang. The surprise dragon's loss is inconsequential to the viewer because of the apprehension of the former Hollywood heavyweights and the British cult idol.

Unintentional humor pervades this Summers-Shaw Brothers spy flick. The aftermath of an unlucky cab driver's interrogation by Girt is funny because it happens to someone else. Girt's propensity for dispatching the players is matched only by his chain-smoking. He winds up being short of breath when he tangles with the wrong sidekick who prefers garrotes to neck ties.

Margaret Lee is seductive as Magda, a duplicitous nightclub singer. Maria Pershy is along for the ride until her character, Margret, has served her purpose. Her sister, Ingrid, is played by Maria Rohm.

Rupert Davies appears to be grateful for the role of Commandant Sanders, a flustered British police inspector working in Hong Kong. Sieghardt Rupp is Peterson, a strange, narcissistic villain who gets his shot at being a dragon although it will serve him no purpose. Roy Chiao plays

Four of the *Five Golden Dragons* are rounded up by Comm. Sanders (Rupert Davies). 1965, Warner-Pathe Distributors Ltd.

Inspector Chiao, a resolute Filipino officer who investigates the odd goings on that place Mitchell at their center.

All Roads Lead to Eddie Jacks

Dan Duryea experienced a major change in his life in 1967 when his wife Helen died of heart failure. One way to deal with the sudden shock and void left by this personal loss was to keep busy. He accepted the role of Eddie Jacks on primetime's first soap opera, *Peyton Place*, after the part was rewritten several times for him.

Eddie Jacks is Dan Duryea's most expansive character and embodies many of the larcenous traits of the actor's best villains. He is the mature culmination of all the scoundrels who hatched a scheme that got the better part of their worst nature. Although Eddie Jacks is a part of this dubious lineage he is a thoroughly unique character. He is more than the end of the line, he is Dan Duryea's most skillful portrait of a low-level con artist who got in over his head.

Peyton Place was based on the 1957 film starring Lana Turner and Jeff Chandler which, in turn, was based on the 1956 novel by Grace Matalious. The book's 1940's setting was adapted by Paul Monash and updated to the modern 60's era and many of the controversial subjects were toned down for the television audience. There were revisions in characters and power mongers but the general adult tone of the book and the movie were retained for the television show.

Dan Duryea was introduced towards the end of Season Three and departed by the end of the following season. For one year, Eddie Jacks was one of the many desperate characters whose squalid life was part of the Peyton Place puzzle. No one who had ill intentions or secret revenge plots was deemed irrelevant. Everyone had an opportunity to play out their drama and affect the general outcome but no one succeeded in maintaining a steady course to dominate the proceedings initiated by the town boss, the crepuscular Martin Payton. Eddie Jacks was no exception.

He may have been a sordid reprobate from the wrong side of the tracks and that put him in another social class than the power brokers and royal hangers-on. It did not matter to Eddie Jacks because he had plenty of connections and he knew how to use them by letting them use

Eddie Jacks is the end of the line for Dan Duryea's lineage of cads and scoundrels. 1967, 20th Century Fox Television.

him. That meant spreading smears and innuendoes before accepting a contract to kill Martin Peyton, the town scion. It all happens in the space of a year.

Episode 364 opens with a shady character walking down the nighttime main street as the narrator tells his story. His name is Eddie Jacks and he once lived in Peyton Place. He had a wife, Ada, and a daughter, Rita. The husband and wife ran the local tavern and were a part of the community, but Eddie "had debts and something to hide. One day he left." Now that he has returned, the narrator tells the viewers that Eddie Jacks "wants most people to forget his past. He wants to take advantage of the few who remember him."

The people he will use in the first stage of his game are his wife and daughter, the town's newspaper publisher and the owner of a mill. That's just in the beginning. He will also affect the people who are related to the people that he's using. Of the four main players, only Elliot, the newspaper publisher and Rita, his daughter, believe that he wants to change his reprobate ways. Ada, his wife, and Leslie, the manager of the mill, do not buy into Eddie's repentant conciliation routine.

It does not matter to him because he has some secrets that he'd like to share unless he can get some leverage for his silence. Charm is part of Eddie Jacks' avaricious personality and he plans to endear himself to everyone he has to use to throw them off guard before he lays down his demands. To understand Eddie Jacks, think of him as an old and desperate combination of Johnny Prince, Karl Benson and Carl Lutcher.

His first connection is Ada (Evelyn Scott), the wife that he walked out on. She knows him better than he knows himself and does not buy into his reformed wayward father act. Ada is shocked when she is awakened at night by somebody fumbling at the front door of the tavern. She emerges from her backroom bedroom and controls her anger when the stranger enters, turns on the light and appears to be her ex-husband.

Eddie Jacks acts as if nothing happened between them.

"See? I got them", he says when he pulls out the pack of cigarettes he went out to buy more than eighteen years ago.

He behaves as if nothing has changed but he could not be more mistaken than he is arrogant and nonchalant. It will not matter to him that most people will not believe that the ex-jailbird has paid his debt to society but they will accept him because he is the father of the beloved Rita (Patricia Morrow) and estranged husband of Ada. The players of Peyton Place know that Eddie Jacks is bad news but he is what they need when they have dirty deeds to be performed undercover.

The soap opera premise of the show means that subplots are constantly creating problems and solutions that are played out in a continual loop. Resolutions turn into new headaches that are eased by short term remedies that fester into tragic circumstances. Eddie Jacks walks into a scenario of relative calm because certain embarrassing situations have been averted by fate and happenstance. He has no qualms about opening these old wounds and applying a poultice of salt and vinegar to aggravate the pain. It is more than a matter of necessity to him; it is a sadistic game that fills him with glee.

Ada is happy that their daughter has married Norman Harrington (Christopher Connelly), the youngest son of Leslie Harrington (Paul

Eddie Jacks thinks that he can mesmerize his estranged wife into thinking that he has noble intentions regarding mending his tomcat ways. 1967, 20th Century Fox Television.

Langton), the manager of the Peyton Place Mill. However, her daughter's weak heart is subjected to the stress of pregnancy. She is attended to by Dr. Rossi (Ed Nelson), one of the good guys of Peyton Place.

Leslie Harrington is harangued by his sons for aiding and abetting the jail escape of a notorious criminal, Jack Chandler (John Kellogg). Chandler had come to the end of his lengthy run on the soap opera as a chiseler and roughneck. Norman witnessed the late night jail house visit of his father before Chandler made his escape. He surmises that his father smuggled in the gun that the con used for his breakout.

This caused Norman to blackmail his father into giving him a day laborer's job at the mill instead of starting at the top. Now, Rodney (Ryan O'Neal), his eldest son, wants to tell the police that his father was responsible for Chandler's escape, only he wants the old man to be by his side to corroborate the charge.

News that the fugitive Chandler was shot dead by the police seems to end the matter but that is not the case when Eddie Jacks returns. The scheming prodigal son later taunts Leslie about the late night snacks he used to make the men when they used the tavern's back room for their secret meetings in the old days. Rodney, Rita's brother-in-law, asks his father if Eddie Jacks knew Chandler after the old man asks his son's help in helping to run the con artist out of town. Suddenly, Jack Chandler is very much alive.

Ultimately, it will be Leslie who will hire Eddie Jacks to kill Martin Peyton (George Macready) the same way he hired Chandler to murder his wife twenty years ago. Blackmail and bargaining are parts of the round robin of avaricious and deceitful games of Peyton Place. Eddie Jacks is in it every step of the way, from extorting money and accepting bribes to becoming a clandestine player who finds himself in the spotlight when he finds the wrong body in the Peyton mansion. It will be the aged Peyton's young fiancée, Adrienne (Gena Rowlands), who is found at the bottom of the stairs with Eddie Jacks standing over her lifeless body.

That is getting ahead of things and why Adrienne took the brutal fall requires filling in the rest of the dirty doings that surround the drama that engulfs the ambitious Eddie Jacks when he is arrested for murder. Until then, a little background information is needed; in the parlance of today's sordid tabloid mentality it would be called gossip. Martin Peyton's impending marriage is not the usual May-December romance. It is a scheme to break up the marriage of his grandson, Steven Cord (James Douglas), an ambitious lawyer who is contesting his grandfather's will on the grounds of incompetence. There is ill will between the two men because Steven was born out of wedlock to Peyton's hallowed and deceased daughter.

Adrienne has been chosen as bait because there is an undeniable attraction between her and Steven. It would be a matter of time before the fuse is lit and the explosion destroys Steven's marriage to Betty (Barbara Parkins). Instead, it eliminates Adrienne when she has a heated meeting with Betty about the resultant infidelity, an exchange that should have not occurred at the top of the stairs. Nothing underhanded occurred because it was a case of an emotionally distraught woman taking one backward step too many. All that Eddie Jacks knows is that he saw Betty bolt through the front door before he entered the mansion to discover the body.

All of this occurs after Eddie Jacks has been wheeling and dealing into making himself an unofficial beneficiary of the Peyton fortune. That is the basis of a plan that started the day he saw a photo of the expectant bride in a Boston newspaper. She was the same New York party girl he had spied on years ago when he worked for a detective agency that specialized in divorces. She was his ticket to riches and all he needed was the alibi of contrition and reconciliation.

The first step was to return home and turn his ex-wife's life topsy-turvy. Ada stares at him in utter disbelief as he walks around the tavern and mentions how nothing has changed. Eddie uses small talk to ingratiate himself to Ada who warns him to keep his hands off her. The conversation switches to Rita, their daughter and this is when maternal instincts kick in and she warns him to stay away from the young woman.

Eddie knows that there are other ways of making inroads. One of them is visiting Leslie Harrington, a man who sees the specter of Jack Chandler come alive in the form of Eddie Jacks.

"It's a matter of courtesy to wait in a man's outer office. Isn't it?", remarks a flustered Harrington when he enters his office and sees a stranger sitting in his chair.

The stranger turns out to be Eddie Jacks and Harrington's annoyance turns into subdued panic. He does not hesitate to ask why the missing link to his past has returned to Peyton Place. The standard answer is, "A man gets awful tired of moving around. Awful tired."

It is the smarmy way that Eddie Jacks makes his case that makes him appear to be untrustworthy. He is always smiling and accentuating his points with a slow arc of the hand or an exaggerated expression and he moves in a slow deliberate style.

Harrington's pointed questions get a claim that Eddie has returned to take care of his little girl but his old friend isn't buying any of it because she is comfortably married to Norman, his son, the grandson of Martin Peyton. Harrington wants to know why Jacks has returned at this particular time because he does not do anything that does not have an angle. Eddie Jacks acts as if he hasn't heard the question and begins to ruminate on Fate.

"Before I left, Martin Peyton was such a magical name…someone to look up to… almost super human."

He finds it that he is now related to the rich old man because of his daughter's marriage to Peyton's grandson, Harrington's youngest boy. That also means that Eddie Jacks and Leslie Harrington are in-laws. When Jacks is told that things have changed and there isn't any room for him in Peyton Place, the hustler ignores the jibe and begins to reminisce about the past, particularly about Jack Chandler.

He thought it was nice how he let Chandler and Harrington use the tavern's back room for their personal business. Weren't the little snacks that he prepared for them really nice? That segues into Eddie's surmising that Harrington must have been the one who helped Chandler escape jail by supplying him the gun.

"Is that what Chandler told you?", asks the nervous miller.

This scene is done with Dan Duryea's talent for understatement. He acts as if he is being pleasant when recalling fond memories but he is really telling Harrington not to be so dismissive of him because he is the one dictating the terms of the deal he is about to broker. What that deal is remains to be seen and Harrington is back to square one concerning his involvement with Chandler's escape and shooting death only now it is from another perspective. That it comes from the newest member of his family makes it ironic because there are no blood ties that can necessitate a compromise. Eddie Jacks does have an angle and he is going to make Harrington sweat before he tells him what it is.

The next stop is to visit Elliot Carson (Tim O'Connor), the editor of The Clarion. This visit shows the other side of Eddie Jacks, the frail and vulnerable individual who is at a crossroads in his life. Redemption is not possible unless the opportunity to reform is available. How can an ex-con get back on his feet and who will hire someone who has done jail time?

Eddie Jacks pretends that this information of serving time will shock Elliot when he knows that the editor will commiserate with him. Elliot spent 18 years in jail for a crime he did not commit so how can he not empathize with Eddie Jacks? Despite his jovial attitude, the self-deprecating humor is meant to throw people off guard, claims Eddie.

"Keep 'em laughing…then people won't know how beat up a guy is on the inside."

Self-pity and groveling are Eddie's ways and means of manipulating the editor. He tells him about the hard luck life of a hustler. You could find him wherever a fast buck could be made. The road from the casinos to the backroom gambling dens led to prison.

"When you get locked up, you have nothing but time on your hands. The worst part is you begin to think…think about the things you missed in life."

Elliot's expression shows that he relates to what he is being told. Eddie Jacks drones on about how he walked out on Ada and his little girl. He wants to see if a phony and a con-artist like himself can make a go out of being a father. The first step is getting a job. That's why he came to The

Clarion. He wants to put a want ad in the classifieds and take a risk that someone will hire an ex-con. Elliot falls for Eddie's story hook, line and sinker. He helps Eddie jacks get a job in the most unlikely place.

Eddie's next step is to see his daughter face-to-face. This happens at the beach after the young woman has witnessed Steven kissing a woman who was not his wife. She was Adrienne, who was sent there by Peyton to compromise his grandson. Rita puts the scene on hold when she meets the mysterious stranger at an abandoned store on the ramshackle boardwalk.

He tells her how he plans to open up a night spot for young people and asks her opinion about his ideas. The stranger tells her about how the boardwalk used to be crowded in the old days and it is a shame that it is a lonely place now. The sad story gives Rita a chance to ask him how he was

Eddie and Ada are at ends about his decision to reenter his daughter's life. She believes that it can only have dire consequences. 1967, 20th Century Fox Television.

involved with Peyton Place in the first place. He tells the story of his life and how his estranged family affair was her story also. Rita's commiseration turns to anger when she realizes that she is the daughter that he abandoned and her mother is the wife that hates him. The distraught woman returns home and is circumspect of her mother, whom she believes has something to do with her father's return.

Eddie Jacks has made contact with the people he needs to use. It is now a matter of them losing composure thinking about him and finding ways to use each other to deal with him. The first step is a job offer arranged by Elliot Carson.

Ada offers Eddie a bartending job insisting that it is for the sake of their daughter. She recites a list of strict stipulations and says that if he violates any of these, he will be fired. Nothing worries Eddie and he laughs at the thinly disguised threats. He hasn't even started the job yet but he acts like he never left the tavern. Ada tells her ex-husband, "If it wasn't for Rita you couldn't get within five miles of this place and you know it."

The declaration can't wipe the smirk off his face. Nothing can. After all, it is a smirk that Duryea has been wearing for almost thirty years as an actor. Ada makes it clear that he has been hired as a bartender and nothing more. She does not want to hear anything about management: "Forget the management bit. I'm hiring you as a bartender, pure and simple. And that means just mix and no talk."

Not content to leave well enough alone, Eddie tells her, "Alright, but you can't separate the two. A bartender's stock and trade is talk. That's one of the reasons why this place caught on in the first place. Remember? See? There's a certain psychology in a bar. It doesn't seem to work with a woman. 3 to 1 business will triple when word gets around that I'm here."

Eddie makes it seem as if he is doing Rita a favor by accepting the offer to tend bar. She still won't let him get the upper hand and tells him, "Get this straight, Eddie. I run a clean place here. That means no gambling, no courtesy drinks, no shills. When a guy's had too much, out he goes. That includes the bartender."

Eddie's acknowledgement is his smirk. It is something that will get him so far in his comeback attempt. His luck is about to change and it won't be for the better because, in the long run, he is still a low-level con artist. His hubris outshines his actual ability and it is when he fails to vary his tactics that his plan will begin to unravel. The first indication is when he rubs Elliot the wrong way when he visits the newspaper man at his headquarters.

Elliot has been alerted to Eddie's possible involvement with Chandler and Harrington because of one of Ada's accusations. The newspaperman tries to be subtle in the way he pumps Eddie about a possible connection between Harrington and Chandler. Elliot's questions finally unnerve Eddie and he becomes unraveled and demands that Elliot stop pressuring him.

The sudden outburst causes Eddie to regain his composure and he does this by putting on his amiable smile. It does not matter because he has been rattled and this causes both men to believe that they are on to something. Eddie tries to smooth things over by inviting Elliot to the tavern for a drink of Eddie's vintage Scotch.

It is an offer that Elliot take up at an opportune time for Eddie. The night that Elliot dropped the tavern was the night had to keep a secret rendezvous with Harrington. Eddie maintains his game face when he shares a drink with Elliot but excuses himself for personal reasons. Elliot gives Eddie enough time to leave before he steps out for some night air. He witnesses Eddie and Harrington speaking to each other in a car before it is driven away into the night fog. It is then that Elliot realizes that Ada may be right in her accusations.

The other subplots begin to unfold and they have nothing to do with Eddie Jacks until he interjects himself into the action. Steven Cord still wants to prove that Martin Peyton is incompetent in court. Cord's marriage to Betty is unraveling because of his involvement with Adrienne, bride-to-be of the elderly millionaire. Leslie Harrington is still nervous because of his connection to Chandler, a man who had a vicious grip on the mill owner because of a vicious past deed. Rodney and Norman still need to prove their independence even though they will be named in their grandfather's will. Meanwhile, Elliot Carson and Dr. Rossi continue to be the town's good guys.

For the time being, Eddie Jacks isn't even remotely related to many of their concerns although he will have affected them after his plan has been exhausted. Right now, he is busy messing with the emotions of his daughter and son-in-law. Eddie's next step is to visit Martin Peyton to size him up. He is totally out of his league when he tries to intimidate the sickly old man. Adrienne maintains a poker face when Eddie Jacks taunts her with mysterious insults and this piques Peyton's interest in what the swindler has on her. Martin Peyton begins to believe that Eddie Jacks has returned to Peyton Place to swindle him.

While Eddie Jacks is implementing his plan, Peyton deals with Steven Cord's lawsuit. During the trial, Adrienne testifies that she was not

One way for Eddie Jacks to size up old man Peyton is through his volatile chauffeur, Lee. 1968, 20th Century Fox Television.

hired to break up his marriage and it is revealed that she was once a party girl. The case is dismissed and the only damage has been to Adrienne's reputation.

While this drama is being played out, Eddie Jacks is visited in his ramshackle rented room by his partner-in-crime. Harrington is becoming nervous and offers Jacks some money to leave him alone. When this can't be done he offers Jacks a larger sum to commit murder. He wants him to kill Martin Peyton.

Jacks finds this amusing because it is the same offer Harrington made to Chandler twenty years ago when he hired the town hustler to kill his wife. Eddie realizes that it is inevitable because his attempts to extort money have failed because it is now common knowledge that Adrienne was a call girl.

Eddie draws up a contract that will force Harrington, who is the executioner of Peyton's will, to bequeath a certain amount of the fortune to Rita and Norman. He also wants a share. Once the agreement it is sealed it is Eddie's turn to be nervous because the Peyton wedding is going to happen the next day. That means he will have to kill him that night.

He makes arrangement by stealing a wrench from Lee (Stephen Oliver), the chauffeur's toolbox so he can bludgeon the old man and have the suspicion fall on the driver. Eddie establishes an alibi by pretending to be sick that night at work and Ada sends him home because she does not wants him to contaminate the bar patrons.

It is a cold night and Eddie feels the chill as he hides in the bushes outside of the mansion. He does not know it but inside the mansion there is a confrontation between Betty and Adrienne. They are reserved in their threats about Adrienne's involvement with Steven. Adrienne loses her cool and steps forward to strike Betty but falls downs the stairs and is killed.

Eddie sees Betty fleeing from the mansion and thinks nothing of it. His world is turned upside down when he finds Adrienne's lifeless body at the foot of the stairs. Martin Peyton comes out of his room and demands to know who is there lurking in the shadows. He finds out it is Eddie when Lee turns on the lights and prevents Eddie from fleeing the murder scene.

Eddie begs him to listen to him as he insists his innocence. Martin Peyton is sardonic with his announcement of guilt. The police tell him that he can tell his story at the arraignment. Steven does not promise Eddie that he will be his councilor but he will listen to his story. Eddie is arrested and taken to the station which is located across the street from where Rita and Norman live. She can't believe that she sees her father in handcuffs and becomes hysterical.

Through happenstance and grim eye witness testimony, Steven Cord defends Eddie Jacks. It is proven that Eddie Jacks did not commit murder and an investigation corroborates his story. This absolution gives Eddie a new chance in life and he takes it.He becomes a model dad and husband until he is drawn into one of his daughter's strange third encounters of the mental kind.

Dr. Rossi's delinquent brother has returned to Peyton Place and he sets off an adverse reaction to Rita because the drifter reminds her of a phantom from the past. His name was Joe Chernak and he was the punk who once led her astray. It is a jolt that was added to the shock of her miscarriage.

Dr. Rossi's brother Joe (Michael Christian) becomes Chernak's twin and he evokes a psychosomatic reaction in Rita when she becomes dazed and withdrawn. This leads to her father into a brutal brawl with the Charnak twin where he is mangled by the younger man. This fight cures Rita of her malady and earns the Rossi kid damnation even though he was trying to convince her that he was not Joe Charnak.

Daddy's hot headedness and battle scars are soothed by Rita's invitation to a family dinner that evening at a restaurant. After all of the trials and tribulations, Eddie Jacks has finally found the respectability that he yearned for. In the long run, he couldn't handle it and all it took was an invitation to a family dinner with Rita, Ada and Norman.

Eddie Jacks couldn't handle the domesticity that he yearned for and writes his daughter a note telling her that her best bet was to put all of her

Eddie finally receives the stamp of approval of his daughter and he can't handle it. 1968, 20th Century Fox Television.

money on Norman because he had the legs to be a winner. It was his way of saying goodbye.

Rita is thunderstruck that her father has left home a second time and, as usual, she takes her pain out on her mother. She accuses her mother of being happy that her father has abandoned them again. Ada is mortified, not because of her daughter's accusation, but for her gullibility and her husband's gumption. She defies her daughter and says that she is glad that he left because she "never had for the use for the bum anyway." Ada slams the door with a thunderous force that shatters all of the illusions that they had built up around the unrepentant heartbreaker.

The last we see of Eddie Jacks is his drunken wobbly self walking to catch the next bus out of town. He hands the driver a bill and tells him to take him as far as the denomination will let him travel. When the driver asks him, "Round trip or one way?", Eddie answers, "One way."

"That's a long one way", answers the driver.

Eddie Jacks smiles and the driver says, "Let's go because I'm behind schedule."

The amiable drunk replies, "That's exactly what I was saying to myself."

Eddie Jacks takes his seat, looks out the window and beams with a drunken smile. He waves good-bye to the wife and daughter he has run out on for the second time.

Conclusion

The Bamboo Saucer

Broadway producers Lee Loeb and Sam Ross were mounting a program of revivals and tried to spark Dan Duryea's interest. They wanted him to star in a series of plays: *The Music Master*, *The Return of Peter Grimm* and *The Auctioneer*. Producer Nicholas Eckert approached Dan Duryea for *The Tivoli Gates*, a movie about the Danish underground during World War II. The movie never went beyond the planning stage.

Dan Duryea may not have returned to the theater or fought with the Danish underground but he did record two spoken LP records for the Edward Garrett's W/G label. His first disc was the self-penned, *The Pitfalls of a Rube Abroad* and that was followed by *It's a Mod, Mod, Mod, Mod World*.

Whether the world was mad or mod was a moot point by 1968. Dan Duryea's last movie would be as real as the Cold War yet other-worldly because of the underlying science fiction theme. The movie is also a lesson in independent production in 1968 the way *Scarlet Street* was a successful experiment of an independent production company and movie studio working in tandem. The only difference was in 1968 there was no studio system, just guilds and unions for indie producers to contend with. To further complicate things, the movie was made two years earlier before finding a way off the shelf.

In *The Bamboo Saucer*, Dan Duryea fought for Truth, Justice and the American Way in his last film role as Hank Peters, a snub-nosed CIA man ready to outdo the Commies in a battle to commandeer a downed UFO in Red China. He is tough with the phone decisions and the snap commands that make staying alive in the field his first priority. Peters leads an Ameri-

A movie poster for *The Bamboo Saucer*. 1968, World Entertainment Corp.

can contingent consisting of an astronaut and scientists that will match wits and brawn with a Russian group made up of belligerent comrades and a sensitive beautiful scientist.

The psychedelic era dominated the late sixties, and everything that existed out of that warped sensibility was considered plastic and quaint. The past was negated by the new hip and former icons and attitudes were now ridiculed, challenged, and discarded. Even Walt Disney was regarded with the same dread and contempt once reserved for Fu Manchu. Movies like *The Bamboo Saucer* were considered insufficient blips on the new radar. Today, they embody the 60s more than most of the tripe that symbolized the era at the time.

Red, white, and blue are some of the colors of this trip inside Red China to destroy a flying saucer that may put an end to American technological dominance as we know it. It's not just the American team that wants to find the saucer but a Russian expedition that collides with the capitalists in intent and motive.

The Russian Communists are not as tight-knit with their Chinese counterparts as one would think, and they have to forge an uneasy alliance with the westerners. The scientists on both sides overrule the military authority and the movie becomes an ode to mutual understanding and international peace by the time it ends. Until then, the nod goes to the Americans thanks to Hank Peters (Dan Duryea), a state department man who leads the Americans with the aid of a Chinese scout named Sam Archibald (James Hong).

Collision Course is one of the alternate titles of the movie and could well be used to describe the antagonism that exists between Hank Peters and Zagersky, the militaristic officers played by Dan Duryea and Vincent Beck. Duryea has the edge because he is wilier and tougher. The Russian is blustery and comes off the way a peasant in uniform would if he had power.

The main mover in his expedition is Anna Karachev (Lois Nettleton), a Russian scientist. She bonds with Norwood (John Ericson), the American test pilot, and they provide the balance of power to the international minded scientists in the group. This includes Bob Hastings and Bernard Fox for the Americans and British and Nick Katurich and Rico Cattani for the Russians. Only Peters and Zagersky have any enmity toward each other.

They finally trust each other until Zagersky tries to hijack the saucer back to Moscow. One of his men is killed trying to figure out a way to fly the saucer. As a result, a blood-and-guts battle goes down to provide cover for the saucer's takeoff. The military men revert to their valiant combative stance against a column of Red Chinese soldiers, as does one of the peaceniks. In the end, universal peace is experienced when three of the survivors take a tour of the universe before deciding to land at Geneva as a display of international cooperation.

Dan Duryea's last screen role is a tough-guy-of-valor part that lets him boss people around and defend his mission with his deadly machine-gun aim. He barks orders and shoots under duress with equal aplomb.

Hank Peters (Dan Duryea) is a two-fisted State Department man who goes toe-to-toe with the Russians and Red Chinese. Bob Hastings (l) watches his back. 1968, World Entertainment Corp.

Peters is fiercely American and does not trust the touchy-feely demeanor of everyone else. It is not his mission to share credit and knowledge with anyone for any reason.

He turns out to be right as the Russian leader tries to pull a *coup de etat*, but fails. It does not matter because the final victory flight is an international affair. All conventions are shattered when the Geneva-bound Bob Hastings' final "Amen" puts a damper on nationalism.

John Ericson is Fred Norwood, the test pilot who first encounters the UFO. He travels to China with Peters' team and gets to take a test run of the craft across the universe before flying to Geneva in a statement about international cooperation. Ericson had been the co-star with Anne Francis on *Honey West*, a hard-driving sensual private eye show that was short-lived and ahead of its time.

Lois Nettleton affects a thick Russian accent as Anna Karachev. Vincent Beck is Zagersky, the Boris Badenov-cartoon-stereotype Russian operative. Bob Hastings is Jack Garson and Bernard Fox is Dave Ephram, both specialists in their respective fields. James Hong is Sam Archibald, Peters' inside man in Red China.

Variety's review of the movie reported that the Times Square audience hissed at the end of the movie. It was not a film critique so much as it was a political opinion that was indicative of the mood of the times. Patriotism and anything pro-Washington invited ridicule. *Bamboo Saucer* was released in 1968, one of the pivotal years of the 60's rebellion. 1968 was the year that Martin Luther King and Robert F. Kennedy were assassinated. The Watts Riots backed up the Black Power slogan, "Burn, Baby, Burn!" The police used their night sticks to keep the peace at the Democratic Convention in Chicago. The war in Vietnam escalated and the nation was besotted with protest marches and demonstrations. Richard Nixon rose from the dead and was elected president.

Hank Peters was the squarest and most clean cut of any of the characters that Dan Duryea played because of his State Department credentials. It's funny how a cynical public could take a character like that and consider him subversive. That was the 60's *zeitgeist*.

The New Amsterdam Theater was the Times Square grind house where *The Bamboo Saucer* played and it was located one block away from The National Theatre, where *The Little Foxes* debut in 1938. In the thirty years that ensued, Dan Duryea appeared in sixty one movies and over fifty television programs, plus a score of plays and radio shows. Not a bad set of credentials for someone who once described himself as "a bread and butter actor."

List of Credits

The Little Foxes
(1941-RKO Radio Pictures-115 min.)

Regina Giddens: Bette Davis. *Horace Giddens*: Herbert Marshall. *Alexandra Giddens*: Teresa Wright. *David Hewitt*: Richard Carlson. *Birdie Hubbard*: Patricia Colinge. *Leo Hubbard*: Dan Duryea. *Ben Hubbard*: Charles Dingle. *Director*: William Wyler. *Screenplay:* Lillian Hellman, based on her play. *Additional dialogue*: Arthur Kober, Dorothy Parker, and Alan Campbell. *Producer*: Samuel Goldwyn. *Cinematographer*: Gregg Toland. *Musical Score*: Meredith Willson. *Editor*: Daniel Mandell.

Ball of Fire
(1941-MGM-111 min.)

Professor Bertram Potts: Gary Cooper. *Katherine "Sugarpuss" O'Shea*: Barbara Stanwyck. *The Professors:* Oskar Homolka, Henry Travers, S.Z. Sakall, Tully Marshall, Aubrey Mather, Leonid Kinsky and Richard Hayden. *Joe Lilac*: Dana Andrews. *Duke Pastraimi*: Dan Duryea. *Garbageman*: Allen Jenkins. *Director*: Howard Hawks. *Screenplay*: Charles Bracket and Billy Wilder. *Story:* Billy Wilder and Thomas Monroe. *Producer*: Samuel Goldwyn. *Musical Score*: Alfred Newman. *Cinematography*: Greg Toland. *Editor:* Daniel Mandell.

Pride of the Yankees
(1942-MGM-128 min.)

Lou Gehrig: Gary Cooper. *Eleanor Twitchell*: Teresa Wright. *Babe Ruth*: Himself. *Sam Blake*: Walter Brennan. *Hank Hanneman*: Dan Duryea.

Christina "Ma" Gehrig: Elsa Janssen. *Henry "Pop" Gehrig*: Ludwig Stoesell. *Myra Tunsely*: Virginia Gilmore. *Bill Dickey*: Himself. *Director*: Sam Wood. *Screenplay*: Jo Swerling and Herman J. Mankiewicz. *Story:* Paul Gallico. *Prologue*: Damon Runyon. *Producer*: Samuel Goldwyn. *Musical Score*: Leigh Hairline. *Cinematography*: Rudolph Mate. *Editor*: Daniel Mandell.

That Other Woman
(1942-20th Century Fox-75 min.)

Emily Borden: Virginia Gilmore. *Henry Summers:* James Ellison. *Ralph Cobb:* Dan Duryea. *Constance Powell:* Janis Carter. *Grandma:* Alma Kruger. *George:* Bud McAllister. *Mrs. MacReady:* Minerva Urecal. *Bailey:* Charles Arnt. *Director:* Ray McCarey. *Screenplay:* Jack Jungmeyer. *Producer:* Walter Morosco. *Cinematography:* Joseph MacDonald. *Editor:* J. Watson Webb, Jr.

Sahara
(1943-Columbia Pictures-97 min.)

Sgt. Joe Gunn: Humphrey Bogart. *Waco Hoyt*: Bruce Bennett. *Jimmy Doyle*: Dan Duryea. *Giuseppe:* J. Carrol Naish. Sgt. Maj. Tambul: Rex Ingram. *Capt. Jason Halliday*: Richard Nugent. *Jean Leroux (Frenchie):* Louis Mercier. With: Lloyd Bridges, Carl Harbord, Patrick O'Moore. *Capt. Von Schletow*: Kurt Krueger. *Director*: Zoltan Korda. *Screenplay:* John Howard Lawson and Zoltan Korda. *Short Story:* Philip MacDonald. *Producer:* Harry Joe Brown (unaccredited). *Score:* Miklos Rozsa. *Cinematography:* Rudolph Mate. *Editor:* Charles Nelson.

Man From Frisco
(1943-Columbia Pictures-97 min.)

Matt Braddock: Michael O'Shea. *Diana Kennedy*: Anne Shirley. *Joel Kennedy*: Gene Lockhart. *Jim Benson*: Dan Duryea. *Russ Kennedy*: Tommy Bond. *Johnny Rogers*: Ray Walker. *Martha Kennedy*: Ann Shoemaker. *Director:* Robert Florey. *Screenplay*: Ethel Hill and Arnold Manoff. *Story and Adaptation*: George Carleton Brown and George Worthing Yates. *Produc-

er: Albert J. Cohen. *Musical Score*: Marlin Skiles. *Cinematography*: Jack Marta. *Editor*: Ernest Nims.

Mrs. Parkington
(1944-MGM-124 min.)

Susie "Sparrow" Parkington: Greer Garson. *Major Augustus "Gus" Parkington*: Walter Pidgeon. *Armory Stilham*: Edward Arnold. *Baroness Aspasia Conti*: Agnes Moorehead. *Edward, Prince of Wales*: Cecil Kelloway. *Alice, Duchess of Bramount*: Gladys Cooper. *Jack Stilham*: Dan Duryea. *With*: Frances Rafferty, Tom Drake, Peter Lawford, Hugh Marlowe, Selena Royale and Fortunio Bonanova. *Director*: Tay Garnett. *Screenplay*: Robert Thoeren and Polly James. *Novel*: Louis Bromfield. *Producer:* Leo Gordon. *Musical Score*: Stanislaw Kaper. *Cinematography*: Joseph Ruttenberg. *Editor:* George Boemler.

Ministry of Fear
(1944-Paramount Pictures-87 min.)

Stephen Neale: Ray Milland. *Carla Hilfe*: Marjorie Reynolds. *Willi Hilfe*: Carl Esmond. Mrs. *Bellane #2, the spiritualist*: Hillary Brooke. *Inspector Prentice*: Percy Waram. *Cost'Travers, the tailor*: Dan Duryea. *Dr. Forrester*: Alan Napier. *George Rennit, private investigator*: Erskine Sanford. *Director*: Fritz Lang. *Screenplay*: Seton I. Miller. *Novel*: Graham Greene. *Producer*: Seton I. Miller. Musical Score: Victor Young and Miklos Rozsa (unaccredited). *Cinematography*: Henry Sharp. *Editor*: Archie Marshek.

None But The Lonely Heart
(1944-RKO Pictures-113 min.)

Ernie Mott: Cary Grant. *Ma Mott*: Miss Ethel Barrymore. *Henry Twite*: Barry Fitzgerald. *Ada Brantline*: June Duprez. *Aggie Hunter*: Jane Wyatt. *Jim Mordinoy*: George Coulouris. *Lew Tate*: Dan Duryea. *Direction and Screenplay*: Clifford Odets. *Novel*: Richard Llewellyn. *Producer*: David Hempstead. *Musical Score*: Harris Eisler. *Cinematography*: George Barnes. *Editor:* Roland Gross.

Woman in the Window:
(RKO Pictures, Inc.-1945-99 min.)

Professor Richard Wanley: Edward G. Robinson. *Alice Reed*: Joan Bennett. *DA Frank Lalor*: Raymond Massey. *Heidt:* Dan Duryea. *Director*: Fritz Lang. *Screenplay*: Nunnally Johnson. *Novel:* J.H. Willis. *Producer*: Nunnally Johnson. *Cinematography*: Milton R. Krasner. *Music:* Arthur Lange. *Editor*: Gene Fowler Jr. and Marjorie Johnson.

Main Street After Dark
(1945-MGM-57 min.)

Lt. Lorgan: Edward Arnold. *"Ma" Dibson*: Selena Royale. *Lefty Dibson*: Tom Trout. *Jessy Bell Dibson*: Audrey Totter. *Posey Dibson*: Dan Duryea. *Keller, the pawnbroker*: Hume Cronyn. *Rosalie Dibson*: Dorothy Ruth Morris. *Director:* Edward L. Cahn. *Story*: John C. Higgins. *Screenplay*: John C. Higgins and Karl Kamb. *Producer*: Jerry Bresler. *Musical Score*: Jackson Rose. *Editor:* Harry Koner.

The Great Flamarion
(1945-Republic Pictures-78 min.)

The Great Flamarion: Erich Von Stroheim. *Connie Wallace:* Mary Beth Hughes. *Al Wallace:* Dan Duryea. *Eddie Wheeler*: Stephen Barclay. *Director:* Anthony Mann. *Screenplay*: Anne Wigton. *Story:* The Big Shot by Vicki Baum. *Producer*: William Wilder. *Musical Score*: Alexander Laszlo. *Cinematography*: James Spencer Brown, Jr. *Editor*: John F. Link.

The Valley of Decision
(1945-MGM-119 min.)

Mary Rafferty: Greer Garson. *Paul Scott*: Gregory Peck. *William Scott*: Donald Crisp. *Pat Rafferty*: Lionel Barrymore. *Jim Brennan*: Preston Foster. *Constance Scott*: Marsha Hunt. *Clarissa Scott*: Gladys Cooper. *William Scott, Jr.:* Dan Duryea. *Director:* Tay Garnett. *Screenplay*: Sonya Levien and John Mehan. *Novel*: Marcia Davenport. *Producer*: Edwin H. Knopf.

Music: Herbert Stothart. *Cinematography*: Joseph Ruttenberg. *Editor*: Blance Sewell

Along Came Jones
(1945-RKO-90 min.)

Melody Jones: Gary Cooper. *Cherry de Longpre*: Loretta Young. *George Fury*: William Demerast. *Monte Jarrod*: Dan Duryea. *Avery de Longpre*: Frank Sully. *Director*: Stuart Heisler. *Screenplay*: Nunnally Johnson. *Novel*: Alan Le May. *Producer*: Gary Cooper. *Music*: Walter Lange. *Cinematography*: Milton R. Krasner. *Editor:* Thomas Neff.

Lady On A Train
(1945-Universal-94 min.)

Nikki Collins: Deanna Durbin. Jonathan *Waring:* Ralph Bellamy. *Wayne Morgan:* David Bruce. *Mr. Sanders:* George Coulouris. *Danny*: Allen Jenkins. *Arnold Waring*: Dan Duryea. *Mr. Haskell:* Edward Everett Horton. *Margo Martin:* Maria Palmer. *Director:* Charles David. *Screenplay:* Edmund Beloin and Robert O'Brien. *Story:* Leslie Charteris. *Producer*: Felix Jackson. *Music*: Miklos Rozsa. *Cinematography*: Elwood Bredell. *Editor*: Ted J. Kent.

The Black Angel
(1946-Universal Pictures-81 min.)

Martin Blair: Dan Duryea. *Catherine Bennett*: June Vincent. *Marko*: Peter Lorre. Captain *Flood*: Broderick Crawford. *Mavis Marlowe*: Constance Dowling. *Joe:* Wallace Ford. *George Mitchell:* Archie Twitchell. *Director*: Roy William Neill. *Screenplay:* Roy Chanslor. *Novel:* Cornell Woolrich. *Producers:* Tom McKnight and Roy William Neal. *Cinematography*: Paul Ivano. *Musical Score*: Frank Skinner. *Editor*: Sal A. Goodkind.

Scarlet Street
(1945-Fritz Lang Productions-103 min.)

Christopher Cross: Edward G. Robinson. *Katharine "Kitty" March*: Joan Bennett. *Johnny Prince*: Dan Duryea. *Milly Ray*: Margaret Lindsay. *Janeway*: Jess Barker. *Patch-Eye Higgins*: Charles Kemper. *Director and Producer*: Fritz Lang. *Screenplay*: Dudley Nichols. *Novel and Play ("La Chienne")*: Georges De La Fouchadiere and Mouezy-Eon. *Music*: H.J. Salter. *Cinematography*: Milton Krasner. *Editor*: Arthur Hilton.

White Tie and Tails
(1946-Universal-International-81 min.)

Charles Dumont: Dan Duryea. *Louise Bradford*: Ella Raines. *Larry Lundie*: William Bendix. *George*: Frank Jenks. *Archer*: Richard Gaines. *Nat Romero*: Donald Curtis. *Director*: Charles Barton. *Screenplay*: Bertram Millhauser. *Novel:* ("The Victoria Docks at Eight"): Charles Beakon and Rufus King. *Producer*: Howard Benedict. *Music*: Milton Rosen. *Cinematography*: Charles Van Enger. *Editor*: Ray Snyder.

Black Bart
(1948-Universal-International-80 min.-C)

Lola Montez: Yvonne De Carlo. *Charles E. Boles (Black Bart)*: Dan Duryea. *Lance Hardeen*: Jeffrey Lynn. *Jersey Brady*: Percy Kilbride. *Sheriff Godon*: Lloyd Gough. *Director*: George Sherman. *Screenplay*: Lucy Ward, Jack Natteford, and William Bowers. *Short Story*: Lucy Ward and Jack Natteford. *Producer*: Leonard Goldstein. *Music*: Uncredited. *Cinematography*: Irving Glassberg. *Editor*: Russell Scoengarth.

Another Part of the Forest
(1948-Universal-International-107 min.)

Marcus Hubbard: Fredric March. Oscar Hubbard: Dan Duryea. Ben Hubbard: Edmond O'Brien. Regina Hubbard: Ann Blyth. Lavinia Hubbard: Florence Eldridge. John Bagtry: John Dall. Laurette Sincee:

Dona Drake. Birdy Bagtree: Betsy Blair. Director: Michael Gordon. Screenplay: Vladimir Pozner. Play: Lillian Hellman. Producer: Jerry Bresler. Music: Daniele Amfitheatrof. Cinematography: Hal Mohr. Editor: Milton Carruth.

River Lady
(1948-Universal-International-78 min.-C)

Sequin: Yvonne De Carlo. *Beauvais*: Dan Duryea. *Dan Corrigan*: Rod Cameron. *Stephanie Morrison*: Helena Carter. *Mike Riley*: Lloyd Gough. *Ma Dunnegan*: Florence Bates. *H.L. Morrison*: John McIntire. *Director:* George Sherman. *Screenplay:* D.D. Beauchamp and William Bowers. *Novel*: Houston Branch and Frank Wuter. *Producer*: Leonard Goldstein. *Music*: Paul Sawtell. *Cinematography*: Irving Glassberg. *Editor*: Otto Ludwig.

Larceny:
(1949-Universal-International-89 min.)

Rick Mason: John Payne. *Deborah Owens Clark:* Joan Caulfield. *Silky Randall*: Dan Duryea. *Tory*: Shelly Winters. *Madeline*: Dorothy Hart. *Charlie Jordan*: Percy Helton. *With:* Dan O'Herlihy, Russ Conway, Paul Brinegar, and Don Wilson. *Director*: George Sherman. *Screenplay*: D.D. Beauchamp and William Bowers. *Novel*: Houston Branch and Frank Waters. *Producer*: Leonard Goldstein. *Musical Score*: Paul Sawtell. *Cinematography*: Irving Glassberg. *Editor*: Otto Ludwig.

Criss-Cross
(1949-Universal-International-87 min.)

Steve Thompson: Burt Lancaster. *Anna Dundee*: Yvonne De Carlo. *Slim Dundee*: Dan Duryea. *Det. Lt. Pete Ramirez*: Stephen McNally. *Vincent*: Tom Pedi. *Frank:* Percy Helton. *Finchley:* Alan Napier. *Pop:* Griff Barnett. *With*: Esy Morales and his Rhumba Band, Meg Randall, Richard Long, Joan Miller, Edna Holland, John Doucette, Marc Krah, James O'Rear, John Skins Miller and Tony Curtis (unbilled). *Director*: Robert Siodmak.

Screenplay: Daniel Fuchs. *Novel*: Don Tracy. *Producer*: Michel Kraike. *Musical Score*: Miklos Rozsa. *Cinematography*: Frank Planer. *Editor*: Ted J. Kent.

Manhandled
(1949-Paramount-97 min.)

Merl Kramer: Dorothy Lamour. *Joe Cooper*: Sterling Hayden. *Karl Benson*: Dan Duryea. *Ruth/ Mrs. Alton Bennett*: Irene Hervey. *Lt. Dawson*: Art Smith. *Dr. Redman:* Harold Vermilyea. *Alton Bennett*: Alan Napier. *Guy Bayard*: Phillip Reed. *Director:* Lewis R. Foster. *Screenplay*: Whitman Chambers and Lewis R. Foster. *Novel ("The Man Who Stole A Dream")*: L.S. Goldsmith. *Producer*: William H. Pine and William C. Thomas. *Music*: Darrell Calker. *Cinematography*: Ernest Laszlo. *Editor*: Howard Smith.

Too Late For Tears aka Killer Bait
(1949-United Artists-99 min.)

Jane Palmer: Lizabeth Scott. *Don Blake*: Don DeFore. *Danny Fuller*: Dan Duryea. *Alan Palmer*: Arthur Kennedy. *Kathy Palmer*: Kristine Miller. *Lt. Breach*: Barry Kelly. *Director*: Byron Haskin. *Screenplay and Story*: Roy Huggins. *Producer*: Hunt Stromberg. *Music*: Dale Butts. *Cinematography*: William Mellor. *Editor*: Harry Keller.

Johnny Stool Pigeon
(1949-Universal-International-76 min.)

George Morton: Howard Duff. *Terry Stewart*: Shelley Winters. *Johnny Evans*: Dan Duryea. *Joey Hyatt*: Anthony (Tony) Curtis. *Nick Avery*: John McIntire. *Sam Harrison*: Gar Moore. *Pringle*: Leif Erickson. *Director*: William Castle. *Screenplay*: Robert L. Richards. *Story*: Henry Jordan. *Producer*: Aaron Rosenberg. *Cinematography*: Maury Gertsman. *Editor*: Ted J. Kent.

One Way Street
(Universal-International-1950-76 min.)

Dr. Frank Matson: James Mason. *Laura Thorson*: Marta Toren. *John Wheeler*: Dan Duryea. *Father Moreno*: Basil Ruysdael. *Ollie*: William Conrad. *Director*: Hugo Fregonese. *Screenplay*: Laurence Kimble. *Producer*: Leonard Goldstein. *Music*: Frank Skinner. *Cinematography*: Maury Gertsman. *Editor*: Milton Carruth.

Winchester '73
(1950-Universal-International-92 min.)

Lin McAdam: James Stewart. *Lola Manners:* Shelly Winters. *Waco Johnnie Dean:* Dan Duryea. *Dutch Henry Brown*: Stephen McNally. *High Spade Frankie Wilson*: Millard Mitchell. *With:* Charles Drake, John McIntire, Will Geer, Jay C. Flippen, Rock Hudson, Tony Curtis, Abner Biberman and James Best. *Director:* Anthony Mann. *Screenplay*: Robert L. Richards and Borden Chase. *Story:* Stuart N. Lake. *Producer:* Aaron Rosenberg. *Cinematography*: William Daniels. *Editor:* Edward Curtiss.

The Underworld Story:
(1950-Allied Artists-91 min.)

Mike Reese: Dan Duryea. *E.J.Stanton*: Herbert Marshall. *Catherine Harris*: Gale Storm. *Carl Durham*: Howard Da Silva. *DA Ralph Munsey*: Michael O'Shea. *Molly Rankin*: Mary Anderson. *Clark Stanton*: Gar Moore. *Mrs. Eldridge*: Frieda Inescourt. *George "Parky" Parker*: Harry Shannon. *With*: Alan Hale, Jr., Roland Winters and Jay Adler. *Director*: Cy Endfield. *Screenplay*: Henry Blankfort. *Story*: Craig Rice. *Adaptation*: Cy Endfield. *Producer:* Hal E. Chester. *Music*: David Rose. *Cinematography*: Stanley Cortez. *Editor*: Richard Heermance.

Al Jennings of Oklahoma
(1951-Columbia Pictures-79 min.-C)

Al Jennings: Dan Duryea. *Margo St. Clare*: Gale Storm. *Frank Jennings*:

Dick Foran. *Alice Calhoun*: Gloria Henry. *Lon Tuttle*: Guinn "Big Boy" Williams. *Judge Jennings*: Raymond Greenleaf. *Fred Salter*: Harry Shannon. *Tom Marsden*: John Dehner. *Director*: ray Nazarro. *Screenplay*: George Bricker. *Book*: Al J. Jennings and Will Irwin. *Producer*: Rudolph C. Flothow. *Music*: George Duning and Paul Mertz. *Cinematography*: Howard Greene. *Editor*: Richard Fantl.

Chicago Calling
(1952-Arrowhead Pictures-75 min.)

Bill Cannon: Dan Duryea. *Mary Cannon*: Mary Anderson. *Bobby:* Gordon Gebert. *Jim*: Ross Elliot. *Nancy Cannon*: Melinda Plowman. *Babs Kimball*: Judy Brubaker. *Peggy*: Marsha Jones. *Pete*: Roy Engel. *Director*: John Reinhardt. *Screenplay*: Peter Berneis and John Reinhardt.

Thunder Bay
(1953-Universal-International-103 min.-C)

Steve Martin: James Stewart. *Stella Rigaud*: Joanne Dru. *Teche Bossier*: Gilbert Roland. *Johnny Gambi*: Dan Duryea. *Kermit MacDonald*: Jay C. Flippen. *Francesca Rigaud*: Marica Handerson. *Phillipe Bagard*: Robert Monet. *Dominique Rigaud*: Antonio Moreno. *Director*: Anthony Mann. *Screenplay*: Gil Doud and John Michael Hayes. *Producer*: Aaron Rosenberg. *Cinemtography*: Wiiliam Daniels. *Music*: Frank Skinner. *Editor*: Rossell Schoengarth.

Sky Commando
(1953-Columbia-69 min.)

Col. Ed (E.D.) Wyatt: Dan Duryea. *Jo McWerthy*: Frances Gifford. *Lt. Holstein "Hobbie" Lee:* Touch (Mike) Connors. *Major Scott*: Michael Fox. *With*: William Bryant, Selmer Jackson and Morris Ankrum. *Director*: Fred J. Sears. *Screenplay*: Samuel Newman. *Story*: Samuel Newman, Arthur E. Orloff and William Sackheim. *Producer*: Sam Katzman. *Cinematography*: Lester White. *Editor*: Edwin H. Bryant.

36 Hours aka *Terror Street*
(1953-Hammer Films- 85 min.)

Major Bill Rogers: Dan Duryea. *Katherine "Katie" Rogers*: Elsy Albin. *Sister Jenny Miller*: Ann Gudrun. *Slossen, the smuggler*: Eric Pohlman. *Henry Slossen*: Kenneth Griffith. *Director*: Montgomery Tully. *Screenplay and Story*: Steve Fisher. *Producer*: Anthony Hinds. *Music*: Ivor Slaney. *Cinematography*: Walter Harvey. Editor: James Needs.

World For Ransom
1954-Allied Artists-82 min.)

Mike Callahan: Dan Duryea. *Alexis Pederas*: Gene Lockhart. *Julian March*: Patric Knowles. *Major Bone*: Reginald Denny. *Frennessey March*: Marian Carr. *Sear O'Connor*: Arthur Shields. *Inspector McCollum*: Douglas Dumbrelle. *Wong*: Keye Luke. *Chan*: Clarence Lung. *Guzik*: Lou Nova. *Dancer*: Carmen D'Antonio. *Director*: Robert Aldrich. *Screenplay*: Hugo Butler and Lindsay Hardy. *Producer*: Robert Aldrich and Bernard Tabakin. *Cinematography*: Joseph F. Biroc. *Editor*: Michael Luciano.

Ride Clear of Diablo
(1954-Universal-International-80 min.-C)

Clay O'Mara: Audie Murphy. *Laurie Kenyon:* Susan Cabot. *Whitey Kincaide:* Dan Duryea. *Kate*: Abbe Lane. *With:* Russell Johnson, Paul Birch, Jack Elam and Denver Pyle. *Director*: Jesse Hibbs. *Screenplay:* George Zuckeman. *Additional Dialogue:* D.D. Beauchamp. *Story:* Ellia Marcus. *Producer*: John W. Rogers. *Music:* Milton Rosen and Herman Stein. *Cinematography*: Irving Glassberg. *Editor*: Edward Curtiss.

Rails Into Laramie
(1954-Universal-International-80 min.-C)

Jefferson Harder: John Payne. *Lou Carter*: Mari Blanchard. *Jim Shanessy:* Dan Duryea. *Helen Shanessy:* Joyce Mackenzie. *Lee Graham:* Barton MacLane. *With:* Harry Shannon, Lee Van Cleef and Myron Healey.

Director: Jess Hibbs. *Screenplay:* D.D. Beauchamp, Borden Chase and Joseph Hoffman. *Producer:* Ted Richmond. *Music:* Henry Mancini, Milton Rosen and Herman Stein. *Cinematography:* Maury Gertsman. *Editor:* Ted J. Kent.

Silver Lode
(1954- RKO Pictures- 81 min.-C)

Dan Ballard: John Payne. *Rose Evans*: Lizabeth Scott. *Ned McCarty*: Dan Duryea. *Dolly*: Dolores Moran. *Sheriff Wooley*: Emile Meyer. *Judge Cranston*: Robert Warwick. *Director*: Allan Dwan. *Screenplay*: Karen DeWolf. *Producer*: Benedict Bogeaus. *Music*: Louis Forbes. *Cinematography*: John Alton. *Editor*: James Leicester.

This Is My Love
(1954-RKO Radio Pictures-91 min.-C)

Vida Dove: Linda Darnell. *Murray Myer*: Dan Duryea. *Glenn Harris*: Rick Jason. *Evelyn Myer*: Faith Domergue. *Eddie Collins*: Hal Baylor. *Connie Russell*: Herself. *With*: Jerry Mathers, Susie Mathers, William Hopper and Carl "Alfalfa" Switzer. *Director*: Stuart Heisler. *Screenplay:* Hugh Brooke and Hogan Wilde. *Short Story ("Fear Has Black Wings"):* Hugh Brooke. *Producer:* Hugh Brooke. *Music:* Franz Waxman. *Cinematography*: Ray June. *Editor:* Otto Ludwig.

Foxfire
(1955-Universal-International-87 min.-C)

Amanda Lawrence: Jane Russell. *Jonathan Dartland*: Jeff Chandler. *Hugh Slater*: Dan Duryea. *Maria*: Mara Corday. *Mr. Mablett*: Barton MacLane. *Mrs. Lawrence*: Frieda Inescourt. *Director*: Joseph Pevney. *Screenplay*: Ketti Frings. *Producer*: Aaron Rosenberg. *Music*: Frank Skinner. *Cinematography*: William Daniels. *Editor*: Ted J. Kent.

Storm Fear
(1955-United Artists-88 min.)

Charlie: Cornel Wilde. *Elizabeth*: Jean Wallace. *Fred*: Dan Duryea. *Edna*: Lee Grant. *David:* David Stollery. *Hank*: Dennis Weaver. *Benjie*: Steven Hill. *Director and Producer*: Cornel Wilde. *Screenplay*: Horten Foote. *Novel*: Clinton Seeley. *Music*: Elmer Bernstein. *Cinematography*: Joseph LaShelle. *Editor*: Otto Ludwig.

The Marauders
(1955-MGM-80 min.-C)

Mr. Avery: Dan Duryea. *Corey Everett*: Jeff Richards. *Hook:* Keenan Wynn. *Hannah Ferber*: Jarma Lewis. *Roy Rutherford*: Harry Shannon. *Albie Ferber*: David Kasday. *Louis Ferber*: James Anderson. *Ramos*: Peter Mamkos. *Director*: Gerald Mayer. *Screenplay*: Jack Leonard and Earl Felton. *Novel*: Alan Marcus. *Cinematography*: Harold Marzorati, A.S.C. *Music*: Paul Sawtell. *Editor:* Russell Selwyn.

Battle Hymn
(1957-Universal-International-108 min.-C)

*Col. Dean Hess:*Rock Hudson. *En Soon Yang*: Anna Kashfi. *Sgt. Herman*: Dan Duryea. *Capt. Skidmore*: Don DeFore. *Mary Hess*: Martha Hyer. *Maj. Moore*: Jock Mahoney. *Mess Sergeant*: Alan Hale, Jr. *Director:* Douglas Sirk. *Screenplay*: Vincent B. Evans and Charles Grayson. *Novel*: D.E. Hess. *Producer*: Ross Hunter. *Cinematography*: Russell Metty. *Music*: Frank Skinner. *Editor*: Russell Schoengarth.

Night Passage
(1957-Universal-International- 90 min.-C)

Grant McLaine: James Stewart. *The Utica Kid*: Audey Murphy. *Whitey Harbin*: Dan Duryea. *Charlotte Drew*: Dianne Foster. *Verna Kimball*: Elaine Stewart. *Ben Kimball*: Jay C. Flippen. *Will Renner*: Herbert Anderson. *Jeff Kurth*: Hugh Beaumont. *Shotgun*: Jack Elam. *Director*: James Neilson.

Screenplay: Borden Chase. *Producer:* Aaron Rosenberg. *Music*: Dimitri Tiomkin. *Cinematography*: William Daniels. *Edito*r: Sherman Todd.

The Burglar
(1957-Columbia Pictures-90 min.)

Nat Harbin: Dan Duryea. *Gladden:* Jayne Mansfield. *Della*: Martha Vickers. *Baylock*: Peter Capell. Dohmer: Mickey Shaughnessy. Police Captain: Wendell K. Phillips. Sister Sara: Phoebe Mackay. *Charlie:* Stewart Bradley. *News Commentator*: John Fracenda. *Newsreel Narrator*: Bob Wilson. Director and Editor: Paul Wendkos. Screenplay: David Goodis, based on his novel. *Producer*: Louis W. Kellman.. *Cinematography*: Don Malkames. *Musical Score*: Sol Kaplan.

Slaughter on 10th Avenue
(Universal-International-1957-103 min.)

William "Bill" Keating: Richard Egan. *Madge Pitts*: Jan Sterling. *John Jacob Masters*: Dan Duryea. *Daisy "Dee" Paisly*: Julie Adams. *Al Dahlke*: Walter Matthau. *Lt. Anthony Vasnick*: Charles McGraw. *Howard Rysdale*: Sam Levene. *Solly Pitts*: Mickey Shaughnessy. *Benjy Karp*: Harry Bellaver. *Midget*: Nick Dennis. *Director*: Arnold Laven. *Screenplay*: Lawrence Roman. *Novel*: William J. Keating and Richard Carter, "The Man Who Rocked the Boat." *Produce*r: Albert Zugsmith. *Music*: Herschel Burke Gilbert-Richard Rodgers-Henry Mancini (uncredited). *Cinematography*: Fred Jackman, Jr. *Editor:* Russell F. Shoengarth.

Kathy O
(1958-Universal-International-99 min.-C)

Harry Johnson: Dan Duryea. *Celeste Saunders*: Jan Sterling. *Kathy O'Roarke*: Patty McCormack. *Helen Johnson*: Mary Fickett. *Ben Melnick*: Sam Levene. *Aunt Harriet*: Mary Jane Croft. *Direction and Screenplay*: Jack Sher. *Producer*: Sy Gomberg. *Music*: Frank Skinner. *Cinematography.*: Arth E. Arling. *Editor*: George A. Gittens.

Gunfight at Sandoval
(Walt Disney Productions-1959-63 min.)

Texas John Slaughter: Tom Tryon. *Ben Jenkins*: Harry Carey, Jr. *Dan Trask*: Dan Duryea. *Mrs. Barko*: Beverly Garland. *Adeline Harris*: Norma Moore. *Captain Cooper*: Judson Pratt. *Director*: Harry Keller. *Producer*: James C. Pratt.

Platinum High School
(1960-MGM-95 min.)

Steven Conway: Mickey Rooney. *Jennifer Evans*: Terry Moore. *Maj. Redfern Kelly*: Dan Duryea. *"Crip" Hastings*: Warren Berlinger. *Lorinda Nibley*: Yvette Mimieux. *Hack Marlow*: Richard Jaeckel. *With*: Christopher Dark, Conway Twitty, Jimmy Boyd, Jack Carr, Elisha Cook, Jr. and Harold Lloyd, Jr. *Director*: Charles F. Haas. *Screenplay*: Howard Breslin. *Story*: Robert Smith. *Producer*: Red Doff. *Executive Producer*: Albert Zugsmith. *Music*: Van Alexander. *Editor*: Gene Ruggiero.

Six Black Horses
(1962-Universal-International- 80 min.-C)

Ben Lane: Audie Murphy. *Frank Jesse*: Dan Duryea. *Kelly*: Joan O'Brien. *Boone*: George Wallace. *Mustanger*: Roy Barcroft. *Charlie*: Dick Pascoe. *Puncher*: Bob Steele. *Cantina Dancer*: Charlita. *Director*: Harry Keller. *Screenplay*: Burt Kennedy. *Producer*: Gordon Kay. *Cinematographer*: Maury Gertsman. *Editor*: Aaron Stell.

He Rides Tall
(1964-Universal--84 min.)

Marshal Rocklin: Tony Young. *Bart Thorne*: Dan Duryea. *Ellie Daniels*: Madlyn Rhue. *Kate McCloud*: Jo Morrow. *Josh McCloud*: R.G. Armstrong. *Dr. Sam*: Joel Fluellen. *Director*: R.G. Springsteen. *Screenplay*: Charles W. Irwin and Robert Creighton Williams. *Producer*: Gordon McKay. *Cinematographer*: Ellis W. Carter. *Musical Score*: Irving Gertz.

Do You Know This Voice?
(1964-Columbia Pictures-80 min.)

John Hopta: Dan Duryea. *Rosa Marotta:* Isa Miranda. *Jackie Hopta:* Gwen Watford. *Supt. Hume:* Peter Madden. *Det. Sgt. Connor:* Barry Warren. *Judy:* Jean Aubrey. *Director:* John Nesbitt. *Screenplay:* Neil McCallum. *Novel:* Evelyn Berckman. *Producer:* Jack Parsons. *Music:* Carlo Martelli. *Cinematography:* Arthur Lavis. *Editor:* Robert Winter.

Taggert
(1964-Universal-85 min.-C)

Taggart: Tony Young. *Jason:* Dan Duryea. *Stark:* Dick Foran. *Consuela:* Elsa Cardenas. *Miriam:* Jean Hale. *Ben Blazer:* Emil Meyer. *Director:* R.G. Springsteen. *Screenplay:* Robert Creighton Williams. *Novel:* Louis L'Amour. *Producer:* Gordon McKay and Associates. *Cinematography:* Will Margulies. *Musical Score:* Herman Stein. *Editor:* Tony Martinelli.

Walk A Tightrope
(1965-Paramount Pictures-69 min.)

Carl Lutcher: Dan Duryea. *Ellen Sheppard:* Patricia Owen. *Jason Sheppard:* Terence Cooper. *Doug Randle:* Richard Leech. *Counsel:* Neil McCallum. *Director:* Frank Nesbitt. *Screenplay:* Jann Rubin. *Story:* Neil McCallum. *Producer:* Jack Parsons. *Music:* Buxton Orr. *Cinematography:* Basil Emmott. *Editor:* Robert Winter.

The Bounty Killer
(1965-Embassy Pictures-93 min.-C)

Willie Duggan: Dan Duryea. *Johnny Liam:* Rod Cameron. *Carole:* Audrey Dalton. *Rideway:* Richard Arlen. *Luther:* Fuzzy Knight. *Youth:* Peter Duryea. *Pianist:* Eddie Quillan. *Inister:* Grady Sutton. *Waiter:* Tom Kennedy. *Red:* Bob Steele. *Seddon:* Boyd "Red" Morgan. *Mike Clayman:* Larry "Buster" Crabbe. *Sheriff Green:* Johnny Mack Brown. *Director:* Spencer Gordon Bennett. *Screenplay:* Leo Gordon. *Producer:* Alex Gordon. *Cin-*

ematographer: Frederick E. West. *Musical Score*: Ronald Stein. *Editor*: Ronald Sinclair.

Flight of the Phoenix
(1965-20th Century Fox-147 min.-C)

Frank Towns: James Stewart. *Lew Moran*: Richard Attenbourough. *Captain Harris:* Ptere Finch. *Heinrich Dorfmann*: Hardy Kruger. *Trucker Cobb:* Ernest Borgnine. *Crow:* Ian Bannen. *Sergeant Watson:* Ronald Fraser. *Dr. Renaud:* Christian Marquand. *Standish:* Dan Duryea. *Bellamy:* George Kennedy. *Gabriele:* Gabriele Tinti. *Carlos:* Alex Montoya. *Tasso:* Peter Bravos. *Farida* : Barrie Chase. *Director and Producer:* Robert Aldrich. *Screenplay:* Lukas Heller. *Novel:* Elleston Trevor. *Cinematography:* Joseph Biroc. *Music:* DeVol. *Editor:* Michael Luciano.

The Hills Run Red
(1967-United Artists-103 min.-C)

Jerry Brewster: Thomas Hunter. *Mendez*: Henry Silva. *Col. Getz*: Dan Duryea. *Seagall*: Nando Gazzolo. *Mary Ann*: Nicoletta Machiavelli. *Director*: Albert Lattuada. *Screenplay:* Dean Craig, Jack Pulman, Luigi Malerba and Alberto Lattuada. *Producers:* Ermanno Donati and Luigi Carpentieri. *Cinematography:* Toni Secchi. *Musical Score*: Enrico Morricone. *Editor*: Ornella Micheli.

Incident at Phantom Hill
(1966-Universal-88 min.-C)

Captain Matt Martin: Robert Fuller. *Memphis*: Jocelyn Lane. *Joe Barlow*: Dan Duryea. *Adam Long:* Tom Simcox. *Dr. Hannaford*: Linden Chiles. *Krausman*: Claude Akins. *O'Rourke*: Noah Beery, Jr. *Gen. Hood*: Paul Fix. *Frontiersman*: Denver Pyle. *Trader*: William Phipps. *Sheriff Drum:* Don Collier. *Director:* Earl Bellamy. *Screenplay:* Frank S. Nugent and Ken Pettus. *Producer:* Harry Tatelman. *Cinematographer:* William Marguiles, A.S.C. *Musical Score:* Hans J. Salter. *Musical Supervision:* Joseph Gershenson. *Editor:* Gene Milford.

Winchester '73
(1967-Universal-97 min.-TVM-C)

Lin McAdam: Tom Tryon. *Dakin McAdam*: John Saxon. *Bart McAdam*: Dan Duryea. *Preacher*: John Drew Barrymore. *Larouge*: Joan Blondell. *High-Spade Johnny Dean*: John Dehner. *Meriden*: Barbara Luna. *Ben McAdam*: Paul Fix. *Dan McAdam*: David Pritchard. *Jake Starret*: John Doucette. *Scots:* Jack Lambert. *Sunrider:* John Hoyt. *Director:* Herschel Daugherty. *Teleplay:* Richard L. Adams, based on screenplay by Bordern Chase. *Producer*: Richard E. Lyons. *Cinematography*: Bud Thackery. *Musical Score*: Sol Kaplan. *Editor*: Richard G. Wray.

Five Golden Dragons
(1967-Commonwealth United Entertainment-104 min.)

Bob Mitchell: Bob Cummings. *Magda*: Margaret Lee. *Comm. Sanders*: Rupert Davies. *Gert*: Klaus Kinski. *Ingrid*: Maria Rohm. *Margret*: Maria Perschy. *Golden Dragons*: Dan Duryea, Brian Donlevy, George Raft and Christoper Lee. *Director*: Jeremy Summers. *Screenplay*: Harry Alan Towers. *Story*: Edgar Wallace. *Producer*: Peter Welbeck (Harry Alan Towers). *Music*: Malcolm Lockyer. *Cinematography*: John Von Kotze. *Editor*: Donald J. Cohen.

Stranger On The Run
(1967-Universal-97 min.-TVM-C)

Ben Chamberlain: Henry Fonda. *Valverde Johnson*: Anne Baxter. *Vince McKay*: Michael Parks. *O.E Hotchkiss*: Dan Duryea. *George Blaylock*: Sal Mineo. *Mr. Gorman*: Lloyd Bochner. *Matt Johnson*: Michael Burns. *Leo Weed*: Tom Reese. *Dickory*: Bernie Hamilton. *Larkin*: Zalman King. *Alma Britten*: Madlyn Rhue. *Berk*: Walter Burke. *Director*: Don Siegal. *Screenplay*: Dean Riesner. *Story*: Reginald Rose. *Producer*: Richard E. Lyons. *Cinematography*: Bud Thackeray. *Music*: Leonard Rosenman. *Editor*: Richard G. Wray.

The Bamboo Saucer aka *Collision Course*
(1968-World Entertainment Corp.-100 min.)

Hank Peters: Dan Duryea. *Fred Norwood*: John Ericson. *Anna Karachev*: Lois Nettleton. *Jack Garson*: Bob Hastings. *Zagersky*: Vincent Beck. *Dave Ephram*: Bernard Fox. *Sam Archibald*: James Hong. *Director*: Frank Telford. *Screenplay*: Frank Telford. *Story*: Frank Telford and Rip (Alfred) Van Ronkel. *Producers*: Charles E. Burns and Jerry Fairbanks. *Music*: Edward Paul and Raoul Kraushaar. *Cinematography*: Hal Mohr. *Editor*: Richard Harris.

Television Credits

Schlitz Playhouse of Stars PG- 01/25/'52

Guest Stars: Dan Duryea, Teresa Celli, John Forsythe, Henry Jones and William Redfield.

Schlitz Playhouse of Stars: Souvenir from Singapore 06/06/'52

Hostess: Irenne Dunne. *China Smith:* Dan Duryea. *Guest Stars:* Phillip Ahn, Edgar Barrier, Everett Glass, Aram Katcher, Guy Kingsford, Walter Kingsford, Keye Luke, Gloria Saunders, Mari Young. *Director:* Arthur Pierson. *Teleplay:* Robert C. Dennis. *Producer:* Edward Lewis. *Cinematography:* Henry Freulich. *Editor:* Fred W. Berger.

The Affairs of China Smith (1952-26 eps)

Regular Characters: China Smith: Dan Duryea. Shira, the Empress: Myrna Dell. Inspector Hobson: Douglas Dumbrille. Mis. Characters: Clarence Lung.

1.1. *The Bamboo Coffin*: Morley: Ben Wright. Mariaman: Rita Moreno. Gresham: Charles Evans. Kolo: Aram Katcher. Chopman: Phillip Tong. DirectorZ: Arthur Pierson. Teleplay: Robert C. Dennis.

1.2 *Celestial Pebbles.*

1.3 *The Corpse with the Purple Ear.*

1.4 *Cruise to Columbo*: *Dolores Barry*: Joy Hodges. *Burton Lambert*: Louis Jean Heydt. *Chow Lee*: Lane Nakano. *Director*: Arthur Pierson. *Teleplay*: Lindsay Hardy.

1.5 *Curse of the River Gods.*

1.6 *Devil-in-th-Godown. Ruth Cotton*: Marjorie Lord. *Han*: Clarence E. Lung. *Constantine*: Peter Mamakos. *Ho-Kow*: Charles Lung. *Director*: Edward Mann. *Teleplay*: Robert C. Dennis.

1.7 *Dynasty of the Dead.*

1.8 *Espionage Express.*

1.9 *High Sea. Alma Rosa Perez*: Marta Roth. *Ping Lien*: Clarence Lung. *Jose Perez*: Ted Hecht. *John Crane*: Nestor Paiva. *Director*: Arthur Pierson. *Teleplay*: Robert C. Dennis.

1.10 *The Jade Trap.*

1.11 *Jungle Dragon. Carmelita Molina*: June Chon. *Lo Seng*: Nestor Paiva.

1.12 *The Kapriellian Cipher. Mr. Rashid/Max Kapriellian*: Nestor Paiva. *Napoleon Nevar*: Clarence Lung. *Marcetta St. John*: Jean Wilkes.

1.13 *Killer in the Kampong.*

1.14 *Kris of Death.*

1.15 *Moon Flower.*

1.16 *My Ship has a Golden Keel.*

1.17 *Pagoda in the Jungle. Chang Po*: Richard Hale. *Andre Gissen*: Walter Coy. *Papa Nogren*: Ralph Dumke.

List of Credits • 459

1.18 *The Phantom Sampan.*

1.19 *Port of Thieves.*

1.20 *Shanghai Clipper. Anya Karenski*: Marian Carr. *Mr. Pilok*: Marc Krah. *Miss Soong*: Mary Marco. *Director*: Robert Aldrich. *Teleplay*: Robert C. Dennis.

1.21 *Straight Settlement.* Sing Ho: Paul Guilfoyle. Maria Torres: Susan Alexander. Johnny Fong: Clarence Lung. Krantz: Lucien Prival. *Director*: Robert Aldrich. *Teleplay*: Lindsay Hardy, based on a short story by Robert C. Dennis.

1.22 *The Tanaka Archive.*

1.23 *The Wondrous Funeral of Sergeant Ko.*

1.24 *Wreath of Poppies.*

1.25 *The Year of the Phoenix. Brasher*: Jack Raine. *Phoebe*: Louis Arthur. *Geraldine*: Claudia Barrett. *Director*: Arthur Pierson. *Teleplay*: Robert C. Dennis.

6: Please insert The New Adventure of China Smith between:

Lux Video Theatre: The Brooch. 04/ 02 / '53

Mrs. Boyd: Mildred Natwick. *Howard Boyd*: Dan Duryea. *Amy Boyd*: Sally Forrest. *Clara*: Tillie Born. *Narrator*: Alan Shayne. *Announcer*: Jay Jackson. *Director*: Fielder Cook. *Teleplay*: William Faulkner. *Producer*: Cal Kuhl.

The New Adventures of China Smith

The Star and the Story: The Lie 01/ 02/ '55
Jim Ripley: Dan Duryea. *Laura Kent*: Beverly Garland. *Matron*: Jo Gilbert. *Doctor*: Mack Williams. *Mr. Spargrove*: Ted Bliss. *Pancho*: Salvador Baguez. *Laura Ames*: Nancy Matthews. *District Attorney*: Ralph Brooks. *Director*: Alvin Ganzer. *Teleplay*: Frederic Brady. *Story*: Kathleen Norris.

Producer: Warren Phillips. *Cinematography:* George E. Diskant. *Editor:* Roland Gross

The New Adventures of China Smith (1954-26 eps.)

Regular Characters: China Smith: Dan Duryea. Empress Steffi: Regina Gleason.

2.1 *A Bandit of Malaya. Krisiva*: Michi Kobi. *Canavan*: Ted Newton. *Marouf*: Werner Klemperer. *Aslug*: David Renard. *Director*: Alvin Ganzer. *Screenplay*: Robert C. Dennis.

2.2 *The Bible of Dr. Quaile. Maggie*: Patricia Wright. *Derby*: Ted Hecht. *Ko Fon*: Victor Sen Yung. *Director*: Leslie Goodwins. *Teleplay*: Herbert Purdum, Wilton Schiller and Jack Laird, based on a short story by Herbert Purdum.

2.3 *Black Wings of the Firebird. Moonflower*: Mae Tai Sing. *Han*: Clarence Lung. *Chan Wu*: Nestor Paiva. *Director*: Gene Fowler, Jr. *Teleplay*: Rik Vollaerts and Lawrence Godlman.

2.4 *The Broken Rice Bowl of Chen Lo. Chen Lo*: Nestor Paiva. *Precious Star*: Frances Tong. *Lu Yang*: Victor Sen Yung. *Director*: Alvin Ganzer. *Teleplay*: Lawrence Goldman.

2.5 *The Devil Chaser. Bergdahl:* Jack Reitzen. *Lim*: Larry Chan. *Tomkins*: Roy Franklyn. *Ward*: Richard Glyer. *Boy*: Terry Yee. *Director*: Gene Fowler, Jr. *Teleplay*: Robert C. Dennis.

2.6 *Double Crosswinds. Helen McCloud*: Sydney Perkins. *Torchlo*: Jack Littlefield. *Dingo Hawkins*: Joe Laurel. *Director*: Gene Fowler, Jr. *Teleplay*: Robert C. Dennis.

2.7 *The Emperor's Teapot.* Guest: Victor Sen Young.

2.8 *Escort to Saigon.*

2.9 *Ferry to Kowloon. Renee:* Maxine Cooper. *Olga*: Marian Carr. *Shepler*: Keith McConnell. *Asbury*: Edward Bartell. *Ferry Captain*: James Buckner.

Director: Alvin Ganzer. *Screenplay*: Robert C. Dennis.

2.10 *Forbidden Atoll*. *Anastasia*: Geraldine Farmer. *Marakow:* Nestor Paiva. *Captain Amon*: Keith McConnell. *Ritter*: Joe Laurie. *Mapes*: John Trigonis.

2.11 *Full Fathom Five*.

2.12 *Grave in Sumatra*.

2.13 *The Manchu Emeralds*. *Kate Orleans*: Patricia Wright. *Gluck*: Ralph Manza. *Qoit*: Roy Franklyn. *Franz*: Charles Lung. *Director*: Leslie Goodwins. *Teleplay*: Geoffrey Homes.

2.14 *The Night the Dragon Walked*. *Min Su*: Ted Hecht. *Marnee*: Joan Morgan. *Mr. Ronald*: Charles Lung. *Justin Kobol*: William Sweeney. *Jade Flower*: Maria Tsien. *Director*: Gene Fowler, Jr. *Teleplay*: Robert C. Dennis.

2.15 *Nightmare in Green*. *Guest*: Frances Fong.

2.16 *The Paper Dragon*. *Gretchen*: Marian Carr. *Flyzig*: Peter Abenheim. *Carol*: Maxine Cooper. *Inspector D'Amico*: Jack Littlefield. *Webster*: Edgar Iverson. *Director*: Gene Fowler, Jr. *Teleplay*: Robert C. Dennis.

2.17 *Plane to Taiwan*. *Iris Clark*: Priscilla Pointer. *Chen Tu*: Conrad Yama. *Malfy*: Werner Klemperer. *Wong*: Keye Luke. *George Loo*: Victor Sen Yung.

2.18 *The Proverbs of Shen-Tze*.

2.19 *The Sea Coffin*. *Guests:* Marian Carr, Joe Laurel.

2.20 *The Sign of the Scorpion*. *Carla*: Priscilla Pointer. *Aban*: Keye Luke. *Commodore Tilson*: Richard Glyer. *Mrs. Tilson*: Linda Sutherland. *Kelly*: Joseph Miksak. *Officer Strangway*: Edgar Iverson. *Director*: Gene Fowler, Jr. *Teleplay*: Robert C. Dennis.

2.21 *Spectacles of Heaven*. *Guests:* Frances Fong, Edgar Iverson.

2.22 *The Tai-Ling Glaze*. *Director*: Alvin Ganzer. *Teleplay*: Lawrence Goldman.

2.23 *The Talons of Tongking. Ming Toy*: Mighi Kobi. *Tony Wan*: Keye Luke. *Ak Chee*:

2.24 *The Tidewalker. Shell*: Ted Hecht. *Norodani:* Mark Sheeler. *Miss Glong*: Maria Tsien. *Director*: Gene Fowler, Jr. *Teleplay*: Robert C. Dennis.

2.25 *The Traveler from Tsing-Tao. Kip*: William Sweeney. *Sgt. Manion*: Joseph Miksak. *Blunden*: Jack reitzen. *Bridgid*: Luba Sharoff. *Director*: Alvin Ganzer. *Teleplay:* Robert C. Dennis.

2.26 *The Yellow Jade Lion. Mei Lin*: Frances Fong. *The Lion*: Maark Sheeler. *Lo Tan*: Charles Lung.

The Ford Television Theatre: Double Exposure. 3/26/'53

Red Findlay: Dan Duryea. *Devlin:* George Brent. *Marvin:* Marvin Kaplan. *Sally Sherman:* Jean Willes. *Mayor:* Pierre Watkin. *Hearkness:* Pat O'Malley. Johnson: Ted Stanhope. Police Chief: Robert B. Williams. Bartneder: Shephard Menken. D.A.: George DeNormand. *Director:* Lew Landers. *Teleplay:* Frederick Brady. *Story:* John D. Weaver. *Producer:* Irving Starr. *Cinematography:* Gert Anderson. *Editor:* Al Clark.

Lux Video Theatre: The Brooch. 04/ 02 / '53

Mrs. Boyd: Mildred Natwick. *Howard Boyd:* Dan Duryea. *Amy Boyd:* Sally Forrest. *Clara:* Tillie Born. *Narrator:* Alan Shayne. *Announcer:* Jay Jackson. *Director:* Fielder Cook. *Teleplay:* William Faulkner. *Producer:* Cal Kuhl.

The Star and the Story: The Lie, 01/ 02/ '55

Jim Ripley: Dan Duryea. *Laura Kent:* Beverly Garland. *Matron:* Jo Gilbert. *Doctor:* Mack Williams. *Mr. Spargrove:* Ted Bliss. *Pancho:* Salvador Baguez. *Laura Ames:* Nancy Matthews. *District Attorney:* Ralph Brooks. *Director:* Alvin Ganzer. *Teleplay:* Frederic Brady. *Story:* Kathleen Norris. *Producer:* Warren Phillips. *Cinematography:* George E. Diskant. *Editor:* Roland Gross.

The Jack Benny Program: Jack's Lunch Counter, 02/20/'55

Regulars: *Charleston T. Gundelfinger*: Jack Benny. *Chubby Wilson*: Don Wilson. *Slugger*: Dennis Day. Guests: *Gang Leader*: Dan Duryea. *First Customer*: Benny Rubin. *Interior Decorator*: Frank Nelson. *Dancer in Diner*: Dick Kallman. *Director and Producer*: Frederick De Cordova. *Writers*: George Balzer, Hal Goldman, Al Gordon, and Sam Perrin. *Cinematography*: Robert De Grasse. *Editor*: Ralph Davis, Jr.

Schlitz Playhouse of Stars: O'Brien, 04/15/'55

Host: James Mason. *Federal Agent Sam Ireland*: Dan Duryea. *Lavinia Corey*: Lillian Bronson. *Carla*: Margaret Field. *Ruby Swanson*: Virginia Lee. *Director*: Sobey Martin. *Teleplay*: Sidney Bidell and DeWitt Bodeen. *Story*: William Brandon. *Producer*: William Self. *Cinematography*: George T. Clemens. *Editor*: Sam Gold.

December Bride: High Sierras, 1955

Studio 57 : Nailed Down, 10/08/ 1955

Narrator: Joel Aldrich. *Lukas*: Gene Barry. *Doc Munday*: Dan Duryea. *Red*: Terry Frost. *Belle*: Natalie Norwick. *Rick Vallin*: Steve Pendleton. *Olaf*: Aaron Spelling. *Sheriff*: Douglas Spencer. *Director*: Don Weis. *Teleplay*: David P. Harmon. *Original Story*: Harry Sinclair Drago. Producer: William Asher. Cinematography: John MacBurnie. Editor: Daniel A. Nathan.

Star Stage: The Marshal and the Mob, 01/06/'56

Host: Jeffrey Lynn. *Jason*: Dan Duryea. *Patterson*: Ward Bond. *Harve*: Kem Dibbs. *Carol*: Barbara Eiler. *Jenks*: Paul Guilfoyle. *Savannah*: Tim Graham.

Chevron Hall of Stars: A Matter of Nerve, 04/06/'56

Guests: Dan Duryea, Leo Gordon, Myron Healey, Gayle Kellogg, James Parnell, Audrey Swanson and Tracey Roberts. *Director:* Tom Gries. *Teleplay:* Richard Carr. *Producer:* Warren Lewis. *Cinematography*: William V. Skall. *Editor:* Chandler House.

Schlitz Playhouse of Stars: Repercussion, 08/10/'56

Pete Richards: Dan Duryea. *Jeanne Richards:* Marcia Henderson. *John Simpson:* Carl Benton Reid. *Ronnie Simpson:* Ross Elliot. *Roy Edwards:* Addison Richards. *Margaret Simpson:* Eve Miller. *Johnson:* Don Shelton. *Nat Strong:* Bing Russell. *Director:* Robert Florey. *Teleplay*:Douglas Morrow. *Story:* A.P. Willson. *Producer:* William Self. *Cinematography*: George T. Clemens. *Editor*: Joseph Gluck.

The 20th Century-Fox Hour: Smoke Jumpers, 11/14/'56

Cliff Mason: Dan Duryea. *Chief Fred Anderson:* Dean Jagger. *Peg:* Joan Leslie. *Ed Miller:* Richard Jaeckel. *Pop:* Robert Armstrong. *Sparks:* Lawrence Dobkin. *Mike Miller:* Robert Bray. *Copter Pilot:* Brett Halsey. *Farnum:* Bobs Watson. *Director:* Albert S. Rogell. *Writer:* Art Cohn (story).

General Electric Theater: The Road that Led Afar, 11/25/'56

Host: Ronald Reagan. *Brad Lawson:* Dan Duryea. *Phoebe Durkin*: Piper Laurie. *Preacher Bailey:* Edgar Buchanan. *Eloise:* Beverly Washburn. *Sally:* Cheryl Callaway. *Trap:* Gary Hunley. *Hutch:* Don Wittenberg. Director: Herschel Daugherty. Teleplay: Hagar Wilde. Story: Lula Vollmer. Producer: Stuart Reynolds. Cinematography: Herbert Kirkpatrick. Editor: Edward Haire.

Cavalcade of Stars: The Frightened Witness, 02/19/'57

Announcer: Dan Riss. *Joe Kohler*: Dan Duryea. *Craig:* Harold (J) Stone. *Harriet Kohler:* Barbara Billingley. *Lt. Folson*: Herbert Rudley. *Jimmy Kohler*: Christian Pasques. *Betty Kohler*: Wendy Winkelman. *Mrs. Little-*

field: Eleanor Audley. *Hood*: Lewis Charles. *Doc Staples*: Edward Jerome. *Police Officer*: Jim Nolan. *Mario*: Philip Van Zandt. *Director*: Anton Leader. *Teleplay*: Malvin Wald and Jack Jacobs. *Story*: Mildred Cramm. *Producer*: Warren Lewis. *Cinematography*: Joe Novak. *Editor*: Marsh Hendry.

Suspicion: Doomsday, 12/16/'57

Eddie Schumaker/McDillard: Dan Duryea. *Jim Adams*: Robert Middleton. *Cal*: Charles Bronson. *Perry Slavins*: Edward Binns. *Fitzgerald*: Robert Cornthwaite. *Vavich*: William Phipps. *Smitty*: Bing Russell. *Angie*: Mike Ragan. *L.M. Tucker*: Howard Wendell. *Director*: Bernard Girard. Teleplay: Sy Bartlett. Producer: Richard Lewis. *Cinematography*: Bud Thackery. *Editor*: Bill Mosher.

Wagon Train: The Cliff Grundy Story, 12/25/'57

Major Seth Adams: Ward Bond. *Flint McCullough*: Robert Horton. *Cliff Grundy*: Dan Duryea. *Craig Manson*: Russell Johnson. *Lucas*: Don Durant. *Charlie Wooster*: Frank McGrath. *Bill Hawks*: Terry Wilson. Director: George waGGner. *Teleplay*: Aaron Spelling. *Story*: Philip MacDonald. *Producer*: Richard Lewis. *Cinematography*: Herbert Kirkpatrick. *Editor*: Gene Palmer.

Zane Grey Theater: This Man Must Die, 1/24/'58

Host: Dick Powell. *Kirk Joiner*: Dan Duryea. *Libby*: Carole Mathews. *Lee Willis*: Karl Svenson. *Chick Braus*: Than Wyenn. *Sheriff Sam Baker*: Walter Coy. *Director*: James Sheldon. *Teleplay*: Russell S. Hughes. *Story*: Jack Guss and Norman Jacob. *Producer*: Hal Hudson. *Cinematography*: Guy Roe. *Editor*: Arthur Hilton.

Climax! : Four Hours in White, 02/06/'58

Dr. Dennis Sullivan: Dan Duryea. Bette Sullivan: Ann Rutherford. Henry Reeves/Anthony Reeves: Steve McQueen. Dr. Skinner: Eduard Franz.

Susan Anders: Gloria Talbott. Luther Reeves: Rusty Lane. Dr. Whittaker: Don Keefer. Dr. Fincannon: Lester Matthews. Director: Buzz Kulik. Teleplay: Oliver Crawford. Story: Ronald Sercombe.

The United States Steel Hour: Hour of the Rat, 5/21/'58

John Woodrufe: Dan Duryea. *Sakamura:* Kaie Deei (Khigh Dhiegh). *Sir Robert Manchester*: Louis Hector. *Captain Peter Raine*: Ronald Long. *Lt. Grahame Saunders:* Arthur Malet. *Sgt. Major Jack Pollard:* John McLiam. *Nakamura:* Tojuro. *Teresa Woodrufe:* Joan Wetmore.

Wagon Train: The Sacramento Story, 6/25/'58

Major Seth Adams: Ward Bond. *Flint McCullough*: Robert Horton. *Dora Gray Fogelberry:* Linda Darnell. *Cassie Tanner*: Marjorie Main. *Cliff Grundy:* Dan Duryea. Julie revere: Margaret O'Brien. Galvin: Reed Hadley. Cleveland 'Clee' McMasters: george Chandler. *Charlie Wooster*: Frank McGrath. *Bill Hawks*: Terry Wilson. *Director*: Richard Bartlett. *Teleplay*: Thomas Thompson. *Producer*: Howard Christie. *Cinematography*: Bud Thackery. *Editor*: Stanley Rabjohn.

Schlitz Playhouse of Stars: Kinsman, 09/19/'58

Guest Stars: Dan Duryea, Anthony Caruso, Edith Barrett, Nesdon Booth, Richard Ever, Robert Ever, Rudy Lee and Helen Wescott. *Director and Producer*: Jules Bricken. *Teleplay*: Tom Seller. *Cinematography*: John L. Russell. *Editor:* Danny B. Landres.

Pursuit: Tiger on a Bicycle, 10/12/'58

Matt Shaw: Dan Duryea. *Kathy Nelson*: Laraine Day. *Mood:* Chester Morris. *Other Guests:* Neville Brand and David Ladd. *Director:* Paul Nickell. *Teleplay:* Joanne Court (Joan Scott). *Story:* Jonathan Latimer. *Producer:* Norman Felton. *Music:* Bernard Herrman.

Cimarron City: Terror Town, 10'18/'58

Mayor Matt Rockford: George Montgomery. *Roy Budinger:* Dan Duryea. *Cora Budinger:* Barbara Lawrence. *Grant Budinger:* Don Megowan. *Judd Budinger:* Jonathan Haze. *Carl Budinger:* Dan Blocker. *Jess Williams*: George Dunn. *Director:* Richard Bartlett. *Teleplay*: Norman Jolley. *Story:* Trebor Lewis. *Cinematography*: Jack MacKenzie. *Editor:* Lee Huntington.

The Jack Paar Tonight Show, 1958

Walt Disney's Wonderful World of Color: Texas John Slaughter: Showdown at Sandoval, 01/23/'59

Host: Walt Disney. Texas John Slaughter: Tom Tryon. Dan Trask: Dan Duryea. Ben Jenkins: Harry Carey, Jr. Mrs. Amanda Barko: Beverly Garland. Adeline Harris: Norma Moore. Capt. Cooper: Judson Pratt. Director: Harry Keller. Teleplay: Frank D. Gilroy and Maurice Tombragel. Director: Harry Keller. Teleplay: Frank D. Gilroy, Maurice Tombragel. Producer: James C. Pratt. Editor: Stanley E. Johnson.

Rawhide: Incident of the Executioner, 1/23/'59

Gil Favor: Eric Fleming. *Rowdy Yates:* Clint Eastwood. *Wishbone*: Paul Brinegar. *Jardin:* Dan Duryea. *Johnny Doan:* Martin Milner. *Madge:* Marguerite Chapman. *Kenley:* James Drury. *The Salesman*: Stafford Repp. *Mary:* Jan Shepherd. *The Salesman:* William Schallert. *Director:* Charles Marquis Warren. *Teleplay*: James Edmiston. *Producer*: Charles Marquis Warren. *Cinematography*: Philip H. Lathrop. *Editor:* George A. Gittens. *Theme Music*: Dimitri Tiomkin. *Lyrics:* Ned Washington. *Singer:* Frankie Laine.

Wagon Train: The Last Man, 2/11/'59
Major Seth Adams: Ward Bond. *Flint McCullough*: Robert Horton. *Survivor (William Capehart)*: Dan Duryea. *Ellen Emerson*: Judi Meredith. *Charlie Wooster*: Frank McGrath. *Bill Hawks*: Terry Wilson. *Mr. Emerson*:

Damien O'Flynn. *Director*: James Neilson. *Teleplay*: Larry Marcus. *Story*: James Gunn. *Producer*: Howard Christie. *Cinematography*: Benjamin Kline. *Editor*: Gene palmer.

Westinghouse Desilu Playhouse: The Comeback, 03/09/'59

*Host:*Desi Arnez. *Cal Thompson:* Dan Duryea. *Joe Grady:* William Frawley. *Beth Jones:* Maggie (Margaret) Hayes. *Arthur:* Scott Morgan. *Duff Jones:* Stephen Wootton. *George Taylor:* Robert Rockwell. *Director:* Arthur Lubin. *Teleplay:* Stanley Niss. *Story*: Harry Essex and John Fante. *Producer:* Quinn Martin. *Cinematography*: Carl E. Guthrie. *Editor:* Robert L. Swanson.

The David Niven Show: The Vengeance, 06/30/'59

Host: David Niven. *Mark Johnson:* Dan Duryea. *Ruth Johnson:* Dorothy Green. *George Hilton:* Adam Williams. *Skipper:* Robbin Warga. *Harry Nichols*: Wright King. *Vance Jefferson:* Tol Avery. *Detective:* Russ Bender. *Director:* Don McDougall. *Teleplay:* John Robinson. *Producer:* Vincent M. Fennelly. *Cinematography:* Charles Burke. *Editor:* Chandler House.

Laramie: Stage Stop, 9/15/'59

Slim Sherman: John Smith. *Jonesy:* Hoagy Carmichael. *Andy Sherman*: Robert Crawford, Jr. *Jess Harper:* Robert Fuller. *Bud Carlin*: Dan Duryea. *Judge Thomas J. Wilkens*: Everett Sloane. *Clint:* Gordon Jones. *Matt*: Jon Locke. *Deputy Marshal:* Don Haggerty. *Marshal*: Dan Riss. *Director:* Herschel Daugherty. *Teleplay:* Robert Pirosh. *Producer:* Robert Pirosh. *Cinematography:* Lionel Linden. *Editor:* John C. Fuller. *Theme:* Cyril J. Mockridge.

The Twilight Zone: Mr. Denton on Doomsday, 10/16/'59

Host and Narrator: Rod Serling. *Al Denton:* Dan Duryea. *Dan Hotaling:* Martin Landau. *Liz:* Jeanne Cooper. *Henry J. Fate:* Malcolm Atterbury. *Charlie:* Ken Lynch. *Pete Grant:* Doug McClure. *Doctor:* Robert Burton.

Director: Allen Reisner. *Teleplay*: Rod Serling. *Producer*: Buck Houghton. *Cinematography*: George T. Clemens. *Editor*: Bill Mosher.

Adventures in Paradise: Judith, 02/15/'60

Adam Troy: Gardner McKay. Theodore Florian: Dan Duryea. Judith: Gloria Vanderbilt. Ruth Brodie: Doreen Lang. Max Brodie: Frank Overton. Renee: Linda Lawson. Director: Paul Stanley. Teleplay: Stanford Whitmore. Creator: James Michen. Producers: Richard Goldstone and Martin Manulis. Cinematography: Perry Finnerman. Editor: James D. Ballas.

Riverboat: Wichita Arrows, 2/29/'60

Captain Brad Turner: Dan Duryea. *Joshua Walcek*: Jack Lambert. *Terry Blake*: Bart Patton. *Albert Scott*: Don Haggerty. *Sheriff*: Robert Armstrong. *Carley*: Roy Barcroft. *Director*: William Witney. *Teleplay*: Bob Duncan and Wanda Duncan. *Producer*: John Francis Larkin. *Cinematography*: Ray Flin. *Editor*: Stanley Rabjohn.

Riverboat: Fort Epitaph, 3/07/'60

Captain Brad Turner: Dan Duryea. *Joshua Walcek*: Jack Lambert. *Terry Blake*: Bart Patton. *Major Louke Daniels*: Charles Cooper. *Lt. Tom Henshaw*: Brad Weston. *Barbara Daniels*: Joan Camden. *Chief Running Bear*: Stuart Randall. *Kicking Bear*: Ronnie Rondell, Jr. *Director*: John Brahm. *Teleplay*: Richard Morgan. *Producer*: Richard H. Bartlett. *Cinematography*: Buddy Harris. *Editor*: Lee Huntington.

Wagon Train: The Joshua Gilliam Story, 3/30/'60

Major Seth Adams: Ward Bond. *Flint McCullough*: Robert Horton. *Joshua Gilliam*: Dan Duryea. Greta Halstadt: bethel Leslie. *Charlie Wooster*: Frank McGrath. *Bill Hawks*: Terry Wilson. Freda Halstead: Irene Tedrow.. *Director*: Virgil W. Vogel. *Teleplay*: Gene Coon. *Producer*: Howard Christie. *Cinematography*: Benjamin H. Kline. *Editor*: Lee Huntington.

General Electric Theater: Mystery at Malibu, 4/10/'60

Host: Ronald Reagan. *Barnaby Hooke*: Dan Duryea. *Olga Lemaire*: Audrey Totter. *Antoinette 'Tony' Warren*: Dianne Foster. *Donald Reisel*: Richard Ney. *Father Randall*: J. Pat O'Malley. *Hank Rogers*: Hal Smith. *Father Serra*: James Bell. *Director*: Richard Irving. *Teleplay*: Ernest Pascal. *Producer*: Josef Shaftel. *Cinematography*: Bud Thackery. *Editor*: Robert Seiter.

The United States Steel Hour: Shadow of a Pale Horse, 5/21/'60

Jack Rigger: Dan Duryea. *Andrew Kirk*: Frank Lovejoy. *Tim Parker*: Jim Boles. *Carlyle*: dean L. Almquist. *Mary Rigger*: Priscilla Gillette. *Tom O'Byrne*: Carrol O'Connor. *Director*: Jack Smight. *Teleplay*: Bruce Stewart, *Story*: Joe Palmer, Jr. *Producer*: George Kondolf.

Bonanza: Badge without Honor, 9/24/'60

Regulars: *Ben Cartwright*: Lorne Green. *Adam Cartwright*: Pernell Roberts. *'Hoss' Cartwright*: Dan Blocker. *'Little Joe' Cartwright*: Michael Landon. *Number One, Hop Sing's Cousin*: james Hong. *U.S. Deputy Marshall Gerald Eskith*: Dan Duryea. *Jason Blaine*: Fred Beir. *Mariette Blaine*: Christine White. *Judge Rand*: Wendell Holmes.

Shirley Temple's Storybook: Tom and Huck, 10/09/'60

Host and Narrator: Shirley Temple. *Tom Sawyer*: Teddy Rooney. *Huckleberry Finn*: David Ladd. *Aunt Polly*: Janet Blair. *Becky Thatcher*: Ruthie Robinson. *Muff Potter*: Dan Duryea. *Marshal Rogers*: Jackie Coogan. *Injun Joe*: Paul Stevens. *Director*: Paul Nickel. *Teleplay*: Bruce Geller (based on characters created by Mark Twain. *Producer*: William Asher.

Laramie: The Long Riders, 10/25/'60

Slim Sherman: John Smith. *Jess Harper*: Robert Fuller. *Andy*: Robert Crawford, Jr. *Luke Gregg*: Dan Duryea. *Ed McKeever*: John Anderson.

Charley Craig: Fred Coby. *Gerber*: 'Red' Morgan. *Franky*: Boyd Stockman. *Director*: Lesley Selander. *Teleplay*: John Dunkel. *Story*: John C. Champion. *Producer*: Robert Pirosh. *Cinematography*: Lionel Linden. *Editor*: John C. Fuller.

Wagon Train: The Bleymeir Story, 11/16/'60

Major Seth Adams: Ward Bond. *Flint McCullough*: Robert Horton. *Samuel Bleymeir*: Dan Duryea. *Justin Claiborne*: James Drury. *Charlie Wooster*: Frank McGrath. *Bill Hawks*: Terry Wilson. *Belle Bleymeir*: Elen Willard. *Director*: Virgil W. Vogel. *Teleplay*: William Raynor and Myles Wilder. *Story*: Milton Krims. *Producer*: Howard Christie. *Cinematography*: Benjamin H. Kline. *Editor*: Gene Palmer.

About Faces, 1960

Here's Hollywood, -1961

Zane Grey Theater: Knight of the Sun, 3/09/'61

Host: Dick Powell. *Henry Jacob Hanley*: Dan Duryea. *Beth Woodfield*: Constance Towers. *Director*: Don Taylor. *Teleplay*: John Furia, Jr. *Producer*: Aaron Spelling.

The Barbara Stanwyck Show: Sign of the Zodiac, 4/03/'61

Hostess: Barbara Stanwyck. *Madge Terry*: Barbara Stanwyck. *Pierre*: Dan Duryea. *Helene Terry*: Joan Blondell. *Elsie*: Helene Hatch. *Guard*: Charles Anthony Hughes. *Director*: Jacques Tourneur. *Teleplay*: A.I. Bezzerides. *Producer*: William H. Wright. *Editor*: Bruce Schoengarth.

Checkmate: Tight as a Drum, 3/23/'61

Don Corey: Anthony George. *Jed Sills*: Doug McClure. *Dr. Carl Hyatt*: Sebastian Cabot. *Major Sam Wilson*: Dan Duryea. *Cadet William Edgerton Gray*: Peter Lazar. *Cadet Danny Slocum*: Phil Grayson. *Cadet C.R. Maphis*: Robert G. Slade. *Henry Creasy*: Dabbs Greer. *Freighter Blaisden*: Dennis Rush. *Mr. Slocum*: Frank Wilcox. *Jasmine da Gama*: Tita Marsell. *Director:* Herschel Daugherty. *Teleplay:* Edwin Blum and Robert C. Dennis. *Story:* Edwin Blum. *Creator*: Eric Ambler. *Producer*: Richard Berg. *Cinematography*: Benjamin H. Kline. *Editor*: Tony Martinelli.

Route 66: Don't Count the Stars, 4/28/'61

Tod Stiles: Martin Milner. *Buz Murdock*: George Maharis. *Mike McKay*: Dan Duryea. *Linda McKay*: Susan Melvin. *Judge Mary Lindstrom*: Mary Jackson. *Ernie Bassard*: Oliver McGowan. *Banker*: Vaughn Taylor. *Director:* Paul Wendkos. *Teleplay:* Stirling Silliphant. *Creators*: Stirling Silliphant and Herbert B. Leonard. *Producer*: Herbert B. Leonard. *Cinematography*: Jack A. Marta. *Editors*: Jack Gleason and Milton Shifman.

Laramie: The Mountain Men, 10/ /'61

Slim Sherman: John Smith. *Jess Harper*: Robert Fuller. *Daisy Cooper*: Spring Byington. *Mike Williams*: Dennis Holmes. *Ben Sanford*: Dan Duryea. *Carl Sanford*: Jason Evers. *Sheriff Mort Cory*: Stuart Randall. *John Sanford*: Alex Cord (Alex Viespi). *Joe Vance*: John Cliff. *Director*: Joseph Kane. *Teleplay*: Lee Erwin and Donn Mullally. *Story*: Daniel B. Ullman. *Producer*: John C. Champion. *Cinematography*: Ray Rennahan. *Editor*: Ray DeVally.

Frontier Circus: The Shaggy Kings, 12/07/'61

Colonel Casey Thompson: Chill Wills. *Ben Travis*: John Derek. *Tony Gentry*: Richard Jaeckel. *Tiber*: Dan Duryea. *Jeb Randall*: Dick York. *Karl Maynard*: Frank DeKova. *Doc Turner*: Paul Newlan. *Hark Baker*: Paul Lambert. *Molly*: Lorrie Richards. *The Circus Cook:* Alan Carney. *Michael*

Smith: Michael Pate. *Chief Shining Knife*: Dennis Cross. *Director*: Richard Irving. *Teleplay*: Samuel A. Peeples. *Cinematography*: Benjamin H. Kline. *Editor*: Lee Huntington.

Tales of Wells Fargo: Winter Storm, 1962

Jim Hardie: Dale Robertson. *Marshal Blake:* Dan Duryea. *Jeb Gaine:* William Demerest. *Tina:* Lory Patrick. *Hanson:* R.G. Armstrong. *Kelly:* Eddie Firestone. *Eddy Pierce:* Jim Beck. *Ruth:* Gale Garnett. *Tom:* Boyd Stockman. *Director:* William Witney. *Teleplay:* Dick Nelson. *Producer:* Earle Lyon. *Cinematography:* Bud Thackery. *Editing:* Edward Biery.

Naked City: Daughter Am I in Thy Father's House?, 1962

Regulars: *Det. Adam Flint:* Paul Burke. *Lt. Mike Parker*: Horace McMahon. *Det. Frank Acaro:* Harry Bellaver. Guest Stars: *Clyde Royd:* Dan Duryea. *Helga Royd:* Barbara Harris. *Dom Capado:* Marco St. John. *Mr. Capado:* Frank Campanella. *Narrator:* Lawrence Dobkin. *Director:* David Lowell Rich. *Teleplay:* Shimon Wincelberg. *Producer:* Charles Russell. *Cinematography:* John S. Priestley. *Editing:* Hugh Chaloupka.

Wagon Train: The Wagon Train Mutiny, 9/19/'62

Christopher Hale: John mcIntire. Hannah barber: Jane Wyman. Amos: Dan Duryea. Charlie Wooster: Frank McGrath. Bill hawks: Terry Wilson. Duke Shannon: Denny Miller. Mr. Hunter: Regis Toomey. Leland barber: Peter Helm. John Hunter: Dick Jones. Renaldo Ortega: Jose De Vega. Major Groff: John Rodney. Director: Virgil W. Vogel. Teleplay: Norman Jolley. Producer: Howard Christie.

Rawhide: Incident of the Wolves, 11/16/'62

Gil Favor: Eric Fleming. *Rowdy Yates:* Clint Eastwood. *Wishbone*: Paul Brinegar. *Abner Cannon:* Dan Duryea. *Julie Cannon:* Patty McCormick. *Luther Cannon:* Paul Carr. *Matt Cannon:* Jack Grinnage. *Director:* Thomas Carr. *Teleplay:* William L. Stuart. *Producer:* Vincent M. Fenelly. *Cinematography:* Jack Swain. *Editor:* James Baiotto. *Theme Music*: Dimitri Tiomkin. *Lyrics:* Ned Washington. *Singer:* Frankie Laine.

Going My Way: **Mr. Second Chance,** 11/22/'62

Father Chuck O'Malley: Gene Kelly. *Father Fitzgibbon*: Leo G. Carroll. *Harold Harrison:* Dan Duryea. *Ken Hamlin*: Ross Elliott. *Mrs. Harrison*: Dorothy Green. *Marilyn Harrison*: Maggie Pierce. *Mrs. Featherstone*: Nydia Westman. *Bill Fleming*: Willis Bouchey. *Elevator Operator*: Frankie Darro. *Director*: Allen Reisner. *Teleplay:* Joe Connelly and Mark Weingart. *Story*: Robert Hardy Andrews. *Producer*: Joe Connelly. *Cinematography*: Fred Mandl. *Editor*: Richard G. Wray.

Wide Country: **Tears on a Painted Face,** 11/29/'62

Mitch Guthrie: Earl Holliman. *Andy Guthrie:* Andrew Prine. *Willie Xeno:* Dan Duryea. *Chris Xeno:* Charles Robinson. *Artie Devan*: Steve Brodie. *Frank Higgins*: Ray E. Teal. *Doc:* Jan Aryan. *Slim Walker:* Slim Pickens. *Director*: Herschel Daugherty. *Teleplay:* Louis Pelletier. *Producer:* Frank Telford. *Cinematography*: Walter Strenge. *Editor:* Danny E. Landres.

The Eleventh Hour: **Why am I Grown So Cold?,** 2/06/'63

Dr. Theodore Bassett: Wendell Corey. *Dr. Paul Graham*: Jack Ging. *Connie Folsom:* Eleanor Parker. *Ben Lorrigan*: Dan Duryea. *Ruth Brewer:* Lori March. *Judge Cavanaugh:* Jan Peters.

Alcoa Premiere: **Blow High, Blow Clear,** 2/14/'63

Host: Fred Astaire. *Harlan Tracy*: Tommy Sands. *Charlie Quinn*: Dan Duryea. *Hannibal Roth*: John Anderson. *Doyle:* Chris Robinson. *Martha Ellison*: Jane Wyatt.
Director: John Braham. *Teleplay:* Harold Swanton.

The Tonight Show Starring Johnny Carson (Talk Show), 4/16/'63

The United States Steel Hour: The Many Ways of Heaven, 5/01/'63

Captain Walker: Dan Duryea. *Jim Hampshire*: Wesly Addy. *Russell Hampshire*: Jonathan Carter. *Cissy Hampshire*: Cathleen Nesbit. *With*: Lloyd Bochner and Robert Burr. *Teleplay*: Ellen M. Violett. *Story*: George Loveridge.

Rawhide: Incident of the Prophecy, 11/21/'63

Gil Favor: Eric Fleming. *Rowdy Yates*: Clint Eastwood. *Wishbone*: Paul Brinegar. *Brother William*: Dan Duryea. *Charlie 'Rabbit' Waters*: Warren Oates. *Gurney*: James Griffith. *Orville*: Raymond Guth. *Dexter*: Harry Dean Stanton. *Dr. Merrill*: Hugh Sanders. *The Sheriff*: Ray Teal. *Director*: Thomas Carr. *Teleplay*: Samuel Roeca. *Producer*: Vincent M. Fennelly. *Cinematography*: Jack Swain. *Theme Music*: Dimitri Tiomkin. *Lyrics*: Ned Washington. *Singer*: Frankie Laine.

Route 66: A Cage in Search of a Bird, 11/29/'63

Tod Stiles: Martin Milner. *Linc Case*: Glenn Corbett. *Jay Leonard Ringsby*: Dan Duryea. *Julie Severn*: Stefanie Powers. *Rick Decatur*: Alex Cord. *Police Officer*: bert Remsen. *Director*: James Sheldon. *Teleplay*: Stirling Silliphant. *Creators*: Stirling Silliphant and Herbert B. Leonard. *Producer*: leo Davis. *Cinematography*: Jack A. Marta. *Editor*: Jack Gleason. *Music*: Nelson Riddle.

The Alfred Hitchcock Hour: Three Wives Too Many, 1/03/'64

Host: Alfred Hitchcock. *Marion Brown*: Teresa Wright. *Raymond Brown*: Dan Duryea. *Lucille Brown*: Linda Lawson. *Bernice Brown*: Jean Hale. *Lt. Storber*: Steven Gravers. *Mr. Bleeker*: Robert Cornthwaite. *Producer*: Herbert Coleman. *Executive Producer*: Norman Lloyd. *Cinematography*: John

F. Warren. *Editor:* Danford B. Greene. *Director:* Joseph Newman. *Teleplay:* Arthur A. Ross. *Story:* Kenneth Fearing.

Kraft Suspense Theater: Who is Jennifer?, 1/16/'64

Mrs. Charlotte Heaton: Gloria Swanson. *Lt. Boyd Manners*: Dan Duryea. *Mark Nelson*: David Brian. *The Mystery Girl*: Brenda Scott. *The Booking Sergeant*: John Dennis. *The Police Woman*: Jan Shepard. *Chief Austin*: Morris Ankrum. *First Policeman*: Gene Roth. *Director*: Alvin Ganzer. *Teleplay*: George Slavin and Paul Tuckahoe. *Story*: George Slavin. *Producer*: Luther Davis. *Cinematography*: Robert Tobey. *Editor*: Robert Watts.

Burke's Law: Who Killed the Paper Dragon?

Capt. Amos Burke: Gene Barry. *Det. Tim Tilson*: Gary Conway. *Det. Les Hart*: Regis Toomey. *Henry:* Leon Lontoc. *Charlie January*: Howard Duff. *Hop Sing Kelly*: Dan Duryea. *Sylvia Hanson*: Barbara Eden. *Sidney Young*: James Shigeta. *Fragrant Lotus*: Ginny Tiu. *Lotus Bud*: Miyoshi Umeki. *Sweet Young Thing*: Kathy Kersh. *Peach Petal*: Tura Satana. *Director*: Marc Daniels. *Teleplay*: Jameson Brewer and Day Keene. Based on characters created by Frank D. Gilroy. *Producer*: Aaron Spelling. *Cinematography*: George E. Diskant. *Editor*: Desmond Marquette. *Music*: Joseph Mullendore.

Wagon Train: The Sam Race Story, 10/11/'64

Christopher Hale: John McIntire. Cooper Smith: Robert Fuller. Charlie Wooster: Frank McGrath. Bill Hawks: Terry Wilson. Sam Race: Dan Duryea. Annabelle Day: Cheryl Holdridge. Julie: Allyson Ames. Digger: Hal Needham. Trinket Seller: Louis Quinn. Director: Joseph Pevney. Teleplay: Calvin Clements, Sr. Producer: Howard Christie.

Bonanza: Logan's Treasure, 10/18/'64

Regulars: *Ben Cartwright*: Lorne Green. *Adam Cartwright*: Pernell Roberts. *'Hoss' Cartwright*: Dan Blocker. *'Little Joe' Cartwright*: Michael Land-

on. *Sam Logan:* Dan Duryea. *Frank Reed:* John Kellogg. *Angie Malone:* Virginia Gregg. *Mike Crawford:* Tim McIntire. *Director:* Don McDougall. *Teleplay*: Ken Pettus. *Story:* Robert Sabaroff.
Producer: David Dortort. *Cinematography*: Haskell Boggs. *Editor:* Ellsworth Hoagland. *Music*: David Rose.

Burke's Law: Who Killed 711?, 12/09/'64

Capt. Amos Burke: Gene Barry. *Det. Tim Tilson*: Gary Conway. *Det. Les Hart*: Regis Toomey. *Henry:* Leon Lontoc. *Pepe Van Heller*: Hans Conreid. *Tristram Corporal*: Broderick Crawford. Sam Atherton: Dan Duryea. Clarissa Benton: Rhonda Fleming. *Harold Harold*: Burgess Meredith. *Aurora Knight*: Mamie Van Doren. *Woman in Lobby*: Allyson Ames. *Man in the Lobby*: Lou Krugman. *Director*: Sidney Lanfield. *Teleplay:* Paul Dubov and Gwen Bagni.

That Regis Philbin Show, 1965 x 2

Daniel Boone: Sound of Fear, 2/11/'65

Regulars: *Daniel Boone*: Fess Parker. *Yadkin:* Albert Salmi. *Mingo*: Ed Ames. *Rebecca Boone*: Patricia Blair. *Jemima Boone*: Veronica Cartwright. *Israel Boone*: Darby Hinton. Simon Perigore: Dan Duryea. Petch: Jack Elam. *Savate*: Jacque Aubuchon. *Toff*: Robert J. Wilke. *Andrew Perigore*: Peter Duryea. Parson: Jim Boles. *Director*: Harry Harris. *Teleplay*: Truman Clay and Dick Nelson. *Story*: Truman Clay. *Producer*: Paul King. *Executive Producer:* Aaron Rosenberg. *Cinematography:* Jack Swain. *Editor*: Orven W.Schanzer.

Combat: Dateline, 2/23/'65

Regulars: *Sgt. Saunders*: Vic Morrow. *Littlejohn:* Dick Peabody. *Caje*: Pierre Jalbert. *Kirby*: Kack Hogan. *Doc:* Conlon Carter. Guests: *Barton*: Dan Duryea. *Reardon*: Douglas Henderson. *Major Mueller*: Henry Beckman. *Director*: Sutton Roley. *Teleplay*: Richard Newhafer. *Producer:* Gene

Levitt. *Music*: Leonard Rosenman. *Cinematography*: Emmett Berglolz. *Editor*: Richard L. Van Enger.

The Long Hot Summer: The Return of the Quicks, 12/16/'65

Regulars: *'Boss'Will Varner*: Edmond O'Brien. *Ben Quick*: Roy Thinnes. *Clara Varner*: Nancy Malone. *Jody Varner*: Paul Geary. Guests: *Chuck Quick*: Dan Duryea. *Phil McDermott*: Whit Bissell. *Bess Quick*: Jan Shepard. *Minnie Littlejohn*: Ruth Roman. *Eula Harker*: Lana Wood. *Director*: Don Richardson. *Teleplay*: James Gunn. *Stories*: William Faulkner. *Producer*: Frank Glicksman.

The Loner: A Little Stroll to the End of the Line

William Colton: Lloyd Bridges. *Matthew Reynolds*: Dan Duryea. *Preacher Whatley*: Robert Emhardt. *Chisholm*: Bart Burns. *Director*: Norman Foster. *Teleplay*: Rod Serling. *Producer*: Andy White. *Cinematography*: Howard Schwartz. *Editor*: Harry Coswick. *Created by*: Rod Serling.

The Virginian: The Challenge, 10/19/'66

Regulars: *John Grainger*: Charles Bickford. *The Virginian*: James Drury. *Trampas*: Doug McClure. Guests: *Ben Crayton*: Dan Duryea. *Jim Tyson*: Don Galloway. *Bobby Crayton*: Michael Burns. *Sarah Crayton*: Barbara Anderson. *Sam Fuller*: Bing Russell. *Dr. Manning*: Byron Keith. *Director*: Don McDougall. *Teleplay*: Joy Dexter and Harry Kronman. *Story*: Joy Dexter. *Novel*: Owen Wister. *Producer*: Joel Rogosin. *Cinematography*: Enzo A. Martinelli. *Editor*: Michael R. McAdam.

The Monroes: Gold Fever, 1966

Regulars: *Clayt Monroe:* Michael Anderson, Jr. *Kathy Monroe:* Barbara Hershey. *Jefferson Monroe:* Keith Schultz. *Fennimore Monroe:* Kevin Schultz. *Amy Monroe:* Tammy Locke. *Major Mapoy:* Liam Sullivan. *Dirty Jim:* Ron Soble. Guest Star: *T.J. Elderbush:* Dan Duryea. *Director*: James

B. Clark. *Teleplay*: Jack Turley. *Producer*: Al C. Ward. *Cinematography*: Monroe P. Askins. *Editor:* Bill Mosher.

Combat: A Little Jazz, 2/21/'67

Regulars: *Sgt. Saunders*: Vic Morrow. *Littlejohn:* Dick Peabody. *Caje*: Pierre Jalbert. *Kirby*: Kack Hogan. *Doc:* Conlon Carter. Guests: *Bernie Wallace*: Dan Duryea. *Hank Davis*: Noah Beery, Jr. *Zack Fielder*: Dennis Hopper. *Will*: Joe Maross. *Woody Jones*: Robert Easton. *Director*: Michael Caffey. *Teleplay*: James Menzies. *Producer*: Richard Caffey. *Music:* Leonard Rosenman. *Cinematography:* Emmett Bergholz. *Editor*: Robert L. Wolfe.

Peyton Place : Eddie Jacks, 3.96 (8/21/'67) - 4.61 (5/09/'68)

Eddie Jacks: Dan Duryea. *Rita Jacks*: Patricia Morrow. *Ada Jacks*: Evelyn Scott. *Steven Cord:* James Douglas. *Martin Peyton*: George Macready/ Wilfred Hyde-White. *Constance MacKenzie*: Dorothy Malone. *Dr. Michael Rossi*: Ed Nelson. *Rodney Harrington*: Ryan O'Neal. *Betty Anderson*: Barbara Parkins. *Leslie Anderson*: Paul Langton. *Norman Harrington:* Christopher Connelly. *Eliot Carson*: Tim O'Connor. *Lee Weller*: Stephen Oliver. *Joe Rossi*: Michael Christian.

Radio Credits

Lux Radio Theater: Woman in the Window, 06/25/'45
Edward G. Robinson, Joan Bennett and Dan Duryea.

Suspense: Will to Power, 01/09/'47
Cathy Lewis and Dan Duryea.

Suspense: Man Who Couldn't Lose, 12/12/'47
Guests: Jack Webb, Dan Duryea.

Family Theater: Toledo Smith, 04/08/'48
Dan Duryea and Skip Homeier

Family Theater: The Postmistress of Laurel Run, 06/22/'49
Virginia Gregg, Parley Baer and Dan Duryea.

Family Theater: Lodging for the Night, 01/25/'50
Guests: Osa Munson, Dan Duryea and Robert Alda.

The Hedda Hopper Show: Guest, 10/21/'50

Man from Homicide:

Suspense: Remember Me, 04/07/'52
Joseph kearns, Charlotte Lawrence, Dan Duryea and Lee Millar.

Suspense: The Driven Snow, 03/08/'52
Harry Bartell, Parley Baer, Byron Kane, Dan Duryea and Jeanne Bates.

Family Theater: Sideman, 01/06/'54
Charlotte Lawrence, Sam Edwards, Jack Kruschen, Dan Duryea, Scotty Beckett and Jo Stafford.

Theater Credits:

Stepping Sisters, Belmont Theatre, 333 performances (Apr.22,1930-Feb., 1931

Dead End, Belasco Theatre, 687 Performances-(10/28/'35-6/12/'37

Drina: Elspeth Eric. *'Babyface' Martin*: Joseph Downing. *Hunk:* Martin Gabel. *Gimpty:* Theodore Newton. *TB*: Gabriel Dell. *Spit*: Charles R. Duncan (replaced by Leo Gorcey). *Dippy*: Huntz Hall. *Tommy*: Billy Halop. *Angel*: Bobby Jordan. *Milty:* Bernard Punsly. *Mrs. Martin*: Marjorie Main. *Francey:* Sheila Trent. *Kay:* Margaret Mullin. *G-Man:* Dan Duryea. *Producer:* Norman Bel Geddes. *Playwright and Director:* Sidney Kingsley. Production Design: Norman Bel Geddes.

Many Mansions, Biltmore Theatre, 158 performances (10/27/'37-3/03/'38)

Auguste Aramini: Petrosino. *Rev. Josiah Ward*: Seth Arnold. *Dean Redmond*: Lewis Dayton. *Bob Edmunds*: Dan Duryea. *Bishop Graves*: Vaughan Glaser. *Morgan Grange*: Wendell Phillips. *Producer*: Many Mansions, Inc. *Playwright*: Jules Eckert Goodman and Eckert Goodman. *Staged by*: Lee Strasberg. *Scenic Design by*: John Koenig. *Music*: Milton Lusk.

Missouri Legend, Empire Theatre, 48 performances (Sept. 19, 1938-Oct., 1938)

Billy Gashade: Jose Ferrer. *Mrs. Howard*: Dorothy Gish. *Thomas Howard*: Dead Jagger. *The Widow Weeks*: Mildred Natwick. *Frank Howard*: Richard Bishop. *Jim Cummins*: Russell Collins. *George*: Vincent Copeland. *Asa*: James Craig. *Bob Johnson:* Dan Duryea. The reverend: Clifford Heckinger. Charlie Johnson: Karl Malden. Producer: Guthrie McClintic (in association with Max Gordon). Playwright: E.B. Ginty. Staged by: Guthrie McClintic. Musical Director: Albert Pearl. Production Design: John Koenig.

The Little Foxes, National Theatre, 410 performances (2/15/'39-2/03/'40)

Regina Giddens: Tallulah Bankhead. *Birdie Hubbard*: Patricia Collinge. *Horace Giddens:* Frank Conroy. *William Marshall:* Lee Baker. *Benjamin Hubbard:* Charles Dingle. *Leo Hubbard:* Dan Duryea. *Val:* John Marriott. *Addie:* Abbie Mitchell. *Oscar Hubbard:* Carl Benton Reid. *Alexandra Giddens:* Florence Williams. *Producer:* Herman Schumlin. *Playwright:* Lillian Hellman. *Staged by*: Herman Schumlin. *Scenic Design:* Howard Bay.

The Front Page, Medford, Conn. Summer Stock, (limited performance)-1947

The Country Girl, Summer Stock (limited performance), 1963

Brecht on Brecht, 1963, Theatre Group Presentation (Auditorium of University of California Extension).

Director: William Allyn. *Adaptation*: George Tahori. *Piano Accompaniment*: Don Ebey. *Cast:* Dan Duryea, Nina Foch, Kim Hamilton, Kevin McCarthy and Dolores Sutton.

Endnotes

1: Table of Contents

1. *Stay As Mean as You Are*; Alyce Canfield; 1951
2. *Not So Bad*; Ed Peters; Motion Picture, 1945
3. *Not So Bad*; Ed Peters; Motion Picture, 1945
4. *Screenland; Screen Monster, Home Treasure*; Lupton A. Wilkinson, 1947
5. *Not So Bad*; Ed Peters; Motion Picture, 1945
6. *Don't Shoot My Daddy*; Robbin Coons; 1949
7. *Sunday News*, 1957; The Merchant of Menace; Pete Coutros
8. *TV Star Parade*; Sure, You Can Raise Normal Kids in Hollywood; Tony Bowen; 1967
9. The Haunting Memories that Guide His Life; Sylvia Resnick; *Movie Life*, 1967

2. The Early Years: Hollywood's Finest

1. Goldwyn; Arthur Marx; Norton, 1st. Edition; 1976
2. *Ball of Fire*; Frank Miller; TCM.Com
3. *The Pride of the Yankees*; Leonard Maltin's Classic Movie Guide; Penguin; 2005,2010
4. *Sahara* (1943); Notes; TCMDb Archive Materials; tcm.com.
5. *Fritz Lang: Interviews* by Barry Keith Grant, p.10;
6. *Fritz Lang: Interviews* by Barry Keith Grant, p. 10;
7. *Fritz Lang: Interviews* by Barry Keith Grant, p.11;
8. *Duryea, the Menace*; Thomas M. Pryor; June 23, 1945, p.107

3: Universal Studios

1. *The Genius of the System*; Thomas Schatz; Panteon Books, New York © 1988. P.354
2. *The Genius of the System*; Thomas Schatz; Panteon Books, New York © 1988. P.357
3. *Hollywood without Makeup*/Pete Martin/Bantam Books, New York/©1938, 1944, 1945, 1946, 1947
4. *Hollywood without Makeup*/Pete Martin/Bantam Books, New York/©1938, 1944, 1945, 1946, 1947
5. *Hollywood without Makeup*/Pete Martin/Bantam Books, New York/©1938, 1944, 1945, 1946, 1947. P. 139/140

4: New Directions

1. *Variety*, Apr. 19, 1949
2. *The New York Times*, July 14, 1949
3. *Variety*, August 9, 1949
4. *Variety*, November 7, 1951
5. *Variety*, Jan. 23, 1962
6. *The New York Times*, April 20, 1954
7. *Variety*, Aug. 29, 1956

6: Sidekicks, Ciphers and Bums

1. *The New York Times*, Oct. 19, 1952.

9: Retro Cowboy

1. *Variety*, Oct. 14, 1964

10: The Cold War

1. Dan Duryea: Had Sense Enough to Recognize His Limitations; David Johnson; Films in Review; June-July, 1971.
2. *Variety* Wed., Oct. 12, 1966

Index

A
Anderson, Mary 148, 158

B
Bankhead, Thallulah-25,
Barrett, Claudia 17(p), 169, 174
Barrymore, Ethel 57, 59, 60
Bennett, Joan 4,5, 68, 71, 90, 92, 93, 94
Bogart, Humphrey 49, 50
Bond, Ward 275, 307 (p)
Burns, Michael 285, 289
Byington, Spring 193, 292

C
Carlo, Yvonne De 7, 106, 107, 108, 109, 115, 125, 134
Carr, Marion 169, 176, 212, 215
Charlita 272 (p), 273
Cooper, Gary 12, 35, 39, 40, 42, 43, 45, 49, 83, 85, 117

D
Davis, Bette 35, 36
DeFore, Don 240
Dell, Myrna 164, 166
Dumbrille, Douglas 164, 166, 212
Durbin, Deanna 88, 89
Duryea, Dan Career Synopsis (1-21); Biography (21-31)

F
Flippen, Jay C 204, 245
Foran, Dick 152, 361, 364

G
Garland, Beverly 189, 315
Garson, Greer 60, 62, 79, 81
Goldwyn, Sam 23, 33, 34, 39, 46
Grant, Cary 57, 58, 60

H
Hellman, Lillian 25, 33, 34
Helton, Percy 122, 124
Hudson, Rock 117, 239, 242

J
Jaeckal, Richard 199, 267, 321

L
Lambert, Jack 318, 321, 324, 386
Lamour, Dorothy 7, 137
Lancaster, Burt 125
Lang, Fritz 3, 5, 7, 64, 67,68, 90, 91, 94
Lockhart, Gene 55, 56, 212
Luke, Keye 171, 180, 181

M
Marshall, Herbert 35, 148, 149
Mason, James 132, 134
McCormick, Patty 19, 262, 265
McGraw, Charles 154, 156, 248
McIntire, John 107, 117, 275, 380
Murphy, Audey 19, 218, 221, 244, 245, 270, 271

Fuller, Robert 288, 271

N
Natwick, Mildred 25, 186, 188

O
O'Shea, Michael 54, 56

P
Paiva, Nestor 169, 180
Payne, John 122, 123, 221, 223, 224, 226, 227

R
Robinson, Edward G. 5, 68, 69, 71, 92, 94
Rooney, Mickey 19, 265
Rosenberg, Aaron 3, 203

S
Scott, Lizabeth 7, 141, 142, 162, 227
Sen Yung, Victor 169, 181
Serling, Rod 92, 313, 380
Shaughnessy, Mickey 247, 251, 256
Silva, Henry 375, 377 (p)
Stanwyck, Barbara 39, 41, 43, 339
Sterling, Jan 247, 251, 262
Stewart, James 12, 117, 120, 203, 206, 244, 245, 404, 405
Storm, Gale 148, 152
Stroheim, Erich Von 5, 75, 76, 79

T
Toland, Gregg 35
Toren, Marta 132, 134
Tryon, Tom 12, 15, 315, 384

W
Wendkos, Paul 16, 257
Wilde, Cornel 16, 235, 237, 238
Winters, Shelley 7, 117, 120, 121, 122, 128, 129
Wyler, William 35, 158
Wyman, Jane 283, 284 (p)
Wright, Teresa 35, 37, 45, 399, 400

Y
Young, Tony 12, 358, 359

Z
Zugsmith, Albert J. 19, 247, 265, 269

www.ingramcontent.com/pod-product-compliance
Lightning Source LLC
Chambersburg PA
CBHW060313230426
43663CB00009B/1691